By the same author

DISRAELI'S FICTION

CONRAD: *ALMAYER'S FOLLY* TO *UNDER WESTERN EYES*

CONRAD: THE LATER FICTION

THE
HUMANISTIC
HERITAGE

*Critical Theories of the English Novel from James
to Hillis Miller*

Daniel R. Schwarz

upp

University of Pennsylvania Press
Philadelphia 1986

First published in the United States 1986 by the
University of Pennsylvania Press

First published in the United Kingdom by
THE MACMILLAN PRESS LTD
Houndmills, Basingstoke, Hampshire RG21 2XS

Library of Congress Cataloging-in-Publication Data

Schwarz, Daniel R.
  The humanistic heritage.

  Bibliography: p.
  Includes index.
    1. English fiction—History and criticism.
  2. Criticism—Great Britain—History.   3. Criticism—
  United States—History.   4. Fiction.   I. Title.
  PR826.S38   1986   801'.953   85–13949
  ISBN 0–8122–7997–2
  ISBN 0–8122–1218–5 (pbk)

Printed in Hong Kong

For Marcia

Contents

Acknowledgements   viii

Introduction   1

1 The Humanistic Heritage of James and Lubbock: the
   Emergence of an Aesthetic of the Novel   16
2 The Importance of E. M. Forster's *Aspects of the Novel*   41
3 Privileging Literary Criticism: the Legacy of F. R. Leavis's
   The Great Tradition   60
4 'The Idea Embodied in the Cosmology': the Significance of
   Dorothy Van Ghent's *The English Novel: Form and Function*   80
5 'Formal Realism': the Importance of Ian Watt's *The Rise of
   the Novel*   99
6 Two Major Voices of the 1950s: Northrop Frye's *Anatomy of
   Criticism* and Erich Auerbach's *Mimesis*   118
7 Reading as a Moral Activity: the Importance of Wayne C.
   Booth's *The Rhetoric of Fiction*   151
8 The Consolation of Form: the Theoretical and Historical
   Significance of Frank Kermode's *The Sense of an Ending*   170
9 Marxist Criticism of the English Novel: Arnold Kettle's *An
   Introduction to the English Novel* and Raymond Williams's
   The English Novel from Dickens to Lawrence   187
10 The Fictional Theories of J. Hillis Miller: Humanism,
   Phenomenology, and Deconstruction in *The Form of
   Victorian Fiction* and *Fiction and Repetition*   222

Selected Bibliography   267
Index   273

Acknowledgements

I am indebted to my colleagues and students at Cornell where I have been teaching for seventeen years. In particular, I have had the privilege of knowing M. H. Abrams, whose example as a scholar and colleague has had an incalculable effect on my work. I also appreciate the friendship, generosity, and encouragement of Anthony Caputi, Michael Colacurcio, Tom Hill, and David Novarr. Some of the material in the book was first presented to an informal colloquium of graduate students with whom I was working during the period I wrote this book. I wish to acknowledge the help of Barrett Fisher, Helen Maxson, Beth Newman, Margaret Nichols, Paul Russell, Steven Sicari, William Thickstun, and Caroline Webb. Directing a 1984 Summer Seminar for College Teachers for the National Endowment for the Humanities helped me clarify my introduction and my final chapter; I am grateful to the participants. The good-natured and thorough secretarial help of Phillis Molock is invaluable to my work. Mira Batra has been helpful with the index and page proofs. As the dedication indicates, I owe a great debt to my wife.

Parts of the manuscript appeared as articles elsewhere and are repeated by permission of the editors. An earlier version of Chapter 4 appeared in *Diacritics* (autumn 1978); a version of Chapter 5 appeared in *The Journal of Narrative Technique* (spring 1983); a version of Chapter 8 appeared in *The Centennial Review* (autumn 1984–winter 1985). Parts of Chapter 7 first appeared in *The Sewanee Review*, 93 (1985) under the title 'Reading as a Moral Activity'. A version of Chapter 2 was published as 'The Importance of E. M. Forster's *Aspects of the Novel*' in *The South Atlantic Quarterly*, 82:2, pp. 189–205, copyright © 1983 by Duke University Press, Durham, N.C.

Cornell University   DANIEL R. SCHWARZ
Ithaca, New York

Introduction

I

I shall be discussing the theory and method of Anglo-American novel criticism in order to understand the way that the novel has been read, taught, and written about since 1900 in England and America. Implicitly and explicitly, I shall be arguing for the importance of an ideology of reading which I call the Humanistic Heritage. My hope is to contribute to a dialogue between traditional formal criticism that has dominated Anglo-American criticism and recent criticism, including structuralism, deconstruction, and Marxism.

In order to be able to make comparisons, my focus is on books that treat the same subject: the English novel from Defoe through Joyce. I shall discuss the trends in novel criticism in England, America, and the English-speaking world since 1900. I have selected major texts which illustrate those trends and which contribute to the Anglo-American aesthetic of the novel. Henry James's fiction criticism and Percy Lubbock's *The Craft of Fiction* (1921); E. M. Forster's *Aspects of the Novel* (1927); F. R. Leavis's *The Great Tradition* (1948); Dorothy Van Ghent's *The English Novel: Form and Function* (1953); Ian Watt's *The Rise of the Novel* (1957); Erich Auerbach's *Mimesis* (1953); Northrop Frye's *Anatomy of Criticism* (1957); Wayne Booth's *The Rhetoric of Fiction* (1961); Frank Kermode's *The Sense of an Ending* (1967); the Marxist novel criticism of Arnold Kettle and Raymond Williams; and J. Hillis Miller's *The Form of Victorian Fiction* (1968) and *Fiction and Repetition* (1982). I have included Auerbach and Frye because, although addressing the English novel less centrally, they have written theoretical studies that have had a major influence on novel criticism. And I discuss Williams and Kettle because Marxist principles have played a significant if subsidiary role in the criticism of the English novel.

While one might quarrel with some of my choices, I believe that these are the books that have been most influential in the reading and teaching of the English novel. I have taken no systematic survey, but I

1

have consulted numerous colleagues in England and America. Were my study to have included criticism of the American novel, I would have surely included Richard Chase's *The American Novel and Its Tradition* (1957); D. H. Lawrence's *Studies in Classic American Literature* (1923), and the work of Edmund Wilson. Were my study to have attempted a survey of important recent work on the novel, it would have included a discussion of feminist criticism.

The tradition of humanistic novel criticism should be understood as a coherent, but heterogeneous, aesthetic. I shall examine the major books of each critic – the books that really make a difference – in terms of their response to prior and contemporary literary theory and practice, as well as to their cultural milieu. Each critical work will be examined as an instance of a particular critical approach and for its critical significance to us. Critical texts, like novels, enact in their form and technique their values. I have sought to enact in my discussions the eclecticism, pluralism, and open-mindedness which I think is the essence of an enlightened humanism. Thus I examine each book according to its own aesthetic and intellectual assumptions before stepping back to consider its limitations and contribution. I am interested in how the various approaches of these critics create and reflect the aesthetic, moral, and intellectual concepts of the culture which produced them. Even as they powerfully respond to the works they examine, our critics often reveal their own desperate search for order, within both traditional and recalcitrant texts, as a response to the historical chaos in the twentieth century. (Is it surprising that most of the critics I discuss enact in their critical practice the criteria and standards they admire in novelists?)

The work of Barthes, Derrida, and their followers has taught us to be wary of simple explanations that privilege thematic unity and to inquire into how literary works signify. But many of us are uncomfortable with their attack on voice, mimesis, and the effort to discover reasonably accurate interpretations. We have not addressed our critical tradition as a subject of serious inquiry, and that may be why recent criticism has conquered the ground so easily. The challenge of structuralism and post-structuralism has often sent traditional Anglo-American critics to the barricades, but little effort has been made to define what principles have been employed to speak about fiction in England and America. That the humanistic tradition of novel criticism has in fact produced a corpus of interpretive material remarkable in its quality and responsive to the literature it addresses is prima facie evidence for the force of its intellectual and methodological assumptions. One of the great achievements of this approach is that it has brought some coherence to the study of fiction by recognizing that fiction has its own unique formal problems.

While Anglo-American critics have not articulated a philosophic basis for their criticism, they have developed a methodology and principles – even, indeed, an implicit theory – that interprets, analyses, and judges novels effectively. To be sure, the defence of Anglo-American criticism of the novels rests, finally, on the quality of the analysis that major English novels have received. I think it can be argued that the tradition of the English novel from Defoe through Conrad, Lawrence, Joyce, and Woolf, has been established and discussed according to aesthetic principles which suit that tradition. Despite some failures, this method has explicated the texts of the major British novelists since Defoe and made these texts more accessible to readers. That complicated and problematic novels, like *Lord Jim* and *Ulysses*, have become part of the consciousness of educated people and that the works of eighteenth and nineteenth century novels have been better understood – more subtly and fully read – is a tribute to the efficacy of this criticism.

Anglo-American criticism of the English novel is in part derived from the very tradition of manners and morals that the English novel addresses. Perhaps from a historical perspective this criticism should be seen as a response to the British novel's interest in content and its moral effects on readers. That is why it has tended to make its aesthetics subservient to its moral values. Anglo-American formalism never abandoned humanism. Its concerns are the accuracy, inclusiveness, and the quality – the maturity and sincerity – of mimesis in the English novel, particularly how people live in a social community. Anglo-American criticism of the English novel would usually subscribe to what Gene Thornton wrote in another context, '[A]rt is about something other than art, and subject matter is important precisely because it distracts the viewer's attention from art and focuses it on something outside the picture – life, the world, God – that is more important than art.'[1] Yet humanistic novel criticism also takes seriously the importance not only of subject matter, but of form, and believes that the doing – technique, structure, and style – is important *because* it reveals or discusses the meaning inherent in the subject.

The differences that separate various strands of Anglo-American criticism seem less significant than they once did. Now we are able to see that the New Critics, Aristotelians, the *The Partisan Review* group, contextualists, and literary historians share a number of important assumptions: authors write to express their ideas and emotions; the way humans live and the values for which they live are of fundamental interest to authors and readers; literature expresses insights about human life and responses to human situations, and that is the main reason why we read, teach, and think about literature. While the emphasis varies from critic to critic, we can identify several concepts that define this criticism:

(1) The form of the novel – style, structure, narrative technique – expresses its value system. Put another way: form discovers the meaning of content.

(2) A work of literature is also a creative gesture of the author and the result of historical context. Understanding the process of imitating the external world gives us an insight into the artistry and meaning of the work.

(3) The work of fiction imitates a world that precedes the text, and the critic should recapture that world primarily by formal analysis of the text, although knowledge of the historical context and author is often important. Humanistic criticism believes that there is an original meaning, a centre, which can be approached by, and often, almost reached, by perceptive reading. The goal is to discover what authors said to their intended audience *then*, as well as what they say to us now. Acts of interpretation at their best – subtle, lucid, inclusive, perceptive – can bring that goal into sight.

(4) Human behaviour is central to most works, and should be the major concern of analysis. In particular, these critics are, with the exception of Frye, interested in how people behave – what they fear, desire, doubt, need. Although modes of characterization differ, the psychology and morality of characters must be understood as if they were real people; for understanding others like ourselves helps us to understand ourselves.

(5) The inclusiveness of the novel's vision in terms of depth and range is a measure of the work's quality.

Examining important works of novel criticism will enable us to discuss the development and evolution of these concepts. The struggle within Anglo-American novel criticism has been between emphasis on form and emphasis on content. In a sense I shall be focusing on two aspects or traditions, the artistic and empirical, and arguing that Anglo-American criticism depends on a dialogue between the formalism of the first and the humanism of the second. The artistic or

aesthetic aspect descends from James and Lubbock through Bloomsbury and the New Critics (in theory, if not always in practice) and,
finally, to proponents of structuralism and deconstruction. All of these
critics are interested in the text as a work of art. The empirical tradition
includes Leavis, Kettle, and Williams, as well as such kindred spirits in
America as Lionel Trilling and *The Partisan Review* critics (notably
Philip Rahv), the Chicago critics, and the Marxist critics. Those in the
empirical tradition are more likely to stress fiction as a mirror of
human life and are more likely to be interested in how fiction shapes
the reader. In keeping with the spirit of moderation and pragmatism of
Anglo-American novel criticism, neither of these traditions is indifferent to the concerns of the other. Indeed, the differences between
them are of degree, not kind. The dialogue between the two aspects is the
essence of what I call humanistic formalism, a formalism that straddles
the borderland where form and content are inextricably fused. Within
humanistic formalism is a rather vast critical territory, inhabited on
one side by James and Lubbock, and on the other, by Williams and
Kettle.

Because Anglo-American criticism has tended to sacrifice theory for
method, philosophic inquiry for practicality and utility, and general
principles for close analysis of texts, even distinguished English and
American critics fail to recognize the full theoretical underpinnings of
Anglo-American criticism. Thus, in what I take to be a paradigmatic
view of our critical heritage, Denis Donoghue has written:

For the past forty or fifty years, teachers of literature in American
colleges and universities have acted upon a few assumptions, mainly
derived from I. A. Richards' early books, *Principles of Literary
Criticism* (1924) and *Practical Criticism* (1929). The first assumption
is that in reading a poem you think of the words on the page as a
transcription of a voice speaking; not necessarily the poet speaking
in his own person, but a hypothetical person, speaking in imagined
circumstances sufficiently indicated by what he says. The second
assumption is that you are interpreting the poem, trying to understand the context, the speaker's sense of it, and the cogency of that
sense. The meaning of the poem is what the speaker means to say.
The third assumption is that you read poems to imagine experiences
you have not had, to exercise sympathy and judgement upon them,
and to take part in richer communications. It follows that it is
essential, in reading a poem as in taking part in a conversation, to
judge the speaker's tone correctly, because tone indicates his

relation to his own feeling and to the person or persons he is addressing. These assumptions, suitably elaborated, prescribe an orthodoxy of reading.[2]

While in many ways, this is an admirably succinct statement, it also reveals a number of misconceptions. In listing my objections, I think I can make clear why I have written this book.

(1) Donoghue collapses the history of Anglo-American criticism into a summary of the New Criticism and ignores the distinction within Anglo-American formalism between the aesthetics of poetry and the distinct aesthetics of the novel that have developed since James and Lubbock.

(2) Donoghue ignores the fact that the author may very well wish the audience to discover something quite different from what the speaker means. To argue that the meaning of the poem is what the speaker says it is ignores the relationship between author and reader which has been the focus of Booth's *The Rhetoric of Fiction* and *A Rhetoric of Irony* (1974).

(3) Donoghue overlooks the historical dimension of the text and the dialogue between the real and fictional world.

(4) He ignores the expressive dimensions of a text, the way the text reveals the creative process of the author, perhaps in relation to his own works, letters, and life.

(5) He slights the importance of several major questions: What kind of work does the reader confront? For what purpose was it created? What view is being urged upon the reader? What significance does it have for a contemporary reader?

I begin with James because he is the father of novel criticism in English. He imported the preoccupation with craft that dominated the discussion of fiction in nineteenth-century France. After examining the codification of James in Lubbock's *The Craft of Fiction*, I turn to E. M. Forster's *Aspects of the Novel*, which somewhat paradoxically emphasizes fictional characters as human beings and art as ineffable mystery. My next chapter demonstrates that the importance of *Scrutiny* and Leavis was in defining a canon for the English novel in terms of the moral intensity of the work. Like Lionel Trilling, Leavis combines an interest in formal questions with Arnoldian high seriousness. But Leavis's concerns are usually confined to questions of individual behaviour and its conflict with community standards. It remained for Watt, Kettle, and Williams – all strongly influenced by Leavis – to define an aesthetic that took greater account of social, political, and historical factors that shaped the novelist's writing and our perception of the work's meaning. Like Leavis, they are concerned less with the process of presentation than with the quality of the world imitated. Watt's *The Rise of the Novel* developed the relationship between a novel's form and its historical antecedents. In considering these implications of subject matter, including how people live in their communities, and in examining their personal relationships, the Marxist criticism of Kettle in his *Introduction to the English Novel* and Raymond Williams in *The English Novel from Dickens to Lawrence* is as much indebted to Leavis as to Marx and Engels and is in the tradition of British empiricism and positivism. It is not until after *The English Novel from Dickens to Lawrence* that Williams becomes more attuned to the subtleties and theoretical rigour of European Marxist theory.

Meanwhile, in America formalists like Van Ghent and Mark Schorer were applying and adopting the New Criticism to fiction. To an extent the New Criticism, with its emphasis on the work of art as a separate and distinct entity to be examined in its own terms, is the result and counterpart of literary modernism. But in part because of the example of Van Ghent and Schorer, the emphasis on technique rarely dominated novel criticism in America. At its best the New Criticism was used by imaginative critics to ask important questions about an author's psychology and philosophy, as well as about the moral values of the work.

Booth's *The Rhetoric of Fiction* emphasizes the importance of understanding how conscious choices of the author – based upon intention and purpose – shape the reader's response. Influenced by the prior Chicago Aristotelians R. S. Crane and Richard McKeon, Booth showed that the imagined world needs to be understood as a formal relationship between the author who creates and the reader who responds.

Auerbach's *Mimesis* and Frye's *Anatomy of Criticism* represent two opposing strands of criticism in the 1950s: the mimetic and the hermeneutical. Auerbach believes that literature's value depends on the accuracy of its representation of the historical forces it describes, while Frye believes that he can create a system that would separate the study of literature from the study of other aspects of the world. Kermode attempts to resolve these strands in *The Sense of an Ending*. Kermode seeks to mediate between the world of fiction and our world by arguing that we use fiction to make sense of our lives. Kermode tries to combine aesthetic and moral criticism by asking what kind of continuities fiction has with our own lives – our hopes, plans, and needs – and implicitly what role does reading play in our lives.

The final chapter focuses on Hillis Miller's two theoretical books on fiction. *The Form of Victorian Fiction* and *Fiction and Repetition*. More than any other major critic of the English novel, Miller comes to terms with theoretical developments of the past fifteen years or so – including phenomenology, structuralism, and post-structuralism – and is therefore an appropriate figure with whom to conclude our study. Miller's call for heterogeneity is very much in the tradition of pluralism that the humanistic tradition has valued. Nor does he turn his back on the world the novel represents or on construing order in novels, even though he simultaneously seeks to undermine such organizing principles.

We shall discover that changing patterns of criticism reflect changing cultural values. One can very roughly outline three phases of the way in which artists regard themselves in the twentieth century. The first is the iconoclastic modernism of turn-of-the-century artists such as Eliot, Pound, and Joyce, as well as Picasso and Matisse, who variously were influenced by French Symbolism, Pater's *The Renaissance*, Wilde, and F. H. Bradley's *Appearance and Reality*. This first generation of modernists rejected the positivism of science and thought of the artist as an exile or ivory tower figure who should be separate from the concerns of the middle class community and indifferent to political action. This stress on form and technique at the expense of serious interests in the world beyond self derives in part from two factors: the alienation of the artist from the world in which he or she lives and the concomitant belief that the artist's experience is special. In the early twentieth century, fiction and poetry often tried to extend the domain of realism by drawing upon the various non-realistic experiments in the visual arts, including Cubism, Fauvism, and other forms of Post-Impressionism. From the perspective of the artist who is interested in the act of artistic creation, James, Lubbock, and Forster in their criticism similarly redefined the concept of realism. To an extent the aesthetic formalism of the New Criticism and the Chicago criticism, with its emphasis on the work of art as a separate and distinct entity to be examined on its own terms, is the result and counterpart of the literary modernism of the century's first decades.

The second phase was the turn in the arts to subject matter of a less rarefied nature – to greater concern with politics and history – under the stress of the world depression and world wars. In America neither the criticism of Lionel Trilling and Edmund Wilson, nor even of such formalists as Dorothy Van Ghent and Kenneth Burke, was ever dominated by an emphasis on technique and aesthetic issues. In England in the 1930s and 1940s Leavis and his *Scrutiny* colleagues spoke of formal matters in relation to content, and kept alive liberal humanistic attitudes in the form of standards of seriousness, maturity, and inclusiveness of vision. From a retrospective point of view, we can see how Leavis and Trilling negotiated a compromise between aestheticism and ideological and polemical criticism. While eschewing this compromise, Marxist criticism of the novels is part of this second phase, a phase which privileges content over style and realism over imagination.

After World War II and the Holocaust, we can see the third stage as art – in such movements as abstract expressionism, minimalism, theatre of the absurd, the New Novel in France and, cacophonous music – becomes once again separate, elite, and difficult. Self-enclosed systems that privilege form over content, imagination over reason, and morphology over the specific entity (*langue* over *parole*) are in this tradition, including much of the work of Frye, Stevens, Derrida, and Barthes, and some of the work of Kermode and Hillis Miller. To be sure, the post-War American Jewish novel, particularly the work of Bellow, and the Angry Young Men in England were notable exceptions. The recent emphasis on realism, expressionism, mythic and symbolic overtones, and historical imagination not only in painting and sculpture, but also in such fiction as Thomas's *The White Hotel*, Eco's *The Name of the Rose*, and Doctorow's *Ragtime* and *The Book of Daniel* may foreshadow a criticism that, while seeking sophistication in matters of form and while interested in verbal play and marginality, will boldly and powerfully address how form serves the interests of content.

II

If only to define differences and similarities, it may be worthwhile to examine the assumptions of the humanistic tradition in light of the central premises of structuralism and post-structuralism. Anglo-American criticism believes that there is an original meaning, a centre, which can be approached by perceptive reading. Traditional humanistic criticism assumes that language and signs do have external references, or at least do take part in mediating between the real world and the imagined ontology created by the author's imagination. Usually, it assumes that there is the possibility of approaching a correct reading based on the discovery of formal and thematic principles. It may be that in its unshaped potential language can only have differences, not values. But a *literary text* is not inchoate but rather the appropriation of language by an author for the specific purpose of creating an imaginative vision. The text becomes an object to be perceived and understood. The relationships between its formal meanings give it a *value*. The Anglo-American humanistic tradition assumes that the reader strives to recreate the perception of reality that the author created.

Structuralism has much in common with Anglo-American formalism, particularly New Criticism. Both define literary works as a system, although the New Criticism eschewed that term because 'system' implied the very mechanistic and scientific (as opposed to humanistic) values that it was trying to challenge. In its search for formal principles within an imagined ontology, structuralism resembles the New Criticism. For both Anglo-American formalism and structuralism stress the formal and self-regulating principles inherent within a work, although the latter does so more at the expense of verisimilitude and intrinsic organic unity than the New Criticism. Like the structuralists, the New critics saw a poem as a system of 'elements such that a modification of any one entails modification of all others', while the New Criticism stressed its relation to a *telos*.[3] Structuralism seeks to define the conventions which enable physical objects or events to have meaning; it thus complements the nominalistic activity of close reading. As Culler reminds us, Levi-Strauss's version of structuralism sees the mind as 'a structuring mechanism which imposes form on whatever material it finds to hand'.[4] At times the structuralists provide a theoretical model for critical processes that much Anglo-American novel criticism takes for granted. For example, the New Criticism could accept the formulation of reading to which Culler subscribed in his 1974 *Structuralist Poetics*: 'The reader must organize the plot as a passage from one state to another and this passage or movement must be such that it serves as a representation of theme. The end must be a transformation of the beginning so that meaning can be drawn from the perception of resemblance and difference.'[5]

Deconstruction rejects the notion of an authoritative reading based on discovering or understanding the author's intention, perceiving thematic patterns, and comparing the world within the text to a world beyond the text. Derrida, its seminal theorist, is part of a traditional radical scepticism that seeks to ask not how we can know but whether we can know. He and his followers question the authority of any interpretation and seek to show that the same text can generate a contradictory interpretation. The rhetorical mode of deconstructive reading is *aporia*, the moment when reading reaches an irreconcilable paradox. Deconstruction stresses that each reading contains the seeds of its own undoing. It privileges the reader rather than the author. The text becomes consubstantial with the reader rather than, as in traditional criticism, with the author and the reader through a process of communication. Deconstruction asks formal questions about how the text exists separate and distinct from the author and tries to define, as Foucault puts it, 'the condition of both the space in which [the text] is dispersed and the time in which it unfolds'.[6] Characteristically, Foucault claims that '[T]hese aspects of an individual which we designate as making him an author are only a projecting in more or less psychologizing terms, of the operations that we force texts to undergo, the connections that we make, the traits that we establish as pertinent, the continuities that we recognize, or the exclusions that we practice'.[7]

Deconstruction regards a text – and for deconstruction, the text is any written work, not merely a literary work – not as a single goal to be approached by a reader, but as a space within the reader's mind where the possibilities of meaning must be explored and sorted out. Deconstruction compellingly argues that heterogeneous readings always co-exist in an irreconcilable paradox or *aporia*. Deconstruction reminds us that all readings are misreadings because they are only partial readings that cannot account for all the possibilities of a text. But, far less convincingly, Derrida and his followers stress that texts lack both ultimate meaning and effects. For them, as Culler writes, 'Interpretation is not a matter of recovering some meaning which lies behind the work and serves as a center governing its structure; it is rather an attempt to participate in and observe the play of possible meanings to which the text gives access.'[8] As Foucault puts it, Deconstruction asks, 'How can a free subject penetrate the substance of things and give it meaning? How can it activate the rules of a language within and thus give rise to the designs which are properly its own.'[9] These critics do not regard literary work as 'representation' and 'expression', but as products of culture with infinite structures and potential meaning. This approach emphasizes the role of the reader as an active presence creating meaning, and in radical versions sometimes seems to turn the reader into the privileged figure if not an *übermensch*. Each reader must rewrite or 'produce' the text as he or she responds to the effects the text has upon him or her.

Deeply influenced by deconstruction, Miller is still part of the tradition which believes that the primary purpose of critical and theoretical discussion is to produce analyses of literary works. Miller's *Fiction and Repetition* shows us the possibility for dialogue between humanistic and post-structuralist criticism. In Miller we see how the subject – the story and themes – of fiction almost inevitably enters through the back door of even the most rarefied discussions and becomes a strong factor in critical discussion. Significance does not inhere in the text but is experienced during a series of interpretive acts. Yet for Miller the reader creates meaning insofar as interpretive acts are a function of the text. And this is not far from the approach of Booth, Van Ghent, and Leavis. When Miller focuses on the tension between the meanings created by the different expectations generated by content and form, he is in the tradition of Anglo-American formalists, including Blackmur and Burke.

We can find other important points of contact between traditional criticism and recent theory, particularly as practiced by American and English followers of Barthes and Derrida. Intertextuality is, to an extent, a new name for 'influence' and 'encounter' studies. For the more penetrating influence studies do more than trace the source of origin, but rather show how the prior work inheres in and transforms its host text. Both Frye and the Chicago critics recognize, as Culler puts it in *The Pursuit of Signs* that, 'to read is always to read in relation to other texts, in relation to the codes that are the products of these texts, and go to make up a culture'.[10] Genre criticism, as practised by Chicago criticism and Frye, relates a literary work to a whole series of other works, treating them not as sources, but as constituents of genre.

As we shall see, the interest in what a text does as a series of linguistic events or acts is not new. The text's effect upon the reader has been a focus of Booth and his fellow neo-Aristotelians, although their emphasis is more on the patterns inherent in texts than on the sense-making of the reader. Booth, for example, speaks of a 'structure of effects' throughout the work. The dominance of the text and the reader is certainly inherent in the ideology of reading propounded by the New Critics. Should we not recall that the traditional formalist stress on ambiguity and paradox produces ironic readings that undermine the supposed centre or essence of the work without necessarily providing an alternative centre? Indeed, is the hetero-geneous reading that Miller calls for in *Fiction and Repetition* so different from a pluralistic one?

The distance between the deconstructionist scepticism of the author as a presence or origin and the intentional fallacy is far shorter than is often imagined. Surely, the effort of deconstruction to banish the author recalls the New Criticism. Understanding the omniscient narrator as a separate and distinct self-dramatizing character and attending to the speaker's performance – his or her theatricality – are early deconstructions of the tradition of the author as authority. Well before deconstruction, Anglo-American criticism had emphasized the temporality of reading by stressing reading as a process, and this has helped it focus both upon the dynamic quality of a novel's movement and the more subtle evolution and transformation of characters. This focus on reading as process has called attention to stylistic and structural patterns that undermine or qualify the author's intention.

Indeed, American deconstructionists, including both Hillis Miller and Jonathan Culler, often write within the same tradition of common sense and shared values as the traditional critics that preceded them. As Culler puts it, 'Interpretation is always interpretation of something, and that something functions as the object in a subject–object relation, even though it can be regarded as the product of prior interpretations.'[11] Are Culler's 'stories of reading' different from traditional modes of interpretation? As he acknowledges: '[T]hese stories reinstate the text as an agent with definite qualities or properties, since this yields more precise and dramatic narratives as well as creating a possibility of learning that lets one celebrate great works. The value of a work is related to the efficacy granted it in these stories – an ability to produce stimulating, unsettling, moving, and reflective experiences.'[12] Ultimately, even if the value of the work derives from the experience it produces, that experience still depends on the text.

But we should not ignore crucial differences between traditional criticism and deconstruction. Anglo-American criticism does believe that there is the possibility of aproaching the meaning that the author expresses in his or her text, even while that criticism acknowledges that there is not one determinate meaning. It believes that human behaviour is central to most works and should be the major concern of analysis. It focuses on the motives of an action and the results and consequences of human decisions. Yet, as we shall see, focus on subject cannot be separated from form and technique. It is the essence of humanistic criticism to locate and define a voice. Thus Anglo-American criticism sees the voice not as a convention but as a necessary condition of art. It regards the voice as the living presence which reveals himself or herself through words and to which we *want* and *need* to respond. Finally, it seeks something beyond the omniscient narrator or ironic persona – namely, the ordering mind that is gradually revealed by the *telos* of the work.

Anglo-American criticism insists on the unique creative energy of the author. Surely, even if thought, speech, and writing are partly controlled by convention, the individual psyche in response to a situation or attitude gives them shape. Cannot the self be both a source and the construct of cultural patterns? If a work is culturally determined, it is also individually expressed by a particular individual at a particular place in time. Anglo-American criticism has shown that texts have meanings other than those in relation to other texts and conventions of reading. Traditional criticism stresses the author's creativity, judgment, and intuition in the structuring process – the expression of his or her unique self in the imagined world. And once we allow the place of judgment or intuition, meaning is no longer 'moving' through the subject, but is a function of the author's mythmaking and ordering propensities.

Literary theory is useful and important when it proposes effective and inclusive ways to discuss imagined works and when it helps us to define their meaning and form. We should ask of literary theory that it provide both the methods to respond to the specificity of our literary experience and the concepts to organize that experience. It should give us an epistemology – a theory of knowledge – to understand and organize our literary experience, and a semiology – a system of signs – to describe that understanding. I shall demonstrate not only how works of literary theory organizes our knowledge of the English novel, but also how they are an indispensible tool for helping us to discover the significance of individual novels.

I have tried to keep in mind diverse audiences: college and university teachers and graduate students who will read my book to clarify their own positions, and also advanced undergraduates who may have read some of the critics I discuss. As literary study in England and America has become more fragmented and polemical, undergraduates are increasingly baffled by the focus on literary theory, particularly in fiction courses, and by the abstract discussion such focus generates. To keep the focus on novels with which readers are familiar, I have chosen, as much as possible, to discuss how my critics treat major English novels. These include *Tom Jones, Tristram Shandy, Emma, Bleak House, Wuthering Heights, Vanity Fair, Jude the Obscure, Lord Jim, The Rainbow*, and *Ulysses*. I hope to show how diverse critics read the same novels and authors. These texts not only span the historical range of the English novel, but present a variety of narrative techniques, styles, modes of characterization, and formal structures.

NOTES

1. Gene Thornton, *New York Times Arts and Leisure*, 12 Feb. 1982: 'P. H. Polk's Genius versus Modernism', pp. 25–6.
2. Denis Donoghue, *The New York Review of Books*, 27:10 (12 June 1980) 37–41.
3. C. Levi-Strauss, *Anthropologie Structurale*, quoted in Jonathan Culler, *Structuralist Poetics: Structuralism, Linguistics and the Study of Literature* (Ithaca, New York: Cornell University Press, 1974) p. 13.
4. Culler, *Structuralist Poetics*, p. 40.
5. Culler, *Structuralist Poetics*, p. 222.
6. Michael Foucault, 'What is an Author', in Josué V. Harari (ed.), *Textual Strategies: Perspectives in Post-Structuralist Criticism* (Ithaca, New York: Cornell University Press, 1979) p. 144.
7. Foucault, p. 150.
8. Culler, *Structuralist Poetics*, p. 247.
9. Foucault, p. 158.
10. Jonathan Culler, *The Pursuit of Signs: Semiotics, Literature, Deconstruction* (Ithaca, New York: Cornell University Press, 1981) p. 12.
11. Jonathan Culler, *On Deconstruction: Theory and Criticism after Structuralism* (Ithaca: New York: Cornell University Press, 1982) p. 74.
12. Culler, *On Deconstruction*, p. 82.

1 The Humanistic Heritage of James and Lubbock: the Emergence of an Aesthetic of the Novel

I

We begin our study with Henry James because James is the first figure whom we can isolate as a major source of the way we have read and taught fiction in England and America for the past fifty years. We can trace back to Henry James the dilemma of Anglo-American novel criticism: how to focus on technique without sacrificing subject matter. Much of the novel criticism of this century has been trying to resolve these two factors into an aesthetic. Given that novels seem to create imagined worlds with distinct time, space, and causality that mime that of the real world, it seems as if subject matter ought not be ignored. But given that novels are, like other literary forms, works of art composed of words, we cannot ignore technique. As we shall see in the ensuing pages, most 'formal' critics of the novel do not neglect content in determining meaning; nevertheless, focus on one always seems to be at the expense of the other.

When in his recent book, *Fiction and Repetition*, J. Hillis Miller speaks of repetition, he is speaking of the same dilemma. What he calls 'Platonic' repetition underlies the concept of true-to-life; as he puts it, 'The validity of the mimetic copy is established by its truth of correspondence to what it copies.' Hillis Miller's 'other, Nietzschean mode' is one in which 'Each thing . . . is unique, intrinsically different from every other thing' and exists 'on the same plane'. This tradition enjoys art for its own sake, 'without reference to some paradigm or archetype', and feels that discussion of differences and similarities in technique is interesting in itself.[1]

In the following pages, without making any claims to completion, I

16

shall briefly sketch the major ideas of James. The stature of James's novel criticism surely depends upon James's stature as a novelist. As Sarah B. Daugherty notes, 'James's Prefaces, though they have been rigidly interpreted by Percy Lubbock and others, constitute his presentation of his own case, not a set of formulae to be applied to the works of other novelists.'[2] We should remember that his discussion of method and theory is shaped by his own experience of writing novels and, in the case of the Prefaces, in response to his memory of his own novels. Still, his writing about the aesthetic of the novel provided an example for discussing the art of the novel, particularly point of view, and for the humanistic perspective that has dominated Anglo-American formal criticism of the novel. While James looks forward to concern with form and technique, he provided continuity with the high seriousness of Arnold who argued for the central place of criticism and defined it as a disinterested act of mind. As Daugherty has shown, James accepts Arnold's definition of criticism – 'to know the best that is known and thought in the world': 'For him, the literary critic was not the narrow formalist, but rather the cultural, social, and moral critic;' James wished, like Arnold, 'to remain aloof from the vulgar herd, to observe the world from an intellectual height, to see life steadily and see it whole.'[3]

According to Wimsatt and Brooks, James and Flaubert 'display, in reaction against romantic inspirationalism, a concern for crafts-manship, and a stress upon form as opposed to the exploitation of privileged "poetic" materials'.[4] But James's focus on art was in part a reaction to naturalism which focused on heredity and environment in shaping human character and on the drab life of the lower-middle and lower classes. That art controls life and that form discovers the moral significance of theme are part of the New Critical credo for which James has been regarded as a source. Wimsatt and Brooks iterate an orthodoxy of New Criticism when they remark: '[T]he general principle governing the relation of individual word to the total work is not changed simply because these are poems and not novels.'[5] For them James is a spokesman in defence of this position when he writes: 'A novel is a living thing, all one and continuous, like any other organism, and in proportion as it lives will be found, I think, that in each of the parts there is something of each of the other parts' ('The Art of Fiction', *M*, p. 36).[6] By stressing the relationship between form and content in his criticism and by creating works that required the most attentive and intense kind of reading, James provides a precedent for the view articulated by Mark Schorer that technique discovers the values of subject matter. By example and critical tenet, James's insistence of the fusion of style and substance and of form and content has been adopted as a premise of the ontological approach of New Criticism and the rhetorical approach of Chicago Aristotelian criticism. James's attention to aesthetic matters – craft, unity, technique – made him a favourite of New Criticism and his interest in narration made him an important figure in rhetorical criticism.

James's interest in technique and form is influenced by the concept of art for art's sake that Gautier, Baudelaire, and Mallarmé made prominent in France, and which Pater, Wilde, and Yeats imported and developed in England.[7] James can sound like a devotee of art for art's sake who is indifferent to the moral implications of reality and content. When in the preface to *The Spoils of Poynton* he speaks of 'technical subterfuges and subtleties' as 'the noblest parts of *our* amusement', James is something of an aesthete and connoisseur: 'My prime loyalty was to the interest of the game, and the honour to be won the more desirable by that fact. Any muddle-headed designer can beg the question of perspective, but science is required for making it rule the scene' (*AN*, p. 137).[8] Whatever sense of fun informs this passage, it still seems to value artistry for its own sake and to patronize moral values and content.

For James, it is the imagination which mediates between life and art. The artist was not, as the naturalists seemed to regard him, a passive objective observer: 'Experience is never limited, and it is never complete; it is an immense sensibility. . . . It is the very atmosphere of the mind; and when the mind is imaginative – much more when it happens to be that of a man of genius – it takes to itself the faintest hints of life, it converts the very pulses of the air into revelations . . . [Experience is] the power to guess the unseen from the seen, to trace the implication of things, to judge the whole piece by the pattern, the condition of feeling life in general so completely that you are well on your way to knowing any particular corner of it' ('The Art of Fiction', *M*, pp. 34–5). James believed that the imagination transformed life into art and that art was something separate and distinct; as James E. Miller puts it:

It may well be that this conception of the mysteriously operating imagination, on both conscious and unconscious levels, was what separated James from other realists of his time. Whereas they tended to locate the criteria for realism in an apprehendable reality in experience or life itself, James tended to locate the criteria inside the author or artist, and in what the crucible of the imagination did to or for the materials gathered from experience and life. Far from believing that there was a single reality to apprehend, James believed that each novelist, in his individual perspective, by the garnering of impressions that in combination were his and his alone, and through the mystifying process of his unique crucible of imagination, actually created a reality that was impossible of duplication by any other writer (*M*, p. 5).

The notion of art as a separate reality is in the romantic tradition and reminds us that James has continuities with those, from Coleridge through Wilde and Stevens, who sought to build in art an alternative space and who believed that literature can create ghostlier demarcations and keener sounds than the real world.

James borrows a good deal of his critical terminology and something of his sense of the artist as a special figure from the visual arts. In 'The Art of Fiction', he wrote 'A psychological reason is, to my imagination, an object adorably pictorial; to catch the tint of its complexion – I feel as if that idea might inspire one to Titianesque efforts' (*M*, p. 41). Perhaps the interest in Europe, and particularly in Paris, in Impressionism and, later, in the more self-conscious experiments in rendering reality more accurately and more closely – such as Cubism, Fauvism, and Post-Impressionism – was a factor in his use of terminology from painting and sculpture. After all, the Prefaces were written in 1907–9 when Cezanne, Matisse, and Picasso were challenging traditional concepts of reality with their foreshortening, their abandonment of traditional perspective, and their inquiries into the relationship between three-dimensional reality and two-dimensional painting. James felt that 'a picture without composition slights its most precious chance for beauty . . .' (*AN*, p. 84). He saw himself as a painter of consciousness, as someone who caught the evanescent processes of the mind and who imposed, by means of deft brush strokes, order and meaning. He often used the term 'painter' interchangeably with 'writer'. Comparing himself to a painter, he wrote: 'Sketchily clustered even, these elements gave out that vague pictorial glow which forms the first appeal of a living 'subject' to the painter's consciousness; but the glimmer became intense as I proceeded to a further analysis'. (*AN*, p. 141).

James borrowed the term 'foreshortening' from painting to, as James E. Miller puts it, 'indicate that infinitely complex task of evoking a sense of reality . . . [B]oth space and time are for the writer a challenge of perspective; and picture, scene, and dialogue will all be determined by the total strategy for foreshortening' (*M*, p. 12). In other words, for the purpose of arousing interest, the artist will reorganize material according to the artistic demands of intensity, economy, and composition. Because James conceived of his novels in spatial terms and wanted to 'build' a shape or design that would hold, he also uses architectural images with their three-dimensional implications (*AN*, p. 109). Thus he describes *The Portrait of a Lady* as 'a structure reared with an "architectural" competence' (*AN*, p. 52). He recalls his plan for *The Awkward Age* in spatial terms: '[T]he neat figure of a circle consisting of a number of small rounds disposed at equal distance about a central object. The central object was my situation, my subject in itself, to which the thing would owe its title, and the small rounds represented so many distinct lamps, as I liked to call them, the function of each of which would be to light with all due intensity one of its aspects' (*AN*, p. 110).

For the most part, James refused to embrace the position that art was an ivory tower or sacred fount. In his essay on Flaubert (1902), James wrote, 'the form is in *itself* as interesting, as active, as much of the essence of the subject as the idea, and yet so close is its fit and so inseparable its life that we catch it at no moment on any errand of its own' (*M*, p. 259). Form enables the artist to present and understand subjects. The artist's imaginative vision implies his morality. Furthermore, he argued that an artist's total work expresses a more inclusive vision than any of the parts. He wrote of Turgenev (1874), a writer he greatly admired for the way he used plot to create a fable about characters without sacrificing a mature vision of life: 'The great question as to a poet or a novelist is, How does he feel about life? What, in the last analysis, is his philosophy? When vigorous writers have reached maturity we are at liberty to look on their works for some expression of a total view of the world they have been so actively observing' (*M*, p. 297).

James's 'The Art of Fiction' (1884), perhaps his most important single piece of novel criticism, was a response to Walter Besant's 'The Art of Fiction' (1884). Because Besant's published lecture expressed some of the critical shibboleths of the day, James chose the same title as Besant. While James becomes more interested in technique as his career progressed, he never abandoned the credo expressed in 'The Art of Fiction' that 'A novel is in its broadest definition a personal, a direct impression of life: that, to begin with, constitutes its value which is greater or less according to the intensity of the impression' (*M*, p. 33). As Daugherty writes: 'Despite his abiding interest in the art of fiction his discussion of technique was always related to his concern for "life".'[9]

At the centre of James's criticism is an interest in life in every aspect, even if in his work we feel that the focus is on the manners and morals of the upper middle class. In a passage that can only be read autobiographically, he says of himself that 'he incurs the stigma of labouring uncannily for a certain fullness of truth' (*AN*, p. 154). In the Preface to *The Princess Casamassina*, he asserts that the novelist 'report[s] with truth on the human scene; to do so, the novelist requires 'the sense of life and the penetrating imagination' (*AN*, pp. 76, 78). The quest for realism is related to the quest for life and truth. Life was the raw material of art; as Miller puts it, 'Life was the source of art, direct and first-hand impressions made up the materials, and the personal and individual consciousness shaped them into a unique image and a form that constituted their value' (*M*, p. 3).

Content, then, is far more important to James than to some of his followers. Usually, James did not give priority in his criticism to technique. In 'The Art of Fiction', James asserts that, ' "The story", if it represents anything, represents the subject, the idea, the *donnée* of the novel; and there is surely no "school" . . . which urges that a novel should be all treatment and no subject. There must assuredly be something to treat' (*M*, p. 40). Of subject matter the key question asks, 'is it valid, in a word, is it genuine, is it sincere, the result of some direct impression or perception of life?' (*AN*, p. 45). The artist must not be content with creating isolated palaces of art remote from either the reader's or his own life. For James, then, the human aspect is central, and he is nowhere more compelling than when discussing *What Maisie Knew*: 'No themes are so human as those that reflect for us, out of the confusion of life, the close connection of bliss and bale, of the things that help with the things that hurt, so dangling before us for ever that bright hard medal, of so strange an alloy, one face of which is somebody's right and ease and the other somebody's pain and wrong' (*AN*, p. 143). As Daugherty writes, 'His conception of character as center, for example, derived not merely from an aesthetic ideal but from a humanistic philosophy . . . .'.[10]

James directed the novel away from its traditional emphasis on plot, an emphasis derived from neo-classicism and the novel's epic and romance antecedents. James regarded character, not plot, as central to the novel. This relates to what Oscar Cargill calls 'his faith in human

will and in character'.[11] In England and America, James contributed
to the making of an aesthetic that values character over plot and the
English novel of manners and morals over novels that either emphasize a romance component or an historical perspective or polemical
vision.' Miller notes, 'James saw this psychological drama (action or
inaction) as in some sense in competition with conventional plot . . .'
(*M*, p. 10). James's interest is in 'a man's specific behavior' rather than
plot: 'What a man thinks and what he feels are the history and the
character of what he does' (*AN*, p. 66). Thus he preferred fiction in
which character was the centre, and felt a lack of structure when the
attention was more diffuse. In James, according to Miller, 'the matrix
of character and action is consciousness. Thus consciousness becomes
the key to fictional interest and feelings, meditations, inner responses,
flow of thought surge to the fore as major material for representation'
(*M*, p. 16). He wrote in the Preface to *The Princess Casamassina*, 'I
confess I never see the *leading* interest of any human hazard but in a
consciousness (on the part of the moved and moving creature) subject
to fine intensification and wide enlargement' (*AN*, p. 67). Not only is
James's interest in the motives and psyche of characters, but he is
certain that the only conceivable interest for reading is our interest in
other human beings. In an essay on Trollope (1883), he wrote,
'Character, in any sense in which we can get at it, is action and action is
plot, and any plot which hangs together, even if it pretends to interest
us only in the fashion of a Chinese puzzle, plays upon our emotion,
our suspense, by means of personal references. We care what
happens to people only in proportion as we know what people are'
(*M*, p. 200).

James was at his best not as a theorist but when dealing with specific
examples in his work and that of others. After 'The Art of Fiction'
(1884), James rarely posited universal standards and usually insisted
on evaluating authors on their own terms. As Daugherty writes,
'Despite his increasing interest in technique, James became less
preoccupied with theoretical formulations and more tolerant of
aesthetic diversity.'[12] This nominalism, this insistence on responding
to texts on their own terms as 'cases', as James would call them, was an
important influence on the critical practice of allowing a text to
generate its own aesthetic rather than either applying an *a priori*
standard or looking for specific thematic patterns. Perhaps related to
nineteenth-century American optimism, James was relatively tolerant
of all kinds of forms and styles. Style is judged according to its
efficiency and form according to its unity. Content is not judged in

terms of whether it satisfactorily illustrates a position or demonstrates an ideology, but rather upon whether it reflects human life as it is actually lived.

That James's criticism eschews dogmatism, and speaks in general for flexibility and openmindedness is illustrated by his critical style. He rarely wrote as if he believed he could promulgate a credo or set of rules. The qualifications, circumlocutions, hesitations, and intricacies of his own style reinforce his pluralism even while implicitly acknowledging the impossibility of precision in aesthetic matters. In all his criticism, but most notably in the Prefaces, the modest tone, qualifications, sensitivity, tolerance, and judiciousness speak for his humanism; as he puts it: 'The house of fiction has in short not one window, but a million . . .' (*AN*, p. 46). We cannot tell the writer what to write or how: 'We must grant the artist his subject, his idea, his *donnée*: our criticism is applied only to what he makes of it' (*M*, p. 38).

James's discussion of the art of fiction revolves around the artist's relation to his art, the presence of the artist in his work, and the importance of the artist's discovering values. As Miller writes, 'James's presence in the form of the first-person singular is felt throughout his own work, and he contended that as a matter of fact an author could not escape his work because be left his stamp everywhere. . . . Although the author's "spiritual presence" was always distinctive though largely unconscious, his "rendering" of his subject was a matter of acute consciousness' (*M*, pp. 11–12). To use current terms, James believed in the metaphysics of presence. Thus while James has been adopted by rhetorical critics and New Criticism, his aesthetic principles are often surprisingly expressionistic and derive from the creative process that precedes the work. James sees a relationship between 'felt life' – the author's perception of experience – and 'the "moral" sense of a work of art;' the artist's sensibility provides the 'projected morality' (*AN*, p. 45).

R. P. Blackmur summarizes James's central tenets in his introduction to 'The Art of the Novel', his title for his 1934 collection of James's Prefaces to the New York edition of his work.

Life itself – the subject of art – was formless and likely to be a waste, with its situations leading to endless bewilderment; while art, the imaginative representation of life, selected, formed, made lucid and intelligent, gave value and meaning to, the contrasts and oppositions and processions of the society that confronted the artist. . . . Then everything must be sacrificed to the exigence of that form, it must never be loose or overflowing but always tight and contained. There was the 'coercive charm' of Form, so conceived, which would achieve, dramatise or enact, the moral intent of the theme by making it finely intelligible, better than anything else. (*AN*, p. xxxviii)

James called attention to the importance of form at a time when talk about real life dominated discussion of fiction. Before agreeing with Miller that for James, 'form is everything – whether it is called execution, treatment, technique – which is done to the unrefined lump of life, the patch of actual experience, to turn it into the finished work of art, product of the imagination' (*M*, p. 17), we must stress that James sought organic or 'found' form as a way of focusing 'interest'. As Wellek notes, 'the harmony of form and substance is James's constant requirement'.[13] But perhaps by focusing on form, Blackmur underestimates James's commitment to life and essential humanistic values. James believed in the inseparability of style and meaning. Although for the later James a complex style was essential to prsent the complexities of life, he felt that style must always be a means of understanding experience.

We should look more closely at James's standards, even while acknowledging that he is rarely concerned with proposing specific tenets. James believes that the intensity of the creative process is the source of economy, organic unity and, hence, artistic excellence. Intensity of creative effort produces within the imagined world intensity that is usually lacking in day to day life: 'Without intensity, where is vividness, and without vividness where is presentability?' (*AN*, p. 66). In the preface to *The Tragic Muse*, he wrote: 'I delight in deep-breathing economy and organic form', and economy and organic unity derive from the intensity of the creative process (*AN*, p. 84). The artist tries 'to preserve for his subject that unity, and for his use of it (in other words for the interest he desires to excite) that effect of a *centre*, which most economise its value' (*AN*, pp. 37–8). Economy means, as Miller writes, 'Making everything "count" to the utmost. . . . [It has] no reference to size or length but full relevance to architecture and shape' (*M*, p. 19). James frequently refers to what he calls 'the rule of an exquisite economy' (*AN*, p. 129). Of such long novels as *War and Peace*, he asks: 'What do such large loose baggy monsters, with their queer elements of the accidental and the arbitrary, artistically mean . . .' (*AN*, p. 84).

For James, 'interest' is crucial. To arouse interest the artist must

discover *representative* experience: 'The art of interesting us in things
. . . can *only* be the art of representing them' (*AN*, p. 9). James never
loses sight of arousing and maintaining the interest of the reader.
Verisimilitude is a value based on the assumption that the reader will
respond to what he believes is real. Yet interest is not simply interest in
the subject matter; but rather it includes a sense on the part of the artist
of the reader's interests. 'The only obligation to which in advance we
may hold a novel . . . is that it be interesting' (*M*, p. 33). In a sense,
the artist represents the reader and prepares a text which, when its
technique and subject matter fuse into a whole, will appeal to the
reader. He admires the 'preserved and achieved unity and quality of
tone. . . . What I mean by this is that the interest created, and the
expression of that interest, are things kept, as to kind, genuine and true
to themselves' (*AN*, p. 97). Thus aesthetic concepts are inextricably
related to content and the reader's response to it. James is extremely
conscious of *earning* the reader's attention, and he realizes that he
needs to create characters in whom we are 'participators by a fond
attention': 'The figures in any picture, the agents in any drama, are
interesting only in proportion as they feel their respective situations;
since the consciousness, on their part, of the complication exhibited
forms for us their link of connection with it' (*AN*, p. 62). Frequently,
James thinks of himself as a surrogate for the reader. When he speaks
of 'we' and 'us', he is making common cause with the community of
readers he as an artist seeks.

The emphasis on point of view is central in James's novel criticism as
well as in his fiction where he modified the traditional omniscient
narrator of Victorian fiction. His interest in point of view is related to
his concern about intensity, interest, and realism. In part James's standard is realism – the sense that art can imitate the essence of life, what
Hillis Miller calls a Platonic sense of reality. According to Booth: 'The
process most like the process of life is that of observing events through
a convincing, human mind, not a godlike mind unattached to the
human condition . . . [I]f the experience is to be more intense than our
own observations, the mind used as an observer must be "the most
polished of possible mirrors" '.[14] James depends, in his major works on
what he calls 'intense *perceivers* . . . of their respective predicaments'
as 'mirrors of the subject' (*AN*, pp. 70, 71). For him, 'A subject
residing in somebody's excited and concentrated feeling about something – both the something and the somebody of course being as
important as possible – has more beauty to give out than under any other
style of pressure' (*AN*, p. 128). In fiction he believes that, '[T]he person

capable of feeling in the given case more than another of what is to be felt for it, and so serving in the highest degree to *record* it dramatically and objectively, is the only sort of person on whom we can count not to betray, to cheapen or, as we say, give away, the value and beauty of the thing' (*AN*, p. 67).

Reading James's criticism shows us how broad his interests were, how seldom he let himself become enmeshed in narrow discussion of narrative perspective, and how point of view is only part of James's aesthetic heritage. He understands that the teller is like a reader of experience in the sense that he disentangles what he perceives in life as the reader does in the text. Proposing an important analogy, James equates his dramatized consciousness with a reader of 'the pages of life':

> The teller of a story is primarily, none the less, the listener to it, the reader of it, too; and, having needed thus to make it out, distinctly, on the crabbed page of life, to disengage it from the rude human character and the more or less Gothic text in which it has been packed away, the very essence of his affair has been the *imputing* of intelligence. The basis of his attention has been that such and such an imbroglio has got started – on the pages of life – because of something that some one has felt and more or less understood. (*AN*, p. 63)

By shifting focus from external action to the drama of consciousness, James foreshadowed interior monologue and stream of consciousness. James was interested not simply in point of view as a technique but in dramatized consciousness as action; as James E. Miller writes: 'For life itself, the important terms are *immediacy* and *application*: for art, these become *reflection* and *appreciation*. We are involved in the action of life, and must act and apply; we are interested in the action of fiction (if we are), and appreciate it most intensely in its reflection on the feelings and thoughts of characters' (*M*, p. 16).

When James argued that novels were incremental to the reader's experience and enlarged the scope of the reader's life, he introduced a staple of humanistic novel criticism that is somewhat different from Horace's 'to teach and to delight'. In 'Alphonse Daudet,' he wrote: '[T]he success of a work of art, to my mind, may be measured by the degree to which it produces a certain illusion; that illusion makes it appear to us for a time that we have lived another life – that we have had a miraculous enlargement of experience' (*M*, p. 6). But James sometimes stressed that the imaginative worlds of novels provided alternative places to which readers could escape. He believed that '[novelists] offer us [readers] another world, another consciousness, another experience' (*M*, pp. 23–4). Thus the novel frees the reader from his everyday self.

The concepts of romance and realism are crucial to James's criticism. He certainly saw himself in the tradition of nineteenth-century realism. As Daugherty writes, 'James accepted the premise underlying all realistic fiction – that it is the task of the novelist to deal with life around him, not with fantasy, mythology, or philosophy.'[15] Wimsatt and Brooks note that James was enough of an Aristotelian to give 'a picture of a real and objective and external world'.[16] In 'The Art of Fiction', James wrote that '[T]he air of reality (solidity of specification) seems to me to be the supreme virtue of a novel' (*M*, p. 35). In the preface to *The American*, he wrote that realism 'represents to my perception the things we cannot possibly *not* know, sooner or later, in one way or another. . . . The romantic stands, on the other hand, for the things that, with all the facilities [sic] in the world, all the wealth and all the courage and all the wit and all the adventure, we never *can* directly know' (*AN*, pp. 31–2). By contrast, the romance lets us loose from the real, and '[operates] in a medium which relieves it, in a particular interest, of the inconvenience of a *related*, a measurable state, a state subject to all our vulgar communities' (*AN*, p. 33).

In his concept of romance, James includes the fairy tale, the ghost story, or any experience that exists in 'an annexed but independent world in which nothing is right save as we rightly imagine it' (*M*, p. 109). Romance represented to James a vacation from seriousness and from intense study of character. James anticipates the crucial distinction between English novels and American romance that Lawrence made in *Studies in Classic American Literature* (1923) and, later, Richard Chase developed in *The American Novel and its Tradition* (1951). 'The people [in Hawthorne's *The Scarlet Letter*] strike me not as characters, but as reprsentatives, very picturesquely arranged, of a single state of mind; and the interest of the story lies, not in them, but in the situation, which is insistently kept before us, with little progression . . . (*M*, pp. 214–15). James believed that the romance frees the artist from reality, from fact, and from observation. Because romance implies something of a play world, it also frees him from the rigorous concept of mimesis that insists that art should imitate life. Thus James becomes more an aesthete and a romantic when speaking of fairy tales or the wonderful. He rejects pure genres – 'romance' and 'novel' or 'novel of character' and 'novel of incident': 'The only classification of the novel that I can understand is into that which has life and that which has it not' (*M*, p. 37). He admired Balzac, Scott, and even Zola for fusing realistic and romantic impulses and, in his fiction, James always tempered his own romance elements with a strong realistic component.

James believed in literary criticism of fiction as an intellectual activity and felt that it could educate novelists and readers. In James's criticism, as Wellek writes, 'The contrast between the English novel and the French novel is drawn so sharply that the English appear as the blundering formless prudish psychologists and moralists and the French as the shallow, immoral masters of the surface and of sensations . . . James himself aims at righting the balance; he himself is creating the psychological, moral novel which is also a work of art and form.'[17] James believed that the comparative positions of the French and English novels had much to do with the differing state of criticism in these two nations: 'The authors of the English studies appear to labor, in general, under a terror of critical responsibility; the authors of the French, on the contrary, to hunger and thirst for it.'[18] Because of his appreciation of the French novelists culminating in his acknowledgement of Balzac as his artistic patriarch and master, he also influenced the tendency to value the European novel – particularly the French novel – despite its bent for the sociological at the expense of the psychological, and to patronize the English novel as less artistic and less inclusive.

II

The story of modern novel criticism continues with Lubbock's codification of James's practice and theory. In his foreword to *The Craft of Fiction*, Schorer aptly summarizes Lubbock's achievement: 'He gave the criticism of the novel not only terms by means of which it could begin to discuss the question of how novels are made ("the only question I shall ask"), but also a model of the way that the question might plausibly be put.'[19] James's criticism, especially the Prefaces, is the Bible and Lubbock's *The Craft of Fiction* (1921) is the Talmud or *Midrash*. Lubbock's book along with Joseph Warren Beach's *The Method of Henry James* (1918) and *The Twentieth Century Novel: Studies in Technique* (1932) did much to turn James's musings on his method as a novelist into an aesthetic with rigid rules. Yet it is ironic that Lubbock and Beach sought to codify James's suggestions, for

James himself cautions about theorizing upon art: '[M]ysteries here elude us, . . . general considerations fail or mislead, and . . . even the fondest of artists need ask no wider range than the logic of that particular case. The particular case, or in other words his relation to a given subject, once the relation is established, forms in itself a little world of exercise and agitation' (*AN*, p. 121). James often thought that a characteristic of novels was their freedom from rules and categories; James Miller notes that this freedom gives the novelist room for experimentation and innovation: 'Such freedom *from* rules and regulations and freedom *for* experimentation and creation should prove exhilarating for both writers and their audience' (*M*, p. 26). James particularly objected to the imposition of extrinsic standards on a work based on critics' preconceptions about what a novel should be; he wrote that the only '*a priori* . . . rule for a literary production [is] that it shall have genuine life' (*M*, p. 24). Subscribing to the latitudinarianism of the later James, Lubbock maintains, 'The best form is that which makes the most of its subject' (p. 40).[20] But in practice, as we shall see, he has a hierarchy of methods, and his paradigm is James's later method of having an omniscient narrator render the consciousness of characters even to the point of effacing himself.

We should not forget that Lubbock was a practising novelist as well as the editor of the final volumes of the New York edition of James's works and of James's letters. Like James, Lubbock believes that criticism affects the writing of novels. For example, he speculates that perhaps the reason for the dearth of dramatic novels like *The Awkward Age*, is 'the state of criticism . . . with its long indifference to these questions of theory' (p. 197). Lubbock's premise is that fiction criticism, on the whole, was languishing and that it had neither developed its principles nor vocabulary: 'In writing about novels one is so rarely handling words that have ever been given close definition (with regard to the art of fiction, I mean) that it is natural to grasp at any which have chanced to be selected and strictly applied by a critic of authority' (p. 110). He regrets 'the chaos in which the art is still pursued. . . . [There is] no connected argument, no definition of terms, no formulation of claims, not so much as any ground really cleared and prepared for discussion' (p. 272). What we need is to discuss the 'technical aspect', 'the question of [a novel's] making' (p. 272). He distinguishes between the novel as 'object of art' and its subject which is 'a piece of . . . life' (p. 6).

Creative reading, Lubbock believes, must strive to understand what goes into the making of the work. Anticipating reader-response criticism, Lubbock recognizes the role of the reader in discovering the form that the writer has used to create art out of life: 'The reader of a novel – by which I mean a critical reader – is himself a novelist. . . . The reader must therefore become, for his part, a novelist, never permitting himself to suppose that the creation of the book is solely the affair of the author . . . [B]oth of them make the novel' (pp. 17–18). As we read, 'we are creating a design, large or small, simple or intricate, as the chapter finished is fitted into its place; or again there is a flaw and a break in the development, the author takes a turn that appears to contradict or to disregard the subject, and the critical question, strictly so called, begins' (pp. 23–4).

Lubbock's codification stresses several concepts crucial to twentieth-century novel criticism. Lubbock taught us that a book is 'a process, a passage of experience', revealing its form – or, rather partially revealing its form, because that form is 'an ideal shape with no existence in space' and lacks 'size and shape' (pp. 15, 22), and therefore can only be approached imperfectly. Lubbock realized that the reading of fiction is a linear process and that patterns take shape and then dissolve or recede, only to be replaced by new patterns which do the same. Lubbock's first three sentences make a telling point about the folly of conceiving of fiction in spatial terms:

> To grasp the shadowy and fantasmal form of a book, to hold it fast, to turn it over and survey it at leisure – that is the effort of a critic of books, and it is perpetually defeated. Nothing, no power, will keep a book steady and motionless before us, so that we may have time to examine its shape and design. As quickly as we read, it melts and shifts in the memory; even at the moment when the last page is turned, a great part of the book, its finer detail, is already vague and doubtful. (p. 1)

Using the qualification and suspension of predicate which are characteristic of the mature Jamesian style, Lubbock describes the ineffability of form to the perceiver in a medium that is temporally defined. Because of a novel's length, the reader cannot retain everything; impressions of character, theme and language inevitably displace one another rather than build towards an architectonic whole.

By using much of the Jamesian vocabulary, Lubbock forges a link to his master. Unlike James, at times it seems that for Lubbock point of view *is* the craft of fiction: 'The whole intricate question of method, in the craft of fiction, I take to be governed by the question of the point of view – the question of the relation in which the narrator stands to the story' (p. 251). Lubbock prefers the dramatized consciousness of the narrator to other methods: 'In the drama of his mind there is no personal voice, for there is no narrator; the point of view becomes the reader's once more. The shapes of thought in the man's mind tell their own story. And that is the art of picture-making when it uses the dramatic method' (p. 256). And this works best if a third person narrator is retained, because he can range over time freely: 'The seeing eye is with somebody in the book, but its vision is reinforced; the picture contains more, becomes richer and fuller, because it is the author's as well as his creature's, both at once . . . [The author] keeps a certain hold upon the narrator *as an object*; the sentient character in the story, round whom it is grouped, is not utterly subjective, completely given over to the business of seeing and feeling on behalf of the reader' (pp. 258–9).

Of course, this is the characteristic method of James. We note that in comparison to James's involved, discriminating and sometimes tentative style, Lubbock's is straightforward, sententious, and, at times, aphoristic. This contributes to our sense that Lubbock is a disciple codifying the Master's words – or, to press my metaphor, explaining his parables. Rereading James's criticism is different from rereading *The Craft of Fiction* because Lubbock is much more clinical, detached and even reductive. Unlike James, it does not seem that his sensibility is seeking the exact distinction and the precise word. At times, one feels that in comparison to James, Lubbock's criticism is inflexible, narrow, and humourless; this feeling occurs especially when he uses prescriptive terms: 'The narrative, then, the chronicle, the summary, which must represent the story-teller's ordered and arranged experience, and which must accordingly be of the nature of a picture, is to be strengthened, is to be raised to a power approaching that of drama, where the intervention of the story-teller is no longer felt' (p. 122; emphasis mine). What he dislikes is information told to the reader which 'reposes upon nothing that [the reader] can test for himself. . . . Everything in the novel, not only the scenic episodes but all the rest, is to be in some sense dramatized; that is where the argument tends' (pp. 121, 123). Even Turgenev, one of James's favourites, is faulted for failure to dramatize.

Lubbock focused on James primarily as a formal and technical master and neglected his interest in truth and life. That Lubbock faults *War and Peace* for its lack of unity shows us his commitment to organic unity at the expense of the quality and breadth of content. 'The

chapters of [*War and Peace*] refuse to adapt themselves . . . to a broad
and single effect . . . [T]hey will not draw together and announce a
reason for their collocation' (pp. 52–3); for 'The uncertainty of
Tolstoy's intention is always getting between the reader and the detail
of his method' (p. 59). But of course James himself did not respond to
Tolstoy's concept of form. Basically, Lubbock zeroes in on James's
concept of organic form: 'The well-made book is the book in which the
subject and the form coincide and are indistinguishable – the book in
which the matter is all used up in the form, in which the form expresses
all the matter' (p. 40). He indicts Tolstoy for failing to integrate 'into
one design' the historical material with 'the drama of the rise of a
generation:' 'a comeliness of form . . . [would have made *War and
Peace*] a finer, truer, more vivid and more forcible picture of life'
(pp. 31, 40–1).

Even if one does not agree with his view of *War and Peace*,
Lubbock's standards are clear. Lubbock objects to *War and Peace*
because 'its loose unstructural form . . . is wasteful to its subject' and
does 'injury . . . to the story' (p. 41), because, in James's terms, it is a
'baggy monster'. Organic unity becomes a Neo-Platonic ideal. Lubbock's objection is that the intention of *War and Peace* cannot be
expressed 'in ten words that reveal its unity' (p. 42). On each reading
of *War and Peace*, 'it becomes harder to make a book of it at all;
instead of holding together more firmly, with every successive
reconstruction, its prodigious members seem always more disparate
and disorganized; they will not coalesce' (p. 41). In contrast to *War
and Peace*, *Madame Bovary* 'is a novel in which the subject stands firm
and clear, without the least shade of ambiguity to break the line which
bounds it. . . . The story stands obediently before the author, with all
its developments and illustrations, the characters defined, the small
incidents disposed in order. His sole thought is how to present the
story, how to tell it in a way that will give the effect he desires, how to
show the little collection of facts so that they may announce the
meaning he sees in them' (pp. 60, 62). To an extent, Lubbock's
preference is for the moral ambiguity of Flaubert over the moral
certainty of Tolstoy; for the novel of manners and motives over the
novel in which the individual is seen as the function of, and placed in
the context of, historical forces; and for artistic economy over scope
and range.

For Lubbock, more than for James, form and unity are values in
themselves, distinct and separate from how they convey meaning. The
shift in emphasis is one of degree, not kind, but it is obvious that

content plays a much lesser role in Lubbock than James. Lubbock wrote to redress the balance between form and content at a time when he justifiably felt that matters of form and artistry had been neglected. Yet if we read Lubbock carefully, we discover that, despite his stress on form, he understands the importance of content. Notwithstanding his emphasis on artistry, Lubbock has not abandoned the content of the work and is interested in the feelings of the author, the consciousness of the teller, the issues that the novel presents, and the richness and variety of the imagined world. Technique is perceived as a way not only to artistic unity, but'to seeing and feeling the external world; unity usually revolves around and is in service to meaning. Indeed, while Lubbock's focus is on isolating the originality of James's technique, we should recall how he recapitulates the *content* of the James's novels he discusses – most notably *The Ambassadors* and *The Wings of the Dove* – as if Lubbock cannot quite eschew plot even if he wants to.

Lubbock's argument enacts his credo for fiction that 'the subject dictates the method' (p. 253). Always writing with his plan in mind, he moves from drama (his specific examination of individual novels) to panorama (his conceptual argument that moves backward and for-wards over the novels). By combining the scenic – specific examples of novels – with an informed, panoramic overview of fiction, he provides both a synchronic and diachronic view of the major novels. For Lubbock there are two precepts to guide 'the best manner of treatment' (p. 150): 'In the first place he wishes the story so far as possible to speak for itself, the people and the action to appear independently rather than to be described and explained' (p. 150). The second precept is 'economy' by which he means the most efficient presentation where nothing is superfluous to the meaning or excres-cent to the form.

Lubbock largely followed those precepts in the shaping of *The Craft of Fiction*. While at first it seems that he presents the novels independently and adheres to discrete, economic presentation of each one, it is apparent to the reader that his own narrative orders these texts according to a teleology climaxing in James. Thus Thackeray represents 'the first step in the dramatization of picture': 'the characterized "I" is substituted for the loose and general "I" of the author; the loss of freedom is more than repaid by the more salient effect of the picture. Precision, individuality is given to it by this pair of eyes, known and named, through which the reader sees it; instead of drifting in space above the spectacle he keeps his allotted station and contemplates a delimited field of vision' (pp. 127–8). But Thackeray is faulted for overusing the convention of "universal knowledge of the story and the people in it' (p. 115). According to Lubbock, 'the characteristic danger' of 'pictorial fiction' is that 'the point of view is *not* accounted for' (p. 117). By contrast, *Madame Bovary* 'is largely a picture, a review of many details and occasions, the question of the narrator is never insistent' (p. 118). For Lubbock, finally, 'drama is the novelist's highest light' (p. 120). While here he acknowledges the superiority of the dramatic, he leaves for the penultimate section (p. xvii) his panegyric for the Jamesian method of a dramatized consciousness, a consciousness which merges the advantages of the methods of Thackeray and Flaubert.

The entire argument moves dialectically to the apocalyptic revelation of James's achievement of the dramatized consciousness. To an extent, Lubbock's ignoring a strict chronological approach disguises this movement. Yet Lubbock does have a strong evolutionary perspective on the novel. For example, when briefly discussing *Clarissa*, he speaks of its epistolary technique as 'a stage in the natural struggle of the mere record to become something more, to develop independent life and to appear as action' (p. 155). While acknowledging Richardson's epistolary method of 'making [Clarissa] tell her story while she is still in the thick of it', he patronizes the 'queer and perverse idea of keeping her continually bent over her pen' (pp. 153–4). This technique enables the 'novelist [to pass] on towards drama, [to get] behind the narrator, and [to represent] the mind of the narrator as in itself a kind of action' (p. 148).

Following James, Lubbock uses imagery from the visual arts. Although he uses 'pictures' and 'drama' somewhat differently, Lubbock is indebted to James for these terms. He distinguishes between the reader's role in these two forms: 'In one case [picture,] the reader faces towards the story-teller and listens to him, in the other [drama] he turns towards the story and watches it' (p. 111). The pictorial method enables the author to range back and forth over a character's life and to provide the necessary background which gives significance to the dramatic action: 'It is the method of picture-making that enables the novelist to cover his great spaces of life and quantities of experience, so much greater than any that can be brought within the acts of a play. As for intensity of life, that is another matter; there . . . the novelist has recourse to his other arm, the one that corresponds with the single arm of the dramatist' (p. 118). In this method, the author 'is behind us, out of sight, out of mind; the story occupies us, the moving scene, and nothing else' (p. 113). On the other hand, 'the general panorama, such as Thackeray displays, becomes the representation of the author's experience, and the author becomes a personal entity, about whom we may begin to ask questions. . . . So much of a novel, therefore, as is not dramatic enactment, not *scenic*, inclines always to picture, to the reflection of somebody's mind' (pp. 114–15). Lubbock has his own narrative order, and that order emphasizes James's discovery of a technique to replace the 'picture' of the mind with the dramatic enactment of the mind.

As for James, characterization is crucial to Lubbock's concept of form. Indeed, he seems to diminish the role of plot even further. Following James, Lubbock insists that characters must be chosen not because they are exceptional, but because of their universality. At one point, it is on the basis of characterization that Lubbock differentiates between the scenic, by which he means a dramatized scene in which the major characters take part, and the panoramic, an overview of the characters' experiences. An artist alternates between 'writing, at a given moment, with his attention upon the incidents of his tale, or . . . regarding primarily the form and colour they assume in somebody's thought' (p. 71); if he is a polished artist he alternates according to '*some* plan' (p. 72), and, for Lubbock, the best plan is one that always keeps the reader's interest in mind.

Lubbock's view of Balzac has been strongly influenced by James's admiration of Balzac, a writer whom, as we have seen, James increasingly thought of as his master. For Lubbock, Balzac's strength is in picture, while Tolstoy's is in drama. Balzac's *Eugénie Grandet* shows 'the value of the novelist's picture, as preparation for his drama' (pp. 230–1). After discussing Balzac's pacing, he writes: 'Everybody feels the greater force of the climax that assumes its right place without an effort, when the time comes, compared with that in which a strain and an exaggerated stress are perceptible. The process of writing a novel seems to be one of continual forestalling and anticipating; far more important than the immediate page is the page to come, still in the distance, on behalf of which this one is secretly working' (p. 234). Tolstoy's *Anna Karenina* lacks 'exposition' and 'retrospect'. While Tolstoy excels at creating dramatic scenes, Balzac's merit is his panorama, his general knowledge of his characters. But here Tolstoy is faulted for *not* using the panoramic method: 'The method of the book, in short, does not arise out of the subject; in treating it Tolstoy simply used the method that was congenial to him, without regarding the story that he had to tell' (p. 247). Like James, Lubbock is insisting upon a strong element of intentionality and reason, although he acknowledges the role of the unconscious in the artistic creation.

The Craft of Fiction has its hagiographic aspect. Lubbock is unstinting in his praise for James. Yet, Lubbock acknowledges that because of James's idiosyncrasy, because James's books 'are so odd and so personal and so peculiar in all their aspects', 'the only real *scholar* in the art – is the novelist whose methods are most likely to be overlooked or mistaken, regarded as simply a part of his own original quiddity' (pp. 186–7). Simply put, James showed how to treat 'dramatically' 'an undramatic subject'. In Lubbock's argument, *The Ambassadors* and *The Wings of the Dove* become the quintessence of fiction, the position to which the history of the novel moves. Lubbock dialectically resolves thesis and antithesis – on the one hand, scenic or dramatic, and, on the other, pictorial or panoramic: 'Everything in [*The Ambassadors*] is now dramatically rendered, whether it is a page of dialogue or a page of description, because even in the page of description nobody is addressing us, nobody is reporting his impression to the reader. . . . And yet *as a whole* the book is all pictorial, an indirect impression received through Strether's intervening consciousness, beyond which the story never strays' (p. 170). Basically, James is credited for discovering a technique which uses the best features of scene and panorama. For Lubbock, this is fiction's version of splitting the atom. He writes: 'I do not know that anywhere except in the later novels of Henry James, a pictorial subject is thus handed over in its entirety to the method of drama, so that the intervention of a seeing eye and a recording hand, between the reader and the subject, is practically avoided altogether' (p. 185). This statement reveals a concept of action that values the drama of consciousness over events and episodes.

If we doubt that the teleology of Lubbock's argument climaxes in James, we might recall his praise of *The Wings of the Dove* in which the four characters – Densher, Kate, Milly, Susan Stringham – 'each in turn *seems* to take up the story and to provide the point of view, and where it is absolutely needful they really do so. . . . They *act* [the progress of the tale], and not only in their spoken words, but also and much more in the silent drama that is perpetually going forward within them. They do not describe and review and recapitulate this drama, nor does the author. It is played before us, we see its actual movement' (pp. 184–5). Lubbock argues that James's method is always determined by the needs of his subject. For example, because the subject of *The Awkward Age*, the maturation of Nanda, is 'capable of acting itself out from beginning to end [and] is made to do so, [it is] one novel in which method becomes as consistent and homogeneous as it ever may in fiction' (p. 194). In *The Awkward Age*, James uses the fully *scenic* method, and 'never deviates from the straight, square view of the passing event' (p. 195).

Like James, Lubbock stresses the presence of the author. He understands that Flaubert's supposed impersonality is impossible: 'But of course with every touch that he lays on his subject he must show what he thinks of it; his subject, indeed, the book which he finds in his selected fragment of life, is purely the representation of his view, his judgment, his opinion of it. The famous 'impersonality' of Flaubert and his kind lies only in the greater tact with which they express their feelings – dramatizing them, embodying them in living form, instead of stating them directly' (pp. 67–8). And what he says about Flaubert's impersonality is true of James's pretence to objectivity – and, indeed, Lubbock's own in *The Craft of Fiction*.

The conclusion summarizes the major premises developed in his preceding pages. Lubbock reasserts his belief that the dramatic scene is central. He praises 'the fully wrought and unified scene, amply drawn out and placed where it gathers many issues together, showing their outcome. Such a scene, in which every part of it is active, advancing the story, and yet in which there is no forced effort, attempting a task not proper to it, is a rare pleasure to see in a book. . . . Drama, then, gives the final stroke, it is the final stroke which it is adapted to deliver; and picture is to be considered as subordinate, preliminary and preparatory' (p. 269). Scenes, he believes, should only be used at crucial moments, because a scene display only 'the whole of the time and space it occupies' (p. 268). (Actually, we might ask, are not time and space foreshortened even in dramatic scenes?) At times, he seems to imply that while picture or panorama is a reflection, a secondary image, the dramatic scene is a primary one, that is, one that is more real. He says that the 'pictorial report of things [is] thin and flat' because it is 'the reflection that we receive from the mind of another' (p. 270). But only when one *dramatizes* the mirror of the mind of the teller as 'a solid and defined and visible object' (p. 271) are the benefits of both pictorial and dramatic realized. Thus 'the story that is centred in somebody's consciousness . . . takes its place as a story dramatically pictured, and as a story, therefore, of stronger stuff than a simple and undramatic report' (pp. 271–2).

The Craft of Fiction played a crucial role in defining the James legacy and giving direction to the humanistic heritage of Anglo-American criticism. Indeed, Lubbock's codification and simplification of James make easier reading than the master himself. The paradox of Lubbock's is that while he is more interested in art than life and form than content, he is much more of a positivist than James and turned firmly away from the Wilde tradition that valued art for creating fictions truer and more intense than reality. In 1921 when Lubbock wrote *The Craft of Fiction* this latter aesthetic tradition was important in the work of Yeats, Joyce, and Woolf.

But *The Craft of Fiction* also has some notable shortcomings.

(1) In addition to, and possibly in place of the synopsis of plots, the reader needs detailed analyses of how specific passages contribute to the meaning and artistry of the novels discussed. Lubbock acknowledges that, rather than analyse complete novels, he has chosen novels to analyse an 'aspect'. But at times Lubbock lacks what James might call the finer discrimination, the subtlety of mind that enables James to make poised and mature distinctions when discussing an artist's techniques. As we shall see, in *Aspects of the Novel* (1927) Forster chose the term 'aspects' – a term Lubbock uses for elements of craft – to express his commitment to content and to aspects of form, such as rhythm and pattern, that resist what Forster would have thought of as Lubbock's scientific positivism.

(2) At times, Lubbock is redundant. It seems as if he is constantly repeating his distinction between on the one hand, drama or scenic, and on the other, pictorial or panorama. What does Lubbock mean when he writes: 'The purpose of the novelist's ingenuity is always the same; it is to give to his subject the highest relief by which it is capable of profiting' (p. 173)? (Indeed, Lubbock is not always clear on these occasions when he imports the language of other art forms.)

(3) To some extent, Lubbock does a disservice to the English novel. Except for short discussions of Dickens and Meredith, and the section on Thackeray, he does not do much with English fiction, unless we consider James as English. Not only does he overrate Meredith, claiming that *Harry Richmond* is a great contemporary work that would have stood as proof to Shakespeare, had he returned from the dead, that literature still lives, but he patronizes Richardson as a primitive; Richardson does not know that 'he . . . is engaged in the attempt to show a mind in action, to give a

dramatic display of the commotion within a breast' (p. 152). That Forster chose to discuss mostly English novels was a deliberate rejoinder to Lubbock's comparative neglect of them.
(4) A minor, but important point: an index and chapter titles would have been very useful.

But we should conclude by paying tribute to both James and Lubbock. While they do not provide cohesive interpretations, they focused attention on the art of the novel and gave their successors an example of systematic and rigorous thought about the genre. The history of novel criticism, more than the criticism of poetry and drama, is, in this century, a progressive and evolutionary one. The immense prestige of James, based on his fiction, combined with James's own self-consciousness of what he did as an artist, gave novel criticism its impetus. By stressing the humanistic and mimetic implications of the transformation of life into art, while not disregarding aesthetic considerations, James influenced the direction of Anglo-American formalism and its efforts to reconcile novels as embodiments of social and historical truth with novels as either well-wrought urns or as the author's imaginative, creative, and even playful action. James's humanistic legacy also owes much to his muted tone, tolerance, and tact, and to what Wellek calls his 'belief in the moral and social order of the universe'.[21]

The Craft of Fiction, Lubbock's critical tribute to James, contributed to the making of a humanistic heritage. Their criticism emphasized three concepts: the dramatized consciousness of the individual character – his emotional and moral life – as subject; the author's creative transformation of art into life, and understanding the artistry involved in that process; and the importance of arousing and maintaining the reader's interest. Each of these three concepts depends upon belief in the ability of a human being to control his life and in the implicit value of one man communicating to another.

NOTES

1. J. Hillis Miller, *Fiction and Repetition* (Cambridge, Mass.: Harvard University Press, 1982) p. 6.
2. Sarah B. Daugherty, *The Literary Criticism of Henry James* (Athens, Ohio: Ohio University Press, 1981) p. 139. In 'Henry James's Literary Theory and Criticism', *American Literature*, 30:3 (Nov. 1958) 293–321, René Wellek condescendingly writes, 'The *Prefaces* are primarily reminiscences and commentaries [on James's own work] and not criticism'

(p. 294). Wellek wants to give equal attention to James's other criticism, but surely it is the Prefaces and 'The Art of Fiction' that have become part of our critical heritage.

3. Daugherty, pp. 3–4.
4. William K. Wimsatt, Jr. and Cleanth Brooks, *Literary Criticism: a Short History* (New York: Vintage Books, 1967) p. 686.
5. Wimsatt and Brooks, p. 686.
6. Page numbers in parentheses preceded by 'M' refer to *Theory of Fiction: Henry James*, ed. James E. Miller (Lincoln: University of Nebraska Press, 1972).
7. James did not admire the work of Swinburne, Wilde, or Pater. See Wellek pp. 300–1.
8. Page numbers in parentheses preceded by 'AN' refer to *The Art of the Novel: Critical Prefaces*, ed. R. P. Blackmur (Scribner: New York, 1934).
9. Daugherty, pp. 193–4.
10. Daugherty, p. 194.
11. *The Novels of Henry James* (New York: Macmillan, 1961) p. 375. Quoted in Daugherty, p. 194.
12. Daugherty, p. 139.
13. Wellek, p. 316.
14. Wayne Booth, *The Rhetoric of Fiction* (The University of Chicago Press, 1961) p. 45. The last phrase is quoted from Blackmur, *The Art of the Novel*, pp. 69–70. Wellek aptly remarks that 'point of view in James . . . serves to heighten the consciousness of the character and hence to increase the reader's identification with him. Ultimately it is another device to achieve the general effect of illusion' (Wellek, p. 313).
15. Daugherty, p. 186.
16. Wimsatt and Brooks, p. 692.
17. Wellek, p. 306–7.
18. 'The Present Literary Situation in France', quoted in Daugherty, p. 150.
19. Mark Schorer, 'Forward' to Percy Lubbock, *The Craft of Fiction* (New York: Viking, 1957) orig. edn 1921.
20. Page references in parentheses refer to *The Craft of Fiction* (New York: Viking, 1957) orig. edn 1921.
21. Wellek, p. 320.

2 The Importance of E. M. Forster's *Aspects of the Novel*

E. M. Forster's *Aspects of the Novel* (1927) remains a cornerstone of Anglo-American novel criticism. Forster's study helped define the values and questions with which we have approached novels for the past several decades. Moreover, today, it still addresses the crucial questions that concern us about form, point of view, and the relationship between art and life. While acknowledging the importance of Percy Lubbock's *The Craft of Fiction* (1921) in extending the James aesthetic, the brilliance of Virginia Woolf's insights in her essays in *The Common Reader* (1925) and elsewhere, and the usefulness of Edwin Muir's *The Structure of the Novel* (1928), I believe that Forster's book is the one of these 1920s books on the novel to which we most frequently return to learn about *how* novels mean and *why* they matter to us. *Aspects of the Novel* is informed not merely by the living experience of Forster's having written novels throughout his adult life but, more importantly, by judgment, perspicacity, and erudition. To be sure, he does not articulate what we now think of as a theory, and he lacks the dialectical and polemical edge of recent criticism. Thus he disarmingly explains that he has chosen the term 'aspects', 'because it means both the different ways we can look at a novel and the different ways a novelist can look at his work' (p. 24).[1] In the early chapters, Forster begins with such traditional aspects as 'story', 'people', and 'plot' before turning in the later ones to less conventional ones such as 'fantasy', 'prophecy', 'pattern', and 'rhythm'.

In the editor's introduction to the Abinger edition of E. M. Forster's *Aspects of the Novel*, Oliver Stallybrass rather patronizingly writes that *Aspects* is 'a set of observations, somewhat arbitrarily arranged . . . of a man who is a novelist first, a slightly uncommon reader second, a friend third, and an analytical or theorizing critic fourth.'[2] Moreover,

Stallybrass contends, 'What most readers will cherish are the numerous particular judgments, instinctive rather than intellectual . . . '.[3] For Stallybrass, *Aspects* is merely 'a useful adjunct to other, more sustained and consistent works of criticism'[4] – although we are not told where we are to find them. That the editor of Forster's collected works makes such modest claims for such an historically significant study shows how far scholarship and theory have drifted apart. Because Forster defines aesthetic goals in terms of the values by which he wrote his own novels, it has been fliply observed that *Aspects of the Novel* is Forster's *apologia*. Thus, Stallybrass quotes the narrator in Somerset Maugham's *Cakes and Ales*: 'I read *The Craft of Fiction* by Mr. Percy Lubbock, from which I learned that the only way to write novels was like Henry James; after that I read *Aspects of the Novel* by E. M. Forster, from which I learned that the only way to write novels was like Mr. E. M. Forster.'[5] Taking issue with this condescension, I shall argue that *Aspects of the Novel* is a seminal text in the criticism of fiction.[6]

The key to understanding Forster is to realize that he writes in two traditions: the humanistic tradition, with its components of positivism, nominalism, and utilitarianism, and its admiration of realism; and the prophetic tradition, with Platonic and biblical origins, which sees art as either an alternative to, or an intensification of, this world. In this first tradition, we find Aristotle, Horace, Arnold and usually James; in the second we find Blake, Shelley, Pater, Wilde, Yeats, Lawrence, and Stevens. The first tradition strives to see life steadily and to see it whole. The second wants art to be superior in quality to life. Forster, and indeed Woolf, were drawn to both these traditions. In *Aspects*, we might imagine that Forster speaks in two voices, as he tries to do justice to the appeals of both these traditions. In the chapters, 'Story', 'People', and 'Plot', the voice of the first tradition dominates. But in the later chapters, beginning with 'Fantasy', and becoming more pronounced in 'Prophecy', 'Pattern and Rhythm', the voice of the second tradition becomes gradually more prominent. At times we feel, as in the chapter on fantasy, that he knows that he cannot resolve the contending claims of these two traditions.

Aspects of the Novel is not only a rough codification of the Bloomsbury aesthetic, but a specific response to Woolf's 'Mr. Bennett and Mrs. Brown'. Writing in 1924, Virginia Woolf insisted that the Georgian writers needed to abandon the 'tools' and 'conventions' of their Edwardian predecessors because the latter 'have laid an enormous stress on the fabric of things':

At the present moment we are suffering, not from decay, but from having no code of manners which writers and readers accept as a prelude to the more exciting intercourse of friendship. . . . Grammar is violated; syntax disintegrated; . . . We must reflect that where so much strength is spent on finding a way of telling the truth, the truth itself is bound to reach us in rather an exhausted and chaotic condition.[7]

In 1928 except for Conrad, the great modern British novelists – Lawrence, Joyce, Woolf – were at their peak even if their achievement and significance were far from clear. But while Lawrence, Joyce, Woolf, and Conrad sought new forms and syntax, Forster had shown in his novel – *Where Angels Fear to Tread* (1905), *The Longest Journey* (1907), *A Room With a View* (1908), *Howard's End* (1910), and *Passage to India* (1924) – that the English language and the novel genre already had the resources to examine human life, including its instincts and passions, and in *Aspects of the Novel* he sought to articulate that view.[8]

Forster's own career as a novelist helps us to understand *Aspects*. His iconoclasm in part derives from his homosexuality, and in part his sense that he is an anachronism who belongs to a social and moral era that has been all but overwhelmed by modernism, progress, and utilitarianism. Forster writes in 'The Challenge of Our Time':

I belong to the fag-end of Victorian liberalism, and can look back to an age whose challenges were moderate in their tone, and the cloud on whose horizons was no bigger than a man's hand. In many ways, it was an admirable age. It practised benevolence and philanthropy, was humane and intellectually curious, upheld free speech, had little colour-prejudice, believed that individuals are and should be different, and entertained a sincere faith in the progress of society.[9]

In the guise of writing objective novels, he wrote personal, subjective ones. For Forster's novels, like those of the other great modern British novelists – Conrad, Lawrence, Joyce, and Woolf – are the history of his soul. His novels not only dramatize his characters' search for values, but dramatize his own quest for values, a quest that reflects his own doubt and uncertainty. As Wilfred Stone writes:

His novels are not only chapters in a new gospel, they are dramatic installments in the story of his own struggle for selfhood – and for a myth to support it. They tell of a man coming out in the world, painfully emerging from an encysted state of loneliness, fear, and insecurity. Forster's evangelism springs as much from self-defense as from self-confidence, as much from weakness as from strength; but the style of his sermon always reflects those qualities about which there can be no compromise: tolerance and balance, sensitivity and common sense, and a loathing for everything dogmatic.[10]

Put another way: what Stephen Dedalus says in *Ulysses* of Shakespeare – 'He found in the world without as actual what was in his world within as possible' – is also true of Forster and, as we shall see, of *Aspects*.[11]

Like Forster's novels, particularly the later ones, *Aspects of the Novel* challenges the artistic and thematic conventions of the novel of manners. Indeed, the early chapters on story, people, and plot roughly correspond to the early period when he wrote *Where Angels Fear to Tread*, *The Longest Journey*, and *A Room With a View*, while the later sections discuss aspects that he tried to make more substantive use of in *Howards End* and, in particular, *Passage to India* – the aspects of fantasy, prophecy, pattern, and rhythm. Not unlike his novels, *Aspects* enacts his quest for the inner life as well as his attempt to rescue himself from the curse of modernism. For *Aspects of the Novel* sometimes strikes an elegiac and nostalgic note when confronting contemporary avant-garde works, such as those of Gertrude Stein and James Joyce.

Forster's book originated as the 1927 Clark lectures given at Cambridge University. His conversational approach and lightness of touch, rather than dating the lectures, recreate the spontaneity of clear-headed, sensible, unpretentious talk. Forster is speaking in a tradition of manners that eschewed sharp conflicts and hyperbole on those occasions when a lowered voice and a tactful gesture would do. While Forster's style is somewhat more informal in *Aspects*, it is marked by the same features as his novels: leisurely pace, self-confidence, lucid diction, and poised syntax. As Lionel Trilling puts it, 'The very relaxation of his style, its colloquial unpretentiousness, is a mark of his acceptance of the human fact as we know it now. . . . This, it seems to me, might well be called worldliness, this acceptance of man in the world without the sentimentality of cynicism and without the sentimentality of rationalism.'[12] As in his novels, Forster's style becomes his argument for the proportion, balance, and spontaneity that are essential to Forster's humanism.

Aspects enacts Forster's values. Like his novels, its tone and style are

objective correlatives for the keen sensibility, the personal relationships, and the delicate discriminations of feeling that he sought.
With its elegant phrasing, tact, balance, and sensibility, it is a protest
against what he calls 'the language of hurry on the mouths of London's
inhabitants – clipped words, formless sentences, potted expressions of
approval or disgust'.[13] Forster never forgets what he calls 'the inner
life' and the 'unseen' – those aspects of life which resist language. By
the 'inner life', he means the passions and feelings which enable man to
experience poetry and romance. For Forster, the 'unseen' means not
the traditional Christian God but a world beyond things that can be
reached by passion, imagination, intelligence, and affection.

Aspects of the Novel is informed, above all, by an intense commitment to the importance of reading and writing. Forster believes that
language, including relatively abstract terms like 'beauty', 'curiosity',
and 'intelligence', refers to a shared cultural heritage and therefore
conveys meaning. Thus he can write:

> Our easiest approach to a definition of any aspect of fiction is
> always by considering the sort of demand it makes on the reader.
> Curiosity for the story, human feelings and a sense of value for the
> characters, intelligence and memory for the plot. (pp. 107–8)

These are the 'demands' that motivated Forster to write novels, and
the *values* that he felt must be central to a criticism of the novel. Forster
is never afraid of being naive, and expresses the full range of emotions
from wonder and awe to impatience, chagrin, and dismay. Forster is,
above all, a humanist. As Stone writes, 'His art, and his belief in it, are
his religion. . . . The religion *is* a coming together, of the seen and the
unseen, public affairs and private decencies. Another name for this
religion is humanism.'[14] With its carefully constructed patterns and
symbolic scenes, the artificial order of the novel was for Forster an
alternative to disbelief.

Forster's aesthetic values cannot be separated from his moral
values. In an important 1925 essay, 'Anonymity: an Enquiry', he wrote
that '[a work of literature, such as *The Ancient Mariner*] only answers
to its own laws, supports itself, internally coheres, and has a new
standard of truth. Information is true if it is accurate. A poem is true if
it hangs together. . . . The world created by words exists neither in
space nor time though it has semblances of both, it is eternal and
indestructible.'[15] For Forster, as for his Bloomsbury colleagues Roger
Fry, Clive Bell, G. E. Moore and, often Virginia Woolf, art is a

surrogate for religion. For those who, like himself, do not believe in the harmony of a divine plan or that a God directs human destiny, it provides 'order' and 'harmony' that the world lacks. At its best, art enables us to see life steadily and to see it whole. Aesthetic order can provide a substitute for, and an alternative to, the frustrations and anxieties of life. In 'Art for Art's Sake' (1949), he argued that what distinguished art from life is form, and that view, articulated by Bell and Fry well before *Aspects*, is implicit in much of Forster's book: 'A work of art . . . is unique not because it is clever or noble or useful or beautiful or enlightened or original or sincere or idealistic or educational – it may embody any of those qualities – but because it is the only material object in the universe which may possess internal harmony.'[16] While life in action is fundamentally disorganized ('the past is really a series of *dis*-orders'), creating and responding to art are ways of putting that disorder behind.[17]

'Form' (which he does not discuss in its own chapter) is another name for the internal harmony achieved by the creative synthesis of other *aspects*: '[The artist] legislates through creating. And he creates through his sensitiveness and his power to impose form. . . . Form of some kind is imperative. It is the surface crust of the internal harmony, it is the outward evidence of order.'[18] But form is not merely the *significant* form of Bell and Fry; it includes – much more than for such a pure art as music – awareness of the complexity of life. Unlike music, the novel inevitably addresses how and for what human beings live. Responding to Lubbock, Forster eschews 'principles and systems' as inappropriate to the novel. He insists on 'the intensely, stifling human quality' as a critical focus, because the novel's subject is humanity: 'Since the novelist is himself a human being, there is an affinity between him and his subject-matter which is absent in many other forms of art' (pp. 24, 44). By beginning with 'story' and 'people', *Aspects of the Novel* shows that novels first and foremost depend on human life. Moreover, Forster does not use the formal term 'character' in the title of the 'People' chapters. And the centrality of people derives in part from Bloomsbury's stress on emotional and moral ties. Virginia Woolf asserted in 'Mr. Bennett and Mrs. Brown': 'I believe that all novels . . . deal with character, and that it is to express character . . . that the form of the novels, so clumsy, verbose, and undramatic, so rich, elastic, and alive, has been evolved.'[19]

Underlying *Aspects of the Novel* is a stress on the quality and intensity of novels' moral visions. Forster implies that a novel's ability to show us something we don't know about the people and the universe is important. Not only does penetrating the secret lives of characters help us as readers to become more perspicacious in life, but our aesthetic experience will enable us for a time to achieve internal harmony. As Forster wrote in 'Anonymity: An Enquiry': 'What is so wonderful about great literature is that it transforms the man who reads it towards the condition of the man who wrote, and brings to birth in us also the creative impulse. Lost in the beauty where he was lost, we find more than we ever threw away, we reach what seems to be our spiritual home, and remember that it was not the speaker who was in the beginning but the Word.'[20] On one hand, Forster is speaking urgently in his prophetic voice, urging the religion of art which enables us to see beyond the real world, and we feel his kinship with Blake and Lawrence. On the other hand, despite his epiphanic language, Forster stresses the use of art in terms of the effects of art, and this stress is typical of Anglo-American criticism, which is influenced by a blend of Horatian *utile* and English utilitarianism.

II

Despite Forster's lack of theoretical sophistication, his lucid, unpretentious discussion of the aesthetics of the novel challenges us to consider the necessary dialogue within fiction between art and life, between the imagined world created by the author and the real one in which we, like the author, live. Forster defines the novel in terms of a dialectical relationship between fiction and reality: 'there are in the novel two forces: human beings and a bundle of various things not human beings, and . . . it is the novelist's business to adjust these two forces and conciliate their claims' (p.105). Forster taught us that interest in the novel as an art form is not incongruous with attention to content and that, paradoxically, the novels with the highest artistic values are the richest in insights about life. But Forster knew that '*homo fictus*' is not the same as '*homo sapiens*'. What differentiates art from life is not only that the novel is a work of art, but that 'the novelist knows everything about [a character in a book] . . . [I]n the novel we can know people perfectly, and, apart from the general pleasure of reading, we can find here a compensation for their dimness in life' (p. 63). Forster's assertion that we know the characters in a novel completely and that they contain, unlike characters in life, 'no secrets' is belied by our experience that characters have secrets that even their creator or his own omniscient narrator does not recognize. (This is not only the point of Kermode's *The Genesis of Secrecy* [1979], but one implication of his own chapters on 'Prophecy' and 'Pattern and Rhythm'.)

Forster's introductory chapter insists on a non-chronological approach which conceives of English novelists 'writing their novels simultaneously' (p. 9) and turns away from questions of influence: 'Literary tradition is the borderland lying between literature and history' (p. 22). Imagining a reader who encounters the total experience of the English novel enables Forster to take a quite different perspective from those who speak of influences and origins. His ahistorical approach – what we now call synchronic – appealed to the formalists of the next generation, and probably, along with James and Lubbock, deterred thinking about the novel in terms of traditional literary history.

Forster's book was a response to James's critical legacy and Lubbock's codification and simplification of that legacy in *The Craft of Fiction* which argued, following James, for the importance of point of view. He believes that critics have overstressed point of view. By speaking in compelling terms of the elements that he thinks are crucial, he rescued the novel from the dogmatism of James and Lubbock. Point of view is not the most important 'aspect' but merely one of many secondary ones that do not deserve a separate chapter. The absence of a chapter on 'point of view' probably affected the direction of novel criticism. With Lubbock (whom he has mentioned a few lines previously) in mind, he remarks that critics feel the novel 'ought to have its own technical troubles before it can be accepted as an independent art' (p. 79). For Forster, a novelist's 'method' resolves 'into the power of the writer to bounce the reader into accepting what he says' (pp. 78–9). By discussing point of view in a few pages in the second chapter entitled 'people,' he is emphasizing that point of view, whether in the form of a persona or omniscient narrator, is significant only insofar as it expresses a human voice. Parting company with James and Lubbock, he writes, 'the creator and narrator are one' (p. 56).

Forster's warning about self-conscious art is a deliberate attempt to separate himself from the James aesthetic: 'The novelist who betrays too much interest in his own method can never be more than interesting; he has given up the creation of character and summoned us to help analyse his own mind, and a heavy drop in the emotional thermometer results' (p. 80). Unlike Lubbock who questions Tolstoy's shifting point of view, he feels that 'this power to expand and contract perception, . . . this right to intermittent knowledge' is not only 'one of the great advantages of novel-form', but 'has a parallel in our perception of life' (p. 81). Finally, he holds, what is important is not the technique but the result. Unlike Lubbock, Forster never loses sight of the role of the reader and, like James on occasion, thinks of himself as the reader's surrogate. Stressing that novels must be convincing to readers, he writes: 'All that matters to the reader is whether the shifting of attitude and the secret life are convincing . . .' (p. 84). Yet despite his avowed catholicity, he has his preferences and prejudices. While he believes that it is fine for an author 'to draw back from his characters, as Hardy and Conrad do, and to generalize about the conditions under which he thinks life is carried on,' he does not like the intimacy of Fielding and Thackeray who take readers into confidence about their characters (p. 82). Perhaps influenced by James on this point, he implies that the artist should use his artistry to shape the reader's response rather than simply tell him what to think. *Aspects of the Novel* shows that Forster had a complicated oedipal love–hate attitude – an anxiety of influence – towards James whose novels and criticism influenced him more than he acknowledged.

Forster's most important contribution to the aesthetic of the novel is the distinction between 'flat' and 'round' characters. While flat characters can be summarized in a single phrase and hence are often caricatures, round characters are as complex and multi-faceted as real people: 'The test of a round character is whether it is capable of surprising in a convincing way. . . . It has the incalculability of life about it – life within the pages of a book' (p. 78). He demonstrates that characterization includes different kinds of mimesis in fiction, each with its own function, and that flat and round characters can co-exist in the same novel. While 'It is only round people who are fit to perform tragically for any length of time and can move us to any feelings except humour and appropriateness' (p. 73), the 'proper mixture of [flat and round] characters' is crucial (p. 80). The advantage of flat characters is that they are convenient for authors and easily recognized; moreover, they are easily controlled, 'provide their own atmosphere', and 'are easily remembered by the reader afterwards' (p. 69). Although they exaggerate one major factor at the expense of all others, they have a place in fiction.

The 1910–12 Post-Impressionist exhibits in London taught Forster and his contemporaries that different kinds of mimesis were possible in the same works; Forster is extending that principle to fiction and showing that the equation of 'lifelike' and good is simplistic. Post-Impressionists intentionally neglect some details, while they distort and exaggerate others. Their abrupt cutting of figures, elimination of traditional perspective, and foreshortening of figures and images, influenced the quest of Lawrence, Joyce, Woolf, and Forster to move beyond realism. The concept of volume to describe character may derive from Charles Mauron, to whom *Aspects of the Novel* is dedicated.[21] But it is also likely that Forster himself had learned from modern painting that objects occupying different places in space could be resolved on the same pictorial plane. It may even be that he has in mind the three-dimensionality of sculpture, particularly modern sculpture, which defines objects in relation to the space the work occupies in comparison to the inevitable two-dimensionality of painting.

With its focus on character in the novel in contrast to form, Muir's *The Structure of the Novel* is probably the most important of Forster's immediate offspring. Very much influenced by Forster, Muir has criticized Forster for depreciating and oversimplifying flat characters. Muir prefers to differentiate between 'pure' characters, whom he generally equates with 'flat' characters, and 'dramatic developing' characters whom he equates with 'round' ones. His case for flat characters depends upon extending the concept to include all characters who remain relatively static: 'All pure characters, formally, are in a sense artificial. They continue to repeat things *as if* they were true. . . . It is this accumulation of habits, dictated by their natures or imposed by convention, that makes every human being the potential object of humour.'[22] Thus, he concludes, 'The co-extensive truth and congruity of its attributes, indeed, makes the flat character no less remarkable as an imaginative creation than the round; it is not less true, it is only different. It shows us the real just underneath the habitual.'[23] But Forster had in mind the differing function of characters, not simply their status within the imagined world. Forster's distinction between flat and round characters is still influential because it showed us that the formal world of art functioned on different principles than the world of life. Subsequent critics, including Wayne Booth, Sheldon Sacks, and Northrop Frye, have focused on the rhetorical function of characterization.

Like the other major British modernists – Conrad, Lawrence, Joyce, and Woolf – Forster understood that human character is a continually changing flux of experience rather than, as depicted in the traditional realistic novel of manners, relatively fixed and static; consequently in his novels he sought to dramatize states of mind at crucial moments. Forster's emphasis on character helped to establish the respectability of the view that character (people) in fiction takes precedence over plot. By stressing the primacy of character over plot while rejecting the emphasis of James and Lubbock on point of view, Forster continued the movement away from the traditional stress on plot. The nineteenth century increasingly became more interested in character than plot; climaxing this trend was the interest in obsessions, compulsions, and dimly acknowledged needs and motives in the works of Browning and Hardy, and, indeed, in A. C. Bradley's *Shakespearean Tragedy* (1904).

Forster emphasized that novels depend on a complicated and, at times, messy dialogue between 'life in time' and 'life by values'. It may appear that life by values is part of content or story, but it is clear that its presence in the novel depends upon what Forster calls the author's 'devices', and what subsequent critics call 'artistry' or 'technique' or discourse (p. 29). While subsequent critics use different terms, Forster demonstrates that discussion of fiction must deal with the two variables – whether we call them life in time and life by values, life and pattern, content and form, or story and discourse. (In his *Introduction to the English Novel*, Arnold Kettle borrows Forster's term 'pattern' to define 'the quality in a book which gives it wholeness and meaning', but his definition is much closer to what Forster means by 'life by values' than to what he means by 'pattern'.)[24]

Forster's distinction between story and plot is similar to the distinction in recent studies of narrative between story and discourse: '[Story] is a narrative of events arranged in their time sequence . . . [I]t can only have one merit: that of making the audience want to know what happens next. And conversely it can only have one fault: that of making the audience not want to know what happens next' (p. 27). By contrast plot is an aesthetic matter, the basic unit of form. Plot organizes story; it is 'a narrative of events, the emphasis falling on causality. . . . The time-sequence is preserved, but the sense of causality overshadows it' (p. 86). Unlike drama, Forster contends, plots in novels rarely comply with Aristotle's 'triple process of complication, crisis, and solution' (p. 85). Forster sees plot as a series of circumstances, often arbitrarily selected and arranged, which enables the author to explore the major characters' personal lives and values: 'In the novel, all human happiness and misery does not take the form of action, it seeks means of expression other than through plot, it must not be rigidly canalized' (pp. 94–5). While Forster accepted the classical notion of an efficient plot, we should note that the terms 'economical' and 'organic' derive from the James influence: '[In the plot] every action or word ought to count; it ought to be economical and spare; even when complicated it should be organic and free from dead matter' (p. 88). But the meaning of plot depends on the active participation of a responsive reader: 'Over [the plot] . . . will hover the memory of the reader (that dull glow of the mind of which intelligence is the bright advancing edge) and will constantly rearrange and reconsider, seeing new clues, new chains of cause and effect, and the final sense (if the plot has been a fine one) will not be of clues or chains, but of something aesthetically compact, something which might have been shown by the novelist straight away, only if he had shown it straight away it would never have become beautiful' (p. 88). This is the very kind of active reader that R. S. Crane had in mind in his famous 1952 essay 'The Concept of Plot and the Plot of *Tom Jones*' and upon whom recent theorists depend. Forster conceived of the structure of the novel as a continuous process by which values are presented, tested, preserved, or discarded, rather than the conclusion of a series which clarifies and reorders everything that precedes. He understood that the importance of a linear pattern within the imagined world relates to the temporal experience of reading the novel. He knew that even if the greatest novels expand infinitely as if they were atemporal, 'It is never possible for a novelist to deny time inside the fabric of his novel' (p. 29). For when one 'emancipate[s] fiction from the tyranny of time . . . it cannot express anything at all' because 'the sequence between the sentences' is abolished, and then 'the order of the words,' until there is no sense (pp. 41–2). Thus he pointed novel criticism away from James's spatial conception of form, a concept derived more from James's understanding of painting, sculpture, and architecture than from Coleridge's organic form. Forster helped keep alive temporality as a critical concept in the years when discussion of novel form in spatial terms predominated due to the influence of James and later Joseph Frank.[25]

Forster's insights about endings influenced the work of Alan Friedman's *The Turn of the Novel* (1966) and anticipated Kermode's *The Sense of an Ending* (1967). Endings, Forster avows in the chapter on plot, are inherently defective: 'Nearly all novels are feeble at the end. This is because the plot requires to be wound up' (p. 95). According to Forster, death and love are ordering principles that end novels neatly, but not in accordance with our own experience of life. The ending should be a part of a process, the last section chronologically in the narrative, but not a completion or a summary because, until death, life is a continuing process. We let authors urge us into thinking love is permanent, even though in reality we know the future would disconfirm this. Because, in his view, life is always open, problematic and unresolved, Forster's own novels end on a deliberately inconclusive and ambiguous note. Characteristically, his ending does not resolve the social and moral problems dramatized by the plot. Rather it is another in a series of episodes in which man's limitations are exposed, rather than an apocalyptic climactic episode which resolves prior problems. Later, as we shall see, in the section on 'rhythm', he speaks of the possibility of novels, like symphony music, expanding and opening out for their audience. But he is speaking of the resonance of a work upon its audience after our reading is completed.

III

As *Aspects* progresses, Forster moves further away from the doctrine of nineteenth-century realism that novels must be imitations of life and begins to introduce categories that his classically trained lecture audience would have found innovative and exciting, if at times provocatively idiosyncratic, whimsical, and even bizarre. By introducing these categories and by refusing to restrict himself to what can be seen and analysed within a novel, Forster re-introduced an imaginative and creative strain to criticism that Lubbock's more positivistic approach had denied. Such a strain was a dominant force in the criticism of Pater, Wilde, and at times, James.

Following the chapter on 'plot', Forster turns to 'fantasy'. Forster's 'fantasy' includes the kinds of extraordinary events that James called Romance, but it also includes very different kinds of speculative, tonal, and stylistic departures from realism. Fantasy asks the reader to 'accept certain things' that are unnatural (p. 108). Fantasy 'implies the supernatural, but need not express it' (p. 112); like prophecy, it has a 'sense of mythology' (p. 109). According to Forster, the devices of a writer of fantasy include: 'the introduction of a god, ghost, angel, monkey, monster, midget, witch into ordinary life; or the introduction of ordinary men into no man's land, the future, the past, the interior of the earth, the fourth dimension; or divings into and dividings of personality; or finally the device of parody or adaptation' (p. 112). As a parody of *Pamela*, Fielding's *Joseph Andrews* is an example of the last kind. Inspired by both 'an already existing book' and a 'literary tradition' (p. 120), *Ulysses* is also a fantasy that depends on parody and adaptation.

If fantasy takes us to a linear world of diversity, difference, and idiosyncrasy, prophecy takes us to a vertical dimension where this world is a shadow of a more intense world. The truth of prophecy is the truth of vision. Thus in the subsequent chapter entitled 'Prophecy', Forster asks us to put aside our logic and reason and look elsewhere for insight and knowledge of the human plight. Forster wants the novel to move beyond local nominalistic insights towards unity and towards truth beyond itself. Stone aptly describes Forster's concept of prophecy as 'the seeing of the visible world as the living garment of God, the miracle of natural supernaturalism'.[26] When novels expand temporally and spatially, they displace the reader's awareness of the world in which he lives, and give him a spiritual experience. Such experience is similar to the moment when all will be one, except here the signified is not Christ, but a sense of wholeness that derives from awareness of man's common plight and a common psychological past.

Thus the theme of 'prophecy' is 'the universe, or something universal' (p. 125). Prophecy 'is a tone of voice'; 'What matters is the accent of [the prophet's] voice, his song' (pp. 125, 135). Forster's examples are Lawrence, Dostoevsky, Melville, and Emily Brontë. The prophetic impulse demands from the reader 'humility and the suspension of the sense of humour' (p. 126). While George Eliot is a preacher, Dostoevsky is a prophet:

> [Mitya] is the prophetic vision, and the novelist's creation also . . .
> The extension, the melting, the unity through love and pity occur in
> a region which can only be implied and to which fiction is perhaps
> the wrong approach. . . . Mitya is a round character, but he is
> capable of extension. He does not conceal anything (mysticism), he
> does not mean anything (symbolism), he is merely Dmitri Karama-
> zov, but to be merely a person in Dostoevsky is to join up with all the
> other people far back. (pp. 133–4)

The prophetic dimension cannot be pinned down in particular sentences or patterns of language: 'The essential in *Moby Dick*, its prophetic song, flows athwart the action and the surface morality like an undercurrent. It lies outside words' (p. 138). But how, one might ask, can we agree on the presence of prophecy? Forster might respond that it is the truth that passes understanding, our epiphanic realization that transcends any single moment of narrative.

Chapter Eight is entitled 'Pattern and Rhythm', terms which are borrowed respectively from painting and from music. First, Forster discusses pattern: 'Whereas the story appeals to our curiosity and the plot to our intelligence, the pattern appeals to our aesthetic sense. It causes us to see the book as a whole' (p. 150). He dismisses as jargon the notion that we see a book as a physical shape: 'Pattern is an aesthetic aspect of the novel, and . . . though it may be nourished by anything in the novel – any character, scene, word – it draws most of its nourishment from the plot' (p. 152). Although Stallybrass thinks Forster is merely paying homage to a friend when he mentions Lubbock's novels, Forster is making a critical point by using a novel by Lubbock to illustrate pattern and by praising it for qualities quite remote from point of view.[27] Pattern is whatever in plot is beautiful: 'Beauty is sometimes the shape of the book, the book as a whole, the unity' (p. 152). Not only is James discussed in the section on pattern rather than in the brief section on point of view within the second 'People' chapter, but Strether's role as an observer, as 'a rather too first-class oculist' is facetiously noted (p. 154). Forster indicts James for giving preference to pattern over life: '[Rigid pattern] may externalize the atmosphere, spring naturally from the plot, but it shuts the doors on life and leaves the novelist doing exercises, generally in the drawing-room. . . . To most readers of fiction the sensation from a pattern is not intense enough to justify the sacrifices that made it' (pp. 163–4). Writing of Forster's concern with pattern and rhythm, Edwin Muir, his contemporary and admirer, made a trenchant remark that accurately establishes Forster's link to the James tradition, notwithstanding Forster's effort to separate himself from James's aesthetic: 'We do not really believe that a novel has a pattern like a carpet or a rhythm like a tune. . . . James is the father of most of those questions–begging terms; he was an incurable impressionist; and he had infected criticism with his vocabulary of hints and nods.'[28]

Rhythm is the relation between 'movements'. Rhythm is a linear version of organic form, for it provides the concept of internal harmony for the temporal process of reading, whereas pattern seems to define internal harmony in more traditional formal and somewhat spatial terms borrowed from painting and sculpture. According to Forster, the function of rhythm in fiction is 'not to be there all the time like a pattern, but by its lovely waxing and waning to fill us with surprise and freshness and hope. . . . [I]t has to depend on a local impulse when the right interval is reached. But the effect can be exquisite, it can be obtained without mutilating the characters, and it lessens our need of an external form' (pp. 167–8). Of course rhythm forms a pattern, too, but a temporal one not a spatial one. Perhaps Forster should have differentiated between 'spatial pattern' and 'rhythmic pattern' – recurrence within a temporal framework which is both ineffable and ever-changing; the latter is a dynamic concept that adjusts continually to the experience of reading, and probably owes something to the substantial influence in the 1920s of Gestalt psychology which sees human events as dynamic patterns that constantly move and shift into new fields of perception. He finds rhythm in 'the easy sense' in Proust's *Remembrance of Things Past*: 'The book is chaotic, ill-constructed, it has and will have no external shape; and yet it hangs together because it is stitched internally, because it contains rhythms' (p. 165). E. K. Brown's influential *Rhythm in the Novel* (1950) derives directly from this discussion, but it also anticipates the kind of order that Hillis Miller discusses in his recent *Fiction and Repetition* and that Gerard Genette speaks of in *Narrative Discourse* a book whose focus is *Remembrance of Things Past*; Genette cites Forster with approval.

He then turns to a more sophisticated and elusive kind of rhythm, which he finds only in *War and Peace*:

> Music, though it does not employ human beings, though it is governed by intricate laws, nevertheless does offer in its final expression a type of beauty which fiction might achieve in its own way. Expansion. That is the idea the novelist must cling to. Not completion. Not rounding off but opening out. When the symphony is over we feel that the notes and tunes composing it have been liberated, they have found in the rhythm of the whole their individual freedom. . . . As we read [*War and Peace*] do not great chords begin to sound behind us, and when we have finished does not every item – even the catalogue of strategies – lead a larger existence than was possible at the time? (p. 169)

In his novels and in *Aspects of the Novel*, Forster is trying to create this 'expansion' for his audience, in part by trying to reach back to the sources of man's humanity. But isn't this passage extremely impressionistic? Do we know from this why *War and Peace* achieves its greatness? Aren't we being simply asked to endorse Forster's responses? Indeed as *Aspects* progresses, the argument becomes weaker and weaker, and depends, beginning with 'Fantasy', more on assertion and apt turns of phrase. It is as if he wishes the book to conclude with a prolonged lyric about the novel's potential to move its readers. Yet in the passage, does he not seek to join with those – Pater, Wilde, and usually Woolf – who see art as greater and more important than life and to participate in Yeats's urgent wish in 'Sailing to Byzantium', to be a golden bird 'to sing / To lords and ladies of Byzantium / Of what is past, or passing, or to come?'

The discussion of prophecy and rhythm (and, to a lesser extent, fantasy and pattern) is part of an effort to define something inexplicable, something spiritual and unseen, which might be an antidote to his own discovery and dramatization of evil in the Marabar caves in *Passage to India*.[29] Forster yearned for something beyond the pedestrian, disorganized, and sometimes banal stuff of novels. When Forster speaks of reaching back and 'expansion' we must not forget the influence of Freud, Frazer, and Jung. Frazer's *The Golden Bough* (1890) had extended the range of the past beyond biblical time and even beyond historical time; later, Jung's emphasis on archetypes stressed that all cultures share common anthropological experience and psychological traits. And Forster believed that, despite differences in breeding, customs, and values, a common heritage united mankind. *Aspects*, like *Passage to India*, written only a few years before, is a quest for something beyond the diurnal life. But his tragedy was finally that he could not believe, with Stevens in 'An Ordinary Evening in New Haven', that 'the words of the world are the life of the world'. At times Forster regretfully concedes that creating and perceiving art cannot compensate for the frustrations and anxieties of daily life, and that concession may be why he stopped writing novels.

IV

Before closing we should acknowledge what now seem as shortcomings of *Aspects of the Novel*. The book does not discuss precisely the means by which life is transformed into art, and would benefit from separate chapters on form and narrative technique and more detailed discussion of style, the reader's role, and setting. Sometimes Forster provides us with little more than an impressionistic, gustatory statement of like and dislike. But lyricism is not the same as argument and his credo that 'the final test of a novel will be our affection for it' (p. 23) is a bit tautological. At times, his generalizations need more precise evidence and tauter supporting argument. Clearly, he is ambivalent about the critical enterprise and worried that it is too scientific, even mechanistic. For this reason, he speaks of holding up 'story' with a 'forceps' (as if it were a part of Tristram Shandy's anatomy.) Even if we attribute the lack of sustained analyses to the limitations of length imposed by the original lecture format, we have to admit that his own ratings of prior English novelists are at times quirky and reductive. For example, Scott, who has 'a trivial mind and a heavy style' (p. 30), is a writer for a time when our brains 'decay'; but 'he could tell a story. He had the primitive power of keeping the reader in suspense and playing on his curiosity' (p. 32).

In the face of the bold and experimental, Forster's fastidious and conservative temper, which prefers order, proportion, clarity, and precision, sometimes leads him astray. Although he praises Lawrence for his 'rapt bardic quality', he completely misunderstands *Ulysses* of which he writes, 'the aim . . . is to degrade all things and more particularly civilization and art, by turning them inside out and upside down' (pp. 143, 122). At times, he suppresses his prophetic strain and sees himself as a custodian of humanistic (some might facetiously say bourgeois) principles in the face of challenges from the avant-garde.

Yet while a contemporary reader, accustomed to either the critical nominalism of the New Criticism or the theorizing of recent European criticism, might find it at times lacking in rigour, *Aspects of the Novel* remains one of our seminal texts of novel criticism. We value it because Forster speaks to us not only as a major novelist and an incisive critic, but as a reader who is concerned with how aspects of the novel relate to aspects of our lives.

NOTES

1. Page numbers in parentheses refer to the accessible Harvest paperback of *Aspects of the Novel* (New York: Harcourt, Brace, & World, Inc., 1954) orig. edn 1927.
2. *Aspects of the Novel*, ed. Oliver Stallybrass (London: Edwin Arnold, 1974) orig. edn 1927, p. xiii.
3. Stallybrass, p. xv.
4. Stallybrass, p. xv.
5. Stallybrass, p. xiii.
6. My essay, focusing on Forster's significance and theoretical implications, seeks to complement S. P. Rosenbaum's '*Aspects of the Novel* and Literary History', in *E. M. Forster: Centenary Revaluations*, eds Judith Scherer Herz and Robert K. Martin (London: Macmillan, 1982) pp. 55–83. Rosenbaum's splendid scholarship establishes the literary context in which *Aspects* was written.
7. Virginia Woolf, 'Mr. Bennett and Mrs. Brown', *The Captain's Death Bed and Other Essays* (New York: Harcourt, Brace Co., 1950) pp. 112, 115–17.

8. See my 'The Originality of E. M. Forster's Novels', *Modern Fiction Studies*, 29:4 (winter 1983) 623–41.
9. *Two Cheers for Democracy*, Abinger edition (London: Edward Arnold, 1972) orig. edn 1951, p. 54.
10. Wilfred Stone, *The Cave and the Mountain: a Study of E. M. Forster* (Stanford, Calif.: Stanford University Press, 1966) p. 19.
11. For a discussion of why and how the British novel changed in the 1890–1930 period, see my ' "I was the World in Which I Walked": The Transformation of the British Novel,' *The University of Toronto Quarterly*, 51:3 (Spring 1982) 279–97.
12. Lionel Trilling, *E. M. Forster* (New York: New Directions, 1964) orig. edn 1943, pp. 22–3.
13. *Howards End*, Abinger edn (London: Edward Arnold, 1972) p. 107.
14. Stone, pp. 18–19.
15. *Two Cheers for Democracy*, p. 81.
16. *Two Cheers for Democracy*, p. 90.
17. 'Art for Art's Sake', *Two Cheers for Democracy*, p. 88.
18. 'Art for Art's Sake', *Two Cheers for Democracy*, p. 92.
19. 'Mr. Bennett and Mrs. Brown', p. 102.
20. *Two Cheers for Democracy*, p. 83.
21. See Rosenbaum, pp. 68–71.
22. Edwin Muir, *The Structure of the Novel* (London: The Hogarth Press, 1954) orig. edn 1928, p. 142.
23. Muir, p. 146.
24. Arnold Kettle, *An Introduction to the English Novel*, 2 vols (New York: Harper & Row, 1961, I. 15).
25. When Rosenbaum writes, 'Time is the enemy of value throughout *Aspects of the Novel*' (p. 63), he fails to distinguish between Forster's understanding that time is inevitable to human mortality and Forster's stress, in his discussion of plot and rhythm, that temporality is essential to the form of the novel as we perceive it in the linear process of reading.
26. Stone, p. 117.
27. Stallybrass, p. xiii.
28. Muir, p. 15.
29. See my 'The Originality of E. M. Forster'.

3 Privileging Literary Criticism: the Legacy of F. R. Leavis's *The Great Tradition*

I

American academics have often been puzzled by claims made by English colleagues for the importance of F. R. Leavis. Leavis's position as a literary critic cannot be separated from his role as leader of an academic revolution in England which established literary criticism as a central activity in British culture. Leavis's premise was, as he argues in *Education and the University* (1943), that literary criticism 'trains, in a way no other discipline can, intelligence and sensibility together, cultivating a sensitiveness and precision of response and a delicate integrity of intelligence – intelligence that integrates as well as analyses and must have pertinacity and staying power as well as delicacy'.[1] For Leavis, literary criticism involves the complete engagement of mind and feeling while reading a text, and the subsequent ability to recreate or render that response in writing.

Before we turn to *The Great Tradition* (1948), some prefatory remarks are necessary. From 1932 until its demise in 1953 the forum for his ideas was *Scrutiny*, which Leavis edited almost from the first issue and to which he made 120 contributions. He argued in an editorial in *Scrutiny* entitled 'Retrospect of a Decade' that the university should be 'a focus of humane consciousness; a centre where, faced with the specializations and distractions in which human ends lose themselves, intelligence, bringing to bear a mature sense of values, should apply itself to the problems of civilization'.[2] Leavis believed that civilization and culture, including written and spoken language, had declined. Like Arnold, he believed that the study of English literature could be a major part of discovering the necessary values for the maintenance of English civilization.

The influential *Culture and Environment: The Training of Critical Awareness* (1933), edited by Leavis and Denys Thompson, expressed Leavis's conviction that, as Heyman puts it, 'literature, properly studied, could protect language against the depredations of mechanization and commercialism'.[3] It follows that the trained literary critic had important work to do in arresting this decline. The opening number of *Scrutiny* declares that its goal is to keep the small minority that is interested in the arts 'informed of "the best that is known and thought in the world" '.[4] Leavis believed that the serious study of literature could improve the quality of civilization: 'a serious interest in literature starts from the present and assumes that literature matters, in the first place at any rate, as the consciousness of the age'.[5] He insisted that the study of *present* authors is crucial to our understanding of contemporary civilization. This view conflicted with the Oxbridge tradition of modelling the study of English on the established pattern for classical studies, and emphasizing Anglo-Saxon philology and textual editing. Leavis stressed a distinction between the critic and the scholar, because he felt that the study of English must break free from this stifling legacy. Despite his iconoclastic tone, Leavis's impulses were fundamentally egalitarian in the sense that he wanted to make culture available to more than just the Oxbridge elite.

In a famous exchange with René Wellek in *Scrutiny* (1937), Leavis insisted on the presence in literary criticism not of philosophy but of issues that the reader could recognize from his life experience and which therefore had relevance to the growth of his moral development: 'The business of the literary critic is to attain a peculiar completeness of response and to observe a peculiarly strict relevance in developing his response into commentary; he must be on his guard against abstracting improperly from what is in front of him and against any premature or irrelevant generalizing – of it or from it'.[6] In his introduction to *Revaluation* (1936), he expressed a crucial principle: 'In dealing with individual poets the rule of the critic is, or should (I think) be, to work as much as possible in terms of particular analysis – analysis of poems or passages, and to say nothing that cannot be related immediately to judgments about producible texts.'[7] Thus eschewing theory for sensibility and judgment is his basic principle. Indeed, in taking issue with Wellek over a passage of Blake's, he claims that Wellek's misreading is an instance 'of the philosopher disabling the critic; an instance of the philosophical approach inducing in the reader of poetry a serious impercipience or insensitiveness'.[8]

To understand the importance of Leavis and *Scrutiny* one has to realize the state of the study of English literature, particularly the novel in England, during the 1930s. On one hand, to the Leavises it seemed that the serious critical analysis of texts took a back seat in the major universities to editing and 'dilettantish' appreciation. Q. D. Leavis wrote: 'A life devoted to the humanities means not following a vocation but taking up the genteelest profit-making pursuit, one which confers a high caste on its members'.[9] And on the other hand in the 1930s, Marxism was not only a political stance but a dominant intellectual attitude among students and fellows. Thus novels and poems were described in terms of their contribution to the 'development of human freedom'. In his retrospective after ten years of publishing *Scrutiny*, F. R. Leavis affirmed the importance of a humanistic anti-Marxism to his concept of *Scrutiny*: 'Though without doubt the human spirit was not to be thought of as expressing itself in a void of 'freedom,' unconditioned by economic and material circumstances, nevertheless there was a great need to insist on the element of autonomy and to work for the preservation of the humane tradition – a tradition representing the profit of a continuity of experience through centuries of economic and material change'.[10]

II

While later books including *D. H. Lawrence: Novelist* (1955) and *Dickens the Novelist* (1970) modified his positions, the essence of his approach to the English novel is in *The Great Tradition*. Moreover, it was that book that influenced the reading of fiction in England and America. Together with Arnold Kettle's two volume *An Introduction to The English Novel* (1951), Leavis's book turned the criticism of the novel in England from the Bloomsbury influence, epitomized by Forster's *Aspects of the Novel* (1927) and Woolf's *The Common Reader* (1925), and from the Jamesian aesthetic epitomized by Lubbock. Rather than stressing the technique of the novel and, in the case of Forster, a kind of longing for the pure aesthetic values of music, Leavis insisted in his critical rubric upon the importance of subject matter and what it signified about the world that it described. Thus artistic values are inseparable from the moral, social, and political significance of a text. Put another way, the author's artistry takes the reader to something beyond the purely aesthetic. In that sense, Leavis's criticism is a version of idealism, even Neo-Platonism, disguised as empiricism and has a kinship with Trilling and others who, writing in the 1940's and 1950's for *The Partisan Review*, saw literature and particularly novels as imagined worlds whose social and moral arrangements reflected – in recent vocabulary 'signified' – those of the real world.

The Great Tradition played a pivotal role in defining the aesthetic and moral values of Anglo-American novel criticism:

(1) Leavis rescued the study of the English novel from vague talk about 'slices of life'.

(2) But he also argued that, rather than being divorced from life, reading experience is, like other cultural activities, central to life and contributes to the development of the mature personality.

(3) He emphasized the necessity of responding to each text on its own terms, and responding with one's full intellectual and imaginative powers.

(4) He showed that reading is a creative process: 'Analysis is not a dissection of something that is already and passively there. What we call analysis is, of course, a constructive or creative process. It is a more deliberate following-through of that process of creation in response to the poet's words which reading is. It is a recreation in which, by a considering attentiveness, we ensure a more than ordinary faithfulness and completeness.'[11] (Note the contrast with 'deconstructive'.)

(5) He showed that fiction, like poetry, is accessible to close analysis, at about the time American New Critics were coming to the same conclusion. By running a series in *Scrutiny* entitled 'The Novel as Dramatic Poem' to which he contributed, Leavis wished to emphasize that the novel could have the same kind of intensity, organic unity, and seriousness as poetry.

(6) He showed how close analysis of texts need not bog down in critical nominalism in which the critic isolates image patterns and narrative methods for their own sake.

(7) He insisted that critics could and should make value judgments about the relative merits of texts.

(8) He radically re-arranged the canon of the English novel. He helped to establish, along with Robert Penn Warren in his introduction to the Modern Library Edition, the position of *Nostromo* in the Conrad canon. He urged the importance of George Eliot and contributed to valuing James's earlier works like *Washington Square*, while he attacked the stature of Dickens, Thackeray, Trollope, Hardy, Fielding, and Richardson.

Leavis sees himself as heir to the critical tradition of Arnold and Johnson. But he felt that Johnson – and, to a lesser extent, Arnold – had an audience who believed in culture and shared values with them, while he felt he himself had. To create such an audience: 'It is only in a coherent, educated and influential reading-public, one capable of responding intelligently and making its responses felt, that standards are 'there' for the critic to appeal to: only where there is such a public can he invoke them with any effect.' Leavis spent his life trying to create such a reading public.[12]

His *Scrutiny* essays on Arnold and Johnson are particularly relevant to understanding his goals and values. He seeks in his criticism the intention he ascribes to Arnold:

> We make (Arnold insists) our major judgements about poetry by bringing to bear the completest and profoundest sense of relative value that, aided by the work judged, we can focus from our total experience of life (which includes literature), and our judgement has intimate bearings on the most serious choices we have to make thereafter in our living.[13]

Like Arnold, Leavis engages a text morally and intellectually and judges it as the expression of the man who wrote it. Leavis wrote in *Nor Shall My Sword* (1972): 'I don't believe in any "literary values" and you won't find me talking about them; the judgments the literary critic is concerned with are judgments about life. What the critical discipline is concerned with is relevance and precision in making and developing them.'[14] He praises Arnold in terms which define his own critical goals:

> The lack of the 'gift for consistency or for definition' turns out to be compensated for, at his best, by certain positive virtues: tact and delicacy, a habit of keeping in sensitive touch with the concrete, and an accompanying gift for implicit definition.[15]

He admired Johnson's judgment, intelligence, and magisterial self-confidence. 'He addresses himself deliberately and disinterestedly to what is in front of him; he consults his experience with unequivocal directness and always has the courage of it.'[16] Writing about Johnson, he is defining his own critical goals:

> When we read him we know, beyond question, that we have here a

powerful and distinguished mind operating at first hand upon literature. . . . The critic knows what he means and says it with unescapable directness and force . . . and what he says is clearly the expression of intense and relevant interest.[17]

Among his twentieth-century influences were T. S. Eliot, D. H. Lawrence, and I. A. Richards. Although Leavis later made much of his differences with Eliot, he was profoundly influenced by him. It was Eliot who 'demonstrated . . . what the disinterested and effective application of intelligence to literature looks like'.[18] The title of *The Common Pursuit* is taken from Eliot's 'The Function of Criticism' which advised the critic 'to discipline his personal prejudices and cranks . . . and compose his differences with as many of his fellows as possible, in the common pursuit of true judgment'.[19] Leavis's conception of tradition is indebted to that of T. S. Eliot; he deliberately evokes 'Tradition and the Individual Talent' when he relates Austen's 'individual talent' to her tradition:

> If the influences bearing on [Jane Austen] hadn't comprised something fairly to be called tradition she couldn't have found herself and her true direction: but her relation to tradition is a creative one. She not only makes tradition for those coming after, but her achievement has for us a retroactive effect: as we look back beyond her we see in what goes before, and see because of her potentialities and significances brought out in such a way that, for us, she creates the tradition we see leading down to her. Her work, like the work of all great creative writers, gives a meaning to the past. (p. 5)[20]

Like Eliot, he is not speaking of 'indebtedness', but of an author's awareness that he writes within a living literary tradition. We might recall Eliot's words in 'Tradition and Individual Talent': 'No poet, no artist of any art, has his complete meaning alone. His significance, his appreciation is the appreciation of his relation to the dead poets and artists. You cannot value him alone; you must set him, for contrast and comparison, among the dead.'[21] Tradition has its significance in terms of a history of 'major writers'. The influence upon subsequent major novelists is one of the criteria of a novelist's importance. James's achievement derives in part from his 'having two novelists [Eliot and Austen] . . . of moral preoccupation in his own language to study' (p. 127). Discussing Austen's influence on Eliot, Leavis anticipates

Harold Bloom's 'Anxiety of Influence': 'One of the supreme debts one great writer can owe another is the realization of unlikeness' (p. 10).

Leavis was drawn to Lawrence's criticism even before he recognized the merits of his novels. Leavis took issue with Eliot's condemnation of Lawrence in *After Strange Gods* on the grounds that Lawrence lacked orthodox Christian beliefs. For Leavis, Lawrence had the religious sense because of his concern for man's relationship to the universe and with the mysteries of life. As Balin notes, 'religious' means what Leavis calls in *The Great Tradition* a 'sense of human solidarity' and an 'intuition of the unity of life'.[22] Lawrence came to represent to him a figure who struggled with the same forces in his fiction and his life – utilitarianism, mediocrity, materialism, and privilege – which Leavis confronted in his own criticism and intellectual life. According to Leavis, 'Lawrence stood for life, and shows, in his criticism . . . an extraordinarily quick and sure sense for the difference between that which makes for life and that which makes against it.'[23] As he came to value Lawrence, he gradually separated himself from T. S. Eliot's influence. Leavis recognizes that, like George Eliot, Lawrence has an Evangelical impulse; Lawrence writes 'from the depth of his religious experience, that makes him . . . so much more significant in relation to the past and future, so much more truly creative as a technical inventor, innovator, a master of language, than James Joyce' (p. 25).

Leavis was influenced by Richards who taught at Cambridge from 1921 to 1939, although he parted company with Richards in 1935 when reviewing *Coleridge on Imagination*. Do we not feel the influence of I. A. Richards's *Practical Criticism* in Leavis's response to Wellek? 'My whole effort was to work in terms of concrete judgments and particular analyses.'[24] But close verbal analysis is not an end, but always a means in Leavis. Leavis appreciated Richards' role in training the literary sensibility, but disdained his Utilitarian impulse and scientific positivism as contrary to Lawrentian 'religious' values of wholeness, spontaneity, and a feeling of unity with the universe.[25]

At first one is struck by the incongruity between the poised, confident, authoritative, and prophetic voice and the ill-natured, petty slaps at opposing views. Although they are really part of Leavis's confidence that he is one of the intellectually elect and *he knows* better than others, it is nonetheless disconcerting to read nasty asides, such as those directed towards J. B. Priestley and Lord David Cecil, that are sometimes barely related to issues under discussion. Possessing himself of something of a Puritan consciousness, he enjoys establishing dichotomies between the Elect and the Damned. Thus because Scott 'could not break away from the bad tradition of the eighteenth-century romance', 'out of Scott a bad tradition came' (p. 6). The Evangelical tone, with its righteous anger and intense moral concern, is never far from the surface. Sometimes Leavis likes a novel not only for its artistry, but for its ideas. Thus, one suspects, he admires *Hard Times* for its attack on James Mill's kind of utilitarianism, which Leavis describes as 'so blind in its onesidedness, so unaware of its bent and its blindness' (p. 20). Because of his own failure to gain recognition within the Cambridge academic establishment and his disdain for the values promulgated by them, Leavis enjoys setting himself apart from the social and intellectual establishment. Thus, I think that Leavis likes George Eliot *because* 'She was not qualified by nature or breeding to appreciate high civilisation, even if she had been privileged to make its acquaintance' (p. 13). He enjoys twitting *Lord* David Cecil *because* of his eminence and title; indeed, Leavis relishes his own distance '[from] the best circles', in which, he tells us, George Moore is held in high esteem, even by those admirers who haven't read his novels (p. 8).

III

The Great Tradition is a reprint of essays that Leavis published in *Scrutiny* except for the introduction and the first section of the James chapter. The Conrad chapter consists of two essays which appeared in June and October 1941; the chapter on Eliot appeared in 1945–6. The second James chapter appeared in 1937. The tradition includes Austen, George Eliot, James, and Conrad, but the book only considers in any depth the work of Eliot, James, and Conrad, perhaps because Austen had been discussed by his wife, Q. D. Leavis, in four *Scrutiny* essays. Later, he admitted Lawrence to the tradition, and still later he re-evaluated his condescending attitude towards Dickens.

In part, Leavis's purpose in these essays was to take issue with the traditional approach to the English novel which, he believed, regarded novels as an artistically naive form: '[T]he critical tradition regarding "the English novel" – if "critical" is the word – deals in the "creation of real characters," measures vitality by external abundance, and expects a loosely generous provision of incident and scene, but is innocent of any adult criterion of point and relevance in art. . . . So when it is offered concentrated significance – close and insistent relevance to a serious and truly rich theme, it sees merely insignificance' (p. 141). Once we understand how to recognize significance, he implies, we shall recognize the preeminence in the English novel of Austen, Eliot, James, and Conrad 'who count in the same way as the major poets, in the sense that they not only change the possibilities of the art for practitioners and readers, but that they are significant in terms of the human awareness they promote: awareness of the possibilities of life' (p. 2).

We can begin our examination of Leavis's critical standards by isolating crucial words and phrases that denote praise and values in Leavis's critical lexicon: 'mature', 'impersonality', 'serious', 'moral seriousness', 'sustained and complete seriousness', 'profound serious- ness', 'moral', 'moral preoccupation', 'moral imagination', and 'moral significance'. All these terms describe qualities discovered in a text, but attributed to the moral imagination of the author. These phrases are iterated until they become a critical litany imbued on the reader's consciousness; thus they are often less a critical grammar by which texts are methodically evaluated than a rhetorical assertion of Leavis's humanistic values. Yet it is difficult not to acquiesce to Leavis's terms – despite their subjectivity – because of the intensity of his intelligence and the energy of his engagement.

For Leavis literature is not merely an extension of life, although its subject matter is how and for what man lives, but the imposition of form upon the material of life. Leavis's central value is significant form. It is defined by a set of terms that have a more aesthetic emphasis: 'essential organization', (p. 150), 'organization of . . . vital interests', (p. 151), 'intensely significant [organization]' (p. 152). Form achieves significance not only when the particular is dramatized as an example of larger issues, but in combination with moral intensity and perspicacity. Leavis not only rejects the then traditional dicho- tomy between discussion of the art of the novel and of novels as the raw material of life; he insists that the great novelists in his tradition are concerned with 'form': 'They are all very original technically, having turned their genius to the working out of their own appropriate methods and procedures' (p. 7). His concept of form and unity includes but transcends the Coleridgean concept of organic unity. To be sure, books must have a totality, and the parts must relate to the whole; *Adam Bede* 'is too much the sum of its specifiable attractions' (p. 36). But Leavis' concept of form is inseparable from the moral implications of the work. 'When we examine the formal perfection of *Emma*, we find that it can be appreciated only in terms of the moral preoccupations that characterize the novelist's peculiar interest in life' (p. 8). The great novels combine an interest in form with 'an unusually developed interest in life. . . . They are all distinguished by a vital capacity for experience, a kind of reverent openness before life, and a marked moral intensity' (pp. 8–9). It is precisely this reverence, this moral intensity, which Fielding and Sterne lack. By 'unusually developed interest in life', he means an understanding at a complex level of the moral conflicts between self and society and of the pressures and demands exerted by the social milieu upon the individual. Thus, unity is also a function of other, less purely aesthetic values: maturity, impersonality, and seriousness. Form has, for Leavis, a moral dimension, judging and evaluating even as it controls, or rather controlling so we can judge and evaluate. His concept of form is close to Schorer's concept of technique or Van Ghent's concept of form, but these critics put more stress on the exploratory dimension of form and emphasize how form discovers meaning even as it gives shape to experience. By contrast, Leavis stresses how the author's *moral imagination* gives shape to form, as it does in the subgenre of what Leavis calls the moral fable.

Impersonality is another important concept. The author must transcend his own ego and look outward; even though a literary work is informed and shaped by a deeply felt personal experience, it is not an overflow of powerful feeling. Thus he writes of George Eliot, 'At her best she has the impersonality of genius' (p. 32). Indeed, great fiction is produced when personal problems are felt as moral problems whose significance transcends the limitations of ego: '[D]istinguished and noble as she is, we have in reading her the feeling that she is in and of the humanity she presents with so clear and disinterested a vision' (p. 123). When he indicts George Eliot for 'a tendency towards that kind of direct presence of the author which has to be stigmatized as weakness' (p. 33), he is following T. S. Eliot's insistence that distance from the artistic material is an essential precondition of great art: 'The more perfect the artist, the more completely separate in him will be the man who suffers and the mind which creates.'[26] Although the artist writes out of 'personal need', he must avoid subjectivity. Conrad's 'complex impersonalized whole' is praised in comparison to Eliot whose novels contain 'unabsorbed intellectual elements – patches, say, of tough or drily abstract thinking undigested by her art' (p. 32). Part of George Eliot's failure in the *Mill on the Floss* is that she shares Maggie's lack of self-knowledge; She does not 'place [Maggie's immaturity] . . . by relating it to mature experience' (p. 42). Writing of *Little Dorrit* in *Dickens the Novelist*, Leavis defines impersonality:

> It has the disinterestedness of spontaneous life, undetermined, and undirected and uncontrolled by idea, will and self-insistent ego, the disinterestedness here being that which brings a perceived significance to full realization and completeness in art. The writer's labour has been to present something that speaks for itself.[27]

As Balin notes, Leavis not only equates impersonality and disinterestedness, but seems to think of 'emotion as personal, and intelligence as impersonal'.[28]

'Maturity,' another of Leavis's standards, is close in meaning to impersonality, but implies an author's understanding his characters in terms of the moral and social forces that shape them. As Bilan remarks, 'Leavis apparently considers a purely emotional response an immature one; maturity includes the play on intelligence that involves self-understanding . . . [T]he impersonality of the *art* is dependent on the maturity of the artist'.[29] Mature also seems to mean complex, inclusive, and realistic, but *not* self-ironic. Indeed, Leavis distrusts authorial irony whenever it suggests a lack of seriousness or intensity towards oneself *or* one's subject matter.

'Seriousness' is not only important to the writer but to the reader; thus, in a judgment that he later recanted, he wrote, 'The adult mind doesn't as a rule in Dickens find a challenge to an unusual and sustained seriousness' (p. 19). At times 'seriousness' becomes a masque for Leavis's moral presence. In a footnote in which he disdains Lord David Cecil's haughty superiority to George Eliot's view, Leavis announces his approval of 'truthfulness and chastity and industry and self-restraint' and disapproval 'of loose living and recklessness and deceit and self-indulgence' (p. 13). It is very much in the spirit of Leavis's intellectual and emotional Nonconformity that he asserts that these values 'seem to me favourable to the production of great literature, (p. 13). For, while Leavis never says so, *The Great Tradition* uses the presence of these moral values in themselves as a kind of standard for measuring excellence. Leavis prefers nineteenth-century realism to eighteenth-century neoclassicism, seriousness to wit, morality to playfulness, engagement to ironic or bemused detachment. His own subjective bias against the wit, values, and subject matter of the Augustan novelists, notably Fielding and Sterne, derives from his psychological and moral attraction to the moral absolutism of Evangelicalism. He praises George Eliot the novelist in terms that are applicable to F. R. Leavis the literary critic: '[W]hat she brought from her Evangelical background was a radically reverent attitude towards life, a profound seriousness of the kind that is a first condition of any real intelligence, and an interest in human nature that made her a great psychologist' (p. 14). Among other things, Leavis is trying to define a peculiarly English humanistic tradition and contrast it with the emphasis on purely artistic values which he attributed to the Flaubert tradition in the French novel. Thus he writes of the depiction of Mrs. Transome in *Felix Holt*: 'To be able to assert human dignity in this way is greatness; the contrast with Flaubert is worth pondering' (p. 60).

Leavis prefers the concrete to the abstract, dramatic moments, dialogue to narrators' telling, and realism to romance. First and foremost, the work must dramatize its values: 'The intention to communicate an attitude . . . [must justify] itself as art in the realized concreteness that speaks for itself and *enacts* its moral significance' (p. 31). Neither George Eliot nor Joseph Conrad has a 'philosophy', but '[Conrad] transmutes more completely into the created world the interests he brings in' (p. 32). However, praising the rendering of Mrs. Transome's agony in *Felix Holt*, Leavis writes: 'There is no touch of the homiletic about this: it is dramatic constatation, poignant and utterly convincing, and the implied moral, which is a matter of the enacted inevitability, is that perceived by a psychological realist' (p. 59). In this sense, realism is not a description of a genre or a mode of narrative but a value term conferred on works which are concrete and dramatic. By 'concreteness' Leavis means the dramatized particularity of a situation or response to that situation. Concreteness usually derives from a dramatic moment. What he writes of the impulse and occasion behind Claudio's words in *Measure for Measure* defines qualities that he values in both the characters and the narrators in fiction:

> Claudio's words spring from a vividly realized particular situation: from the imagined experience of a given mind in a given critical moment that is felt from the inside – that is lived – with sharp concrete particularity.[30]

Leavis helped perpetuate the preference of the James–Lubbock aesthetic for showing over telling. Of Wells he writes, 'there is an elementary distinction to be made between the *discussion* of problems and ideas, and what we find in the great novelists' (p. 7). But what Leavis condemns is not so much telling itself but the failure to make the abstract concrete and particular (we might think of Eliot's objection to the failure to fuse thought and feeling, the failure which he calls the 'disassociation of sensibility'.)

Leavis's humanism takes precedence over a narrow formalism. If he is dogmatic in his tone and judgments, he is often flexible and pluralistic in his method, allowing, within basic guidelines, his reading – his *personal* reading – of each writer to generate his critical approach. It is worth noting that Leavis does not eschew any evidence he finds helpful, including biography and letters. Thus, unworried about the intentional or biographical fallacy, Leavis discusses authors as engaged presences in novels: 'Only a novelist who had known from the inside the exhaustions and discouragements of long-range intellectual enterprises could have conveyed the pathos of Dr. Casaubon's predicament' (p. 61). The stress on the author as an engaged presence in the text is important to Leavis's humanism. Partly as a result of Leavis's influence, it remained rather more respectable to discuss the author in England than in America where, in the face of the joint assault of the New Critics and the Chicago Critics, the author almost disappeared from criticism.

IV

Since he completely changed his judgments in *Dickens the Novelist*, we might ignore his disparaging comments about Dickens, were it not that his praise of *Hard Times* gives us insight into the moral fable, a concept he employs to describe such various works as *Silas Marner*, *Nostromo*, and *Roderick Hudson*: '[In the moral fable], the representative significance of everything in the fable – character, episode, and so on – is immediately apparent as we read' (p. 227). For *Hard Times*, 'the fable is perfect; the symbolic and representative values are inevitable, and, sufficiently plain at once, yield fresh subtleties as the action develops naturally in its convincing historical way' (p. 20). According to Leavis's judgment of Dickens's novels in *The Great Tradition*, only *Hard Times* has a 'sustained and complete seriousness' 'in which [Dickens's] distinctive creative genius is controlled throughout to a unifying and organizing significance' (pp. 19–20).

Since Leavis prefers showing to telling and dramatic concreteness to abstractions, and speaks of *Heart of Darkness* as being told from Marlow's 'specific and concretely realized point of view,' it is surprising that he complains in *Heart of Darkness* of 'adjectival insistence upon inexpressible and incomprehensible mystery' (p. 177).

For that insistence is a deliberate part of Conrad's characterization of
Marlow's quest to understand and articulate his experience. Failure to
realize that Marlow is a character whose behaviour is presented
ironically causes Leavis to misunderstand all the Marlow works. Rather
than exploring the complex relationship between Conrad and Marlow
in the way that he explores the relationship between George Eliot and
her omniscient narrator, he complains that Marlow is 'both more and
less than a character and always something other than just a
master-mariner' (pp. 184–5). His preferences of *Typhoon* to *Heart of
Darkness* and *Nostromo* to *Lord Jim* derive from his preference for the
Victorian omniscient narrator, whose moral values are explicit, over a
dramatized narrator's search for values. This preference is, of course,
in conflict with his preference for the dramatic. Although Leavis prefers
moral complexity, he seems to feel more comfortable with a very
clearly defined and even simplified point of view.

The reasons for his admiration of *Nostromo* provide the best
demonstration in *The Great Tradition* of how Leavis applies his
standards. In *Nostromo*, incidents are chosen for their representative
or paradigmatic value rather than being merely nominalistic; the
strands of individual lives reveal something about the way life was lived
at a specific time; and we feel, in the selection and arrangement of the
materials, the presence of the author's moral imagination indicating to
the reader what the appropriate moral standards are. Leavis's praise
for *Nostromo* depends upon its pattern of 'moral significance'. Thus,
'The whole book forms a rich and subtle but highly organized pattern
. . . [The] informing and organizing principle [is] what do men find to
live *for* – what kinds of motive force or radical attitude can give life
meaning, direction, coherence?' (p. 191). In *Nostromo*, '[Conrad's]
organization is devoted to exhibiting in the concrete a representative
set of radical attitudes, so ordered as to bring out the significance of
each in relation to a total sense of human life. The dramatic
imagination at work is an intensely moral imagination, the vividness of
which is inalienably a judging and a valuing' (p. 30). The discussion of
Conrad depends upon the standard of how accurately a writer mimes
the world in which he lives, a standard that depends on the critic's own
experience. Leavis praises Conrad for being 'one of those creative
geniuses whose distinction is manifested in their being peculiarly alive
in their time . . . [and their being] sensitive to the stresses of the
changing spiritual climate as they begin to be registered by the most
conscious' (pp. 21–2). Conrad, argues Leavis, 'is a greater novelist than
Flaubert because of the greater range and depth of his interest in

humanity and the greater intensity of his moral preoccupation' (p. 30).

'Interest' is a crucial concept in humanistic criticism from James to Booth. It expresses the kinds of commitments and engagements which a writer brings to his materials. In the first section of the James chapter Leavis wrote, 'By "interests" I mean kinds of profound concern – having the urgency of personal problems, and felt as moral problems, more than personal in significance – that lie beneath Jane Austen's art, and enable her to assimilate varied influences and heterogenous material and make great novels out of them' (p. 127). Interests must have scope and depth. Thus, in *Roderick Hudson*, James is 'a writer with mature interests, who shows himself capable of handling them in fiction. The interests are those of a very intelligent and serious student of contemporary civilization' (p. 130). Since 'interests', according to Leavis, must be explored and evaluated dramatically within the narrative process and must be part of significant form, it follows that the 'interests' of a writer as *revealed in his art* one criteria for judging his art. Leavis is also taking issue with James and Lubbock about the emphasis on the *art* of the novel, particularly point of view; Leavis is stressing that undue concern with technique can lead criticism astray. In a crucial comment he makes of George Eliot, Leavis asks whether form can be anything but a humanistic concern: 'Is there any great novelist whose preoccupation with 'form' is not a matter of his responsibility towards a rich human interest, or complexity of interests, profoundly realized? – a responsibility involving, of its very nature, imaginative sympathy, moral discrimination and judgment of relative human value?' (p. 29). For Leavis, this responsibility is not only to the fictional materials, but to the prospective reader.

At times, it is almost as if he appropriates James from Lubbock and indeed James himself – or at least the James of the Prefaces to the New York edition, where we learn about James's self-conscious and fastidious artistry. Disagreeing with the usual argument that James turned to Flaubert from the English tradition, he claims that James turned *from* the Flaubert tradition *to* the English tradition of George Eliot; he notes, 'It was James who put his finger on the weakness in *Madame Bovary*; the discrepancy between the technical ("aesthetic") intensity, with the implied attribution of interest to the subject, and the actual moral and human paucity of this subject on any mature valuation' (pp. 12–13).

In the second section of the James chapter Leavis raises questions about the importance of The Prefaces which had become the sacred texts of Lubbock and other of James's followers; he criticizes the inveterate indirectness of the later James . . . [which] appears there, in criticism, as an inability to state – an inability to tackle his theme, or to get anything out clearly and finally' (p. 158). *The Golden Bowl* and *The Ambassadors* show a 'too specialized' 'interest in his material'; they produce 'an effect of disproportionate "doing" – of a technique the subtleties and elaborations of which are not sufficiently controlled by a feeling for value and significance in living. . . . Isn't, that is, the energy of the "doing" (and the energy demanded for the reading) disproportionate to the issues . . . that are concretely held and presented?' (p. 161). In praising *The Portrait of a Lady*, Leavis refers to the overestimation of *The Ambassadors* in *The Craft of Fiction*. For James, 'being a novelist came to be too large a part of his living; that is, he did not live enough' (p. 163). 'Living' – experiencing life fully and responsively – is a Leavis value. James's later style did not sufficiently engage the reader's moral interests: '[I]t exacts so intensely and inveterately analytic an attention that no sufficient bodied response builds up: nothing sufficiently approaching the deferred concrete immediacy that has been earned is attainable' (p. 168).

V

The limitations of *The Great Tradition* can be divided into those of scope and those of method. First, let us turn to those of method.

(1) Leavis does not articulate his method for approaching a text; he only demonstrates it, and does so in a way which often seems quirky and idiosyncratic. Some of Leavis' criteria, like 'range and depth of interest in humanity', are really subjective. At times the standards of quality of subject matter and accuracy of subject matter are not defined in terms of aesthetic standards; on these occasions Leavis is in danger of becoming hopelessly impressionistic and dogmatically opinionated. Thus Eagleton has a point when he writes that '*Scrutiny*'s naive sensuous empiricism, epitomised in the act of "practical criticism", was a "progressive" testing of aesthetic categories against the immediacies of lived experience. . . .'.[31]

(2) Leavis does not really focus on the language of fiction, in particular what he calls 'the exploratory–creative use of words upon experience', although in his criticism of poetry he is more attentive to the creative function of language.[32]

(3) By focusing on crucial passages, and even isolating successful parts and thematic strands of novels from the unsuccessful ones, he does not give us a sense of the whole. To be sure, novel criticism, unless of vast length, does not have the scope for the kind of exhaustive analysis that we expect of criticism of poetry: yet if it is to be true to the narrative movement of the text, its analyses require amplitude that Leavis's readings of novels often lack.

(4) Indeed, for a critic who prides himself on addressing the text, much in his book is *ex cathedra* generalization; for example, neither the dismissal of *Lord Jim*, nor the claim that Conrad is superior to Flaubert and George Eliot, is argued. Where, we ask, are the discussions of such qualities as creative imagination, rhetoric, and stylistic concerns? Except for occasional moments, such as Leavis's misguided objection to Conrad's 'adjectival insistence', they are missing. He has a limited understanding of the dramatized perspective in Conrad's Marlow tales and in much of James.

(5) *The Great Tradition* does not stand on its own. To recognize its stature, it has to be placed in the context of other work as if it were a chapter in the *oeuvre*.

Now let us turn to the problems of scope and inclusiveness. The omissions of *The Great Tradition* are obvious:

(1) It has to be said that as a book which is concerned with establishing an historical tradition that emphasizes the peculiarly humanistic unFlaubertian strand in the English novel, its failure to include both a chapter on Austen and a chapter on the eighteenth-century novel is striking. Dismissing Defoe and Sterne in a footnote hardly suffices. And had he developed the Richardson–Burney–Austen 'line', which he mentions, perhaps he would have traced it to James and provided an important context for James's stress on the psychology of character. Given that this book was Leavis's major work on fiction, one wonders why he never added a chapter on both Austen and Lawrence to later editions, so as to complete the symmetry of his 'tradition', or why he neither went back and expanded the introduction nor provided an index.

(2) Surely, establishing a great tradition means considering at some length the pretenders to that tradition. Yet he patronizes Thackeray as a writer whose 'attitudes, and the essential substance of interest' are extremely limited, and dismisses Trollope with the

flip remark, 'Thackeray is a greater Trollope' (p. 21). We hardly have confidence that Leavis has reached these judgments after a careful reading of the entire canon of both novelists. To discuss Meredith and Hardy in one breath is not very satisfactory. Consigning the Brontës to a note at the end of the opening chapter, Leavis implies that they are hardly deserving of serious attention. And he begins the note with the snide remark that 'there is only one Brontë'. After acknowledging Emily's genius, he calls *Wuthering Heights* 'a kind of sport' (p. 27). Basically, rather than explaining the shortcomings of the major novelists that he omits – the Brontës, Thackeray, Trollope, Hardy, Woolf – he provides facetious remarks punctuated by an occasional insight in the form of an aside.

(3) At times, for all his sophistication, Leavis turns himself into one of those bluff Dickensian figures, a kind of critical Mr. Podsnap, who seems to value intuitively all things English for their own sake. Leavis's provincialism, at times approaching xenophobia, is rather striking when he writes 'that James [sees] life through literature – and English literature' (p. 132). Leavis writes with some pique of '[James's] anti-English stories of cultural comparison' (p. 145), but is offended that in *Daisy Miller* and *The American*, he 'takes an American stand on insufficient ground' (p. 143). Can we accept Leavis's claim that it was only Dickens who 'helped [James] to see from the outside, and critically place, the life around him' (p. 132). Not Hawthorne or Melville? not Stendhal or Balzac? or even Flaubert?

Nevertheless, *The Great Tradition* is a seminal book. Leavis's strength is that he convinces us that he speaks for the educated reader; at best, we feel that, yes, he is *our* self-elected delegate, as when he testifies that his own reading experience caused him to re-evaluate *The Rainbow* and *Women in Love* when his original 'stupidity and habit-blindness' were corrected by subsequent reading (p. 27). Leavis strives for the very qualities that he admires in novelists – maturity, seriousness, impersonality, and awareness of the possibilities of life – and wishes, as a critic, to be 'one of the significant few' – to use his phrase for the great novelists – in the critical great tradition, composed of such figures as Johnson and Arnold (p. 3). The terms he values in literary criticism – 'clear', 'coherent', 'consistent' – become values that he finds in the novels he admires (pp. 5–6). Leavis admires novelists for the very qualities he wishes to achieve in his criticism – imaginative sympathy, moral discrimination, and judgment of relative value. When Leavis praises James for '[bringing] to the business of the novelist a wide intellectual culture, as well as, in an exceptionally high degree, the kind of knowledge of individual humans and concrete societies that we expect of a great novelist' (p. 135), Leavis is praising him for the qualities he values in the critic. If Leavis has come to regard the novelist as a disguised critic, it is because to Leavis the humanistic literary critic has the same relationship and responsibility to texts as the novelist has to life.

NOTES

1. Cited in Ronald Heyman, *Leavis* (Totowa, New Jersey: Rowman & Littlefield, 1976) pp. 64–5.
2. *The Importance of Scrutiny*, ed. Eric Bentley (New York University Press, 1964) p. 9.
3. Heyman, p. 38.
4. *Scrutiny*, p. 4.
5. *Scrutiny*, p. xxv.
6. *Scrutiny*, p. 32.
7. *Revaluation* (London: Chatto & Windus, 1936) pp. 3–4.
8. *Scrutiny*, p. 36.
9. *Scrutiny*, p. 48.
10. *Scrutiny*, p. 6.
11. *Education and the University* (London: Chatto & Windus, 1943) p. 70.
12. Cited from *Letters in Criticism* ed. John Tasker, by Gary Watson, *The Leavises, The 'Social' and the Left* (Swansea, Wales: Brynmill, 1977) p. 5.
13. *Scrutiny*, p. 93.
14. Quoted in R. P. Bilan, *The Literary Criticism of F. R. Leavis* (Cambridge University Press, 1979) p. 70.
15. *Scrutiny*, p. 96.
16. *Scrutiny*, p. 70.
17. *Scrutiny*, pp. 57–8.
18. *The Common Pursuit* (New York: Penguin, 1962) orig. edn 1952, p. 280.
19. *T. S. Eliot, Selected Essays*, new edn (New York: Harcourt, Brace, & World, 1950) p. 14.
20. Page numbers in parentheses refer to *The Great Tradition* (New York University Press, 1964) orig. edn 1948.
21. T. S. Eliot, p. 4.
22. Bilan, p. 201; see *The Great Tradition*, p. 163.
23. *The Common Pursuit*, p. 284.
24. *Scrutiny*, pp. 33–4.
25. See *Education and the University*, pp. 41–2 for a particularly patronizing view of Richards that reflects Leavis's own anxiety of influence.
26. T. S. Eliot, 'Tradition and the Individual Talent', pp. 7–8.

27. *Dickens the Novelist* (Harmondsworth: Penguin Books, 1970) pp. 291–2; quoted in Bilan, p. 175.
28. Bilan, p. 175.
29. Bilan, p. 177.
30. *Revaluation*, p. 226.
31. Terry Eagleton, *Criticism and Ideology* (London: NLB, 1976) p. 15.
32. *The Common Pursuit*, p. 109.

4 'The Idea Embodied in the Cosmology': the Significance of Dorothy Van Ghent's *The English Novel: Form and Function*

I

For the past few decades the teaching of fiction in England and the United States has been radically affected by the appearance of two books: Wayne Booth's *The Rhetoric of Fiction* (1961) and Dorothy Van Ghent's *The English Novel: Form and Function* (1953). While Booth may be more widely discussed in professional forums, Van Ghent is the more influential in terms of her effects upon the teaching of fiction in America and England. Van Ghent's essays have provided models for teachers of fiction on how to approach a novel in terms of its organizing aesthetic principles. Prior to Van Ghent, high school courses discussed plot in terms of the students' own lives, while undergraduate novel courses wavered uneasily between plot synopsis, biography, history, and sociology. Yet although Booth's importance has been recognized by both Anglo-American critics and European theorists who appreciate his methodological clarity, Van Ghent's significance has been neglected. I think that there are two reasons for this neglect. Because her theory is gradually presented in a series of essays about specific novels, the implications of her conceptual framework have not been acknowledged even by those who appreciate the subtlety and power of her readings of English novels that span a spectrum from *Moll Flanders* to *A Portrait of the Artist as a Young Man*. But the more important reason is that the book's deliberate

80

effort to emphasize method rather than theory has made her less interesting to the present generation of theorists. She wrote in a tradition which used method to illuminate theory. Van Ghent's remarkable book is worth renewed attention for several reasons: (a) It is the best history of the *form* of the English novel; (b) virtually every one of its brilliant and provocative readings has fathered a plethora of derivative articles and books; (c) implicit in its individual readings is a formal theory of the novel which is not only applicable to any text, but, along with Booth, forms the intellectual base of much current Anglo-American novel criticism and probably the majority of under-graduate and graduate surveys of the English novel. With Booth, Van Ghent is responsible for the non-contextualist approach that often distinguishes courses in the English novel from courses in American fiction. While Booth focuses on what a novel does, specifically how it persuades the reader, Van Ghent treats a novel as a representation of human experience. Each novel is a discrete ontology with its own physical and moral geography. But Van Ghent's concept of the novel includes an awareness that the imagined world was created at a specific time and place and necessarily reflects them. She attempts to show how major novels mime both the external world of the time they were written and the world inhabited by the contemporary reader. Generally she uses internal rather then contextual evidence to establish the world in which the novel was written.

At a time when the aesthetic formalism of the New Criticism was struggling with fiction, Van Ghent realized that fiction's length and variety require different critical assumptions. She found the model she needed in Gestalt psychology which seeks to apprehend phenomena as functions with organized configurations rather than as distinct, isolated, discrete perceptions. 'A novel itself is one complex pattern, or Gestalt, made up of component ones. In it inhere such a vast number of traits, all organized in subordinate systems that function under the governance of a single meaningful structure, that the nearest similitude for a novel is a 'world'. This is a useful similitude because it reflects the rich multiplicity of the novel's elements and, at the same time, the unity of the novel as a self-defining body' (p. 6).[1] Gestalt psychology sees human events as dynamic patterns that constantly move and shift into new fields of perception, fields that are only static until modified by the next perception. It seeks to locate the fun-damental principles which tie disparate data together and to propose self-regulating principles which will account for new data.

Van Ghent's major aesthetic values are the intensity of mimesis and the quality and integrity of mimesis. The first is the traditional New Critical standard which measures the excellence of a work according to the unity and coherence of the imagined world. Like the New Critics, she takes unity and coherence as values, and admires highly organized works. The second seeks to evaluate by objective, formal standards the degree to which novels reflect the world in which they are written and the degree to which they have meaning in our world. 'Integral structure' has both an objective and a subjective dimension. Since books have no meaning prior to their being read by readers, integral structure depends primarily on our perception of the quality, intensity, integrity, and authenticity of the imagined world it presents. But, our other experiences inform and shape our responses to our reading experience. Her tenet that a novel is 'the idea embodied in the cosmology' recalls a crucial statement in Richards' *Principles of Literary Criticism* (1925): 'To make the work "embody", accord with, and represent the precise experience upon which its value depends is the [artist's] major preoccupation, in difficult cases an overmastering preoccupation.'[2] Van Ghent's concept of value is derived from Richards' example: 'The critic cannot possibly avoid using some ideas about value. His whole occupation is an application and exercise of his ideas on the subject, and an avoidance of moral preoccupations on his part can only be either an abdication or a rejection under the title of 'morality' of what he considers to be mistaken or dishonest ideas and methods.'[3] Following Richards, she believed that aesthetic experience is not radically different from other experience:

The sound novel, like a sound world, has to hang together as one thing. It has to have integral structure. Part of our evaluative judgment is based on its ability to hang together *for us*. And like a world, a novel has individual character; it has, peculiar to itself, its own tensions physiognomy, and atmosphere. Part of our judgment is based on the concreteness, distinctness, and richness of that character. Finally, we judge a novel also by the cogency and illuminative quality of the view of life that it affords, the idea embodied in its cosmology. . . . All these tests test the value of the novel only *for us*, and value for us is all the value that matters. But if the particular novel has been integral and characterful and meaningful for other individuals and other generations as well, however different its appearance to them, the book automatically extends our lives in amplitude and variousness. (pp. 6–7)

The above passage not only advances claims for technique to those who would ignore that element, but also insists on the quality of the author's vision as an aesthetic standard. ('The cogency and illuminative quality of the view of life it affords.') In the *Tess of the D'Urbervilles* essay she explains *the way a novel means*:

What philosophical vision honestly inheres in a novel inheres as the signifying form of a certain concrete body of experience; it is what the experience 'means' because it is what, structurally, the experience *is*. When it can be loosened away from the novel to compete in the general field of abstract truth – as frequently in Hardy – it has the weakness of any abstraction that statistics and history and science may be allowed to criticize; whether true or false for one generation or another, or for one reader or another, or even for one personal mood or another, its status as truth is relative to conditions of evidence and belief existing outside the novel and existing there quite irrelevant to whatever body of particularized life the novel itself might contain. But as a structural principle active within the particulars of the novel, . . . the philosophical vision has the unassailable truth of living form. (p. 197)

Novels are meaningful not because they accurately mime external reality but because they are coherent, consistent, and plausible. But I would argue that some kinds of novels do in part depend for their structural principles upon how the imagined world mimes the actual one. These novels are inseparable from their historical context and cannot be perceived intelligently without some knowledge of their factual background; certainly Dostoevsky's *Notes from Underground*, Tolstoy's *War and Peace*, and Disraeli's *Sybil* fall into this category.

In addition to our own response, Van Ghent argues, a book has meaning in terms of how prior generations responded to it. I think she means not only that the history of a novel's critical readings will tell us something about the history of taste, but that each reading modifies the text and that the history of a text would be a history of a text's readings. Her explanation for the order of chapters clarifies this concept:

The reason for the chronological order of the series is chiefly that examples of an art are developments of the history of the art, and understanding and just appraisement of the examples ask for experience of the history. Furthermore, a novel does change to our perception when set in a special environment of other novels. In the environment provided here – that of well-known English novels in their historical sequence – each of these familiar books inevitably acquires an aspect of freshness, of newness, just by the special juxtaposition with its neighbors. By sheer arrangement, they illuminate each other – and us. (p. vii)

Van Ghent's chronological sense is informed by three basic premises: (a) novelists talk to one another and learn from one another; (b) literary works are more comprehensible if seen as part of the evolution of a tradition; (c) juxtaposing two or more novels from different periods can create exciting contexts for the texts and increase our sense of chronology by the very act of chronological disruption. Thus she often recalls prior chapters in order to give another perspective on the novel under discussion.

Van Ghent's sense of literary history recalls Eliot's concept of tradition which I cited in my Leavis chapter: 'No poet, no artist of any art, has his complete meaning alone. His significance, his appreciation is the appreciation of his relation to the dead poets and artists. You cannot value him alone; you must set him, for contrast and comparison, among the dead.'[4] It is worth remarking that Eliot's famous passage has its historical and ahistorical aspects. In its emphasis on an evolving tradition it is historical, but it is ahistorical in its emphasis on the reader's perception of the simultaneity of past and present as phenomena within a continuum. Van Ghent would have found in this ahistorical aspect a parallel to her Gestalt model.

The influence of Eliot reminds us that important critics are themselves understood as part of an historical process. It is always tempting to believe that past decades represent the dark eras of literary criticism, and that currently fashionable practices are the critical Holy Grail. In an essay that seeks to establish the importance of a major figure, it would be tempting to survey the wasteland of novel criticism prior to 1953. But the principal features of Van Ghent's criticism can best be discerned and understood in the context of prevailing literary theory, and particularly of novel theory, at the time her book appeared in 1953, because her work brought together the ideas of a number of seminal figures.

There can be no denying the influence on Van Ghent of the New

Criticism, and of the classicism of Pound, Hulme, and Eliot. She knew Brooks' and Warren's *Understanding Fiction* (1943) and Gordon's and Tate's *The House of Fiction* (1950), and understood the difficulties that the New Critics had in applying their aesthetic formalism to longer prose works. She was profoundly influenced by two seminal essays by Mark Schorer, 'Technique as Discovery' (1948) and 'Fiction and "Analogical Matrix" ' (1949);[5] while she acknowledges the debt to the latter piece in her Austen essay, the former pervades her argument, and is perhaps most explicit in the following remark: 'Technique elongates or foreshortens, and while the rudimentary relationships of common experience remain still recognizable, it reveals astonishing bulges of significance, magnifies certain parts of the anatomy of life, of whose potentialities we had perhaps not been aware, humbles others' (p. 173).

But her view of the relationship between poet and reader was influenced by Kenneth Burke who argued that

> a poem's structure is to be described most accurately by thinking always of the poem's function . . . [A] poem is designed to 'do something' for the poet and his readers, and . . . we can make the most relevant observations about its design by considering the poem as the embodiment of this act. In the poet, we might say, the poetizing existed as a physiological function. The poem is its corresponding anatomic structure. And the reader, in participating in the poem, breathes into this anatomic structure a new physiological vitality that resembles, though with a difference, the act of its maker, the resemblance being in the overlap between writer's and reader's situation, the difference being in the fact that these two situations are far from identical.[6]

Nor can there be much doubt that R. P. Blackmur was a major influence on Van Ghent. We might recall that most of Blackmur's essays that were to appear many years later in *Eleven Essays in the European Novel* (1967) had been published as articles and that his *Language as Gesture* appeared in 1952. Perhaps the best gloss on Van Ghent's work comes from Blackmur's preface to *Eleven Essays*: 'For me every good novel is a speculation – a theoretic form, a fresh psychology – a speculation in myth which reaches into the driving psyche: the psyche which endures and even outlives human behavior.'[7] In his essay entitled 'A Feather-Bed for Critics', Blackmur articulates the unspoken assumption behind Van Ghent's work: 'The composition of a great poem is a labour of unrelenting criticism, and the full reading of it only less so; and it is in this sense too, that the critical act is what is called a "creative" act, and whether by poet, critic, or serious reader, since there is an alteration, a stretching, of the sensibility as the act is done.'[8]

As these parallels with Burke and Blackmur suggest, Van Ghent parts company with the emphasis of James and Lubbock on point of view and with those of the New Critics who, in the pages of *Kenyon Review* and *Sewanee Review*, insisted on the supremacy of form over content. With Lionel Trilling, she understood that novels deal with timeless values that are relevant to successive generations of readers. In her preface, Van Ghent acknowledges that the decision to open with Don Quixote was influenced by Lionel Trilling's remark in a 1948 *Kenyon Review* piece entitled 'Manners, Morals, and the Novel', a remark she quotes: 'In any genre it may happen that the first great example contains the whole potentiality of the genre. It has been said that all philosophy is a footnote to Plato. It can be said that all prose fiction is a variation on the theme of *Don Quixote*' (p. viii).[9] In the same essay, Trilling provides justification for Van Ghent's stress on the quality of the content in her work: "For our time the most effective agent of the moral imagination has been the novel of the last two hundred years. . . . Its greatness and its practical usefulness lay in its unremitting work of involving the reader himself in the moral life, inviting him to put his own motives under examination, suggesting that reality is not as [he sees] it.'[10] Thus Van Ghent is part of a tradition, stretching from Plato and Horace through Arnold, Leavis, Trilling, and Burke (as well as the European Critics, Lukàcs and Benjamin), that is primarily concerned with the moral effects and moral values of art. Typical of the positivistic, empiricist Anglo-American tradition, Trilling, Leavis, and Arnold emphasize method rather than theory. Her criticism has an urgency that most Anglo-American criticism now lacks, an urgency that recalls Leavis's and Arnold's certainty that the reading of literature can affect the quality of one's moral life. We should hear a note of Arnold's 'high seriousness' and Leavis's twin standards of tangible realism and moral seriousness in Van Ghent's phrase 'the cogency and illuminative quality of the view of life that [the text] affords'.

As part of this tradition, Van Ghent refuses to separate moral and aesthetic considerations when confronting a text. For her, literary form is the moral shape imposed upon characteristic events that make up a narrative. The 'value' of a novel depends upon its 'meaningfulness

– its ability to make us more aware of the meaning of our lives' (p. 7). Form, then, is the means by which an artist controls, interprets, and evaluates life, and she is unwilling to dissociate formal analysis of the text from the quality and persuasive power of the content. 'The form of the book . . . *is* the content. The form . . . is the book itself.' When she insists that 'we cannot dissociate an author's conception of life, and its "value" and "significance" from the aesthetic structure of the literary work' (p. 113), she is stressing the importance of the integral relation between form and content and insisting that neither can be ignored. To be sure, discussion of content is often disguised in formal terms. Van Ghent presupposes a strong connection between moral and aesthetic values. This connection enables her to see a novel's structure as equivalent to the author's moral attitudes and to his suggestions about how man ought to order his life. A novel's form is equivalent to its persuasive powers added to its revelations and insights. To speak of a work of art independent of its form is thus impossible.

Not infrequently, a critic's discussion of books he or she regards as inadequate gives us a good sense of the critic's aesthetic criteria and method. For in those works the critics must necessarily establish the standards by which the works fail. Thus Van Ghent's discussion of *The Egoist* and *The Heart of Mid-Lothian* enables her to clarify her basic premise. In her view, *The Egoist* fails because it does not transform the nominalistic into the representative. That is to say, it does not achieve the universality that great fiction requires. A novel achieves this by 'spiritual *contextualism*' of the lives within its imagined world: 'Where such context strongly exists and style subserves it, is not the concreteness there too – the concreteness that makes the created world of a novel excitedly meaningful "for us"?' (p. 193). In *The Egoist*, style takes the place of spiritual context. The problem with *The Heart of Mid-Lothian* is that Scott refuses to explore moral issues in terms of 'aesthetic structure – presumably because he does not know that they are there. His neglect of their inherence in his materials is an index of confusion. . . . This deflection of vision is what we mean by disorderliness and disorganization of structure' (p. 120).

For Van Ghent, language is a crucial component of structure which she defines as 'the arrangement and interrelation of all the elements in a book, as dominated by the general character of the whole' (pp. 65–6).

Each author does not consult the whole body of the language in selecting words for his meanings; . . . he is driven, as if compulsively, to the selection of a highly particular part of the language; . . . the individual character of his work, its connotations and special insights, derive largely from the style he has made his own – that is to say, from the vocabulary and verbal arrangements he has adopted out of the whole gamut of words and rhetorical patterns available in the language. . . . He is acting partly under compulsions of the culture in which he has been bred and whose unconscious assumptions – as to what is interesting or valuable or necessary or convenient in life – are reflected in the verbal and rhetorical selections common in that culture; and he is acting partly also under compulsions that are individual to his own personal background, but that still maintain subtle links with the common cultural assumptions. (p. 110)

If this seems naive today, we might recall that fiction criticism, until Schorer's essay 'Fiction and the "Analogical Matrix" ', had neglected the importance of language. Van Ghent shows that the verbal texture does not merely reinforce theme and form, but *creates* new levels of significance. In 1953 critics of fiction usually did not emphasize that the individual word was as important to prose as to poetry and that the critic must attend to each word. Until it was realized that language exists prior to other elements and is the element on which the other elements depend, criticism of fiction was more comfortable with narrative structure and theme. The focus on voice and persona in recent decades derives from closer scrutiny of the individual sentence, image, and word. In 1953 it was not a commonplace to argue that the style a character uses is 'a mimesis of an action of the soul,' that various styles differentiate characters and situations, and that the language an author uses reveals both his consciousness and his *Zeitgeist*. Thus, her *Pride and Prejudice* essay from which the quotations in this paragraph are taken is crucial to the development of Anglo-American criticism. In that essay she shows how the materialistic 'language Jane Austen inherited from her culture and to which she was confined' shaped every aspect of her novel's imagined world – the family, community and personal relationships (p. 109). Her focus upon diction and syntax, the least common denominator of a novel, influenced David Lodge's important *Language of Fiction* (1966).

II

Van Ghent is very conscious that she writes at a time 'when society has failed to give objective validation to inherited structures of belief, and when therefore all meanings, values, and sanctions have to be built up from scratch in the loneliness of the individual mind' (p. 267). Modern criticism's preoccupation with form and structure doubtlessly derives, in part, from a widespread sense of personal and cultural failure. When the meaning of our personal lives and the values of our culture are uncertain, we become obsessed with the shapes and patterns rather than the values of experience. As Van Ghent puts it, 'the problems of modern life have appeared intransigent indeed; and, in general, the growth of the intransigence has been reflected in an increasing concern with technique on the part of the artist' (p. 245). The artist (and for Van Ghent the critic is a version of the artist) discovers forms and patterns in the phenomenal world: 'art is the discovery of order' (p. 132). Order, harmony, form, schematization – all these words, taken in the context of references to Hiroshima, the Holocaust, concentration camps, show how art for Van Ghent becomes what Frye has called the 'secular scripture'. In a sense, there is a note of desperation in Van Ghent's search for unity and meaning in her book.

Van Ghent's dedication is extremely revealing. The book is dedicated to Ben Lehman, 'who first illuminated for me the critical approach to literature as a search for the principle of form in the work and implicitly as a search for form in the self'. Within every essay, generalizations about the nature of the human soul and about the modern *Zeitgeist* are part of her urgent search for form within the self. We need not dwell on her troubled and tumultuous life to appreciate the intensity of her quest for order and to feel her straining for the appropriate word and organization. Her search for personal order in literature derives from her gloomy evaluation of the world: 'In a time of cultural crisis, when traditional values no longer seem to match at any point with the actualities of experience, and when all reality is therefore thrown into question, the mind turns inward on itself to seek the phase of reality there – for the thinking and feeling man cannot live without some coherent schematization of reality' (p. 263).

While Van Ghent did not write under such dramatic circumstances as Erich Auerbach who had left Nazi Germany and wrote *Mimesis* while teaching in Turkey, the cloud of historical crisis hovers over her work. She identifies with Coleridge (whom she quotes more than any other writer) who also saw himself writing in an 'age of anxiety', the term Auden borrowed to describe the modern era (p. 124). She is implicitly arguing that man must turn back to the humanistic tradition of which the novels that she writes on are a central aspect: 'Fielding looks upon humankind and all its proclivities as offering an ideal of intelligent order; whereas two world wars and the prospect of a third, universally disintegrating, offer to the modern view a notion of humankind as governed by irrational motives, self-destructive, incognizant of what civilized order might mean. Our own "nature", as representing humanity, we see as incalculable, shadowy, dark, capable of inexplicable explosions' (p. 77). (On the next page, she makes clear that she has the spectre of 'a concentration camp' in mind.) But beyond Van Ghent's desperate quest for order are the tenets of idealism and romanticism, tenets which provided the philosophic underpinning for the New Criticism. Van Ghent believes that the mind constructs its world. For Van Ghent, the life of the mind is the significant reality, and it is the human mind from which originates shape and order in life.

In the final chapters, her voice loses its objectivity and takes on a tone of moral urgency; the critic gives way to the teacher and prophet. The impulse she attributes to Lawrence is also hers: 'Lawrence's missionary and prophetic impulse, like Dostoevski's, was to combat the excesses of rationalism and individualism, excesses that have led – paradoxically enough – to the release of monstrously destructive irrationals and to the impotence of the individual' (p. 259). Van Ghent, like Lawrence, wishes to urge that the imaginative energy of literature is an important kind of experience. In the book's last pages, the voice of the critic and the voice of the artist she is discussing merge:

> Joyce's doctrine of the epiphany assumes that reality does have wholeness and harmony – even as Stephen as a child premises these, and with the same trustfulness – and that it will radiantly show forth its character and its meaning to the prepared consciousness, for it is only in the body of reality that meaning can occur and only there that the artist can find it. This is essentially a religious interpretation of the nature of reality and of the artist's function. It insists on the objectivity of the wholeness, harmony, and meaning, and on the objectivity of the revelation – the divine showing-forth. (p. 275)

If the artist is shaman, his rite of passage is language. In a moving, almost lyrical moment, Van Ghent describes her beliefs in terms of her reading of Joyce. She shares Joyce's belief in the redemptive power of language. Indeed, she reminds us how the early modernists' belief in the autonomy of art created the necessity for a literary criticism that espoused that credo. Van Ghent believes that the novelist can use language to create an alternative to the real world where principles of wholeness, harmony, and meaning exist. Her conclusion is not only the climax of her critical reading of Joyce and her theory of fiction, but a statement of her faith in the ability of language to order lives, most especially her own. In her final sentences Van Ghent implicitly becomes a kind of artist because she has created order and meaning in her critical essays: 'The epiphany of "everything and everywhere" as one and harmonious and meaningful . . . [is] found in the labyrinth of language that contains all human revelations vouchsafed by divine economy, and to be found by the artist in naming the names' (p. 276).

The form and technique of Van Ghent's book enact her idealism, an idealism dependent on using the faculty of imagination as Coleridge understood it: 'To Coleridge, imagination was the faculty likest in kind to the primary faculty of perception which gives spatial and temporal and causal organization to the world; a creative faculty because synthetic in function, a maker of unities' (pp. 123–4). The critic uses his imagination to organize into comprehensible patterns the welter of words and events in the novel. Her ideal critic is what Harold Bloom would call a strong misreader. Van Ghent believes that the critic, like the novelist, creates his or her own order. Van Ghent's concept of mimesis is more romantic than realistic. When she rejects George Eliot's idea that the mind of the novelist is 'a mirror from whose "reflections" of "men and things" he draws his account', she is articulating her own view of the *critic's* role:

> The "mirror" of the mind shapes what it sees. It does not passively "reflect" things-as-they-are, but creates things-as-they-are. Though we can clearly discriminate the quality of intention shown by a realistic art – and it usually reduces finally to a choice of materials from the field of the quotidian, the commonplace, the mediocre – yet its aim of veraciousness is necessarily one of veraciousness to what the artist sees in the shape-giving, significance-endowing medium of his own mind, and in this sense the mythopoeic art of *Wuthering Heights* is as veracious as the realistic art of *Adam Bede*. (p. 172)

Once one sees the novel as a cosmology, then it is a short step to see the artist as a God figure, a creator with a capital C. The novel becomes a secular scripture, because its origins, movement, and ingredients correspond to the parts of biblical history of the world stretching from Genesis to Revelation. *The Rainbow* is based on Lawrence's perception of the novel's potential to rewrite the scripture and carry his prophetic message. While it remained for Frye's *Anatomy of Criticism* (1957) and Kermode's *The Sense of an Ending* (1967) to show how novels create their own internally ordered world with their own genesis, apocalypse, prolepses, and typology, Van Ghent perceived novels as imagined worlds with their own system of correspondences.

> Folk magic is, after all, in its strategy of analogy, only a specialization and formalization of the novelist's use of the symbolism of natural detail, a symbolism of which we are constantly aware from beginning to end. Magical interpretation and prediction of events consist in seeing one event or thing as a "mimicry" of another – a present happening, for instance, as a mimicry of some future happening; that is, magic makes a system out of analogies, the correlative forms of things. . . . Novelistic symbolism *is* magical strategy. (pp. 207–8)

If Van Ghent seems to argue for the autonomy of the text, it is in part because the autonomy depends upon her belief that the text contains shared systems of correspondences that will heal a secular age.

III

To be sure, Van Ghent's book has its limitations. The contemporary reader will find Van Ghent's political vision rather thin and dated. Her political idealism is almost a stereotype of the liberal imagination in the early 1950s. She is not particularly interested in a grammar of historical or economic cause and effect; one has only to think of the work of Benjamin or Lukàcs to realize that this dimension is missing from Van Ghent's world view. In his preface to *Studies in European Realism*, Lukàcs contended that 'every action, thought, and emotion of human beings is inseparably bound up with the life and struggles of the community, i.e., with politics; whether the humans themselves are conscious of this, unconscious of it or even trying to escape from it, objectively their actions, thoughts and emotions nevertheless spring from and run into politics'.[11] While her interest in a grammar of motives and of manners is particularly suited to the characteristic concerns of the English novel, Van Ghent rarely focuses on the way that a novel's social, economic and political milieu shapes the characters, or the way that milieu mimes the actual world at the time the novel was written. If, as she writes of *Great Expectations*, 'the child–parent situation has been disnatured, corrupted, with the rest of nature', should she not relate this to the social and economic factors that have caused this strain – industrialism, child labour, and the displacement of an agrarian family-oriented culture by an urban, material one? (p. 135). Of course, the very brevity of her essays prevents her from developing these aspects of the imagined world in which characters dwell. Yet, despite the scientific model, Van Ghent's bent is for the brilliant *aperçu* rather than the carefully reasoned argument. At times, as in the above instance, she eschews mustering evidence in favour of extending the implications of her ingenious insights.

The brilliant *Great Expectations* chapter illustrates another of Van Ghent's shortcomings. Because Van Ghent concentrates on one novel of each author, she does not locate the consciousness of the author that informs an author's entire canon. Where an author has expressed quite different values in prior or later novels, some of the statements about the author may seem reductive. In the *Great Expectations* chapter, references to a broad range of Dickens' novels would make statements like the following more compelling: 'The principle of reciprocal changes, between the human and the nonhuman, bears on the characteristic lack of complex "inner life" on the part of Dickens' people – their lack of a personally complex psychology' (p. 131). I am not sure that is true of the troubled adolescent Esther Summerson or her mother, to cite two obvious examples. And this brings me to another problem. Sometimes Van Ghent's impressive generalizations lack specificity; at other times they become overly abstract. (To be fair she tries to encompass the Dickens world in her 1950 *Sewanee Review* piece, 'The Dickens World: a View from Todgers', but in that essay, too, she lacks a sense of Dickens' artistic evolution.)

Van Ghent's range and boldness sometimes lead to oversimplification and imprecision. For example, we need some sense of the intellectual and social milieu before we can accept the following: 'For it is the community that is the protagonist of [*Tess of the D'urbervilles*], the community as the repository of certain shared and knowledgeable values that have been developed out of ages of work and care and common kindness' (p. 177). I am not sure she explains exactly how in *Tess*, 'the earth is most actual as a dramatic factor – that is, as a factor of causation' (p. 201). Or her effort to make the grand rhetorical gesture may lead to such obfuscation as the following: 'But the earth is "natural," while, dramatically visualized as antagonist, it transcends the natural. The integrity of the myth thus depends, paradoxically, upon naturalism; and it is because of the intimate dependence between the natural and the mythological, a dependence that is organic to the subject, that Hardy's vision is able to impregnate so deeply and shape so unobtrusively the naturalistic particulars of the story' (p. 201). Surely the success of Hardy's vision is related to aspects of Hardy's language, technique, and imagination, but the above passage deflects us from specific discussion of these matters. The tendency to posit issues in large terms at times creates a word world peripheral to the novel under discussion. Her desire to teach us *how to perceive* causes her to miss important historical relationships. The above passage implies that Hardy is as much a mythic writer as a realist, something more people are beginning to recognize but which few readers other than D. H. Lawrence understood at that time.

Writing nearly a decade before Booth and the Anglo-American preoccupation with narrators, she is at times inattentive to this aspect of fiction, although it does play a large part in some of the essays. She does not consider the implications of an omniscient narrator as a self-dramatizing character within the novel's imagined world. She is in a long line of critics who mistakenly condemn Thackeray for telling rather than showing. Furthermore, the problem with *Vanity Fair* is that the omniscient narrator 'becomes a personal convenience for relaxation of aesthetic control, *even a means to counterfeit* his creative vision' (p. 141). Moreover, the Amelia world is not sufficiently strong to 'act as [the] judge and corrector' of the Becky-world (p. 142):

> As the convention of the omniscient author allows Thackeray to keep up a maladroit "sound track" of personal interpolations, so it also collaborates with his confusion as to where the compositional center of his book lies; for though the Becky-world and Amelia-world, having no common motivation, confront each other with closed entrances, so to speak, yet the author is able, by abuse of his rights of omniscience, to move facilely through these closed doors. (p. 143).

Van Ghent is wrong on two counts. Thackeray is perfectly aware that the Amelia-world is morally anaemic, and he means his narrator to be a self-dramatizing character whose language reveals complex values and emotions. The narrator reminds us that the reader, too, is part of the corrupt world of *Vanity Fair*: 'Which of us is there can tell how much vanity lurks in our warmest regard for others, and how selfish our love is? . . . Always to be right, always to trample forward, and never to doubt, are not these the great qualities with which dullness takes the lead in the world?' (ch. 35). In fact the narrator, the man who in spite of himself is part of the world he detests and whose evolving personality takes an increasingly cynical view of the world he observes is 'the morally meaningful' alternative to Becky (p. 143). While Becky's vitality and energy transcend the simple Amelia and the ineffective, submissive Dobbin, these qualities are modified by passages like the following:

> In describing this syren, singing and smiling, coaxing and cajoling, the author, with modest pride, asks his readers all round, has he once forgotten the laws of politeness, and showed the monster's hideous tail above water? No! Those who like may peep down under waves that are pretty transparent, and see it writhing and twirling, diabolically hideous and slimy, flapping amongst bones, or curling round corpses. (ch. 64)

By equating her, a few sentences later, with 'the fiendish marine cannibals', Thackeray establishes through his narrator a moral standard that judges her and places her in context by means of the concrete image which Van Ghent says is indigenous to the technique of the English novel (pp. 144–5).

Van Ghent's shortcomings derive from her need to believe literature matters more than other kinds of experience. At times the prophetic bent subsumes her critical powers. Her desire to teach us how to live displaces the more subtle activity of teaching us how to read. Neglect of the *Zeitgeist* and of narrative technique derives from the desire to define the thematic implications in terms of our life. Moreover, the supplementary classroom guide that accompanied the original hardcover edition indicated that she saw herself not as a theorist, but as a teacher urging her fellow teachers as well as their students to be more discriminating readers. Clearly at one level she saw her book as a kind of sequel for fiction to Richards' *Practical Criticism* (1929).

IV

Van Ghent's influence has been pervasive. Because her essays follow the order of a syllabus for a very demanding two semester course in the British novel (or three different one semester courses, one in the eighteenth century, one in the Victorian period, and one from Hardy through Joyce), her study has become a kind of companion for teachers of English novel courses. To be sure, there are rival texts, but Arnold Kettle's two volume *An Introduction to The English Novel* (1951), for all its intelligence, in the guise of a Marxist approach often becomes a nostalgic rhapsody for pastoralism. Elizabeth Drew's *The Novel: A Modern Guide to Fifteen English Masterpieces* (1963) is a perspicacious 'reader's guide' but no rival in either its theoretical control or critical intelligence. A later Marxist study by Raymond Williams, *The English Novel From Dickens to Lawrence* (1970), effectively places a group of novelists in a sociological context, but does not approach Van Ghent's analytic intensity of specific works.

As we have seen, the Gestalt model perceives experience as a dynamic process, although it isolates a configuration within the mind. Van Ghent uses this model to define not only how a novel is written, but how it is perceived. She emphasizes the common ground shared by the author and skilled reader. Her book shows us that novels are about how man makes sense of his world and that novels are about testing, discarding, recreating perceptions – a process central to writing and reading novels and also to living. A completed novel is an evolving and developing linear pattern that each reader experiences as he or she moves through the book's time. Since reading is a linear process, a novel looks different at every point along its narrative as it moves towards its apocalypse – the fulfilment of its form. She influenced the movement away from the conception of fictional structure as static and three-dimensional, a conception that derives from non-linear art forms such as sculpture and architecture.

The test of a major critic is whether the critic creates a paradigmatic community, that is, a community of critics who recognize him or her as a seminal theoretical and conceptual thinker whose work provides a paradigm to be studied. Van Ghent has done this. Van Ghent provided the direction for a generation of formal critics of the novel who were not satisfied with limiting their discussion to internal 'facts', but insisted on discovering the implications of those 'facts' in terms of the author's psychological development, his literary and intellectual milieu, and his ideas. Along with Schorer and Blackmur, she taught a generation of students to use analytic methods to ask larger questions, and she did so at a time when close analysis threatened to become obsessed with categorizing colour, animal, and weather images. And Van Ghent is sufficiently eclectic to accommodate diverse kinds of mimesis, unlike Booth and Auerbach who, as we shall see, are troubled by the ethical implications of indefinite and unreliable narration.

Van Ghent's major legacy is that she provides a theory and critical examples to those who wished to apply aesthetic formalism to novels. She taught us that close reading can be used to make crucial, if speculative statements about the culture that produces novels. Her radically inductive method, by which she draws sweeping conclusions from limited but carefully chosen data, enables her to comment boldly on the implications of the fictive work. Her frequent analogies to the visual arts and science provide a context in which these novels must be taken seriously among the major products of Western civilization. In a way, her book is a defence of reading – indeed, of civilization. Behind every sentence is a testimony that these books matter to us. In this sense, she is as oriented to the effects on the individual reader as Booth or Burke. She showed how a critic can discover ordering principles in the seemingly diverse, recalcitrant material of a novel. Just as the author imposes order on the chaotic world of life, so the critic and reader not only create their organizing principles for books, but use those principles to order their own lives. While her ingenuous moral fervour often appears in the guise of political comment, she assumes and implicitly urges us as readers to use novels to expand our perceptual range and to question the world to which we return after the reading of a major novel is completed. As Charles Rosen wrote of Walter Benjamin, she teaches us that:

> The significance of the work is not exhausted by the meaning given to it by the author and his contemporaries, and it is not even adequately realized by them. The work is "timeless" in that it is not limited to the moments of its appearance. It transcends history, but this transcendence is only revealed by its projection through history. The transcendence is double: on the one hand the work gradually reveals a meaning accessible without a knowledge of the time in which it arose, and on the other it preserves for posterity some aspect of that time.[12]

NOTES

1. Page numbers in parentheses refer to Dorothy Van Ghent, *The English Novel: Form and Function* (New York, Rinehart & Co., 1953). The original 1953 edition had a supplementary classroom guide entitled 'Problems for Study and Discussion'. These notes have been omitted from the paperback edition (New York: Harper & Row, 1961).

2. I. A. Richards, *Principles of Literary Criticism* (New York: Harcourt, Brace, & World, 1925) pp 26–7.
3. Richards, p. 35.
4. T. S. Eliot, *Selected Essays* (New York: Harcourt, Brace, & World, 1960) p.4.
5. These essays are reprinted in Mark Schorer, *The World We Imagine* (New York: Farrar, Straus, Giroux, 1968).
6. Kenneth Burke, *The Philosophy of Literary Form*, rev. edn (New York: Vintage, 1957) pp. 75–6.
7. R. P. Blackmur, *Eleven Essays in the European Novel* (New York: Harcourt, Brace, & World, 1967) p. vii.
8. Quoted in Stanley Edgar Hyman, *The Armed Vision* (New York: Alfred A. Knopf, 1948) pp. 241–2.
9. This essay is reprinted in Lionel Trilling, *The Liberal Imagination* (New York: Viking, 1951).
10. Trilling, *The Liberal Imagination*, p. 222.
11. Georg Lukàcs, *Studies in the European Novel* (New York: Grosset & Dunlap, 1964) p. 9.
12. 'The Ruins of Walter Benjamin', *The New York Review of Books*, 24:17 Charles Rosen (27 Oct. 1977) p. 33.

5 'Formal Realism': the Importance of Ian Watt's *The Rise of the Novel*

I

In 1957, Ian Watt published *The Rise of the Novel*. It was viewed as a response to the New Critical orthodoxy of the day, although we now see that it was more of a modification than a refutation of formalism. To appreciate its impact, we need to recall the supremacy of New Criticism in 1957, and its insistence upon the autonomy of the text. Furthermore, it is also important to recall the distinction the New Critics and the *Scrutiny* group encouraged between criticism and scholarship, a term that became increasingly associated in the minds of younger professors and graduate students with the editing of texts, philological inquiry, and rather remote and antiquarian activities.[1] In a 1968 retrospective essay in *Novel*, Watt expressed the credo that informs *The Rise of the Novel*, 'The whole question of the historical, institutional and social context of literature is very widely ignored, to the great detriment not only of much scholarly and critical writing, but of the general understanding of literature at every educational level.' Rejecting the view that the work is an autonomous object, he insists that ideas and novels do not exist 'independently of each other'.[2] Nor can an artist be perceived separately from the social and moral conventions of his time. Deftly combining historical criticism with formal criticism in *The Rise of the Novel*, Watt relates the growth of the novel's form to changes in the intellectual and social milieu of the eighteenth century.

He relates 'the distinctive literary qualities of the novel [to] those of the society in which it began and flourished' (p. 7)[3]; the major works of Defoe, Richardson, and Fielding are in part the result of changes in the reading public, of the rise of economic individualism, and of the 'spread of Protestantism, especially in its Calvinist or Puritan forms'

(p. 60). These factors influenced the movement to individualize characters and to present detailed descriptions of setting and situation. Watt demonstrates that biographical, sociological, and historical knowledge explains the forms of works of art and are necessary for understanding their meaning. He shows that this knowledge not only enables us to retrieve the text that the author wrote, but also enables us to understand patterns of cultural history of which the author and his original readers were unaware. Literature is important because it not only expresses the *Zeitgeist*, but also in turn becomes a significant part of cultural and intellectual history.

Watt's method is his most important argument. While he does not articulate a critical theory, we can extrapolate his method for extending the meaning of a novel beyond its imagined ontology, and for viewing the novel as an expression of an author, a culture, and a literary history. Watt places the creation of each work in the context of the development of an art form. He provides us with a model for reading literature in terms of contexts without sacrificing formal analysis of a work's unique imagined world. He regards the work in part as a particular expression of the author who is shaped by, and is responding to, codes and conventions of his time. His encyclopaedic knowledge of the seventeenth and eighteenth century enables him to show that the works of Defoe, Fielding, and Richardson take their meaning from the world which produced them.

Given the current self-consciousness about theory, and the tendency of some critics to speak dismissively of humanistic criticism as if it were obsolete and irrelevant, it is time to ask ourselves why we read as we do. We need to identify the common humanistic heritage of Anglo-American novel criticism – its humanism, its search for unity, its pluralism – and to distinguish between its various strands, such as the New Criticism, Neo-Aristotelianism, and contextualism. Today Watt's book remains an important methodological refutation of those critics who restrict their attention to the autonomous text and of those who emphasize the reader's response to the text. His book speaks to us as a significant alternative to the tendency to see every work as about the writing and reading of itself, and to insist that the possibility of meaning is a fiction in which authors and readers participate. Watt's belief that criticism should explain the historical conditions which gave rise to the text and shaped its meaning takes issue with the current position that the reader is an heroic figure who creates the text or that the major task of criticism is 'that of making the text interesting, of combating the boredom which lurks behind every work, waiting to move in if reading goes astray or founders'.[4] By contrast, while conceding that interpretations may vary, Watt contends that literary criticism can be true or false insofar as it provides the *correct* material for understanding the text and insofar as it *accurately* reads the text.

Along with Leavis, Booth, and Van Ghent, Watt permanently changed the way novels were read in England and America. The importance of his study depends on a number of factors:

(1) Watt stresses the challenge to the Augustan values by the middle class writers Defoe and Richardson and places that challenge in an historical context. The 'rise' of the novel becomes an expression – a revolutionary challenge – to the traditional class hierarchies, to the dominance of the aristocracy, to the central position of the Anglo-Catholic Church in the nation's religious life, and to the accepted conventions of literary genres and decorum.

(2) By focusing on the relationship between culture and society, Watt helped release novel criticism from the often claustrophobic and stultifying atmosphere of the New Criticism. In its search for patterns of imagery and organic unity, even in second and third rate texts, the New Criticism had become something of a parody of itself.

(3) In a brilliant fusion of historical scholarship with responsive and sensitive reading, Watt helped establish the canon of the English novel in the eighteenth century, particularly the current position of Richardson. He challenged the then orthodox views, promulgated most notably by the Chicago Aristotelians, that Richardson was inferior to Fielding.

(4) Anticipating Frank Kermode and more recent narratologists, Watt sees novels as solving formal 'problems' and conducting 'inquiries' into the possibilities of the genre. He emphasized that novelists were conducting researches into the relationship between art and reality; thus he writes, '[Sterne] proceeds to take to its logical extreme the ultimate realist premise of a one-to-one correspondence between literature and reality' and 'achieves a *reductio ad absurdum* of the novel form itself' (p. 292).

(5) He argues that readers' desires for kinds of vicarious experience that would express and dramatize their interest in private lives, their individualism, and their economic motives were themselves factors in creating the eighteenth-century novel.

(6) He conceives the development of the novel in terms of a movement from simple to more complex forms. The very title –

the 'rise' of the novel – promulgates an evolutionary teleology. This teleological view argues that the English novel reaches its major phase in the Victorian novel (or, in another version, in the early modern novel of James, Conrad, and Joyce) because of the prior experiments with form in the earlier novel. Thus the eighteenth-century novel is seen as a *necessary* stage in the progressive development of English fiction, standing in the same kind of relation as early Elizabethan drama does to Shakespeare. This perspective derives in part from the emphasis on historicism in the visual arts where every painter and sculptor is viewed as a stepping stone, as a necessary precursor to major figures and movements, and figures like Raphael or Cezanne, or movements like the Renaissance or Impressionism, are defined in terms of a grand synthesis of what has preceded. Thus for Watt the novel is incomplete before Austen: 'It cannot be claimed that either [Richardson or Fielding] completely achieved that interpenetration of plot, character, and emergent moral theme which is found in the highest examples of the art of the novel' (p. 15). But Austen is the historical result of the efforts of her predecessors: 'Jane Austen faces more squarely than Defoe, for example, the social and moral problems raised by economic individualism and the middle class quest for improved status; she follows Richardson in basing her novels on marriage and especially on the proper feminine role in the matter; and her ultimate picture of the proper norms of the social system is similar to that of Fielding although its application to the characters and their situation is in general more serious and discriminating' (p. 298). Watt not only reinforced the teleological implications of Leavis's *The Great Tradition* and Kettle's *The English Novel*, but he confirmed Leavis's judgment that Austen was the first novelist of the great tradition.

(7) He demonstrates that this historical or contextual approach is not incompatible with the aesthetic formalism of the New Criticism; for in his readings he relies heavily on the latter method to confirm his generalizations about historical and sociological forces. He did not want to turn his back on the close reading of the New Criticism, but rather wanted to enrich its critical nominalism – its dissection of a text for its own sake. Thus in his praise of Austen's achievement, Watt intrinsically employs the New Critical standard of organic form: 'She was able to combine into a harmonious unity the advantages both of realism of presentation and realism of assessment, of the internal and of the external

approaches to character; her novels have authenticity without diffuseness or trickery, wisdom of social comment without a garrulous essayist, and a sense of the social order which is not achieved at the expense of the individuality and autonomy of the characters' (p. 297).

(8) By arguing that the author might be more profitably understood with reference to historical background and the world reflected in the novel, he took issue with the then fashionable reliance upon Freud and Jung. He showed that authors cannot be understood without the text and vice versa; they must be studied together.

(9) Finally, he suggests that there need not be an absolute dichotomy between external and internal approaches to character and characterization, between Fielding's omniscient narrator and Richardson's dramatization of the psyche of his characters.

II

In the first chapter, 'Realism and the Novel Form', Watt quite intentionally addresses his subject as if it were a social and historical problem open to factual solution: 'The present inquiry therefore takes another direction: assuming that the appearance of our first three novelists within a single generation was probably not sheer accident, and that their geniuses could not have created the new form unless the conditions of the time had also been favourable, it attempts to discover what these favourable conditions in the literary and social situation were, and in what ways Defoe, Richardson, and Fielding were its beneficiaries' (p. 9). Watt is a positivist and empiricist who believes that the principles of scientific and historical inquiry can be applied to the humanities and that valid hypotheses can be developed for studying literature as cultural phenomena. The novel's rise in response to social and historical forces can be explained in the same way as the rise of European universities in the middle ages or the decline of the monasteries in England. Thus, he argues that, 'It is therefore likely that the Puritan conception of the dignity of labour helped to bring into being the novel's general premise that the individual's daily life is of sufficient importance and interest to be the proper subject of literature' (p. 74). Or, relating the rise of economic individualism to the rise of the novel, he demonstrates that, 'It is very likely that the lack of variety and stimulation in the daily task as a result of economic specialization is largely responsible for the unique dependence of the individual in our culture upon the substitute experiences provided by the printing press, particularly in the forms of journalism and the novel' (p. 71).

Watt contends that the novel's conception of mimesis derives from the premises of philosophical realism: 'The distinctive narrative mode of the novel . . . is the sum of literary techniques whereby the novel's imitation of human life follows the procedures adopted by philosophical realism in its attempt to ascertain and report the truth' (p. 31). The method of philosophical realism 'has been the study of the particulars of experience by the individual investigator, who, ideally at least, is free from the body of past assumptions and traditional beliefs; and it has given a peculiar importance to semantics, to the problem of the nature of the correspondence between words and reality' (p. 12). Similarly, literary plots in novels no longer illustrated universals, but 'had to be acted out by particular people in particular circumstances, rather than, as had been common in the past, by general human types against a background primarily determined by the appropriate literary convention' (p. 15). Realism, then, deflects plot from the classic Aristotelian model. Verisimilitude, including specificity of time and space, is essential to realism. Watt writes: 'We have a sense of personal identity subsisting through duration and yet being changed by the flow of experience' (p. 24); another criterion is a fully visualized space, an 'actual physical environment' (p. 26).

In what may be the book's crucial conceptual statement, Watt defines the term 'formal realism' as the novel's embodiment of the particulars of life:

> The narrative method whereby the novel embodies this circum-stantial view of life may be called its formal realism; formal, because the term realism does not here refer to any special literary doctrine or purpose, but only to a set of narrative procedures which are so commonly found together in the novel, and so rarely in other literary genres, that they may be regarded as typical of the form itself. Formal realism, in fact, is the narrative embodiment of a premise that Defoe and Richardson accepted very literally, but which is implicit in the novel form in general: the premise, or primary convention, that the novel is a full and authentic report of human experience, and is therefore under an obligation to satisfy its reader with such details of the story as the individuality of the actors concerned, the particulars of the times and places of their actions, details which are presented through a more largely referential use of language than is common in other literary forms. (p. 32)

Realism depends upon significant correspondence between language and the world imitated: 'The function of language is much more largely referential in the novel than in other literary forms; . . . . the genre itself works by exhaustive presentation rather than by elegant concentration" (p. 30).

Some problems are raised by the above passages that are never quite resolved. First, 'narrative procedures' are discussed in reference to specific texts, but are not inductively defined. Lacking such a synchronic taxonomy, Watt does not really show us how to recognize realistic strategies elsewhere. Ultimately, we are left with nothing more rigorous than 'if a novel resembles other realist novels, then it is in all likelihood one'. Another problem is that the novel is only exhaustive when compared to shorter forms, like the lyric or short story; for its efficacy depends on economical selection and arrangement. The semiotics of realism – the way realism chooses its signs from all possibilities – is not discussed except as discrete phenomena within individual texts. In fact, the novel works by rather elegant concentration of exhaustive particulars, but its concentration and inclusiveness – akin to what we are now calling discourse and story – vary not only from text to text but within a given text.

Finally, we soon discover that Watt is not always clear whether formal realism is a process of mimesis, a goal of mimesis, or an achieved result, and whether it has any *inherent* value or not. Take the following puzzling formulation: 'Formal realism is only a mode of presentation, and it is therefore ethically neutral: all Defoe's novels are also ethically neutral because they make formal realism an end rather than a means, subordinating any coherent ulterior significance to the illusion that the text represents the authentic lucubrations of an historical person' (p. 117). The logic of indicting *Moll Flanders* for its lack of form depends upon conceiving of formal realism as an end, not as a process: 'If [a novel] is to be considered a valuable literary form it must also have, like any other literary form, a structure which is a coherent expression of all its parts' (p. 104). Here it is the selection and design of realistic material that transform life into formal realism: '[T]he accurate transcription of actuality does not necessarily produce a work of any real truth or enduring literary value' (p. 32). Yet at times within the Defoe and Richardson chapters, formal realism is a value to which prior literature has teleologically moved: 'The formal realism of the novel allows a more immediate imitation of individual experience set in its temporal and spatial environment than do other literary forms' (p. 32). If it is preferable (not 'neutral') to establish immediate imitation of individual experience, in terms of the logic of Watt's argument, formal realism cannot be ethically neutral.

Realism for Watt means not only the concept of formal realism, but the very idea that novels reflect the outside world. *The Rise of the Novel* is not always clear whether formal realism is within the work of art or the goal of the artist – whether it is a mode of perception, a philosophic stance, or a narrative strategy, or all three. If it is a narrative 'embodiment', we may ask, can it lack, formal properties and be simply a mode of presentation? Unlike Austen and Flaubert, Defoe, says Watt, did not incorporate 'conflicts and incongruities into the very structure' of his work (p. 130). But is this to imply that Defoe's realism is less embodied in the text than the realism of other writers? Notwithstanding the word 'formal', formal realism becomes in effect a stage in reporting, an imitative process that produces an ur-text in between the artist's perception and the finished work of art. We need to differentiate between realism of subject matter and a narrative which successfully integrates its subject matter into a realistic form. The degree of formal coherence in realistic narrative will vary from text to text. Defoe's selection and arrange- ment of story into narrative are less taut and intensive than that of the organic form of a James or an Austen novel, but Defoe's form is far from inchoate.

At times, Watts' concept of realism is more a subjective than an objective concept, as when he writes that Sterne's realism depends on 'the particularisation of time, place and person; to a natural and lifelike sequence of action; and to the creation of a literary style which gives the most exact verbal and rhythmical equivalent possible of the object described' (p. 291).[5] But this is understandable since what seems natural and lifelike will depend on the reader's past experience; realism, like other qualities attributed to a text, does not simply inhere in texts but depends on the dialogue between readers and texts.

To discuss characters in terms of their truthfulness to life may be a naive position, but to understand that realism is a narrative mode that creates its audience as it discovers particular kinds of meaning is not. Realism enables the reader to participate vicariously and fully in the imagined world of the novel. Realism implies that literary works mediate between the world of the author and the world of the reader; that they do so depends upon the reader sharing with the author enough of a common perception of reality to make possible com- munication of the author's presentation and interpretation of his subject. According to Watt, the bourgeois reader recognizes, in the novel's depiction of upper middle class and lower upper class life, the life he lives or might live.

Jonathan Culler has written that the reader's movement 'back from world to text so as to compose and give meaning to what has been identified' is 'troubled if the text undertakes an excessive proliferation of elements whose function seems purely referential'.[6] But how does one determine excessive? Watt contends that eighteenth-century readers read not to 'compose' meaning but to enter the imagined world. Culler cites Barthes' claim that 'the pure representation of reality [is] a resistance to meaning, an instance of "referential illusion", according to which the meaning of a sign is nothing other than its referent'.[7] If readers respond vicariously to a world which reflects the hopes, anxieties, and conflicts of their own, and if readers respond to 'pure representation of reality' and 'referential illusion,' can we say that it is 'resistant to meaning?' Novels move readers from text to an imagined world, a world that the reader judges in terms of his or her own experience of the real world. Isn't the illusion created by language for the reader the referent? – and the resistance to meaning a patronizing notion on the part of iconoclastic critics who cannot conceive of ordinary readers responding to depictions of complex worlds that include some pedestrian detail?

III

Believing that literature, is among other things, a criticism of life, Watt draws upon his life experience to make comments on the behaviour of fictional characters. The intrusion of comments on how human beings behave, unless wrapped in Freudian or Lacanian terms, is now thought by many to be sentimentalism, or, as some might dismissively put it, 'old-fashioned humanism'. But Watt enacts in his criticism the argument that a literary critic must also be an experienced, mature, judicious observer of human behaviour. Watt is a traditional humanist who believes literature tells us something about ourselves and the world in which we live; as he eloquently puts it, 'writing about literature should somehow convey its awareness of that honor; and . . . it should also embody . . . the notion that it is the product neither of a card index nor of a divine oracle, but of a putative human-being communicating with other putative human beings'.[8] Watt judges behaviour and motives from the stance of his own rational, humanistic, and egalitarian impulses. But since literary criticism, like other forms of writing, is in part disguised autobiography, and since no critic can completely exclude his own biases from his method, this should not surprise us.

Influenced at Cambridge by the Leavises and the *Scrutiny* group, Watt believes that the literary critic has simultaneously the modest task of serving the author he interprets and the magisterial task of speaking in defence of culture and civilization. With his standards of 'moral intensity', 'profound seriousness', and 'total sense of human life', F. R. Leavis preserved the Arnoldian strain of high seriousness which, along with his stress on close reading, influenced Watt. Leavis's standards are not only writ large in Watt's argument, but in his preface where Watt acknowledges 'the great stimulus [I] received at the outset of my research' from Q. D. Leavis's *Fiction and the Reading Public* (p. 8). Like Mark Schorer, Albert Guerard, and Dorothy Van Ghent, Watt seeks in his fiction criticism to use the techniques of New Criticism to ask larger questions about the author's values, psychology, and intellectual milieu, as well as about the social structure which gave rise to the author. In asking questions about the relation between individual and historical forces, and in seeing the particular lives of characters as typifying social issues and historical patterns, he is indebted to Lukàcs and Kettle as well as Leavis.

He sees characters in a novel not only as very particularized individuals signified by signs of unusual specificity, but also as signifiers of historical developments. Such an approach can yield impressive results when he locates the social conventions and issues that provide a novel's context: 'Clarissa, therefore, is without allies, and this is fitting since she is the heroic representative of all that is free and positive in the new individualism, and especially of the spiritual independence which was associated with Puritanism; as such she has to combat all the forces that were opposed to the realisation of the new concept – the aristocracy, the patriarchal family system, and even the economic individualism whose development was so closely connected with that of Puritanism' (p. 222). Indeed, the extent to which a novel signifies the complexity of the historical, sociological, and cultural aspects in which the author lives becomes an aesthetic standard. *Clarissa* is 'the first masterpiece of the novel form' because 'Richardson's very responsiveness to the dictates of his time and his class . . . make it a more modern novel in a sense than any other written in the eighteenth century. Richardson's deep imaginative commitment to all the problems of the new sexual ideology and his personal devotion to the exploration of the private and the subjective aspects of human experience produced a novel where the relationship between the protagonists embodies a universe of moral and social conflicts of a scale and a complexity beyond anything in previous fiction' (p. 220).

He regards decisions about the form and technique of art both as expressive of cultural history and as indications of decisions an author makes: 'It would seem, then, that Defoe's importance in the history of the novel is directly connected with the way his narrative structure embodied the struggle between Puritanism and the tendency to secularisation which was rooted in material progress. At the same time it is also apparent that the secular and economic viewpoint is the dominant partner, and that it is this which explains why it is Defoe, rather than Bunyan, who is usually considered to be the first key figure in the rise of the novel' (p. 83). Watt argues that literary history is not merely the history of forms or even of how artists solved thematic problems, but must include conditions that gave rise to those problems. Thus the novel must be understood in terms of cultural patterns and vice versa: 'This use of the conflict between social classes is typical of the novel in general; its literary mode is radically particular, but it achieves a universality of meaning by making its individual actions and characters represent larger social issues' (p. 166). Literary works mime the social and historical world in which the author lives. They also actually contribute to the creation of the culture; for example, 'the conception of sex we find in Richardson embodies a more complete and comprehensive separation between the male and female roles than had previously existed' (p. 162); or 'Richardson played an important part in the adjustment of language to the new feminine code' (p. 163).

Yet while Watt sees the history of the novel in terms of the history of culture prior to Defoe, he neglects such traditional staples of literary history as influence and generic transformation. Despite his title, at times he proposes an alternative more lateral historicism. In current terms, he emphasizes a synchronic view of culture while neglecting the importance of Bunyan and other English and continental antecedents as origins of the novel. To be sure, Watt is also concerned with causes, but his inductive question is, 'What are the distinctive features of the novel?' Perhaps he should have stressed that the kind of binary formal structure on which *The Pilgrim's Progress* and so much earlier narrative depends (including the *Faerie Queene* and *Paradise Lost*) clearly informs the novels of Defoe, Richardson, and Fielding. And his discussion of the rise of the novel might have accounted for *Clarissa* as a transformation of earlier Romance, as an allegorized struggle between good and evil in the mode of earlier epics and romances, and for *Moll Flanders* as the transformation of primitive Elizabethan experiments with realism.

If Chicago criticism is most valuable for considering Fielding's use of character and form to shape the reader's perception of the moral values, Watt's 'formal realism' works best for Richardson's interest in the idiosyncracies of the psyche and in particulars of manners, setting, and speech. Watt's discussion of Richardson taught us to respond intelligently to a figure who at the time was patronized and misunderstood. Arguing with the then current fashion, Watt felt that it was a mistake to stress Richardson's sentimentalism: 'What is distinctive about Richardson's novels is not the kind or even the amount of emotion, but rather the authenticity of its presentation' (p. 174). Characteristic of Richardson's formal realism is 'the more minutely discriminated time-scale, and the much less selective attitude to what should be told the reader' (p. 175). But much more important is his 'delineation of the domestic life and the private experience of the characters' (p. 175). We should note that Watt praises Defoe and Richardson but not Fielding for temporal and spatial realism and for attention to particulars. Since one of Watt's criteria for fiction is specificity, and since he admires those writers whose 'exclusive aim is to make the words bring his object home to us in all its concrete particularity' (p. 29), Fielding becomes an aberration and Richardson a standard. Watt's skewed structure, in which Fielding is not given equal place with Richardson, combines with Watt's own sympathies to make *The Rise of the Novel* something of an *apologia* for Richardson.

Because I believe it essential that we create a dialogue between Anglo-American criticism and more recent criticism and that we recognize that they often pursue common goals, I would like briefly to look at Watt through the perspective of criteria suggested by Culler in *The Pursuit of Signs* (1981). Watt's approach actually has much in common with structural explanations which, as Culler writes in *The Pursuit of Signs*, 'relates objects or actions to an underlying system of categories and distinctions which make them what they are'.[9] Indeed, Watt demonstrates Culler's observation that 'Social reality includes paradigms of organization, figures of intelligibility; and the interplay between a literary work and its historical ground lies in the way its formal devices exploit, transform, and supplement a culture's way of producing meaning.'[10] Watt has moved us towards understanding the novel as a sign of culture because he sees each novel 'in relation to other texts, in relation to the codes that are the products of these texts and go to make up a culture'.[11] Thus he explains Richardson's stress on individualism and private experience in terms of the codes and conventions of his day. Like recent narratologists, he 'relates a literary work to a whole series of other works, treating them not as sources, but as constituents of a genre'.[12] And his teleological view of literary history considers texts 'in relation to other texts which they take up, cite, parody, refute, or generally transform'.[13] To be sure, Watt does believe in the existence of a world prior to the existence of signs, and he does not see the text simply as a function of conventions to which an author responds. While he sees human behaviour – of authors and characters – affected by codes and conventions, he still believes in the separateness and uniqueness of human character and the capacity of author and characters to define themselves.

It must be remembered that Anglo-American criticism is addressing, in the English novel at least, a tradition of novels of manners and morals where the individuals' choices are central to the theme and form. This tradition of manners and morals for the most part assumes the possibility of people achieving a coherent self which can determine its own fate and which through a strong will and a steady core of moral beliefs separates itself from the forces and situations that are shaping it. While social relationships, including courtship and marriage, are more central to the English novel, they are only one of many foci in, say, Balzac and Tolstoy. It is the interaction between individuals as well as the tension between the community and the individual personality that defines the subject of the English novel; its prototypes are *Clarissa*, *Tom Jones*, *Emma*, and *Middlemarch*. Characteristically, traditional Anglo-American fiction criticism speaks about a character's struggle to discover a coherent self within an indifferent society. From *Moll Flanders* through *Vanity Fair* and *Jude the Obscure*, we see a version of this in the orphan theme; an orphan struggles to maintain his independence at the same time as he or she seeks to exploit society's values to work in his behalf. We should not be surprised, then, that some of Watt's generalizations about the novel genre are more applicable to the peculiarities of the English novel of manners and morals than to the European novel with its more inclusive historical vision that takes account of social and economic forces. 'The novel requires a world view which is centered on the social relationships between individual persons. . . . Until the end of the seventeenth century the individual was not conceived as wholly autonomous, but as an element in a picture which depended on divine persons for its meaning, as well as on traditional institutions such as Church and Kingship for its secular pattern' (p. 84). Even such Marxist critics as Kettle and Raymond Williams domesticate the historical dialectic of the English novel into a struggle of both men and women to woo and marry whomever they please.

Watt shows how the recovery of historical contexts is not simply literary archeology, but can be the prelude to richer readings. To be sure, taking account of the relationship between a work and its causes and conventions does not recover 'original' meaning or pretend to solve all interpretive problems. This is clear from Watt's discussion of Defoe which convincingly shows that the tension between 'rational economic individualism' and 'concern for spiritual redemption' is crucial to Defoe's art (p. 130), but which does not resolve the problem of Defoe's irony. We can accept Watt's discussion of Defoe's values, and still reject his view that *Moll Flanders* is not ironic because Defoe fails to shape our attitude towards the material: 'If [there] are ironies, they are surely the ironies of social and moral and literary disorder. Perhaps, however, they are better regarded not as the achievements of an ironist, but as accidents produced by the random application of narrative authenticity to conflicts in Defoe's social and moral and religious world, accidents which unwittingly reveal to us the serious discrepancies in his system of values' (pp. 129–30).

IV

Watt's chapter on *Tom Jones* is to some extent a response to Chicago Aristotelians, particularly to R. S. Crane's seminal essay, 'The Plot of *Tom Jones*' (1950). If we recall Richard McKeon's disparaging comments about 'digging into the soul of the artist' or 'exploring the structures of experience and cultures', we can see how Watt, who not only presents the historical context but speculates on the author's psyche, is implying that the focus of the Chicago critics had been too narrow.[14] According to Watt, in the central tradition of the novel, 'the Aristotelian priority of plot over character has been wholly reversed, and a new type of formal structure has been evolved in which the plot attempts only to embody the ordinary processes of life and in so doing becomes wholly dependent on the characters and the development of their relationships' (p. 280). But because Fielding was more interested in characters as representative figures than in their idiosyncrasies, he employs a traditional plot: 'It follows logically that if human nature is essentially stable, there is no need to detail the processes whereby any one example of it has reached full development; such processes are but temporary and superficial modifications of a moral constitution which is unalterably fixed from birth' (p. 275). Watt proposes an interesting rule for a grammar of plot:

Tom Jones, then, would seem to exemplify a principle of considerable significance for the novel form in general: namely, that the importance of the plot is in inverse proportion to that of character. This principle has an interesting corollary: the organization of the narrative into an extended and complex formal structure will tend to turn the protagonists into its passive agents, but it will offer compensatingly greater opportunities for the introduction of a variety of minor characters, whose treatment will not be hampered in the same way by the roles which they are allotted by the complications of the narrative design. (p. 279)

Crucial to the book's structure and argument is Watt's distinction between what he calls the 'realism of presentation' of Richardson and Defoe and the 'realism of assessment' of Fielding. By 'realism of assessment', Watt means what Leavis means by 'moral intensity' and 'moral earnestness'. According to Watt, 'Fielding brought to the genre something that is ultimately even more important than narrative technique – a responsible wisdom about human affairs which plays upon the deeds and the characters of his novels. . . . The stimulation has come from a mind with a true grasp of human reality, never deceived or deceiving about himself' (p. 288). While 'realism of assessment' enters into the argument in the closing pages, it should have been a central concept in the book, for Richardson and Defoe also use 'assessment' to select and arrange their materials. What Watt says of Fielding is true of Richardson and even Defoe, 'Fielding's realism of assessment did not operate only through direct commentary; his evaluations were also made explicit by organizing the narrative sequence into a significant counterpoint of scenes which usually reflected ironically upon each other . . .' (p. 293). For unless one is merely presenting a sequence of unselected experience, realism of assessment is always taking place.

Watt may be his own most perceptive critic. In his unusually candid retrospective essay in *Novel*, Watt considers some of the limitations of *The Rise of the Novel*. He realizes that by abandoning three putative final chapters – one on *Tom Jones*, one on Smollett, and one on Sterne,

he no longer had a balance between 'realism of assessment' and
'realism of presentation'. Because technique is discovery in critical as
well as fictional works, the clear implication that we derive from the
structure of *The Rise of the Novel* is that realism of presentation is
better and more important than realism of assessment. Watt also
acknowledges that he overemphasized the independence of the novel's
development from more traditional Augustan social and cultural
values, especially the Augustan interest in 'private life' which influenced 'the novel's relatively detailed description of the domestic life;
and . . . the novel's interest in individual self-definition'.[15] We might
add that his book needs a chapter on Austen, even a short one, to make
credible the argument that Austen combines realism of presentation
and realism of assessment 'into a harmonious unity', and it needs a
longer discussion of Sterne's experiment with parody and realism in his
anti-novel, *Tristram Shandy*.

He concedes also 'an unavoidable asymmetry in the terms':

> For one thing, "realism of assessment" implied an evaluative – and
> implicitly approbative – moral judgment by its user, whereas
> "realism of presentation" referred to narrower and more technical
> matters; and for another, "realism of presentation" was specifically
> related to my subject, the novel, whereas "realism of assessment"
> was obviously a concept which was applicable to all forms of
> literature.[16]

And he further concedes that it may not be possible to separate these
kinds of realism since to some degree they happen simultaneously.
Furthermore, Watt notes that realism of assessment continues on the
reader's part during even the most particular presentation:

> That is, the reader finally concerns himself with Defoe's assessment
> of reality as it is implicit in words and phrases and sentences just as
> much as he does with Fielding. The difference is only that Fielding's
> words and phrases intentionally invoke not only the actual narrative
> event, but the whole literary, historical, and philosophical perspec-
> tive in which character or action should be placed by the reader.[17]

Yet all presentation is selection and arrangement, and selection and
arrangement are inevitably modes of assessment. Perhaps Watt could
better discriminate between the two kinds of realism if he restricted

'presentation' to content, the raw material of the narrative, and confined 'assessment' to the order that the narrative imposes and the rhetorical implications of that order upon the reader. To use current terms, realism of presentation is concerned with story, and realism of assessment with discourse. While the emphasis of Watt's realism of assessment is less on how the text shapes the reader's emotional responses and judgments than upon the value dramatized within the imagined world, the two are inseparable. Realism of assessment is in fact close to Booth's concept of rhetoric. Where Watt is weakest as a 'formal' critic is where Booth is strongest, that is, in showing how responses to texts are the result of specific choices that the artist makes as he creates his imagined world.

Watt does not really articulate an aesthetic of fiction. For while he claims 'formal realism' is a convention, it is really a goal of a set of conventions. At times he speaks of the novel's mode of imitating reality as if it were just a gathering of particulars. He might have shown how realism of presentation is a spectrum of possibilities for presenting story. He might have differentiated among the ways that authors present experience – between scenes which bring out the character's psyche; scenes that provide the moral and geographical setting; and scenes that define the relationships among classes or different segments of the community. He might have shown how realism of presentation and realism of assessment are umbrella terms for a wide variety of functions and effects. But it is unfair to insist upon a morphology or semiotics of realism from a book that has other purposes. Even if Watt has not given us the language for elucidating the efficacy of realism and describing kinds of realism, he has shown us how realism as a mode of perception is essential to the development of the English novel.

It behooves us to conclude with an expression of gratitude and admiration. Because of the poise and polish of Watt's prose, the forcefulness and logical rigour of his erudition, his humane response to the eighteenth-century novel and its background as well as his wit and good nature, *The Rise of the Novel* remains a compelling argument and a pleasure to read. As we respond to the clarity, subtlety, and elegance of Watt's discussion, we might recall what F. R. Leavis wrote of Dr Johnson, 'When we read him we know, beyond question, that we have here a powerful and distinguished mind operating at first hand upon literature.' [18]

NOTES

1. For example, Q. D. Leavis wrote in 'The Discipline of Letters: a Sociological Note', 'The ability to edit texts and make piddling comments on them is no mere qualification by itself for an English university post than a certificate of librarianship, since it is an ability that can be readily acquired by quite stupid people with no interest in literature.' *The Importance of Scrutiny*, ed. Eric Bentley (New York University Press, 1964) orig. edn 1948, p. 53.

2. Ian Watt, 'Serious Reflections on *The Rise of the Novel*', 1 (Spring 1968) p. 213. For two important essays on *The Rise of the Novel*, see David H. Hirsch, 'The Reality of Ian Watt', *Critical Quarterly*, 2:2 (Summer 1969) 164–79 and Mark Spilka, 'Ian Watt on Intrusive Authors: or the Future of an Illusion', *Hebrew University Studies in English* 1:1 (Spring 1973) 1–24. Spilka stresses the implications of Watt's book, implications that he claims Watt does not understand: 'Watt furnishes the social history . . . but he fails to supply the conceptual synthesis which his own materials demand. . . . Once we assume, that is, that realism offered a means of exploring as well as reflecting reality, then its relation to individualism becomes dynamic and the whole question of the novel's function changes, becomes at once social and informing as well as private and authentic, enlightening as well as moving' (pp. 9–10) Hirsch's complaint is not only that Watt oversimplifies Locke, but that he is unable 'to bring about a coalescence between the philosophical outline and actual literary works' (p. 170).

3. Page numbers in parentheses refer to *The Rise of the Novel* (The University of California Press, 1957).

4. Jonathan Culler, *Structuralist Poetics: Structuralism, Linguistics, and the Study of Literature* (Ithaca, New York: Cornell University Press, 1975) p. 262.

5. According to Hirsch, 'Although [Watt] attempts to demonstrate that reality can be sufficiently defined as particulars situated in a locus of time and place, and though he asserts that realism in the novel descended from the legacy of the empirical philosophers who ostensibly defined reality as particulars located in time and place, yet when Watt comes to speak about realism in the novel he can speak of it only as a feeling or belief or an intuition. That is to say that Watt, who represents himself as a wholly objective critic, is in truth a most subjective critic' ('The Reality of Ian Watt', p. 178).

6. Culler, *Structuralist Poetics*, p. 193.

7. Culler, *Structuralist Poetics*, p. 193.

8. Watt, 'Serious Reflections', p. 208.

9. Jonathan Culler, *The Pursuit of Signs: Semiotics, Literature, Deconstruction* (Ithaca, New York: Cornell University Press, 1981) p. 30.

10. Culler, *The Pursuit of Signs*, p. 13.

11. Culler, *The Pursuit of Signs*, p. 12.

12. Culler, *The Pursuit of Signs*, p. 117.

13. Culler, *The Pursuit of Signs*, p. 38.

14. Richard McKeon, *Thought, Action, and Passion* (The University of Chicago Press, 1954) p. 215.
15. Watt, 'Serious Reflections', p. 217.
16. Watt, 'Serious Reflections', p. 213.
17. Watt, 'Serious Reflections', p. 214.
18. F. R. Leavis, *The Importance of Scrutiny*, pp. 57–8. For discussion of Watt's *Conrad in the Nineteenth Century* (University of California Press: Berkeley and Los Angeles, 1979), see my review in *Conradiana*, 13:1 (1981) pp. 73–9.

6 Two Major Voices of the 1950s: Northrop Frye's *Anatomy of Criticism* and Erich Auerbach's *Mimesis*

In this chapter, I shall examine Northrop Frye's *Anatomy of Criticism* (1957) and Erich Auerbach's *Mimesis* (1953). Neither book is primarily concerned with the English novel, but both influenced the way that the novel has been taught in England and America for the past twenty-five years. These books represent opposing approaches to literature. While Auerbach assumes that literature reveals an *a priori* reality, Frye is, with Wallace Stevens and Harold Bloom, in the tradition of those for whom art builds vast imaginative alternatives to the real world.

I

Auerbach's *Mimesis* (1953) has been an important book because it focuses on the way imaginative literature imitates and reflects reality, including the culture in which it was written. His subject is, as he puts it, 'the history of the literary treatment of reality' (p. 116).[1] For Auerbach, art is about something other than art, the writing of novels, or the investigation into how language means. He is interested not only in how people behave and in what people believe, but in what historical forces shape behaviour and belief. Like Georg Lukàcs, Auerbach believes that an appropriate aesthetic standard is whether the artist establishes a compelling link between individual events or relationships and a specific social and economic milieu. Like his fellow Hegelian Lukàcs, Auerbach judges a work's importance by its

118

inclusiveness and its response to historical forces, and thus his concern with the work as literature is inseparable from his interest in the work as intellectual history.

Auerbach is a philologist whose curiosity about language asks questions about which historical conditions produced the written words we read. *Mimesis* inquires into the style that the author uses to present his interpretation of reality. Angus Fletcher has aptly written of Auerbach: 'He sought contexts for poetic forms and believed that these forms were significant only when they were placed against recaptured, supposedly unique historical contexts. To perform this feat required the most imaginative choice of "point of departure" so that each would allow the maximum radiation of meaning with a maximum of philological control. Usually this meant choice of a stylistic element, since style could be controlled by the history of language, while it could be given general, even universal human relevance through its connection with decorum and the entertainment of particular audiences.'[2]

In his 'Introduction: Purpose and Method' to *Literary Language and Its Public in Latin Antiquity and the Middle Ages*, Auerbach cites Vico as his major mentor in his effort to use cultural evidence, including literature to 'form a lucid and coherent picture of this civilization and its unity'.[3] Like Vico, Auerbach assumes that language is the repository of cultural history and that the study of literature, language, and myth in a given period enables us to understand the other major aspects of its culture. Auerbach wrote of Vico: 'For him the world of the nations . . . embraces not only political history but also the history of thought, of expression (language, literature, the fine arts), religion, law, and economics. Because all these follow from the cultural state of human society in a given period and consequently must be understood in relation to one another or else cannot be understood at all, an insight into one of these facets of human creativity at a given stage of development must provide a key to all the others at the same stage.'[4] He praised Vico for seeing literature as 'an autonomous mode of human perception and self-orientation'.[5] Historical and aesthetic understanding derives from specific experience of particular texts, from what Holdheim calls an 'interplay of concepts and forces in which literary understanding coincides with historical understanding, in which the text radiates in all directions and on many levels'.[6] But this understanding is not reducible to a static pattern, but is a matter of the critic's temporal cognition – the same kind of cognition that *Mimesis* demands of its readers. Like Leavis, Auerbach was suspicious of generalities and wanted to describe historical trends with continued reference to particulars.[7]

Auerbach is indebted to Vico for a conception of philology that 'investigated what the various peoples regarded as true at each cultural stage (although this truth was a product of their limited perspective) and what accordingly formed the basis of their actions and institutions'.[8] Auerbach uses passages from novels as his points of departure: '[A] starting point must be strictly applicable to the historical material under investigation. . . . The starting point should not be a category which we ourselves impose on the material, to which the material must be fitted, but a characteristic found in the subject itself, essential to its history, which, when stressed and developed, clarifies the subject matter in its particularity and other topics in relation to it.'[9]

Auerbach admires Vico for perceiving history not in 'abstract or extrahistorical terms, but only as a dialectic, dramatic process'.[10] To the extent that Vico focused on what man himself made of the world by means of his thoughts and actions, Auerbach admired him: 'Vico . . . offers a clear statement, if not a logical justification, of an important and inescapable fact, namely, that we judge historical phenomena and all human affairs, whether of a private, economic, or political nature, according to our own experience . . .'.[11] But Auerbach did not agree with Vico that history was a working out of a pattern ordained by Divine Providence, and that this pattern or 'universal law' was illustrated by stages of development. For Auerbach, history has causation – events occur because of given conditions which can be identified – but not immutable laws.[12]

Let us examine Auerbach's concept of historiography, for as Holdheim notes, he wants to illustrate 'how literary history *should* be written'.[13] The historian, like the novelist, selects and interprets material according to his own understanding. Thus Auerbach prefers the inductive method to a deductive method that relies upon applying *a priori* laws or categories to historical events: 'We cease, it is true, to judge on the basis of extrahistorical and absolute categories, and we cease to look for such categories, precisely because the universally human or poetic factor, which is common to the most perfect works of all times and which should consequently provide us with our categories of judgment, can only be apprehended in its particular historical forms, and there is no intelligible way of expressing its absolute essence. In the historical forms themselves we gradually learn to find the flexible, always provisional, categories we need.'[14] When he speaks of '*a priori* laws', he has in mind a divinely inspired providential pattern as well as dialectical materialism. As Holdheim understands, for Auerbach, 'History is not linear; its events are not merely stages in a demonstrative progression; . . . historical events are . . . not dogmatic but speculative – not staunchly self-identical entities, invariably and reliably "this" or "that", but inherently variable complexes contextually related to the whole of historical reality, subject to infinite modifications, radiating and opalizing in manifold ways.'[15] Auerbach calls this approach 'historical relativism' because it sees an event or a text in terms of its historical context, and asks what conditions determine a deed or work: 'To grasp the special nature of an epoch or a work, to perceive the nature of the relations between works of art and the time in which they were created, is an endless problem which each of us, exerting the utmost concentration, must endeavor to solve for himself and from his own point of view. For historical relativism is relative in two respects – of the material and of those who are striving to understand it.'[16] Understanding our historical predecessors 'on the basis of our own experience' is another aspect of Auerbach's historical relativism.[17] Auerbach's sceptical humanism derives from his own literary and life experience. Rather than propose an overall theory, he proposes 'an historical process, a kind of drama, which advances no theory but only sketches a certain pattern of human destiny. . . . What can thus be achieved under the most favorable circumstances is an insight into the diverse implications of a process from which we stem and in which we participate, a definition of our present situation and also perhaps of the possibilities for the immediate future'.[18] Thus, historical relativism is both a diachronic and synchronic concept.

Auerbach writes of Flaubert's concept of art: 'The universe is a work of art produced without any taking of sides, the realistic artist must imitate the procedures of Creation, and every subject in its essence contains, before God's eyes, both the serious and the comic, both dignity and vulgarity' (pp. 429–30). Auerbach is less concerned with the work as an organic whole than with what the work reveals of the structure of society, the *Zeitgeist*. His critical method is based on sharing Flaubert's belief that 'the truth of the phenomenal world is also revealed in linguistic expression' (p. 429). At one point, he categorizes Flaubert's technique as 'objective seriousness, which seeks to penetrate to the depths of the passions and entanglements of a human life, but without itself becoming moved, or at least without betraying that it is moved' (p. 432). Auerbach maintains critical objectivity to penetrate to the depths of 'the passions and entanglements. But for him there is a second reflective stage when he is moved by those emotions.

Auerbach begins by differentiating between two major traditions of narrative presentation: the Homeric or classical which depends on 'earthly relations of place, time, and cause' and the Biblical one which depends on a 'vertical connection, ascending from all that happens, converging in God' (p. 65). In Homeric literature, details are 'scrupulously externalized and narrated in leisurely fashion' (p. 1). The basic impulse of the Homeric style is 'to represent phenomena in a fully externalized form, visible and palpable in all their parts, and completely fixed in their spatial and temporal relations' (p. 4). The Homeric style 'knows only a foreground, only a uniformly illuminated, uniformly objective present'; the 'descriptive adjectives and digressions' displace the reader's attention (pp. 5, 8). By contrast, the story of Abraham's sacrifice of Isaac in the Old Testament focuses completely on current events and signifies something else. Auerbach brilliantly draws the contrast when he writes:

> On the one hand, externalized, uniformly illuminated phenomena at a definite time and in a definite place, connected together without lacunae in a perpetual foreground; thoughts and feeling completely expressed; events taking place in leisurely fashion and with very little of suspense. On the other hand, the externalization of only so much of the phenomena as is necessary for the purpose of the narrative, all else left in obscurity; the decisive points of the narrative alone are emphasized, what lies between is nonexistent; time and place are undefined and call for interpretation; thoughts and feeling remain unexpressed, are only suggested by the silence and the fragmentary speeches; the whole, permeated with the most unrelieved suspense and directed toward a single goal (and to that extent far more of a unity), remains mysterious and 'fraught with background'. (p. 9)

In the second chapter, he shows that the subjective point of view begins with Petronius. By contrasting Petronius with the New Testament narrative of Peter's denial, he introduces further basic distinctions in terms of *his* teleology. Auerbach claims that Petronius anticipates our modern realists: 'Petronius' literary ambition, like that of the realists of modern times, is to imitate a random, everyday, contemporary milieu with its sociological background, and to have his characters speak their jargon without recourse to any form of stylization. Thus he reached the ultimate limit of the advance of realism in antiquity' (p. 26). Auerbach contrasts Petronius' realism with the more sophisticated realism of the nineteenth-century Europeans whose 'technique of imitation can evolve a serious, problematic, and tragic conception of any character regardless of type and social standing, of any occurrence regardless of whether it be legendary, broadly political, or narrowly domestic' (p. 27); unlike Petronius, these writers 'make clear the social forces underlying the facts and conditions which they present' (p. 27) – in other words, they help us understand action in terms of its economic and political context.

Auerbach asserts that 'Historiography in depth – that is, methodological research into the historical growth of social as well as intellectual movements – is a thing unknown to antiquity' (p. 33). Thus, on one hand, the Ancients' way of viewing things does 'not see forces, it sees vices and virtues, successes and mistakes. [Their] formulation of problems is not concerned with historical developments either intellectual or material, but with ethical judgements' (p. 33). On the other hand, the New Testament authors do view the events in terms of a historical process in a changing world. But change, we should note, in this world is related to God's providential pattern rather than historical or social or economic forces. While the classical mode presents the 'visual' and 'sensory' (p. 41), the moral and historical imagination of the author of St. Mark's 'observes and relates only what matters in relation to Christ's presence and mission' (p. 42). Auerbach faults the classical texts for not entering into a common life: 'The antique stylistic rule according to which realistic imitation, the description of random everyday life, could only be comic (or at best idyllic), is therefore incompatible with the representation of historical forces as soon as such a representation undertakes to render things concretely' (pp. 38–9). Secondly, antique historiography is rhetorical; speeches in Tacitus 'are products of a specific stylistic tradition cultivated in the schools for rhetors' (p. 34). But the Bible does not adhere to specific forms of style: 'A scene like Peter's denial fits into no antique genre. It is too serious for comedy, too contemporary and everyday for tragedy, politically too insignificant for history – and the form which was given it is one of such immediacy that its like does not exist in the literature of antiquity' (p. 40). The New Testament contained direct discourse to render 'the dramatic tension of the moment' (p. 40).

The biblical writer is interested not in realism but in significance in terms of truth about what events reveal about God's purpose:

The Homeric poems present a definite complex of events whose boundaries in space and time are clearly delimited; . . . . The Old Testament, on the other hand, presents universal history: it begins with the beginning of time, with the creation of the world, and will end with the Last Days, the fulfilling of the Covenant, with which the world will come to an end. Everything else that happens in the world can only be conceived as an element in this sequence. . . . As a composition, the Old Testament is incomparably less unified than the Homeric poems, it is more obviously pieced together – but the various components all belong to one concept of universal history and its interpretation. (pp. 13–14)

The unity of each biblical episode depends in part on its place in this universal history. In other words, events are seen retrospectively in terms of a perspective informed by full knowledge of a history stretching from Genesis to the Apocalypse. Thus, in the Bible the fragmentary, discrete presentation of events depended upon interpretation in terms of a teleology.

Events in the Old Testament prefigure those in the New Testament. In a crucial passage, which builds upon implications of the first two chapters, Auerbach writes:

Figural interpretation 'establishes a connection between two events or persons in such a way that the first signifies not only itself but also the second, while the second involves or fulfills the first. The two poles of a figure are separated in time, but both, being real events or persons, are within temporality. They are both contained in the flowing stream which is historical life, and only the comprehension, the *intellectus spiritualis*, of their interdependence is a spiritual act'. . . . The here and now is no longer a mere link in an earthly chain of events, it is simultaneously something which has always been, and which will be fulfilled in the future; and strictly, in the eyes of God, it is something eternal, something omni-temporal, something already consummated in the realm of fragmentary earthly event. (pp. 64–5)

While his example of figuration – the Bible – transcends the temporal world, his *concept* does not, for figuration is when a later passage fulfills the meaning of an earlier one which contains in itself latent significance that requires the later passage to reveal or complete it. That the ontology of a literary work borrows from both the empirical (classical) and figurative (biblical) framework is an argument that

Auerbach, always sceptical of generalizations, does not press. Yet the development of Western realism is implicitly perceived in terms of a dialectical process that tries to resolve the biblical and classical styles. The development of realism is also perceived in terms of his submerged dialectical process that moves between seeing a passage in historical terms and seeing it in terms of its formal qualities. For the meaning of a fragment or word is viewed not only as a reflection of actual historical circumstances but also as part of the *self-contained* ontology and teleology of the literary work.

In a sense, the Bible provides Auerbach with a model for significant form, form in which the resonance of the whole is felt in each part and the resonance of each part reveals the whole. In the kind of literary criticism that some now call narratology, figural interpretation becomes secularized. For events are not only crystallizing moments 'complete' in themselves, but part of the larger pattern of the narrative. They depend for additional meaning or 'fulfilment' – as the reader discovers in subsequent reading – on the incident's relationship to the whole. And because it is a fiction and because to the reader every element is intensive and purposeful, the literary work, like the biblical style, implies a 'transformation . . . whose course progresses to somewhere outside of history, to the end of time or to the coincidence of all times, in other words upward, and does not, like the scientific concepts of evolutionary history, remain on the horizontal plane of historical events' (p. 39).

The unity of the Bible exists on both a vertical and a horizontal axis. For, paradoxically, while the separation of styles and the static quality of character enable us to examine readily the historical contexts of classical literature, it is biblical figures more than Homeric ones that develop through time. God shows us their formation and development: 'Time can touch the [Homeric figures] only outwardly, and even that change is brought to our observation as little as possible; whereas the stern hand of God is ever upon the Old Testament figures' (p. 15). While Homer reserves the elevated style for certain events, in the Old Testament, 'the sublime, tragic, and problematic take shape precisely in the domestic and commonplace [scenes]' (p. 19). Moreover, the biblical figures produce 'a more concrete, direct, and historical impression' precisely '*because* the confused, contradictory multiplicity of events, the psychological and factual cross-purposes, which true history reveals, have not disappeared in the representation but still remain clearly perceptible' (p. 17). And *Mimesis* is 'true history' precisely because it tries to render 'the confused, contradictory multiplicity of events, the psychological and factual cross-purposes'. If we pursue Auerbach's terms somewhat further than he does, we may understand his implication that realistic novels combine the classical and biblical narrative modes.

Auerbach regards modern realism as the integration of these two impulses – the classical one that imitates reality by crystallizing a culture and the biblical one that seeks to render historical process – into a genre whose meaning depends on a relationship to its teleology or organizing principle or radial centre: 'Insofar as the serious realism of modern times cannot represent man otherwise than as embedded in a total reality, political, social, and economic, which is concrete and constantly evolving – as is the case today in any novel or film – Stendhal is its founder' (p. 408). Auerbach summarizes the foundation of modern realism as 'the serious treatment of everyday reality, the rise of more extensive and socially inferior human groups to the position of subject matter for problematic–existential representation, on the one hand; on the other, the embedding of random persons and events in the general course of contemporary history, the fluid historical background' (pp. 433–4).

To be sure the lyric more than the novel depends more upon interpretation in relation to the teleology of the whole and less upon 'rational, continuous, earthly connections between things' (p. 66). In the 'Ode on a Grecian Urn', we cannot possibly know who the lovers on the urn are and what will happen to them, but in *Jude the Obscure* or *Emma*, the narrator provides the reader with knowledge of the evolving relationship between Emma and Knightley and between Jude and Sue. Hence the realistic novel respects earthly relations of place, time, and cause. Yet forms of novels echo the form of the biblical universe, as described by Auerbach, in their resonance of events in terms of a teleology. Although enclosed within the cycle of human life, within the novel's imagined world, Clarissa's death, Tom Jones' restoration to his people, and Emma's marriage represent something beyond themselves; we find 'something which has always been, and which will be fulfilled in the future' (p. 64). Auerbach conceives of the artist as a kind of God who not only breathes life into his imaginary universe as he creates, but orders it according to a teleology in which an episode takes its meaning from the whole. The patterns among scenes in relation to the whole – the codes of narrative – are the realistic novel's version of figurative relations.

Take *Clarissa* in which the central character is a prototype (or figuration) of Christ. *Clarissa* seems to be an apt model for the vertical teleology that fulfills Auerbach's biblical mode, but actually becomes a striking example of a new secular model based on earthly linear relationships. Richardson had to convince his readers that Clarissa would ascend and take her place among the heavenly hosts, but Richardson knew that his audience (in contrast to the audience of Donne's *The Anniversaries*) would not accept a literal dramatization of Clarissa's rising soul. Richardson's version of the teleology in which later events fulfil expectations revealed by prior ones – the relation of the New Testament to the Old – is a narrative 'code' that explains the pattern of her 'fortunate fall'. We *know* that Clarissa will go to heaven, because a process of deferred action has been built into the form of the text. Let me illustrate. First, the reader hears so often that she is going to run away that he is virtually convinced it has happened before he learns about it. It is then reported to have happened, although we never have a letter that quite describes this process. Secondly, the reader hears so much about the putative rape that he comes to 'know' that Clarissa is going to be raped. It is as if it has happened even before we find out that she has been raped; yet neither Clarissa or Lovelace ever speak of the actual event. Finally, we know that her soul is going to take its place in heaven because the two prior events that have been the subject of endless speculation have occurred. The pattern of deferral and retroactive fulfilment becomes the code of the text; the expected event is transformed into what has happened without the event ever being described. Since we never *see* the prior events, we do not expect within this code to see the climactic one. But because of the increasingly intense talk that had preceded prior major events, we are taught to assume that the talked about event will occur and that she will ascend to heaven.

Within this code rhetorical patterns rather than events become the confirmation of fulfilment, and if this is true in a *Clarissa*, it should often be true in more secular literature, especially realistic fiction. Thus our reading of *Tristram Shandy* depends upon our expectations of how the teleology of the conventional novel reveals itself, for Sterne's novel stands in a figurative relation to a paradigm based on our prior reading of novels. It defers the kind of coherent fulfilment of prior patterns – such as what happens *because* of Tristram's early accident, or what is his relationship to Jenny, or what was the effect of the various deaths, especially the deaths of his brother, and in later life, his parents – that we expect based on our prior reading experience. The greatness of *Mimesis* depends upon a rich and subtle dialogue between the work of art and the external world as well as upon the historical perspective. Thus Auerbach understands how Flaubert's language proposes alternative values to those described: 'True reality . . . is in the writer's language, which unmasks the stupidity by pure statement; language, then, has criteria for stupidity and thus also has a part in that reality of the "intelligent" which otherwise never appears in the book' (p. 432). Language does not merely transcribe an external world, but, taken in context of its voice, tone, and style, can signify something other than the world described.

We cannot but be impressed with Auerbach's ability to discuss the historical and philosophical contexts of every period as if he were a specialist. Auerbach examines every conceivable narrative form from courtly romance to twentieth-century fiction. Among Auerbach's essential contributions is his ability to generalize from style, tone, and subject matter. He believes that literature reveals vital historical facts. Thus, writing of Bishop Gregory he can assert, 'Here lies the difference between the Christian and the original Roman conquest: the agents of Christianity do not simply organize an administration from above, leaving everything else to its natural development; they are duty bound to take an interest in the specific detail of everyday incidents; Christianization is directly concerned with and concerns the individual person and the individual event' (p. 81). Or, writing of a 'French heroic epic', *The Song of Roland*, he relates the paratactic and rigid style to the culture: 'The subject of the *Chanson de Roland* is narrow, and for the men who figure in it nothing of fundamental significance is problematic. All the categories of this life and the next are unambiguous, immutable, fixed in rigid formulations' (p. 96). In *Chanson de Roland* he notes that mimesis is limited to 'an elevated style in which the structural concept of reality is still extremely rigid and which succeeds in representing only a narrow portion of objective life circumscribed by distance in time, simplification of perspective, and class limitations' (p. 106). He explains that while the French heroic epic discusses the upper strata of society, it speaks to the common people who cherish similar ideals.

Valuing the classical standards of *prodesse* and *delectare*, he believes that art should seek to *affect* the lives of man morally, politically, and practically. Auerbach uses as aesthetic criteria the quality of the writers' insight as it appears from his perspective in the twentieth century. Insight includes 'any interest, any understanding [of serious problems], any sense of responsibility, in the face of the problems which we recognize in retrospect as having been the decisive ones' (p. 444). Thus, he measures works and genres by what they contribute to 'the development of a literary art which should apprehend reality in its full breadth and depth' (p. 124) – by which Auerbach means attentiveness to historical process. For example, the courtly love tradition is criticized for not meeting this standard: 'Courtly culture gives rise to the idea, which long remained a factor of considerable importance in Europe, that nobility, greatness, and intrinsic values have nothing in common with everyday reality' (p. 122). Also because courtly culture's 'sublimation of love . . . led to mysticism or gallantry', it was 'decidedly unfavorable' to an inclusive realism (p. 124).

Like so many critics in this study, Auerbach's book is organized according to narrative theories he admires in the texts he examines. His book enacts and fulfills his critical standards. Both Auerbach's critical method and the structure of his book fuse the biblical mode and the classical mode. The teleology of *Mimesis* – illustrated by such nineteenth-century French realists as Stendhal, Flaubert, and Balzac – is the movement to do justice to the 'changes . . . taking place in the structure of life' (p. 229). His style *enacts* the biblical style – 'certain parts brought into high relief, others left obscure, abruptness, suggestive influence of the unexpressed, "background" quality, multiplicity of meanings and the need for interpretation, universal-historical claims, development of the concept of the historically becoming, and preoccupation with the problematic' (p. 19). Auerbach's praise of Stendhal provides us with his own critical paradigm: 'The characters, attitudes, and relationships of the dramatis personae, then, are very closely connected with contemporary historical circumstances; contemporary political and social conditions are woven into the action in a manner more detailed and more real than had been exhibited in any earlier novel, and indeed in any literary works of art except those expressly purporting to be politico-satirical tracts' (p. 403). Again, when he praises Stendhal's attentiveness to 'temporal perspective', for letting 'the concept of incessantly changing forms and manners of life [dominate] his thoughts' (p. 407), he is also calling attention to one of the most important features of his own work. And he praises Balzac for stressing the very historical context that is central to his own work. 'Balzac . . . not only, like Stendhal, places the human beings whose destiny he is seriously relating, in their precisely defined historical and social setting, but also conceives this connection as a necessary one' (p. 417). Auerbach stresses the role of the reader in making narrative patterns for himself. Auerbach argues that Balzac's realism 'is directed to the mimetic imagination of the reader, to his memory-pictures of similar persons and similar milieux which he may have seen'; and this is not only true more or less of all realism but of Auerbach's own focus on specified passages – his 'memory pictures' – to which he continually refers in his analyses (p. 415).

In his final chapter he turns to focus on the inner life which in modern fiction has replaced the focus on external reality. Characteristically, Auerbach focuses on a crucial passage as his starting-point – in this case the fifth section of Part One of *To the Lighthouse* – when the thoughts and feelings of Mrs. Ramsay are rendered as she measures her son James's leg for a stocking she is knitting for the lighthouse-keeper's son. Auerbach has a number of objections to modern fiction personified by Woolf. For one thing, the telling (or, in current terms the narrative discourse) is disproportionate to the event (or story). The stress is on the inner event: 'In Virginia Woolf's case the exterior events have actually lost their hegemony, they serve to release and interpret inner events, whereas before her time (and still today in many instances) inner movements preponderantly function to prepare and motivate significant exterior happenings' (p. 475).

Perhaps, more importantly, he objects to Woolf's failure to understand her characters, a failure which derives from her lack of authorial knowledge: '[T]here actually seems to be no viewpoint at all outside the novel from which the people and events within it are observed, any more than there seems to be an objective reality apart from what is in the consciousness of the characters' (p. 472). Auerbach indicts Woolf for the very dubiety that is part of her questing intelligence: 'The author looks at Mrs. Ramsay not with knowing but with doubting and questioning eyes – even as some character in the novel would see her in the situation in which she is described, would hear her speak the words given . . . [T]he author at times achieves the intended effect by representing herself to be someone who doubts, wonders, hesitates, as though the truth about her characters were not better known to her than it is to them or to the reader' (p. 472). But I would argue that our responding to the author's lack of certainty and inability to impose a moral order on the actions she dramatizes is part of reading modern literature. In a related objection, Auerbach contends that, while earlier writers gave us 'subjective, individualistic, and often eccentrically aberrant impression[s] of reality, . . . [T]he essential characteristic of the technique represented by Virginia Woolf is that we are given not merely one person whose consciousness (that is, the impressions it receives) is rendered, but many persons, with frequent shifts from one to the other . . .' (p. 473). We approach Mrs.

Ramsay 'from many sides as closely as human possibilities of perception and expression can succeed in doing' (p. 473). Thus objective reality is approached by means of several subjective perspectives.

Stepping back from Woolf, Auerbach argues that the realistic novel between the two wars was marked by 'multipersonal representation of consciousness, time strata, disintegration of the continuity of exterior events, shifting of the narrative viewpoint' (pp. 482–3). Some writers, including Woolf and Proust, 'have discarded presenting the story of their characters with any claim to exterior completeness, in chronological order, and with the emphasis on important exterior turning points of destiny' (p. 483). When contrasting 'multipersonal consciousness' to the unipersonal method, Auerbach thinly disguises his own preference for the latter. That his preference is clearly with the earlier techniques is given away by words such as 'peculiar' to describe Woolf's technique (p. 478). In Proust, Auerbach objects to the layers of reality that are presented to the reader from diverse points in time. 'Freed from its various earlier involvements, consciousness views its own past layers and their content in perspective; it keeps confronting them with one another, emancipating them from their exterior temporal continuity as well as from the narrow meanings they seemed to have when they were bound to a particular present' (p. 479). Auerbach misses in Proust a consistent fabric of reality in which the moral significance of action is perceived as part of a series of events in a fully realized world. But he believes it is a 'wrong direction' for the novel to strive for the 'concentration of space and time such as can be achieved by the film' (p. 482).

Auerbach believes, finally, that dissolving reality into 'multiple and multivalent reflections of consciousness' shows loss of confidence in a 'clearly formulable and recognized community of thought and feeling' (pp. 486–7). Thus Auerbach believes that this method provides 'a certain atmosphere of universal doom' and is 'a symptom of the confusion and helplessness, . . . a mirror of the decline of our world' (p. 487). But in the final pages of the last chapter he qualifies his scepticism and moves to a dramatic affirmation that undermines his own argument and contradicts his temperamental discomfort with dubiety and uncertainty. In a rather startling reversal, he begins to stress the new realism of Proust and Woolf as a continuation of realism in Stendhal and Balzac. It is as if while writing the book in exile and wondering whether civilization would survive the onslaughts of the War and National Socialism, he had an epiphanic moment in which he saw that the new realism has much in common with his own method and perhaps his own attitudes.

In modern fiction according to Auerbach:

> [T]he great exterior turning-points and blows of fate are granted less importance; they are credited with less power of yielding decisive information concerning the subject; on the other hand there is confidence that in any random fragment plucked from the course of a life at any time the totality of its fate is contained and can be portrayed. There is greater confidence in syntheses gained through full exploitation of an everyday occurrence than in a chronologically well-ordered total treatment which accompanies the subject from beginning to end, attempts not to omit anything externally important, and emphasizes the great turning points of destiny. (p. 484)

Indeed, he hopes that modern techniques which reflect the breakdown of shared reality may also show men the common strands of life that bind them. For if we see a common bond among men, then the 'formation of numerous mutually hostile groups' and the positions of sects 'which [solve] all problems with a single formula' seem foolish (p. 486). He realizes that in Woolf, 'something new and elemental appeared: nothing less than the wealth of reality and depth of life in every moment to which we surrender ourselves without prejudice' (p. 488). Because this method also shows the common life that we all share, Auerbach (like many of the great moderns including Lawrence, Conrad, Joyce, and Woolf) sees it as a humanistic affirmation: 'In this unprejudiced and exploratory type of representation we cannot but see to what an extent – below the surface conflicts – the differences between men's ways of life and forms of thought have already lessened. The strata of societies and their different ways of life have become inextricably mingled' (p. 488). In a final, lyrical moment he looks forward to a 'common life of mankind on earth' where there will be no 'exotic peoples'; '[This] goal begins to be visible. And it is most concretely visible now in the unprejudiced, precise, interior, and exterior representation of the random moment in the lives of different people' (p. 488). The final paragraph of the epilogue is a statement of humanistic faith that a common bond will unite Western civilization and implicitly that his book, covering the works of the divided nationalities, will contribute to that. The last paragraph is a testament to Auerbach's humanistic faith that Western civilization will survive the Holocaust and cataclysmic strife of World War II.

Given his personal history, the concluding pages are the humanistic version of Abraham's faith in God. Written as it was while the war continued and Auerbach, a Jewish exile from Nazi Germany, lived in Istanbul, *Mimesis* is a most moving testament to Auerbach's faith in Western civilization and humanism. For has not the spectre of siege hovered over the book in references to the 'current world crisis' (p. 459), to a Europe in dissolution and to the rise of National Socialism? Auerbach is self-conscious of his position as an exile not only from Germany but from the culture that he loves.

Auerbach's references to the Jews are quite moving. Speaking of the Apostle Paul beginning his missionary work of Christianity, he notes that such work 'was characteristically begun by a member of the Jewish diaspora' (p. 42) – and, Auerbach is, of course, a member of another diaspora. An egalitarian in politics if not in literature, he is uncomfortable with classical writers who 'look down from above' and write for 'a social and literary elite', while he believes that the Old Testament is written for every man (p. 41). Auerbach's humanism penetrates every chapter. He speaks of the Ancients' aristocratic reluctance to become involved with the 'vulgar' life of the ordinary people. Thus he identifies with Petronius's wronged soldiers and sympathizes with the spiritual strivings of the common people. Auerbach objects to those who fail to recognize the majesty and tragedy of human life. Ammianus is criticized because he excludes 'the great vital forces of the human soul: . . . love and sacrifice, heroism in the service of conviction, and the ceaseless search for possibilities of a purer existence' (p. 52). Auerbach also objects to Jerome's 'somberly suicidal ethos, the immersion in horror, in distortion of life and hostility to life' – what he calls Jerome's 'murderous hatred of the world' (p. 57). And he patronizes the Gauls as 'people whose instincts and passions were violent and whose rational deliberations were crude and primitive' (p. 79). Implicitly, is he not comparing the first century terror of Frankish rule in Gaul to the Nazis in Germany?: 'There is a progressive and terrible brutalization. . . . Lusts and passions lose every concealing form; they show themselves in the raw and public immediacy. This brutal life becomes a sensible object; to him who would describe it, it presents itself as devoid of order and difficult to order, but tangible, earthy, alive' (p. 79). Thus, for Auerbach, as for most if not all of the critics whom we are studying, criticism is disguised autobiography.

Let us examine some of the problems in Auerbach's approach:

(1) Because he does not define realism theoretically or even systematically, the book at times lacks an argument. Yet, we could respond, its argument – its insistence on focusing upon the way that texts reveal historical transitions and disruptions – is its method. Indeed, the energy of Auerbach's book is often not in his thesis but in his reading of the books he discusses.

(2) The difference between the classical and biblical texts is one of degree not kind. Auerbach argues that the Old Testament and the New Testament depict incidents whose significance transcends themselves. But, we might ask, are *we* not in part providing the transcendent interpretation to incidents which fit into a teleology that has been revealed as the total Bible from Genesis to Apocalypse? In a sense we do the same when, as readers, we relate in our interpretations the parts or episodes of a literary work to the teleology of the whole. Do not even classical texts such as the Homeric epic also have a teleology in which episodes in the text refer to or 'figure' other episodes? Re-reading earlier episodes, the later moments of a narrative exist in our mind as points of reference within the teleology of the narrative. Thus our response to Odysseus' temptation by Circe, Calypso, and the Sirens is shaped by our knowledge that he returns home to Penelope. And, since we are likely to know the Greek myth, is the relation dissimilar in kind from the presence in our mind of God's grand pattern as we read the Bible? We read episodes of the Bible in view of subsequent chapters of its universal history, chapters which we know in the same way as when we reread a novel. But in all texts, our vantage point as readers creates our sense of the teleology of the narrative. It might be said that we always approach the Bible as rereaders because we know its stretch from Genesis to Apocalypse. Yet, I would respond, the way in which its individual incidents are providential is not clear until we carefully read and untangle the narrative lines of the text.

(3) Auerbach sees realism as an end, whereas it may be more useful to think of it as a process by which authors try to transform the external world into a structured, imagined world, a process which by the very act of transformation into another medium – words – inevitably distorts the reality being rendered. In his splendid recent study *The Realistic Imagination*, George Levine aptly defines realism as 'a self-conscious effort, usually in the name of some moral enterprise of truth telling and extending the limits of human sympathy, to make literature appear to be describing

directly not some other language but reality itself'.[19] Levine also shows how the urge for realism is always in a tension with a latent urge for romance which often subverts the process of creating realistic fiction.

(4) He is not attentive to the unity and structure of the complete work and often does not even consider the formal relationship of the passage or episode he discusses to the whole.

II

Northrop Frye had a much greater impact on English studies than Auerbach whose book announces no revolutionary programme and whose work entered English studies through the back door of such post-war programmes as Romance studies and comparative literature. Frye believes that the study of literature can produce intelligible hypotheses about what literature is. He believes that literature is 'the order of words', that criticism is to literature as science is to nature, and that just as science provides intelligible hypotheses about what nature is, criticism can provide a coherent and systematic study of literature. Thus a self-contained literary universe can be studied as physicists study nature; rather than study '*a* poem as *an* imitation of nature', we 'should study the order of nature as a whole as imitated by a corresponding order of words' (p. 96).[20] Typical of his non-referential poetic is the following: 'Wherever we have an autonomous verbal structure of this kind, we have literature. Wherever this autonomous structure is lacking, we have language, words used instrumentally to help human consciousness do or understand something else' (p. 74). Frye strives for what he calls anagogic criticism which conceives of literature 'existing in its own universe, no longer a commentary on life or reality, but containing life and reality in a system of verbal relationships' (p. 122). In this view, literature includes nature rather than vice versa: 'Nature is now inside the mind of an infinite man who builds his cities out of the Milky Way. This is not reality, but it is the conceivable or imaginative limit of desire, which is infinite, eternal, and hence apocalyptic. By an apocalypse I mean primarily the imaginative conception of the whole of nature as the content of an infinite and eternal living body which, if not human, is closer to being human than to being inanimate' (p. 119). Thus for Frye, literature collectively forms a self-regulating, coherent but ever-changing structure.

Frye thinks of himself in many ways as a student of Aristotle, 'formulating the broad laws of literary experience and in short writing as though he believed that there is a totally intelligible structure of knowledge attainable about poetry which is not poetry itself, or the experience of it, but poetics . . . [T]he opening words of the *Poetics* . . . remain as good an introduction to the subject as ever, and describe the kind of approach that I have tried to keep in mind for myself' (p. 14). That categories (genres, myths, kinds of heroes) – the answering of the question 'What kind of?, – are crucial has a kinship with Aristotelian criticism. According to Frye, 'the basis of generic criticism in any case is rhetorical, in the sense that the genre is determined by the conditions established between the poet and his public' (p. 247). (Remarks such as these provoked Wimsatt's remark about the proximity of Toronto to Chicago.)[21]

Frye helped liberate literary criticism from the stultifying positivism and niggling nominalism of the less gifted devotees of New Criticism. At a time when New Criticism was at the height of its influence, he proposed an alternative by insisting that criticism must go beyond close analysis of details. Thinking no doubt of New Criticism, Frye attacks what he calls an 'ironic provincialism, which looks everywhere in literature for complete objectivity, suspension of moral judgments, concentration on pure verbal craftsmanship, and similar virtues' (p. 62). Frye made an important impact on the study of literature because he opened up the possibility that it could be a distinct, self-contained discipline with its own systems and codes.

Frye also wished to rescue criticism from the obligatory search for moral meanings and what he calls 'social dialectics' within criticism, by which he means the practice of universalizing in terms of the contemporary historical *Zeitgeist*. Thus he is implicitly responding to the tendency in the 1950s for critics of all persuasions to feel compelled to address the Holocaust and the spectre of nuclear war. (Van Ghent's *The English Novel: Form and Function* and the work of Kenneth Burke show how even the best formal criticism felt compelled to include these issues.)

While Auerbach focuses on style, Frye's unit is the myth, the hero, and the genre, all of which Frye thinks of as archetypes or structural organizing principles of literature: 'In its archetypal aspect, art is a part of civilization, and civilization we defined as the process of making a human form out of nature. The shape of this human form is revealed by civilization itself as it develops; its major components are the city, the garden, the farm, the sheepfold, and the like, as well as human society itself. An archetypal symbol is usually a natural object with a human meaning, and it forms part of the critical view of art as a civilized product, a vision of the goals of human work' (pp. 112–13). The poet draws upon external archetypes whether he wills to do so or not: 'Poetry is the product, not only of a deliberate and voluntary act of consciousness, like discursive writing, but of processes which are subconscious or preconscious, or half-conscious or unconscious as well' (p. 88). Hartman acutely notes, 'the archetype is simply the typical at the highest power of literary generalization'.[22] (This position takes issue with the Chicago critics' emphasis on the poet as maker.)

Poets are severely defined by conventions (or archetypes), but these conventions are structures of which, as indicated, the poet may be unaware. Frye's system or morphology stands in the relation to the individual work as *langue* does to *parole*. In *Fables of Identity* Frye has written that, '[the poet] is concerned not with what happened but with what happens. His subject-matter is the kind of thing that does happen, in other words the typical or recurring element in action. There is thus a close analogy between the poet's subject-matter and those significant actions that men engage in simply because they are typical and recurring, the actions that we call rituals'.[23] Like recent deconstructionists, Frye somewhat deprives the author of his creative role, because the author's decision about subject matter is shaped by the available archetypes. As Frank Lentricchia notes, the individual voice loses its importance in Frye's system much as it does in structuralism: '[The] individuated distinctive voice is overpowered by the systematic voice that speaks through it.'[24] Wimsatt and Brooks complain that for Frye, 'the poet is only the *efficient* cause of the poem, but the poem, having form, has a formal cause, that is to be sought. . . . Frye finds the formal cause to be the archetype'.[25] Rather oracularly, Frye writes; 'Originality returns to the origins of literature, as radicalism return to its roots' (pp. 97–8).

Focus on myth, whether in Joyce or Levi-Strauss creates a synchronic or spatial perspective rather than a diachronic or temporal one. We might recall Eliot's speaking of the mythical method, in his review of *Ulysses* in *The Dial*, as 'simply a way of controlling, or ordering, of giving shape and significance to the immense panorama of futility and anarchy which is contemporary history'.[26] The concept of archetype is strongly influenced by Jung, although Frye maintains that the concept of collective unconscious is unnecessary for his purposes.[27] While Wimsatt and Brooks believe that Frye's history moves from 'primitive' to 'sophisticated' forms and that he sees folk myths as simple underpinnings of more intricate forms, I believe that he affirms the opposite – namely a synchronic view that sees complex and recurring structures in forms of every era.[28] Frye rejects the view that art has improved or evolved to a higher form: 'What does improve in the arts is the comprehension of them, and the refining of society which results from it. It is the consumer, not the producer, who benefits by culture, the consumer who becomes humanized and liberally educated' (p. 344). Originally published in 1950, Frye's contribution to novel criticism is contained in the section entitled 'Specific Continuous Forms (Prose Fiction)'. It is part of the Fourth Essay, 'Rhetorical Criticism: Theory of Genres'.

Frye divided prose fiction into four forms or genres: novel, romance, confession, and Menippean satire:

> The novel tends to be extroverted and personal; its chief interest is in human character as it manifests itself in society. The romance tends to be introverted and personal; it also deals with characters but in a more subjective way. (Subjective here refers to treatment, not subject-matter. The characters of romance are heroic and therefore inscrutable; the novelist is freer to enter his characters' minds because he is more objective). The confession is also introverted, but intellectualized in content. Our next step is evidently to discover a fourth form of fiction which is extroverted and intellectual. (p. 308)

The fourth category is the Menippean satire. It 'resembles the confession in its ability to handle abstract ideas and theories, and differs from the novel in its characterization, which is stylized rather than naturalistic, and presents people as mouthpieces of the ideas they represent. . . . At its most concentrated the Menippean satire presents us with a vision of the world in terms of a single intellectual pattern. The intellectual structure built up from the story makes for violent dislocations in the customary logic of narrative, though the appearance of carelessness that results reflects only the carelessness of the reader or his tendency to judge by a novel-centered conception of fiction' (pp. 309–10). The value of Frye's approach for prose was that he asked, 'What kind of?' And his categories were the basis of useful distinctions, for surely it is helpful to think of *Wuthering Heights* as a romance and *Emma* as a novel. Showing how the four forms intersect in *Ulysses* in 'practically equal importance' provides an important perspective on that novel (p. 314).

The Anatomy of Criticism is itself in the genre of the anatomy or Menippean satire (he uses these two terms interchangeably). Fletcher observes, 'Evidently the genre assumes wholeness and hence becomes encyclopedic, but within this wholeness it cuts out endless fragments, whose coherence is a given of the argument and whose correspondence with historical reality will be based on a kind of humorous observation.'[29] One model is Burton's *Anatomy of Melancholy*, where, as Frye writes, 'The word "anatomy" . . . means a dissection or analysis, and expresses very accurately the intellectualized approach of his form' (p. 311). Another source is Sterne's Menippean satire, *Tristram Shandy*, in which one idea generates its successor and which depends upon a hyperbolic, allusive style which never quite catches up to its subject but creates an alternative to that subject.

Frye provided an antidote to the dominant classicism of T. S. Eliot, T. E. Hulme, and the New Critics. His *Anatomy* is in the romantic tradition of imposing a grand imaginative scheme on reality in terms of the structure of man's consciousness; we think of Blake, Yeats, and Lawrence. In contrast to Auerbach's episodic method, Frye wrote an 'epic' or at least a prophetic, visionary poem. For Frye, as Krieger notes, literature has an 'obligation to minister to the creative human desire rather than to open for us the destructive realities of the human condition'.[30] Thus the critic becomes a poet who, by an act of desire, achieves freedom of imagination. By the force of his imagination, he regains the freedom he has lost by the Fall.

The scope of Frye's scheme suggests other twentieth-century works such as *Ulysses*, *The Rainbow*, and Yeats's *A Vision* in that it purports to contain nature and all history. Like these prophecies and epics, his work includes a self-regulating structure which will accommodate future events (in Frye's case, works that are not written). Frye's analysis of Blake provides a model for his own work: 'Everything that has ever happened since the beginning of time is part, Blake says, of the literal Word of God. The ordinary historical conception of human existence as a dissolving flux in linear time is therefore the literal approach to life, the corporeal understanding based on memory. History as the total form of all genuine efforts of human culture and civilization is the canon or Scripture of human life. History as linear time is the great apocrypha or mystery which has to be rejected from it.'[31] Frye is in the great romantic tradition described by Abrams: 'Whatever the form, the Romantic Bard is one "who present, past, and futures sees"; so that in dealing with current affairs his procedure is often panoramic, his stage cosmic, his agents quasi-mythological, and his logic of events apocalyptic. Typically this mode of Romantic vision fuses history, politics, philosophy and religion into one grand design, by asserting Providence – or some form of natural teleology – to operate in the seeming chaos of human history so as to effect from present evil a greater good' (p. 54).[32]

But Frye is also part of the modernist movement. Like the work of Kafka, Freud, Joyce (another Viconian), Brecht, or Pollock, Frye's *Anatomy* is a twentieth-century attempt to question the possibility and significance of temporality, progress, and indeed any concept of unity that is dependent on movement. Frye departs from the progression of linear history. According to Fletcher, 'For the mere profanity, secularism, thingness, and progressivism of the purely linear historian, Frye would seek to enlist a mixed methodology, where that linear history is combined with the ritual periodizing of the poet's imaginings.'[33] The ebullience and energy of Frye's mind, reflected in his style, and the very spontaneity of his associations as he moves rapidly from point to point, suggest not only the internal logic of Blake, but the free association of Freud's psychoanalytic method. Frye's wit, sense of fun, and uninhibited associations among unlike texts may also reflect the influence of surrealism in his formative years. Surrealism also would have taught him that something might exist in the same place at different times or in different places at the same time.

In the *Anatomy* Frye creates a literary analogue to the Bible which he describes as a 'definitive myth, a single archetypal structure extending from creation to apocalypse' (p. 315). His description of the biblical cycle in the section, 'Specific Encyclopaedic Forms' – immediately following 'Specific Continuous Forms' in the fourth essay – is useful to understanding Frye's own work: 'The Bible as a whole . . . presents a gigantic cycle from creation to apocalypse, within which is the heroic quest of the Messiah from incarnation to apotheosis. Within this again are three other cyclical movements, expressed or implied; individual from birth to salvation, sexual from Adam and Eve to the apocalyptic wedding; social from the giving of the law to the established kingdom of the law, the rebuilt Zion of the Old Testament and the millennium of the New' (pp. 316–17). The first section of the *Anatomy* is a gigantic cycle within which are the other three cycles: the ethical, archetypal and rhetorical chapters. The *Anatomy* implies cycle rather than fulfilment of a single teleology. Since, according to Frye, literature contains not a developmental pattern but a recurring one, the reader's apocalypse (or epiphany) is his understanding of the coherence of literature and his awareness that in the *Anatomy*, Frye, the twentieth-century critic-prophet, has, like Blake, created his own space from emptiness – in a sense, reiterated Genesis – and so must his reader. Well before Kermode's *The Sense of an Ending*, Frye saw the possibility of using the biblical myth, and particularly the concepts of Genesis and Apocalypse, as metaphors for understanding literary and life experience.

Let us test Frye's usefulness by looking at a novel that he mentions in several contexts. In 'Essay I, Historical Criticism: Theory of Modes', we learn that *Lord Jim* is a novel in the mode of low mimetic tragedy – the mode of most realistic fiction – which is concerned with the 'isolated mind'. 'The best word' for the hero of low mimetic tragedy is 'Pathos' but he does not say *for whom* it is the best word – the author or the other characters within the imagined world: 'Pathos presents its hero as isolated by a weakness which appeals to our sympathy because it is on our own level of experience. . . . The root idea of pathos is the exclusion of an individual on our own level from a social group to which he is trying to belong' (pp. 38–9). But this does not take us very far; Jim can be categorized as an *alazon* 'which means imposter, someone who pretends or tries to be something more than he is'; as an obsessed character, he is a 'lineal descendent of the *miles gloriosus*' (pp. 39–40). But when in the same paragraph he uses Kurtz, not Jim, as an example of 'an unconditioned will that drives its victim beyond the normal limits of humanity' (p. 40), we realize that he does not really see the psychological kinship between Kurtz and Jim.

In the third essay, 'Archetypal Criticism: Theory of Myth', *Lord Jim* is cited as an example of a 'phase of irony' which is associated with 'sincere, explicit realism' and which 'looks at tragedy from below, from the moral and realistic perspective of the state of experience. It stresses the humanity of its heroes, minimizes the sense of ritual inevitability in tragedy, supplies social and psychological explanations for catastrophe, and makes as much as possible of human misery seem, in Thoreau's phrase, "superfluous and evitable" ' (p. 237). In the interests of range Frye sacrifices depth. Nor are Frye's comments on Stein very precise: 'One of the central themes [of this phase of irony] is Stein's answer to the problem of the 'romantic Lord Jim in Conrad: "in the destructive element immerse". This remark, without ridiculing Jim, still brings out the quixotic and romantic element in his nature and criticizes it from the point of view of experience' (p. 237). But Frye not only fails to note Stein's resemblance to Jim but does not shed much light on Jim's character or on Stein's role as the oracle manqué.

Nor does Frye establish the meaning of the term 'destructive element' within *Lord Jim*.

In the second essay, 'Ethical Criticism: Theory of Symbolism', he mentions Conrad's image of the sea as one both the poet and the reader unconsciously 'expand[s] over many works into an archetypal symbol of literature as a whole' (p. 100); but the sea for Conrad has very specific meaning in terms of his own life; it represents a past where he had succeeded and an experience to which his imagination could return. For Conrad, the sea was the place where he achieved a coherent personality as an exile *before* he became a writer. And it was to the memory of his sea years to which he resorted during periods when he had difficulty writing. For the sea provided memories of order and control; the voyage with its purposeful intent, limited number of characters, and defined beginning and end enabled Conrad to order a recalcitrant narrative.[34] Even if we concede the importance of the archetype, we cannot neglect, given his unique personal history, that it is in his individual use of the sea that Conrad's meaning primarily resides. And Frye's comments on Conrad's oral narrative and the structure of his novel are not incremental for those who have read the novel seriously. For example, does the following help us see the novel differently? 'In Conrad, too, the dislocations in the narrative – working backwards and forwards, as he put it – are designed to make us shift our attention from listening to the story to looking at the central situation' (p. 267). Finally in the fourth essay, 'Rhetorical Criticism: Theory of Genres', he mentions Jim in the section 'Specific Continuous Forms' as an example of 'a parody of the romance and its ideals', but a parody which ironically becomes an 'ironic compound' of the novel and romance (p. 306). But Frye does not explain how the parody – a criticism of a prior perspective – dissolves into an ironic compound. At times it seems as if 'system' replaces criticism.

It is difficult to overestimate the esteem in which Frye was held in the late 1950s and 1960s. That in 1965 critics of the stature of Wimsatt and Hartman were participating in a conference on his work at The English Institute and writing for the volume *Northrop Frye in Modern Criticism*, testifies to his importance. In the 1960s younger critics and students were anxiously trying to apply Frye's models to every author and to every thematic and generic distinction. In recent years, while his brilliance has still been acknowledged, his influence has ebbed, in part because of the emphasis among structuralists – where he might have expected to find some of his natural allies – on meaning's dependence on the relationship of words to other words rather than on references to prior patterns. It has also ebbed because his limitations have become more apparent. It is possible to question the woodenness of his method without sacrificing its conceptual framework. What Frye ignores is the dialogue within the creative process between the individual temperament and archetypes. His work raises a number of major problems:

(1) By conceiving of the critic as a kind of poet, he creates a system which is often indifferent to the needs of those who read criticism to understand the subtle intricacies of the formal and thematic organization of a work. Hartman has noted how 'Archetypal analysis can degenerate into an abstract thematics where the living pressure of mediations is lost and all connections are skeletonized.'[35] And one can sympathize with Wimsatt's and Brooks's objection that 'inert and valueless' poems can be classified within Frye's system, and their concomitant fear that literary criticism can become like a social science, more interested in classification than evaluation.[36]

(2) Frye is a neo-Platonist for whom literary works refer to ideal paradigms. But he does not explain where the objective literary universe exists in which one finds these paradigms. Is it in the critic's imagination or does it exist as forms *a priori* to individual works? Precisely, how does the work catalyse these forms into being? Wimsatt's facetious remark about 'the imagination of the critic' making up myths to produce 'the myth of myth' is to the point.[37]

(3) Frye ignores the temporality of a *work*; as Hartman notes, 'Frye's concept of literary structure is consciously spatial. It depends on a disjunction between our immediate experience of literature, which is guided by the tempo of the work, and criticism, which lays out the completed pattern spatially.'[38]

(4) Frye overlooks the temporality of the world, the very historical process that interests Auerbach. Spatialization of a literary universe and the diminishment of time create a cosmos that undermines Frye's desire that the *totality* of the literary universe stand in a mimetic relationship to the real one. As Hartman puts it, 'He seems relatively unconcerned with the exact dialogue or status of words in the individual consciousness and the particular society.'[39]

(5) Frye neglects the creative process, the process of transforming the real world into the imaginative one. For many who believe that something must precede the literary universe and be the basis of

the creative act, the problem of criticism is both to do justice to the imaginative world of art *and* to mediate between the world of art and the real world. Frye ignores the dialogue between the real world and the imaginary one – whether it be author and text, reader and text, author and *Zeitgeist*. He does not account for the determining pressure of nonliterary factors, including both psychological forces that make the author unique and historical factors that make him speak as a representative figure of a particular set of temporal and spatial circumstances. Of course, any approach that depends upon autonomy will create problems for studying the novel which, more than any other genre, depends not only on the contents of the external world for its subject but upon the reader's willingness to enter the imagined world and remain there for the period of reading.

(6) Nor do his archetypes account for the individuality in expression – the stylistic signature that differentiates one author's work from another and each of an author's works from his other ones. Thus he ignores voice, style, and tone.

(7) Although he rejects the aesthetic approach which thinks of literature as a palace of art, as a partial refuge for the imagination, isn't he guilty of this, too?

(8) Frye invents his own word world in which he ambitiously assigns definitions as if he were a king in a critical wonderland. Thus objecting to the use of 'tropical' to mean 'figurative,' Wimsatt writes, 'Frye's vocabulary is not an accident but a necessary engine for the projection of some of his slanted visions.' [40]

(9) As my discussion of Frye's response to *Lord Jim* indicates, Frye operates at a level of generalization that limits the value of his insights. To take another example, once we say that Becky in Thackeray's *Vanity Fair* is in the "low mimetic mode", but the rest of the characters are in an "ironic mode" because we feel superior in power and intelligence to them, how far have we advanced? Do we learn something about *Vanity Fair* that we don't know? Thus, at times the usefulness of his categories seems limited.

We should stress that behind Frye's text is a human presence speaking to us with, as he describes the hero of the high mimetic mode, the 'authority, passions, and power of expression far greater than ours' (p. 34). Frye's categorizing sensibility is informed by intellectual energy, confidence, and an encyclopedic knowledge of world literature, most notably English literature. But his classifications and categories, his myths and types, seem to have much more relevance for Shakespearian comedy than for novels. He prefers comedy and romance, which free man from consciousness of this world, to satire and tragedy which calls attention to our limitations, fallibility, and mortality.

We may ask, can any overview from a remote perspective that reduces a novel to a single sentence do justice to the complexity of the novel? If, as Frye implies, the New Critics are like viewers of a painting, who get lost in a welter of detail from a perspective that is too close, one could complain that Frye does not allow us to see the wall, let alone the canvas. Thus he cites the works of Conrad (along with Hawthorne, Poe, Hardy, and Woolf) as examples of '[I]ronic litera-ture [which] begins with reason and tends toward myth, its mythical patterns being as a rule more suggestive of the demonic than of the apocalyptic, though sometimes it simply continues the romantic tradition of stylization' (p. 140). He considers the above an example of 'standing back', but without analyses of works, one could argue that it is such a long view that we can – to use his metaphor of examining pictures – barely see the picture or indeed, the *wall* on which it hangs. Yet at a time when abstract art began to dominate the visual arts, Frye produced an original work with its own unique form, a form that was perhaps influenced by the stress on abstraction in contemporary visual arts. Indeed, by taking a distant view, the traditional madonna can be perceived as 'a large centripetal blue mass, with a contrasting point of interest at its center' (p. 140). Like much modern painting, especially that of the Abstract Impressionists, *The Anatomy of Criticism* is, in Fletcher's words, 'periodic, festive, memorial, and dancelike. Man as a creature and creator of the imaginative period is free within controls, a musical being.'[41]

III

Perhaps we should conclude by comparing Frye and Auerbach. Frye believes that literature can be discussed in a closed literary universe. Auerbach uses the text to reveal not so much the literary values but the historical forces in the real world in which it was written. Frye examines the data of literature and induces hypotheses about the phenomena of literature much as a lepidopterist examining butter-flies posits his tentative conclusions. Auerbach deduces from individual passages – the data of literature – generalizations about the world that the passage describes. Auerbach would be distrustful of the paradigms which Frye believes give the text its structure. For Frye, myths and archetypes underlie literature and are rediscovered and reinvigorated by each work. The critic's job is to show the unity in apparent chaos. While for Frye myths are Platonic, for Auerbach prior narratives are empirically necessary responses to historical conditions. Thus, for Auerbach, recent narrative modes develop from prior ones to make sense of the changes in the real world. Put another way: the dynamic real world necessarily produces mutations in artistic forms.

If, to use Frye's terms, Frye is in the high mimetic mode, superior to the world in which he lives, Auerbach is in the low mimetic mode in which he claims no superiority to the work he surveys, and we respond to Auerbach's 'sense of his common humanity' (*Anatomy*, p. 34). For Frye subject matter is not the focus of interest except insofar as it fulfils his paradigms; for Auerbach the subject matter as well as the rendering of it are significant. Auerbach is interested in an 'historically active dynamism' (*Mimesis*, p. 38) which traces growth and transformation while Frye believes in timeless categories. Auerbach sees man's actions as part of an historical process, while Frye sees them as fulfilling archetypes or literary paradigms. But Auerbach, differentiating what he calls figurative relationships from allegory, insists that both the literal and figurative maintain their particular identities and that authors do not cease to be literal when they become figurative. Thus, in a figural scheme, both figure and fulfilment 'have a significance which is not incompatible with their being real. An event taken as a figure preserves its literal and historical meaning. It remains an event, does not become a mere sign' (*Mimesis*, p. 171). Thus while Frye is interested in a synchronic [spatial] perspective, Auerbach focuses on a diachronic [temporal] perspective.

For Auerbach movement in the form of change, development, and modification is crucial to his understanding of the relation between works. For Frye the ideal – what Frye would call 'desire' – expresses itself in literary works like comedy and romance; they release us from the real world, a world shared presumably by reader and author, but defined as distinct from the ideal world where he places literary works. For Auerbach the ideal is realized in a literary work that is attentive to the substance and meaning of the real world, an attentiveness shared by author and reader; the sharing is the axis on which realism depends.

Frye ignores the real world as much as possible, or at least he thinks he does. According to Frye, 'There is thus an objective mythical structure, which is the world of literature itself, and which criticism as a whole seeks to articulate, and a subjective one, which the student achieves as a result of his literary experience.'[42] Frye neglects the forces in the external world which shape literature, whereas Auerbach argues that the imagined world is significant insofar as it crystallizes those forces. While Frye, like Structuralists and Post-structuralists, seeks to free texts from human history, Auerbach wants to recapture history's role in shaping texts by deductively extrapolating those factors from the text. To put it boldly, Frye's impulse is to move away from the *a priori* world, while Auerbach moves towards it. But Frye does not acknowledge that discussions of literature must be mimetic in their very use of seasons, of the cycle of birth and death, of Freudian terms like displacement, and of the words and syntactical formations that we recognize in the real world. Thus, Frye's texts inevitably mediate between the real world and his literary ontology, just as any critic or writer of imaginative literature or, indeed, of any writing must. As the following passage illustrates, Frye cannot turn his back on the nonliterary world, 'Tragedy belongs chiefly to the two indigenous developments of tragic drama in fifth-century Athens and seventeenth-century Europe from Shakespeare to Racine. Both belong to a period of social history in which an aristocracy is fast losing its effective power but still retains a good deal of ideological prestige' (p. 37). The first sentence depends on historically placing a genre in social history, and the second is an elaboration which links the rise of tragedy to the particular position of the aristocracy. Does not Frye's insight partially depend on the very kind of historical understanding, based on prior experience, that Auerbach admires? Had Frye made up out of whole cloth the condition of the aristocracy in fifth-century Athens and seventeenth-century Europe, the sentence would be false not simply in terms of Frye's hypothesis but empirically untrue because it would not correspond to the world we know.

Realism is different in degree but not in kind from romance; at times it quickly becomes anti-realism, for the very order and control which we associate with 'realism' is *not* the order and control of life, but that of the fictive world of romance. The continuities and connections which we associate with 'real life' are often the continuities of hopes, plans, and dreams.[43] Frye's hermeneutical approach and Auerbach's concept of mimesis illustrate a crucial paradox: As we move away from the external world and move centripetally towards the literary text as the centre of our attention, we find ourselves inevitably approaching the external world. As we move centrifugally away from the literary text as centre towards the real world, we soon find ourselves moving in the opposite direction. It is like the myth of Sisyphus or Kafka's Hunter Gracchus on the stairs to heaven. Frye's method cannot avoid empirical observation, and Auerbach refers to the timeless and Platonic world of Christian teleology. Nor can Auerbach's efforts to describe simply the reality of historical forces behind a work entirely avoid becoming the inevitable victim of necessarily reductive patterns, simplifying fictions, and illuminating distortions. The form of all literary criticism, like other modes of descriptive narratives, including history, always creates as it selects its data and imposes an order, and that order enacts in some degree the presence of the author. In 'Tea at the Palaz of Hoon' Stevens's words are as applicable to the modern critic as to the modern poet or novelist, for both seek to find an order in literary works to compensate for the disorder of life:

I was myself the compass of that sea:

I was the world in which I walked, and what I saw
Or heard or felt came not but from myself;
And there I found myself more truly and more strange.

NOTES

1. Page numbers in parentheses refer to Erich Auerbach, *Mimesis: the Representation of Reality in Western Literature*, trans. by Willard R. Trask (New York: Doubleday, English 1957) orig. English edn 1953; orig. pub. 1946.

   My approach will stress that Auerbach is both a formal and historical critic. For an important essay on Auerbach's historiography, see W. Wolfgang Holdheim's, 'Auerbach's *Mimesis*: Aesthetics as Historical Understanding', *CLIO*, 10:2, (1981) pp. 143–54. Also see Thomas M. DePietro, 'Literary Criticism as History: the Example of Auerbach's *Mimesis*, *CLIO*, 8:3 (1979) pp. 377–87.

2. Angus Fletcher, 'Utopian History and *The Anatomy of Criticism*', in *Northrop Frye in Modern Criticism*, ed. Murray Krieger (New York: Columbia University Press, 1966) pp. 70–1.

3. Erich Auerbach, *Literary Language and Its Public in Late Latin Antiquity and in the Middle Ages* (Princeton University Press, 1965) p. 6. In *Mimesis*, he praises Vico for having a vision of man 'as being profoundly embedded in the historical order of his existence' (p. 382).

   As Fletcher notes, 'Auerbach wrote history in the Viconian tradition, bringing the past into the present by linguistic comparisons, through the biography of the language poets use' (Fletcher, p. 71).

4. Auerbach, *Literary Language*, p. 8.

5. Auerbach, p. 14.

6. Holdheim, p. 151.
7. See Holdheim, p. 147.
8. Auerbach, p. 16.
9. Auerbach, p. 19.
10. Auerbach, p. 13.
11. Auerbach, p. 17.
12. See Auerbach, p. 20.
13. Holdheim, p. 144.
14. Auerbach, p. 13.
15. Holdheim, p. 146.
16. Auerbach, p. 12.
17. Auerbach, p. 8.
18. Auerbach, p. 21.
19. George Levine, *The Realistic Imagination: English Fiction from Franken-stein to Lady Chatterley* (The University of Chicago Press, 1981) p. 8.
20. Page references in this section refer to Northrop Frye, *Anatomy of Criticism: Four Essays* (New York: Atheneum, 1967) orig. edn 1957.
21. William K. Wimsatt, 'Northrop Frye: Criticism as Myth', in *Northrop Frye*, p. 88.
22. Geoffrey H. Hartman, 'Ghostlier Demarcations', *Northrop Frye*, p. 116.
23. Northrop Frye 'New Directions from Old', *Fables of Identity: Studies in Poetic Mythology* (New York: Harcourt, Brace, & World, 1963) p. 53. Quoted by Hartman, p. 67.
24. Frank Lentricchia, *After the New Criticism* (The University of Chicago Press, 1980) p. 12.
25. William K. Wimsatt and Cleanth Brooks, *Literary Criticism: a Short History* (New York: Vintage, 1967) orig. edn 1957, p. 709.
26. 'Ulysses, Order, and Myth', repr. in *The Modern Tradition*, ed. Richard Ellmann and Charles Feidelson, Jr. (New York: Oxford University Press, 1965) p. 681. Hartman also quotes this passage, pp. 119–20.
27. See Frye, pp. 111–12.
28. Wimsatt and Brooks, p. 703.
29. Fletcher, p. 58.
30. Murray Krieger, 'Frye and Contemporary Criticism' in *Northrop Frye*,' p. 10.
31. *Fearful Symmetry* (Princeton University Press, 1947) p. 340; quoted in Fletcher, p. 68.
32. M. H. Abrams, 'English Romanticism: the Spirit of the Age', in *Romanticism and Consciousness*, ed. Harold Bloom (New York: Norton, 1970) p. 103.
33. Fletcher, pp. 72–3.
34. See my *Conrad: 'Almayer's Folly' through 'Under Western Eyes'* (London: Macmillan; Ithaca, New York: Cornell University Press, 1980) esp. ch. 3.
35. Hartman, p. 118.
36. Wimsatt and Brooks, p. 711.
37. Wimsatt in *Northrop Frye*, p. 97.
38. Hartman, p. 121.
39. Hartman, p. 128.
40. Wimsatt in *Northrop Frye*, pp. 99–100.

41. Fletcher, p. 73.
42. Northrop Frye, 'Reflections in a Mirror', in *Northrop Frye in Modern Criticism*, p. 145.
43. Barbara Hardy, 'Toward a Poetics of Fiction: 3) An Approach through Narrative,' *Novel*, 2:1 (Fall, 1968) 5–14.

7 Reading as a Moral Activity: the Importance of Wayne C. Booth's *The Rhetoric of Fiction*

I

Wayne C. Booth has produced one of the most important achievements of literary criticism of our time. Beginning with *The Rhetoric of Fiction* (1961), and including *Now Don't Try to Reason with Me* (1970), *Modern Dogma and the Rhetoric of Assent* (1974), *A Rhetoric of Irony* (1974), and *Critical Understanding: the Powers and Limits of Pluralism* (1979), Booth has conducted a brilliant, impassioned, and ebullient defence of reading, communication, and reason. 'For me,' he writes in *A Rhetoric of Irony*, 'one good reading of one good passage is worth as much as anything there is, because the person achieving it is living life fully in that time' (*RI*, p. xii).[1] While *A Rhetoric of Irony* is an immensely learned and useful discussion and *Critical Understanding* is an important defence of humanistic criticism, our focus will be on *The Rhetoric of Fiction*, which stands more than two decades after publication as a critical masterwork.

In *The Rhetoric of Fiction*, Booth demonstrates that the author's meaning is accessible and provides an alternative to the now fashionable belief that, since there is neither hope nor purpose in trying to approach the meaning of a text, we can virtually make our own text. For Booth the critic has the more modest task of discovering the author's intended meaning by responding to specific effects created by the author for the reader. As he recalled six years later in a retrospective essay entitled '*The Rhetoric of Fiction* and the Poetics of Fiction':

The book began as an attempt to show that Gordon and Tate

(among many others) were radically confused about point-of-view and so-called objective narration; it was originally to be what parts of it still are, a polemical essay accepting the main premises of the various "schools of autonomy," and defending the artistic respectability of the visibly "rhetorical" elements that have been under attack at least since the time of Flaubert. It grew into a book on the rhetorical dimension of all fiction. (*Novel*, p. 111)[2]

If Booth began his research with the intention of responding to the New Critics who discussed novels as self-enclosed ontologies, it is clear that he soon expanded his audience to include those who would make the practice of Henry James into prescriptive Rules; those for whom the revival of art for art's sake seemed a comfortable intellectual position after the horrors of World War II and The Holocaust and what seemed in the 1950s to be the ubiquitous threat of nuclear war; those who, like F. R. Leavis, Erich Auerbach, and *The Partisan Review* critics, insisted upon extrinsic standards of moral seriousness and tangible realism; and those who, like Arnold Kettle, under a vague Marxist influence, saw the value of a work of literature in terms of its contribution to 'the achievement of human freedom'.[3]

In the retrospective essay on *The Rhetoric of Fiction*, Booth differentiates between a poetics ('Study of what the work *is*, what it has been made to *be*') and a rhetoric ('What the work is made to *do*'): '*The kinds of actions authors perform on readers* differ markedly, though subtly, from *the kinds of imitations of objects they are seen as making*, in the poetic mode' (*Novel*, pp. 113, 115). Implicitly responding to the New Critics whom he believed focused on poetics and minimized rhetoric – the role of the author–reader relationship, Booth defines the relationship among author, text, and audience. In *The Rhetoric of Fiction* he shows that the 'autonomous' text derives from conscious or unconscious decisions made by the author to shape the reader's response: 'Nothing is real for the reader until the author makes it so, and it is for the reader that the author chooses to make this scene as powerful as possible' (*RF*, 108). Booth insists that an author affects the reader as the author intends, and communicates human emotions and values to an audience; the reader in turn responds to the felt presence of a human voice within the text.

Booth takes the position of a man of reason defending the house of fiction which is under siege. He shows that the 'house of fiction' – the term James used to argue for the pluralism of fiction – has been appropriated by the New Critics for their own purposes; Caroline

Gordon and Allen Tate had used the title *The House of Fiction* (1950) for their seminal text that applied New Criticism to fiction. We must not forget the prestige still enjoyed in 1961 by those New Critical sacred texts, Brooks' and Warren's *Understanding Fiction* (1943) and Gordon's and Tate's *The House of Fiction* (1950). For the New Critics, telling was only acceptable in fiction when it was spoken by a distinct self-dramatizing narrator; for then it most resembled the dramatic lyric and provided the irony, tension, and ambiguity that were values in themselves and hence the focus of their analytic attention. They had been influenced by Henry James and T. S. Eliot, who insisted on the fusion of thought and feeling. Booth shows how 'objective' general rules become the 'subjective' values by which works are measured. But, as Booth puts it, general rules derive from the 'abandonment of the notion of peculiar literary kinds, each with its unique demands that may modify the general standards' (*RF*, p. 34).

Central to Booth's credo is the premise that each work is unique and must be read on its own terms. In his closing paragraph of *The Rhetoric of Irony*, he writes, 'The worst enemy of good reading as of good criticism is the application of abstract rules that violate the life of particular works' (*RI*, p. 277). Certainly Booth is a nominalist. He does not propose rhetorical principles, but discusses rhetorical processes in specific works. He teaches us how authors build 'aesthetic form . . . out of patterned emotions as well as out of other materials' and, by example, how to locate and define the implied author in individual works (*RF*, p. 248). Since the form of each novel is dynamic and evolving, we need to show how the implied author proposes, tests, qualifies, and discards values. Part One of *The Rhetoric of Fiction* examines and ultimately discards the then accepted critical shibboleths – what he ironically calls General Rules – before presenting his own principle that there can be no general rules. He systematically organizes his argument to undermine rules that claim that 'true novels must be realistic', or 'all authors should be objective', or 'true art ignores the audience', or 'tears and laughter are, aesthetically, frauds'. Part One then climaxes with an inclusive discussion of types of narration based on the premise that each text generates its own aesthetic principles dependent on its thematic and moral purpose.

In *The Rhetoric of Fiction* Booth is responding to James and the codification of James by Percy Lubbock in *The Craft of Fiction* (1921). He wrote at a time when New Critics had adopted the Jamesian aesthetic for their own purposes and insisted on the superiority of telling to showing. Booth is ambivalent about the example of James.

On the one hand, Booth shows that James himself is not the formalist critic that some of his followers have made him out to be, because he is not interested in the dramatic for its own sake but as part of the intensity that all good fiction requires. He appropriates James to his cause by arguing that James never thought that the author should be banished; rather, he was concerned with how 'to achieve an intense illusion of reality, including the complexities of mental and moral reality' (*RF*, p. 50). But, on the other hand, Booth has misgivings about James's pursuit of a rhetoric in the service of realism rather than for the purpose of eliciting specific effects: 'From the beginning James's passion for the reader's sense of traveling in a real, though intensified, world dictates a general rhetoric in the service of realism, rather than a particular rhetoric for the most intense experience of distinctive effects' (*RF*, p. 50).

Booth insists that James's method of 'push[ing] all summary back into the minds of the characters' has its price (*RF*, 173). The author surrenders the ability to be an 'unequivocal spokesman' (*RF*, p. 175). And this, finally, is the difficulty of modern literature and the focus of his last chapter, 'The Morality of Impersonal Narration': 'As unreliability increases, there obviously can come a point at which such transformed information ceases to be useful even in characterization of minds, unless the author retains some method of showing what the facts are from which the speaker's interpretations characteristically diverge' (*RF*, p. 175). Booth rejected the then fashionable argument that fiction had evolved from simpler to higher forms and that Flaubert or James represents a turning point. Comparing James to Austen in the *Emma* chapter, he writes, 'By combining the role of commentator with the role of hero, Jane Austen has worked more economically than James, and though economy is as dangerous as any other criterion when applied universally, even James might have profited from a closer study of the economies that a character like Knightley can be made to achieve' (*RF*, pp. 253–4).

II

To understand Booth, we must understand his intellectual tradition. While avoiding polemics, he makes clear in the preface to the *Rhetoric of Fiction* that he is a Chicago Aristotelian who is concerned with 'the art of communicating with readers – the rhetorical resources available to the writer of epic, novel or short story as he tries, consciously or unconsciously, to impose his fictional world upon the reader'. He dislikes criticism which ignores genres and rhetoric, and creates, in the mode of Leavis, 'great traditions' based on subjective standards disguised as objective ones: 'The abandonment of distinctions of species in the face of demands for universally desired qualities is one of the most interesting events in modern literary history' (*RF*, p. 35). For example, in Chapter VIII he convincingly argues that, notwithstanding the unreliability of *Tristram Shandy*, Steine has written a formally coherent novel once one understands its generic contexts and antecedents: 'the comic novel exploded, the sugar-coated collection of philosophical essays, and the miscellaneous satire' (*RF*, p. 224). This is the classic Chicago approach of answering the question, 'What kind of?' It is based on the Aristotelian premise that literary material can be better understood if it can be classified. *The Rhetoric of Fiction*, like *A Rhetoric of Irony*, has a three-part structure with a clearly defined beginning, a middle, and an end. Its first part establishes the folly of applying abstract rules to literary works. Part II effectively shows how traditional narrators control and shape the responses of readers. Part III shows what happens when interest in the narrator's psyche for its own sake makes that impossible.

Booth's work depends on the ideas developed by his mentors, Richard McKeon and R. S. Crane. In his essay 'Imitation and Poetry', McKeon stresses Aristotle's tripartite focus on the act of mimesis; the product of mimesis, or the literary work; and the effect of the work upon the audience. 'Aristotle, thus, says that the poem *imitates* actions and *makes* plots, and he describes the effect of dramatic poetry as a *catharsis*.'[4] But, as McKeon continues, ' "Makes" in the Greek, is "creates" without benefit of the Book of Genesis' and thus imitation means not copying but transforming nature:

> [A] poem is "made," and it possesses, therefore, a unity and an order which are not dependent on the truth or falsity of any statement it contains or on the moral consequences to which it may lead; for its form, if it is a poem, is self-contained, and its "likeness" is not a repetition or copy of a natural object, such as the actions of man, but their presentation in the distinct and heightened necessity and probability achieved by use of the poetic medium.[5]

Thus for McKeon, literary works are not simply facsimiles of the world but heightened and intensified imagined worlds. R. S. Crane's concept of plot is an unstated premise of Booth's argument:

> Plot . . . is not merely a particular synthesis of particular materials
> of character, thought, and action, but such a synthesis endowed
> necessarily, because it imitates in words a sequence of human
> activities, with a power to affect our opinions and emotions in a
> certain way. . . . The positive excellence [of a good plot] depends
> upon the power of its peculiar synthesis of character, action, and
> thought, as inferable from the sequence of words, to move our
> feelings powerfully and pleasurably in a certain definitive way.[6]

Crane's emphasis is upon the relationship between the plot and the
results of the author's imaginative vision upon the audience. Booth's
credo, like McKeon's and Crane's, is based on what he calls 'the
essential poetic truth first formulated by Aristotle – that each
successful imaginative work has its own life, its own soul, its own
principles of being, quite independently of the prejudices or practical
needs of this or that audience, and that our poetic devices should be an
"integral part of the whole" ' (*RF*, p. 93).

Booth believes that novels are purposeful imitations of the real
world on the part of an author who desires to affect his audience in a
particular way. The work of McKeon and Crane made Booth's work
both possible and necessary.[7] While McKeon stresses the kinds of
imitations literature makes and Crane's major concern is the way that
authors make their works, Booth's is upon the response of the
audience. Booth focuses on the *effects* of literary works, and he
invokes the authority of Aristotle who, he says, 'clearly recognizes that
one thing the poet does is to produce effects on audiences', and those
effects are not static but dynamic (*RF*, p. 92). Or, as he puts it in *Now
Don't Try to Reason With Me*, 'Pity and fear, in the tragedies, are not
emotions arrived at *finally*, at the moment when disaster strikes. In any
good tragedy, there is a structure of rising pity and rising fear. Pity and
fear are shorthand terms for the structure of the thought and emotion
embodied in the play. . . . There is . . . a *structure* of effects in all great
art.'[8] At a time when, due to the influence of Joseph Frank's 'Spatial
Form in Modern Literature', the concept of spatial form was extremely
influential, Booth showed that a novel should be perceived more as a
linear temporal process of experience than as a three-dimensional
structure.[9]

In stressing the effects of literature, Booth was influenced by the
work of I. A. Richards, and more directly, by Kenneth Burke who
contended that a literary work does something to the reader and that

what it does depends on prior decisions of the author. Burke writes in the essay 'The Philosophy of Literary Form':

> If we try to discover what the poem is doing for the poet, we may discover a set of generalizations as to what poems do for everybody. With these in mind, we have cues for analyzing this sort of *eventfulness* that the poem contains. And in analyzing this eventfulness, we shall make basic discoveries about the *structure* of the work itself. . . . And I contend that the kind of observation about structure is more relevant when you approach the work as the *functioning* of a structure.[10]

Unwilling to be restricted to Crane's pursuit of '*knowledge* of the *literal* causes that have produced a *particular poem*', Booth found Burke's focus on 'poems and criticism as manifestations of a universal human activity, symbolic action' attractive because it sees literary works as deeds which reveal, like other deeds, the moral quality of the creator.[11]

If Booth finds his intellectual paradigm in Aristotle, it is not merely as a model for rhetorical criticism, but as a central figure in the Western humanistic tradition. According to this tradition, within a world whose patterns can at least partially be understood by a rational mind, man has the intellectual capacity to impose order on the world and to discover a purposeful self. Literature can be central to our knowledge of ourselves and community. If we only read one more book, if we only think a little bit more rigorously, we will be able to solve the problems of texts – and of life. Booth wants to teach us both how to read and how to live; he believes that books can teach us to live better lives because they contain truths. If this seems naive, let us recall that he shares this belief with Aristotle, Horace, Pope, Shelley, and Arnold. Thus in *Now Don't Try to Reason With Me*, he is making a moral as well as an aesthetic statement: 'There is no more satisfactory proof of the existence of the good, the true, and the beautiful, than experiencing their fusion in the unique, particular achievement of a story like "Clay".'[12] For Booth, the major function of criticism is to explain literary works in terms of values and experiences that are common to author, reader, and critic. By 'rhetoric' Booth means both how books communicate with readers and, specifically, how books arouse our interest about the issues and characters in the imagined world and how they affect us morally.

Booth insists that a work be *interesting*. Interest may depend on the discovery of facts, the fulfilment of formal expectations aroused by the cause–effect of plot, the response to conventions, or the recognition of patterns of language. While most great works are interesting in all these ways, our primary concern is for characters whose words and deeds illustrate human behaviour with which we can identify. For Booth, characters are 'people who matter, people whose fate concerns us not simply because of its meaning or quality, but because we care about them as human beings' (*RF*, p. 130). Booth speaks indirectly to the New Critical fear that we will commit the 'affective fallacy' and respond in terms of our own emotional life. Isn't he saying that while books shape our responses, an element of reader subjectivity is inevitable and desirable for a full humanistic response? As E. D. Hirsch has remarked, the criterion of 'being interesting . . . is another way of saying that fiction should please and instruct'.[13]

Booth offers a method that stresses the primacy of two questions: 'Who is speaking to whom?', and 'For what purpose?' That the author creates both a second self and an audience is central to Booth's discussion about the importance of rhetoric. The concept of the implied author is the most original part of Booth's approach: '[An Author] creates not simply an ideal, impersonal "man in general" but an implied version of "himself" that is different from the implied authors we meet in other men's works. To some novelists it has seemed, indeed, that they were discovering or creating themselves as they wrote' (*RF*, pp. 70–1). Seeking unity, the reader strives to locate a coherent presence in the text, a human voice to whom he can respond. Booth goes on to equate the implied author with the artistic whole: 'Our sense of the implied author includes . . . the intuitive apprehension of a completed artistic whole; the chief value to which *this* implied author is committed, regardless of what party his creator belongs to in real life, is that which is expressed by the total form. . . . The 'implied author' chooses, consciously or unconsciously, what we read; we infer him as an ideal, literary, created version of the real man; he is the sum of his own choices' (*RF*, pp. 73–5). Thus Booth's 'implied author' is a strategy to eliminate the author without sacrificing the artist as a creative figure who speaks to us through the text. The author creates readers through a pattern of effects: 'The author creates, in short, an image of himself and another image of his reader; he makes his reader, as he makes his second self, and the most successful reading is one in which the created selves, author and reader, can find complete agreement' (*RF*, p. 138). He provided a paradigm for those who believe with E. D. Hirsch that 'Validity implies the correspondence to a meaning which is represented by the text' and that 'the only compelling normative principle that has ever been brought forward is the old-fashioned ideal of rightly understanding what the author meant'.[14]

One of Booth's major legacies is his distinction between reliable and unreliable narrators: 'I have called a narrator *reliable* when he speaks for or acts in accordance with the norms of the work (which is to say, the implied author's norms), *unreliable* when he does not' (*RF*, pp. 158–9). (I prefer the terms "perceptive" and "imperceptive", since a narrator might be reliable and yet unaware of the implications of his behaviour.) For Booth reliability is itself a *value*: 'The art of constructing reliable narrators is largely that of mastering all of oneself in order to project the *persona*, the second self, that really belongs in the book' (*RF*, p. 83). The function of reliable commentary is to shape the beliefs of the reader, in part by convincing him that the material is morally significant.

With its precise control of narrative distance, its lucid moral vision, and deft ironic tone, *Emma* provides an ideal example for his critical approach and, in particular, the concept of implied author. Booth cogently argues that the implied author represents Jane Austen within the form of the novel, and that Austen's decisions on what to reveal and what to withhold are essential to the values of *Emma*. Booth's focus is not on intention in the biographical sense, but on revealed intention in the text; while Jane Austen never proposed a narrative theory, and we cannot know 'whether Jane Austen was entirely conscious of her own artistry', she is 'one of the unquestionable masters of the rhetoric of narration' (*RF*, p. 244). He shows how Austen's decisions about point of view shape our reading: 'Nothing Knightley says can be beside the point. Each affirmation of a value, each accusation of error is in itself an action in the plot' (*RF*, p. 253). We respond to the implied author as a character. In *Emma*, as in *Tom Jones*, the implied author is a paragon: 'She is, in short, a perfect human being, within the concept of perfection established by the book she writes' (*RF*, p. 265). He demonstrates how Austen's novel presents 'a much more detailed ordering of values than any conventional public philosophy of her time could provide' (*RF*, p. 262). Booth's discussion of Austen's control of distance in *Emma* serves as a rejoinder to those who feel that every work is open and problematic.

Reading a critic at his best can also reveal his limitations because a compelling argument for one approach may deflect him from noticing the possibilities of others. Thus, we might note, Booth does not speak as precisely as he might about the 'rightness' of the final marriage. It is not enough to say, 'We do not ordinarily like to encounter perfect endings in our novels – even in the sense of "perfectedness" or completion, the sense obviously intended by Jane Austen' (*RF*, p. 260). Endings in fiction are crucial to our response to novels and have a disproportionate effect upon our memory of the whole and to our perception of the moral vision of a work. The ending of *Emma* works as the perfect fulfilment of our expectations; in Aristotelian terms, it is necessary and probable.

III

The Rhetoric of Fiction enacts the rhetorical principles for which Booth is arguing. His implied voice is humane, learned, poised, gently authoritative, logical, and, yes, insistent on making moral distinctions. Booth engages us readers as a reasonable man who respects us and wants to share with us his reading and thinking. By referring not merely to his vast literary experience, but to ordinary life experience, he presumes the continuity between reading and living, and the importance of reading well to living well. For Booth believes that reading is a mode of understanding, and understanding is the highest good. His conception of the author–reader relationship and his own relationship to his readers are based on a tradition of manners and morals that values sincerity, maturity, integrity, and dignity. As a critic he practices the social amenities and enacts the subtle moral distinctions that he admires in fiction. Despite occasional lapses, he demonstrates in his work the civilized virtues of good will, tolerance, and honesty. Booth has been accused of dogmatism, but his moderate tone, at least until the final chapters, and his ability to respond to diverse if not all kinds of narration, belie this. Does not Booth aspire to the position he ascribes to the narrator of *Tom Jones*? 'The author is always there on his platform to remind us, through his wisdom and benevolence, of what human life ought to be and might be' (*RF*, p. 217). Like Fielding's host he is presenting a smorgasbord for the readers, gently urging them to discriminate between morsels, to reject this one and savour that one in order to educate subtly their moral taste. Or he recalls the voice of Austen's mature moral imagination, gently showing us the difference between pride and perspicacity.

Booth successfully examines such diverse novels as *Emma*, *Tristram Shandy*, and *Tom Jones* because he allows each of these books to generate its own aesthetic assumptions. In a sense, Part II, 'The Author's Voice in Fiction', is an essay on three major English novels written before 1820, and this restricted focus may be a limitation. It is certainly true that Booth is more comfortable with neoclassic works whose lucid, precise, logical rhetoric; stress upon communication; and articulated moral vision are accessible to his method. Even in periods prior to our own, he argues, the use of authorial silence has produced confusion. Showing that confusion is not restricted to the current period of fragmented moral and aesthetic values enables him to make the point that he is speaking about problems inherent in this technique. While Part III addresses the difficulties in twentieth-century fiction when the author begins to withdraw from his work, Booth might have done more with the Victorian novel as a transitional form between the neoclassical novel as moral philosophy and the modern novel as psychic and moral quest.

I think we need to go beyond Booth in order to differentiate between kinds of implied authors. Some authors may be clearly conveying values as they control the narrator as in *Tom Jones* or *Emma*, but others may, especially in more modern works, be seeking values through a surrogate, as Conrad does with Marlow, or through both the narrative voice and the major characters, as in *The Rainbow* or *Ulysses*. Booth does not convincingly discuss works where the author is writing to discover his values and to define his psyche, and he some-times simplifies the distinction between the expressive and rhetorical aspects of a work. To define the presence of the implied author – the degree of his involvement, the kind of involvement – we need to know something about the author's life and the time in which he lived. For the implied author is also the disguise for the author's repressed and sublimated 'real' self, and the reader feels that presence, too, particularly in modern authors. To experience fully that unacknow-ledged 'real' self, it is often essential to know the author's other works, biography, and letters. That knowledge enables the reader to under-stand ambiguous issues and difficult passages; it also gives the reader the tools to discover complexities of a text where it may appear that none exist. Booth concedes that 'The emotions and judgments of the implied author are . . . the very stuff out of which great fiction is made,' but I would add 'and real' after 'implied' (*RF*, p. 86). The real author may be immersed in a quest for self-definition, and he may be using his art to find refuge from the compelling problems in his life. When the author is in crisis, the distinction between the real and implied author may at times dissolve and blur; or, rather the author's effort to objectify himself and to create an implied author may become part of the drama.

As I have argued elsewhere, in many modern novels, including *Jude the Obscure*, *Sons and Lovers*, *Ulysses* and *The Rainbow*, the author has not 'mastered' himself and has allowed, consciously or unconsciously, the process of understanding himself to become part of the novel.[15] *Sons and Lovers* is better because we see an author struggling to come to terms with Paul. Yet the self that Lawrence reveals is different from the one he thinks he is presenting. *Lady Chatterley's Lover* fails, according to Booth, because 'no literary technique can conceal from us the confused and pretentious little author who is implied in too many parts of the book' (*RF*, p. 81). But that 'little author', I would suggest, is precisely the self-dramatizing figure in the process of creating himself that Booth's theory gives short shrift. Booth has a distinct preference for a second self that excludes the author's doubts and anxieties, as if he accepted the insistence of the early Eliot upon the separation of the man who suffers and the poet who creates. Thus Booth oversimplifies the distinction between expressive and rhetorical aspects of a work when he writes: 'To express this *public* self and to affect a public made up of similar selves become identical processes, and the distinction between expressive and rhetorical theories of literature disappears' (*RF*, p. 109).

Booth's analyses of James and Joyce, as well as other modern writers, are sometimes informed by a nostalgia for both different aesthetic values and different moral ones. He indicts authors for having failed to *articulate* to the reader their moral vision. He does not like the ambiguity – intentional or unintentional – of modern literature because it implies for him a breakdown in values. With characteristic clarity, he argues that the 'difficulty' of reading modern fiction – and 'difficulty' means the inability to discover the meaning intended by the author – derives from three sources: 'There is no warning, either explicitly or in the form of gross disparity of word and deed; the relationship of the ironic narrator to the author's norms is an extremely complex one, and the norms are themselves subtle and private; and the narrator's own mental vitality dominates the scene and wins our sympathy' (*RF*, p. 324). Speaking disparagingly of 'prevailing neutralists theories', Booth would return to a time when art's moral purpose was acknowledged (*RF*, p. 385). Like Arnold and Leavis, Booth believes in the moral function of art: he equates 'writing well' with presenting a coherent moral vision, with 'successful ordering of your reader's view of a fictional world. . . . The artist has a moral obligation, contained as an essential part of his aesthetic obligation to "write well", to do all that is possible in any given instance to realize his world as he intends it' (*RF*, p. 388).

For Booth, Joyce is particularly guilty of moral ambiguity. Commenting on the critical controversy surrounding the ending of *A Portrait of the Artist as a Young Man*, Booth writes: 'Unless we are willing to retreat into babbling and incommunicable relativism, we cannot believe that it is *both* a portrait of the prisoner freed *and* a portrait of the soul placing itself in chains' (*RF*, p. 328). By ignoring the book's expressive qualities, Booth fails to see that the novel dramatizes Joyce's efforts to resolve the problem. Booth resents *Ulysses* because the implications of the ending cannot be agreed upon by competent critics: 'Can two readers be said to have read the same book if one thinks it ends affirmatively and the other sees the ending as pessimistic?' (*RF*, p. 325). (We can respond in the affirmative and ask, 'What about *Clarissa* and *Bleak House*?')

Sometimes Booth confuses his moral and aesthetic standards. When he disapproves of a book's themes, Booth disavows the novel's rhetorical effects and substitutes his own judgments. At such points he judges the imagined world according to his personal standards of sane and moral behaviour. He insists that we must never surrender our moral judgment to the text or to the author: '[T]o claim that we can make ourselves into objective, dispassionate, thoroughly tolerant readers is in the final analysis nonsense' (*RF*, p. 147). He objects to those modern quest novels in which the narrator does not define the values which the character needs to discover to make his life whole or to grow into moral maturity. Finally, Booth is an aesthetic pluralist and a moral absolutist. Booth's own judgments are not simply in terms of artistic integrity, but also in terms of his concepts of true, sincere, honest, and humane behaviour. His own moral norms are derived from the Judeo–Christian tradition; when these norms are threatened or outraged in the face of his perception of nihilism, relativism, or narcissism, he criticizes author and text. As E. D. Hirsch has written, for Wayne Booth, 'If an author does not implicitly take an ethical stance, and if that stance is not one we can respect, then his devices will not effectively work upon us'.[16] Thus Booth's failure to deal sympathetically with ambiguous texts and with uncertainties and excesses within texts is less methodological than personal, resulting from his values and temperament. While he is less tolerant of novels that do not make their moral standards explicit, his rhetorical method would have worked for these texts were he to have used it consistently. One has only to look at casebooks on *A Portrait of the Artist as a Young Man* or *The Turn of the Screw* to see how subsequent critics have used this method to approach the meaning and define the values of some of the very modern texts that trouble him.

Indeed, as he discusses modern works, his objections to their moral opacity conflict with his aesthetic appreciation of their irony. For he acknowledges that authorial reticence may enhance our pleasure: 'We find our ironic pleasure heightened as we travel with less sympathetic protagonists whose faults are never described directly' (*RF*, p. 306). And, indeed in *A Rhetoric of Irony*, he is more open-minded about modern works: 'We should be able to accept, in novels, plays, and poems, the emotional power and interest of many views which we think untrue. . . . The totally ironic view is, we should know by now, one of the plausible views of the human condition; intelligent people have held it in the past and will hold it in the future, and it is thus not inherently ridiculous for an author to ask us to take it seriously' (*RI*, pp. 276–7).

Nothwithstanding the aforementioned problems, the effect *The Rhetoric of Fiction* had upon readers and teachers of fiction can hardly be overestimated. Quite simply, Booth called attention to narrative technique as communication and persuasion. He has provided a model for discussing literary works in terms of their meaning and effects. Highlighted by *The Rhetoric of Fiction*, his career has eloquently and compellingly demonstrated that reading is a dialogue between author and reader, and that the author's meaning can be accurately recovered. But more broadly, in all his work Booth's major assumption is that 'not just the practice of literary criticism but life itself can and should be enhanced by looking to our language' (*RI*, p. xii).

IV

The second edition (1983), except for a fifty-seven page Afterword, and a supplementary bibliography compiled by James Phelan, is virtually the same as the original 1961 edition. The Afterword puts what James would call the 'finer discrimination' on some of Booth's major ideas and answers some of the objections that have been raised. The avowed purpose of the Afterword is to 'extend and clarify' the book (*RF*, p. 402). For the most part the Afterword is a series of discrete footnotes to the original edition, footnotes that reflect the evolution of Booth's thinking since the original publication. In his

Afterword, Booth reaffirms his ties to the Chicago Aristotelians, expressing surprise that his readers had not fully understood his intellectual heritage.

The Afterword is often more an apologia than an argument, and it does not substantially change either the importance or the limitations of the book. Yet it is very much worth having Booth's second thoughts. For one thing, he provides an interesting and potentially important chart of the various possible authors and readers, although the chart really should have been presented in a well-argued chapter of its own. And he adopts from Peter Rabinowitz the valuable distinction between the authorial audience, which knows that the events of a story are false, and the audience, which 'unlike the authorial audience and the breathing reader, believe that the events of the story are real' (*RF*, p. 423). In 1983 Booth is more aware of the role of silence in defining the reader: 'The reader whom the implied author *writes* to can be found as much in the text's silences as in its overt appeals' (p. 423). Finally, by applying to Beckett's recent novella *Company* many of the same sentences and phrases with which he had discussed a Boccaccio tale in the first chapter, he demonstrates that his method is applicable to the struggles and suffering of the morally and spiritually confused narrators of modern texts.

V

It might be valuable to see how *The Rhetoric of Fiction* could take part in a dialogue with more recent critical theory. E. D. Hirsch has best summarized the challenge to those who believe with Booth that the author's meaning is accessible to the attentive and discerning reader:

> Some French theorists, Derrida and Foucault, for instance, along with their American disciples, hold to the doctrine that since genuine knowledge of an author's meaning is impossible, all textual commentary is therefore really fiction or poetry. Emancipated by this insight, we can face the *écriture* of the past without illusion, as representing no stable or accessible meaning. We can write about writing with new-found creativity and freedom, knowing that we ourselves are creating a new fiction which will itself be fictionalized by those who read us. The challenge is to make these fictions creatively, interestingly, valuably.[17]

According to these critics, since there is neither hope nor purpose in trying to approach the meaning of a text, we can virtually make our own text. Thus the reader, not the author, becomes the central figure in giving a text meaning. Booth would not agree with Jonathan Culler that 'the major task of criticism [is to make] the text interesting, [to combat] . . . the boredom which lurks behind every work, waiting to move in if reading goes astray or founders'.[18] For Booth, the critic has a more modest task of discovering the author's intended meaning by responding to specific effects created by the author.

To Culler's objection that the convention of limited point of view may be seen as 'a last-ditch strategy for humanizing writing and making personality the focal point of the text', Booth offers a more inclusive system that considers limited point of view as one aspect of narrative technique.[19] To Barthes' view that 'Writing becomes truly writing only when it prevents one from answering the question, "who is speaking" ',[20] Booth offers a method that stresses the primacy of two questions: 'Who is speaking to whom?' and, 'For what purpose?' To Derrida's distinction between two kinds of interpretation: ' "The one tries to decipher, dreams of deciphering a truth or an origin which lies outside the realm of signs and their play, and it experiences the need to interpret as a kind of exile', an exclusion from the original plenitude that it seeks; the other accepts its active, creative function and joyfully proceeds without looking back',[21] Booth insists that intelligibility and recovery of the meaning intended by the author are values. For Culler, identifying narrators is a process of naturalizing fiction, a process that tends to emphasize the representative at the expense of 'the strange, the formal [and] the fictional'[22]. But, for Booth, the major function of literary criticism is to explain the text in terms of values and experiences that are common to author, reader, and critic; he seeks to 'naturalize' texts by proposing how they create a purposeful and intensive response. And in practice this is not a restrictive strategy for it necessarily includes aspects of the strange (experiences that defy the ordinary), the formal (aesthetic organization of the experience), and the fictive (imaginary experience which, in the form of dream, fantasy, and plans, is part of human life)'. While explaining how works communicate, Booth does not stress the moments of incongruity and excess valued by recent criticism; but he does try to resolve these moments and indicate why they fall short as communication. For Booth, the language of a text *creates* an intensive and purposeful world; in other terms, words are a *sign* of an imagined world, but, once brought into life by language, that world displaces the reader's consciousness of the words as *signifiers*. The text's silences, gaps, and opacities are important insofar as they indicate qualities about the imagined world. However, our attention to the text itself must not take precedence over the ontology signified by that language, for with E. D. Hirsch, Booth would deny that linguistic signs can somehow generate their own distinct meaning as self-sufficient objects.

We might ask why it has become fashionable to focus upon a few moments of doubt and confusion in otherwise unified and lucid texts and whether this does not lead to critical psychosis. As we doubt our social and political standards, as we doubt ourselves, it is hardly surprising that we seek to make discontinuity a model of our thinking, or that we search for the irrational or incoherent in the text. Instead of reaching towards the reality behind literary texts or participating in the imagined worlds created by texts, some critics read to validate *a priori* theories that all works are 'about' reading and writing. In the process, what the author wrote becomes less significant than the moments when the reader – however ignorant he may be of the author's life and other works – perceives inconsistency and incoherence. Criticism becomes a way not of discovering what texts mean but of importing excitement into the life of the mind by raising the stakes of intellectual activity so that it seems to resemble the more 'serious' world of sexuality and politics. Thus terms like 'subversive' text and 'guilty' text have an odd appeal to some academics. A major figure in avant-garde criticism, who customarily speaks dismissively of 'old-fashioned humanism', hyperbolically remarked at a recent conference, 'Universities are constructed for teachers to bully young readers'. A word like 'bully' imports into the academic world the community tensions and political violence that pervade the outside world. Moreover, following Barthes' *Le Plaisir du texte* (1973), it has become fashionable to use a sexual analogy to describe the interpretive process by which the mind has intercourse with the text. Booth's stress on the author's effort to create readers through effects and his belief that books are purposeful imitations of the real world stand as alternatives to such criticism.

NOTES

1. I have used the letters *RF* to designate *The Rhetoric of Fiction*, 2nd edn (University of Chicago Press, 1983) and *RI* to designate *The Rhetoric of Irony* (University of Chicago Press, 1974). Except for the Afterword, every passage I cite is the same in the original 1961 edition of *The Rhetoric of Fiction*.
2. *Novel*, 1:2 (Winter, 1968) pp. 105–17. Subsequent references to this

article are designated by *Novel* and included within the text. The essay has been reprinted in *Now Don't Try to Reason with Me: Essays and Ironies for a Credulous Age* (University of Chicago Press, 1970).

3. Arnold Kettle, *An Introduction to the English Novel*, 2 vols (New York: Harper, 1960) orig. edn 1951, I. 13.
4. Richard McKeon, *Thought, Action, and Passion* (University of Chicago Press, 1960) p. 215.
5. McKeon, pp. 215, 113.
6. R. S. Crane, 'The Concept of Plot and the Plot of *Tom Jones*', *critics and Criticism*, ed. R. S. Crane (University of Chicago Press, 1952) pp. 621–2.
7. For Booth's recent account of the Chicago school, see his 'Between Two Generations: the Heritage of the Chicago School', *Profession 82*, pp. 19–26.
8. 'How Not to Use Aristotle: *the Poetics*', in *Now Don't Try to Reason with Me* (University of Chicago Press, 1970) p. 109.
9. *The Sewanee Review*, 53 (1945) 227–40, 433–56, 643–53; repr. and rev. in his *The Widening Gyre: Crisis and Mastery in Modern Literature* (New Brunswick: Rutgers University Press, 1963).
10. *The Philosophy of Literary Form* (1941), quoted in Stanley Edgar Hyman's *The Armed Vision* (New York: Alfred A. Knopf, 1948) pp. 385–6.
11. *Critical Understanding: the Power and Limits of Pluralism* (University of Chicago Press, 1977) pp. 45, 100.

In the 1967 retrospective essay in *Novel* Booth defines what a rhetoric of fiction is in terms which acknowledge his debt to Burke:

> *The Rhetoric of Fiction* asks, as Kenneth Burke has been doing in a different way, that we think of the poem not primarily as *meaning* or *being* but as *doing*. In place of analyses of poetic form, descriptions and interpretations of types of action or plot (with their power to produce an effect indicated, but not exclusively dominant), I look at effects, at techniques for producing them, and at readers and their inferences. In place of a classification of literary kinds, I give an analysis of *interests* and (as in the *Emma* chapter) manipulations of interests. In place of an analysis into the poetic elements of the internal structure (plot, character, thought, diction) my elements become identical with the three that one finds in all rhetorics, author, work, audience: authors and their various surrogates and spokesmen; works, and their various arrangements for effect; audiences, and their preconceptions and processes of inference. (*Novel*, p. 113)

12. 'How to Use Aristotle', *Now Don't Try to Reason with Me*, p. 129.
13. E. D. Hirsch, Jr, *The Aims of Interpretation*, (University of Chicago Press, 1976) p. 156.
14. E. D. Hirsch, Jr, *Validity in Interpretation*. (New Haven and London: Yale University Press, 1967) pp. 10, 26.
15. See my "I Was the World in Which I Walked": the Transformation of the British Novel,' *The University of Toronto Quarterly*, 51:3 (Spring 1982) pp. 279–97.

16. *The Aims of Interpretation*, pp. 125–6.
17. *The Aims of Interpretation*, p. 147.
18. Jonathan Culler, *Structuralist Poetics* (Ithaca, New York: Cornell University Press, 1974) p. 262.
19. Culler, *Structuralist Poetics*, p. 201.
20. See Culler, p. 200; Culler is paraphrasing a passage from *S/Z* which he has quoted on his p. 159.
21. See Culler, pp. 247–8. The quotation within the Culler quote is taken from Derrida, *Writing and Difference*; the rest of the passage is Culler's.
22. Culler, p. 134.

8 The Consolation of Form: the Theoretical and Historical Significance of Frank Kermode's *The Sense of an Ending*

I

The publication of Frank Kermode's *The Sense of an Ending: Studies in the Theory of Fiction* in 1967 caused considerable excitement among literary faculties in America. For at a time when the relevance of literary study was being called into question by the Vietnam War, the Anti-War protest movement, and the resulting fissures between university and society, Kermode's book argued that literary study was central to our lives; or, as Kermode puts it in his first paragraph, to 'making sense of the ways we try to make sense of our lives' (p. 3).[1] He shows that our imaginative responses to life (including the category of life which we call literature) are shaped by our condition of mortality and by our desperate desire to repress, overcome and ignore that condition by means of sense-making structures provided by our imagination. For, we are 'in the middest, desiring these moments of significance which harmonize origin and end' (p. 48).

Some historical perspective is necessary, and my perspective is that of one who was in graduate school from 1963 until I came to teach at Cornell as an assistant professor in 1968. In a sense the early 1960s were the Golden Age of graduate education in the Humanities. Attracted by financial support, students flocked to graduate schools. Some of the fellowships were underwritten by the government, under the auspices of the National Defense Act, to fill a genuine need for college teachers. Along with generous fellowships and assistantships, rising salaries, and the breakdown of social barriers opened university teaching in the humanities to a much more varied ethnic and economic mix, a mix that for a variety of reasons other fields had begun to achieve somewhat sooner. A plentiful job market fuelled by rising enrolments and concomitant expansion, including the opening of new branches of state universities handsomely underwritten by state legislatures, provided ample job opportunities for all but the most unemployable. At times, universities recruited students finishing Ph.D.'s the way industry now recruits senior engineering students. Graduate programmes also offered an exemption from the draft, because university teaching had been among those jobs designated under the National Defense Act as crucial to the nation's welfare. Originally, this exemption merely relieved one from an inconvenient burden. However, with the involvement of American troops in Southeast Asia, the exemption provided a refuge not only from the strong possibility of being maimed or killed, but it also provided a free zone for those who did not wish to go underground or into exile. Studying literature became a way of joining this generation's version of the Abraham Lincoln Brigade without suffering, as did those idealists of the 1930s, the inconvenience of disrupting one's life. Campus leaders of the anti-war movement often were graduate students and assistant professors in the humanities. In response, many local draft boards no longer recognized universities as inviolable sanctuaries and withdrew exemptions.

Given these circumstances, it is not surprising that English departments in the mid-1960s suffered from a kind of intellectual schizophrenia. On the one hand they were intensely political. On the other hand, as the original energy of the New Criticism lapsed, graduate programmes seemed bogged down in what I call critical nominalism, the watchword of which was 'A poem must not mean but be.' All too often the study and teaching of literature were reduced to close reading of a work for its own sake without reference to either a theoretical or historical framework. Thus in 1966 there was a powerful urge to discover a justification for literary study. Or, in Kermode's terms, literature students needed new fictions to make sense of their lives.

I can recall the enthusiasm with which graduate students and young faculty read *The Sense of an Ending* as a subversive book that challenged the orthodoxy of the day. Here was a literary critic who did not merely present 'readings', but spoke eloquently about the importance of literature in our lives. For Kermode argued that literary works are fictions that help us order our lives in the face of death and crisis. Implicitly and explicitly, Kermode made a statement about the appropriate concerns of the study of literature. He demonstrated that literary criticism need not be merely a series of moves rather mechanical in nature, but could be an avenue to philosophical and historical understanding. Graduate students and academics enjoyed being told that the study of literary criticism had something to do with the real world, and that not only imaginative writing but even criticism had importance – the buzzword by the late sixties was 'relevance' – to the world of action. That a critic could discuss how man lives and what he lives for appealed to those in universities who had begun to lose confidence in their function. To be sure, there were important exceptions, but I am speaking of the general malaise among young academics whose careers and lives were just beginning to take shape and who fretted about the intellectual sterility of their activities in the face of nightly pictures on the network news of carnage and devastation.

II

The Sense of an Ending is Kermode's elaborate response to the inexplicable evil of the Holocaust and the World War and the knowledge that the Post-War world had acquired the potential to destroy itself instantly. Kermode assumes that we can no longer believe that we live in a providentially ordered world or a benevolent cosmos. Faced with a reality that promises evil and offers no salvation, man has an existential need to give shape and meaning to his life: 'Whether you think time will have to stop or that the world is eternal; there is still a need to speak humanly of a life's importance in relation to it – a need in the moment of existence to belong, to be related to a beginning and to an end' (p. 4).

Our needs for fictional ends correspond to the needs of prior eras for Apocalypse; we have a 'deep need for intelligible Ends. We project ourselves – a small, humble elect, perhaps – past the End, so as to see the structure whole, a thing we cannot do from our spot of time in the middle' (p. 8). This, of course, happens whenever we hope or dream of our future. For our fictions have and 'must continue to have . . . a real relation to simpler fictions about the world' (p. 6). Kermode takes the biblical story with its beginning, middle, and apocalyptic end as a paradigm because it has provided our Judeo-Christian culture with an imaginative explanation for the conditions of human life on earth:

'Ideally, it is a wholly concordant structure, the end is in harmony with the beginning, the middle with beginning and end. The end, Apocalypse, is traditionally held to resume the whole structure . . .' (p. 6). By 'concordant', Kermode means consistent within itself. According to Kermode, 'to make sense of their span [men] need fictive concords with origins and ends, such as give meaning to lives and to poems' (p. 7).

Kermode takes as his subject the dialogue between the human imagination and the real world. His goal is to relate 'the theory of literary fictions to the theory of fictions in general' (p. 36). Specifically, Kermode urges that the clichés about 'the alienation of the artist' and 'despair at the decay of the world' about which he spoke in his earlier *Romantic Image* (1957) might be reexamined in light of the needs of all men for fictions and of the kinship of mankind's common imaginative activity with artistic activity.[2] Because, he argues, we do not believe in the Christian fictions of death as the birth of the eternal soul and the movement of history towards the fulfilment of Apocalypse, we require literary fictions and history to give us a sense of order: '[Literary fictions] find out about the changing world on our behalf. . . . [T]hey do this, for some of us, perhaps better than history, perhaps better than theology, largely because they are consciously false; but the way to understand their development is to see how they are related to those other fictional systems. It is not that we are connoisseurs of chaos, but that we are surrounded by it, and equipped for coexistence with it only by our fictive powers' (p. 64).

Beginning with the principle that 'there is a humanly needed order which we call form' (p. 123), Kermode is concerned with how and why imagination organizes experience. Man's one possibility for order in his life is not God, but his own imagination. Imagination is a 'form-giving power, an esemplastic power . . . a maker of orders and concords. We apply it to all forces which satisfy the variety of human needs that are met by apparently gratuitous forms. These forms console; if they mitigate our existential anguish it is because we weakly collaborate with them, as we collaborate with language in order to communicate' (p. 144). As readers our imaginations have access to the imaginations of others. Thus literature helps us make sense of the world, and making sense of our world is our primary imaginative activity. Fictional characters give us the opportunity to watch others deal with their mortality as we must in our own lives; for 'What human need can be more profound than to humanize the common death?' (p. 7).

Literary fictions affect our perception and understanding of the conditions in which we live, displacing the concatenation of time with significant structures. Our literary plots provide temporary models of consonance; they are models of the way man makes coherent patterns: 'Men in the middest make considerable imaginative investments in coherent patterns which, by the provision of an end, make possible a satisfying consonance with the origins and with the middle. That is why the image of the end can never be *permanently* falsified' (p. 17). We are naturally sceptical of our fictions and respectful of facts. Yet the facts of life on earth insist upon certain kinds of fictions: 'We think in terms of crisis rather than temporal ends; and make much of subtle disconfirmation and elaborate peripeteia. And we concern ourselves with the conflict between the deterministic pattern any plot suggests, and the freedom of persons within that plot to choose and so to alter the structure, the relations of beginning, middle, and end' (p. 30). Conceding that we need truth and reality, as well as fiction, Kermode stresses that when we are awake and sane, 'there is a recurring need for adjustments in the interests of reality as well as of control' (p. 17). Fiction imitates history by providing concords 'between past, present, and future, [by providing] significance to mere chronicity' (p. 56). But because we know that this order or any order defies our sense of reality, our imaginative patterns give way in our waking moments to our knowledge of reality.

Kermode equates form with order. In our present moment of crisis – when we do not believe in providential history or death as the birth of the eternal soul – form consoles. It does so because 'form' is 'systematic submission' to 'fictive patterns' (p. 57). And these patterns provide the order we so desperately need. For the *as if* of fiction to be more than 'mere fantasy,' the making of a fiction must not only impose form, but include contingency (p. 146). In contrast to the then prevailing spatial conceptions of form which borrowed their metaphors from the visual arts and spoke of the architectonics of literary works, Kermode insists that form has a temporal dimension. It is 'an inter-connexion of parts all mutually implied: a duration (rather than a space) organizing the moment in terms of the end, giving meaning to the interval between *tick* and *tock* because we humanly do not want it to be an indeterminate interval between the *tick* of birth and the *tock* of death' (pp. 57–8). In particular Kermode stressed that narrative was linear and temporal. It followed that we must think of reading as an active process within time, not simply as a response organized after the physical act of turning pages is completed.

But we might ask, need form as duration be conceived in quite so rigid terms? Once we free form from spatiality and give it a temporal dimension and imagine it as a process and a sequence, should we not think of it as flexible and variable rather than rigid and patterned? We need to stress the varying degrees of submission or organization within texts. Form at any given moment is a series of elastic systems, some functioning far more tautly than others; put another way, some facts resist the predominant concords of a text. On a first reading of *Ulysses*, for example, when we first meet Bloom or Stephen (particularly if we have not read *Portrait*) much of the material resists taut systematic organization, despite the patterning of the *Odyssey*. Upon rereading, much more but by no means all of the material (for example, the catalogues in 'Cyclops' or in 'Ithaca') is organized into sequential narrative. Moreover, narrative material signifies differently; it is not simply that it proposes a hierarchy of meanings, but that it means in several different ways simultaneously. A unit of narrative as short as a paragraph can present necessary background material; atmosphere for a scene or character's mood; information about an action; exploration of a character's psyche; insight into the moral and intellectual fabric of a community; and indications of the attitudes and values of the narrative voice. But the meaning of each unit is distributed differentially among these various components. Furthermore, the ordering principles of narration may turn inchoate and recalcitrant material into grist for its mill, homogenizing and simplifying the story. Conversely, the story may resist form and reveal a problematic status; in current terms, each may deconstruct the other.

But what do we do with passages that resist or undermine our systems of perception? Kermode's theory ignores the fact that the fabric of prose fiction – the multiplicity and randomness of everyday life, and the descriptive observations that the multiplicity and randomness require – resists pattern and challenges the reader to define its significance. And when passages or details go beyond (or fall short, or seem inappropriate, or miss entirely) the requirements of the story and the apparent demands of form or discourse, the reader struggles with the resistance to pattern. In his subsequent work, particularly *The Genesis of Secrecy* (1979), Kermode realized that the urge for order may conflict with the existential desire to live poised dangerously between order and disorder. Put another way, the reader may be more interested in ghostlier demarcations and keener sounds than the order imposed by sequence.

Kermode heightened our awareness of time in fiction. He prefers the term 'time-redeeming' for 'spatial': 'The questionable critical practice of calling literary structures *spatial* . . . is a critical fiction which has regressed into myth' (p. 52). It is time that is central to 'the concords books arrange between beginning, middle, and end' (p. 178): 'Ignoring [time], we fake to achieve the forms absent from the continuous world; we regress towards myth, out of this time into that time. Consulting it, we set the word against the word, and create the need for difficult concords in our fictions' (p. 176). Kermode's distinction between *chronos*, passing time, and *kairos*, significant time, has become influential. It enables us to see that 'in every plot there is an escape from chronicity, and so, in some measure, a deviation from this norm of "reality" ' (p. 50). It qualitatively defines the author's and reader's epiphany of significant relationships.

Kermode used the term *aevum* to talk about things which 'can be perpetual without being eternal' (p. 72). As he wrote in a later *Critical Inquiry* piece, 'We have, that is, experiences which, though they do not belong to the temporal sequence, are undoubtedly within the element of time; they do not belong to eternity and they do not belong to space.'[3] The concept of *aevum* enables Kermode to retain a sense that characters in novels are independent of *our* time and succession even while, within the ontology of the work, they operate in time and succession; put another way, although characters are fictive they operate in conditions which approximate the real. Speaking of how Marcel's life comes together on the climactic day of *Remembrance of Things Past*, Kermode writes, 'The experiences reserved for permanent meaning, carried out of the flux of time, surely do not make a pattern in space; they punctuate that order of time, free of contingency, in which only the ur-novel wholly exists, the *durée* if you like, or the *aevum*' (p. 178). In a sense, as readers we always experience *aevum*.

Notwithstanding its usefulness, Kermode's distinction between *kairos* and *chronos* creates some problems. There are other conditions besides pure *chronos* and pure *kairos* and there are degress of losing ourselves in *kairos* and suspending our sense of time; for there are differences both in the duration and intensity of moments of *kairos*. It seems a simplification to say that in Richardson, where we are relentlessly conscious as readers of passing time, 'everything became *kairos* by virtue of the way in which letters coincided with critical moments' (p. 51). We should think of a spectrum stretching from the pedestrian, even tedious moments that resist the ordering of form (or discourse) to the kind of heightened moments, exemplified in

Lawrence's *The Rainbow*, when Tom and Lydia achieve transfiguration in their passionate embrace, a transfiguration symbolized by the climactic rainbow image at the end of the first section. Although Kermode led us to distinguish between kinds of time in fiction (and life), it would have been valuable had he explored in greater depth distinctions among kinds of time: the imagined effect of time on experience in the fictive world of the story; narrative or 'discourse time' – disruption of chronology, omissions, extended focus on some episodes and summary of others. He should have addressed, too the temporal experience of reading (and rereading) a text, a concept which is far more complex than simply the time it takes to read.

In the late sixties, Kermode's argument that we read because we *need to* appealed to young humanists. Readers, he contends, demand 'constantly changing, constantly more subtle, relationships between a fiction and the paradigms, and . . . this expectation enables a writer much inventive scope as he works to meet and transcend it' (p. 24). Since each era has its own needs, 'the fictions must change, or if they are fixed, the interpretations must change' (p. 24). For one thing, we read fictions differently as we ourselves change; for another, each era reads the same fictions differently. Fictions and reality affect one another: 'When the fictions change . . . the world changes in step with them' (p. 42). Thus because we change and the 'reality' we experience changes, the 'concord-fictions' change. In recent time, literary fictions changed in response to a change in the fiction-making from the one that accounts for 'a common End' to those fictions that account for personal death, crisis, or epoch (p. 35). We think we are in 'eternal transition', and 'perpetual crises': 'The fiction of transition is our way of registering the conviction that the end is immanent rather than imminent; it reflects our lack of confidence in ends, our mistrust of the apportioning of history to epochs of this and that' (p. 101).

Kermode emphasizes the reader's role in giving meaning to literary texts and thus questions the New Critical and neo-Aristotelian notion that meaning inheres in the text as a result of the author's intended or unintended pattern. When he writes 'the making of a novel is partly the achievement of readers as well as writers' (p. 139), he anticipates reader-response criticism, which emphasizes the 'sense-making' of the reader. It followed that if each of us responded to fictions according to our needs, then each reader would produce a different text. And, perhaps encouraged by Barthes and Derrida, Kermode's criticism moved somewhat in that direction. In *The Genesis of Secrecy* (1979), he stresses that literary texts, like biblical texts, contain 'secrets' which are at odds with 'sequence' and contain hidden meanings that challenge and undermine traditional narrativity. The secrets may be missed by those who read chronologically through a work and attend only to story. The stress is more on the reader's creativity and less on the text, although Kermode continues to insist on the reader's collaboration with the text.[4]

III

It is important to understand the critical and historical context in which Kermode wrote because he is engaging in a dialogue with the influential critical perspectives of the post-war period. Kermode wanted to place himself in the humanist tradition, but to separate himself from the critical nominalism of the New Critics for whom close analyses often was an end not a means. Kermode wants to retain the ontological perspective of those who reinvigorated New Criticism for the novel – Mark Schorer, Albert Guerard, and Dorothy Van Ghent; thus he sees novels as self-enclosed, imagined fictive universes with their own cosmology, geography, and moral geography; as he puts it, 'the book is a bibliocosm' (p. 52). But, unlike some prior ontologists, especially Van Ghent, who tended at least partially to see the world as arrested in spatial configurations (this in part because of her debt to Gestalt psychology), Kermode shows how temporal expectations are crucial to our perceptions: 'The "virtual" time of books . . . is a kind of man-centered model of world-time' (p. 52).

Part of the historical importance of Kermode's book was to contest Joseph Frank's widely accepted idea that literary structures, particularly modern ones, were conceived and experienced in spatial terms. Frank had argued that in the great modern writers,

> Past and present are seen spatially, locked in a timeless unit which, while it may accentuate surface differences, eliminates any feeling of historical sequence by the very act of juxtaposition. The objective historical imagination . . . is transformed in these writers into the mythical imagination for which historical time does not exist – the imagination that sees the actions and events of a particular time merely as the bodying forth of eternal prototypes. These prototypes are created by transmuting the time-world of history into the timeless world of myth, and it is this timeless world of myth forming the common content of modern literature, which finds its appropriate esthetic expression in spatial form.[5]

When Kermode draws a crucial distinction between fiction and myth and belittled myths as 'degenerate' fictions, Kermode has in mind what he considers to be Frank's spatial myth and perhaps Frye's archetypes as articulated in *Anatomy of Criticism* (1957).

Myth operates within the diagrams of ritual, which presupposes total and adequate explanations of things as they are and were; it is a sequence of radically unchangeable gestures. Fictions are for finding things out, and they change as the needs of sense-making change. Myths are the agents of stability, fictions the agents of change. Myths call for absolute, fictions for conditional assent. Myths make sense in terms of a lost order of time, *illud tempus* as Eliade calls it; fictions, if successful, make sense of the here and now, *hoc tempus*. (p. 39)

When we forget that fictions are tools for making sense, they degenerate into myths, and 'are not consciously held to be fictive' (p. 39). Because we can provisionally give our assent to fictions and then withdraw it, fiction-making is a *process* of mind and thus a temporal activity. But, myth-making, on the Frank or Frye model, is a 'spatialization' because it arrests phenomena and imposes arbitrary shapes in the form of categories.

Frank has insisted in 'Spatial Form: an Answer to Critics' (*Critical Inquiry* [Winter 1977]) that spatialization does not abolish time and that Kermode's own concept of '*aevum*' is a spatial one. He praises Kermode for the insight that 'Plots therefore seem to work *against* the flow of time, and to keep alive, or to create, an indigenous kind of unity which overarches and reshapes the constraints of pure temporal linearity.'[6] In fact, spatiality and temporality depend upon one another and cannot be separated. Even a three-dimensional object, such as a sculpture or a painting, exists and is experienced temporally. Conversely, even the most pedestrian moments are not pure duration but have a spatial dimension. Form knits temporal moments into patterns or concordances which, because of their reflexive quality – their references to the past and their anticipation of the future – are experienced spatially. And the concept of *kairos*, significant time, does have an implication of the suspension of our sense of time.

It may be that part of the problem is that Frank is thinking more of the author's activity, his act of creation, and Kermode is thinking more of the reader's perception of and participation in the imagined world which cannot, in his view, exclude the temporal dimension. Both Kermode and Frank could be clearer about whether they are speaking about authors, imagined worlds, or readers. Kermode insists on the distinction between intemporality and temporality, and is reluctant to accept that the necessary complement of time is space and that one cannot be defined without some reference to the other. But surely he wishes us to understand that the fullness of time is defined by its place (or space) within a linear structure. He seems unaware that he himself does not entirely eschew spatialization; '*kairos*' involves an arrest of time, which inevitably takes on a three-dimensionality, and occupies space for reader and writer within an imagined world. Finally, if we perceive significant relations between temporal events, do we not spatialize those events in our mind in the very act of perception?

In part, Kermode meant his book to be a rejoinder to Frye's archetype theory. For Kermode, Frye's categories are limited because they exist in a closed literary universe divorced from reality, a universe which may be coherent in itself but which lacks reference to the real world. Kermode rejects the view that fictions can ignore the objective world and the concomitant view that criticism of literature should create its own ontology. Fiction depends on a continuing dialogue between imagination and reality, a play of mind that never ceases and is continually modifying its perceptions, while myth depends upon imposition of patterned hierarchies. Put another way, fiction is messy and unruly; myth is neat and hygienic.

Because the neo-Aristotelians's influence on literary study has severely diminished, we might forget the importance of that position in 1968. While Kermode lacks the methodological rigour of the Chicago critics and while he later abandoned some of their principles, in *A Sense of an Ending* he is an Aristotelian in a number of ways.

(1) He accepts Aristotle's assumption that literary plots are not mere reflections of the external world. 'The world a novel makes . . . is unlike the world of our common experience because it is created and because it has the potency of a humanly imaginative creation'. (pp. 137–8)

(2) Because plots move through time from beginning to end, ends have a teleological function. What distinguishes novels from life is that 'In a novel the beginning implies the end:. . . . All that seems fortuitous and contingent in what follows is in fact reserved for a later benefaction of significance in some concordant structure' (p. 148). In *Physics* III, 6, Aristotle had written, 'Nothing is complete (*teleion*) which has no end (*telos*); and the end is a limit.'[7]

(3) As for Aristotle, peripeteia or irony of action is essential to a

complex action. Peripeteia is 'a falsification of expectation, so that the end comes as expected, but not in the manner expected' (p. 53). Moreover, the ironic reversal must be necessary and probable: 'The more daring the peripeteia, the more we may feel that the work respects our sense of reality; and the more certainly we shall feel that the fiction under consideration is one of those which, by upsetting the ordinary balance of our naive expectations, is finding something out for us, something *real*' (p. 18).

(4) In part, meaning inheres in the text and depends on how conscious and occasionally unconscious decisions of the author are embodied in the text: 'As soon as it speaks, begins to be a novel, it imposes causality and concordance, development, character, a past which matters and a future within certain broad limits determined by the project of the author rather than that of the characters. They have their choices, but the novel has its end' (p. 140). Kermode examines the effects of these decisions upon readers. In stressing manipulation of expectations, Kermode speaks of *our* responses to urge us that he is describing patterns of imaginative experience common to us all. Much of his argument revolves around how fictions depend upon expectations which in literature and life are shaped by conventions.

(5) He assumes, like Aristotle, that 'It is through character that plot is actualized' (p. 139).

(6) Empiricism and pluralism are preferable to rigid categories and hierarchies. Kermode is Aristotle to Frye's Plato. While Frye sees phenomena as instances of a system, Kermode is interested in fictions in themselves and for what they do.

Kermode is also responding to Auerbach's *Mimesis*, which was an important precursor in its focus on how works internalize the reality of the world in which they are created. Auerbach also insisted that we understand the 'meaning' of narrative in terms of the way that episodes fulfilled expectations of prior episodes. His model was the relationship between the Old and New Testament: The New Testament *required* that the Old Testament be reinterpreted in terms of expectations that the New Testament fulfilled. What Kermode describes as the immanence of the end, the presence of the end, in our lives and reading derives in part from Auerbach's discussion of figural interpretation: 'Figural interpretation establishes a connection between two events or persons in such a way that the first signifies not only itself but also the second, while the second involves or fulfills the first. The two poles of a figure are separated in time but both, being real events or persons, are within temporality.'[8] However, there is a crucial difference between Auerbach and Kermode. Figural interpretation becomes Kermode's 'concords', but his argument depends less on a relationship between different texts and more upon our seeing within literary texts both figurations of our own lives and figurations of the concords we desire. By allowing for the play between reader and text, Kermode opens the window of Auerbach's essentially closed literary universe.

By insisting upon asking what fictions do for us, Kermode, like Arnold, I. A. Richards, and Leavis is very much in the tradition of English utilitarianism and English positivism. We recall I. A. Richards' influential argument that 'pseudo-statements' were the main instruments by which we order our attitudes to one another and the world. For Richards, poetry could not be true except in terms of its own integrity, unity, and necessity, but it is useful as an ordering principle. Kermode argues that fictions have played a *useful* role in man's historical and cultural evolution because their mode of inquiry, their truth of reference, and their internal necessity tell us something about the world. Kermode's inquiry into the history and ambiguity of language is in the English tradition of Richards and Empson, a tradition influenced by A. J. Ayer and the logical positivists as well as traditional Germanic philology. He understands that our reading is a function of 'cultural and linguistic conventions – the shared information codes upon which literature, like any other method of communication, depends' (p. 105). But he is also aware that each of us is a captive of his own linguistic system. Thus he acknowledges in his discussion of *chronos* and *kairos* that we make up words to play our own games.

Despite his modest tone, Kermode along with Frye and Bloom helped change the critics role in England and America from humble scholar-teacher sharing his insights with other readers to the commanding figure who creates in his own romantic agony a system of texts that makes sense to him. Urged on by his rage for order, the critic like the poet is an heroic figure who uses his creative imagination to interpret not only texts but the real world. In this tradition, the models for which include Nietzsche, Freud, and Marx, the critic is a prophetic figure, a *vates*, who dominates the material he discusses.

In *After The New Criticism* (1980), Frank Lentricchia calls Kermode a 'conservative fictionalist'. Because, Lentricchia contends, reality is privileged and horrible, the fictionalist poet and critic seek refuge in fiction-making, which has a kinship with aestheticism and other self-indulgent strategies that turn away from the external world: 'Imagination makes space between us and chaos and thereby grants momentary release from sure engulfment, madness, and death.'[9] What Lentricchia says of Stevens and Frye is apropos of Kermode, too: 'Both Stevens and Frye imply systems of last-ditch humanism in which human desire, conscious of itself as "lack", to cite Sartre's term, and conscious of the ontological nothingness of its images, confronts a grim reality which at every point denies us our needs.'[10] Kermode might respond to Lentricchia that even if man perceives of himself as estranged from any simple plan of God, as a helpless figure in an amoral, indifferent cosmos, he need not seek refuge in solipsisms of art for art's sake, on the one hand, or in desperate existential tightrope-walking, on the other; for man has the potential to establish a working relationship, a dialogue with the not-I-world. Like Stevens, Kermode enacts an imaginative journey which asserts the power of the mind to enlarge freely and creatively the space of the human prison by creating fictions of order, dances of intellectual play, which push aside our thoughts of death, our ultimate destiny. What Kermode says of the *as if* of novels becomes true of the *as if* of criticism: 'The *as if* of the novel consists in a . . . negation of determinism, the establishment of an accepted freedom by magic. We make up *aventures*, invent and ascribe the significance of temporal concords to those "privileged moments" to which we alone award their prestige, make our own human clocks tick in a clockless world' (pp. 135). But unlike Frye, who seeks refuge in a system, and Stevens, who seeks refuge in the play of his imagination, Kermode confronts the chaos boldly and confidently.

Lentricchia reductively describes Kermode's dialogue between fiction and reality in terms of a simple dichotomy. 'Reality is truth *because* we do not create it; our fictions are lies just *because* they are constructions of our consciousness.'[11] Kermode for the most part avoids oversimplifying the dialogue between life and death, time and space, *chronos* and *kairos*, form and content. He is arguing that there are different kinds of truth. He borrows from physics the 'Principle of Complementarity' (what he calls a 'concord-fiction') to argue how 'propositions may even yet be true and false at the same time' (p. 62). Thus a fiction can be both true – to its perceptions of the real world, to the integrity of its own vision, and to the sincerity of its creator – and *false* at the same time.

Criticizing Kermode's argument, Gerald Graff has written, 'It is not clear how fictions can help us make "discoveries" unless they refer to something that is not a fiction, and how anybody can refer to something that is not a fiction in Kermode's epistemological universe is not clear.'[12] But Kermode is clear that what is not a fiction is the amoral indifferent cosmos in which man lives his mortal span. Graff fails to realize that fiction, for Kermode, is a verb (an activity, as to make fictions) as well as a noun and as a verb it enables us to cope with that cosmos. Fiction-making is a process as well as a goal, a process that enables man to take part actively and creatively with the cosmos in the dialogue.

To Graff's objection that he does not show 'how we can choose intelligently between one fiction and others',[13] Kermode might respond that those fictions that depend on taking account of the world out there and its conditions will be least escapist and sentimental and thus the most illuminating. Just because we must create our own order does not mean it has to be solipsistic; it may be part of a pattern of perceptions shared by others. This shared imaginative activity itself becomes a fact within the real world, and creates, despite individual variations, a kind of community of perception beyond the self. For some, this occurs at concerts and performances of plays; perhaps it occurred in New York in 1980 during the monumental Picasso exhibit at the Museum of Modern Art.

IV

Before concluding we should note that in *The Sense of an Ending*, Kermode seems to slip into the habit of measuring value by the extent to which works or movements conform to his patterns. Like Wayne Booth, he is wary of books that do not conform to his own sense of order. To use his terms, at times he lets his fictions of modernism degenerate into myths. Thus he claims that a decadent phase followed the first great moderns of the early twentieth century. Unlike the later avant-garde, those modernists sustain tradition: 'However radical the alterations to traditional procedures implied [in the early modernists], . . . they are extensions, in a recognizable sense, of a shared language' (p. 123). He praises Joyce and Yeats for resisting myths: 'What saved [Yeats] was a confidence basic to the entire European tradition, a confidence in the common language, the vernacular by means of which from day to day we deal with reality as against justice' (p. 107). In other words, Kermode believes, with Eliot, that early modernism preserved its continuity with the past. By contrast, he attacks the avant-garde for its nihilism and triviality, for ignoring the past humanistic cultural heritage as a source of order. Yet at the same time he acknowledges that the avant-garde, particularly Robbe-Grillet, conducts research into the relation between form and reality – which is, of course, Kermode's own subject. When he indicts avant-garde literature for lacking sequence, he seems to be dismissing the possibility that moments of disorder, even chaos, when material resists the sequence of narration and makes its own counter-statement, are part of literature.

Writing in an age of anxiety, Kermode lives with the knowledge that he attributes to De Quincey: 'We accept the knowledge that our inherited ways of echoing the structure of the world have no concord with it, but only, and then under conditions of great difficulty, with the desires of our own minds' (p. 173). In such an age, Kermode implies, the critic cannot be content with simply calling attention to the complexity and subtleties of a literary work. Kermode not only writes with the modesty, manners, and decorum of an English don, but addresses anti-Semitism and Fascism with the intensity and commitment that appealed to those who believe, with Leavis and Trilling, that literature, and even criticism, is central to our culture. Like Arnold, Kermode implies that literature is a surrogate for religion in a faithless age.

One could argue that Kermode's study is a kind of grand romantic metaphor posing as cultural history; for he synthesized philosophy, religion, and history into a fiction which discovers for him concords between literature and life. Kermode argues very much in the tradition of the Romantic bard seeking a grand visionary synthesis. While Kermode can be faulted for not providing sufficient evidence to support his argument about cultural history and the changes in our fictions, his learning, wit, and strategic use of quotation create its own fiction of concord to which we provisionally assent. Yet when we step away we realize that quoting Stevens is hardly the same as providing logical evidence and, indeed, reminds one of those who select biblical texts to *prove* an argument. *The Sense of an Ending* is, finally, a humanistic fiction in a post-Christian world. It *enacts* the making of the kind of concords that we need in an age of disbelief even as it fulfils a need in Kermode and in us to 'speak humanly of a life's importance in relation to [the world]' (p. 4). Fifteen years after publication it still speaks to our needs, still remains what Stevens would call "a poem for our climate".

NOTES

1. Page numbers in parentheses refer to *The Sense of an Ending: Studies in the Theory of Fiction* (New York: Oxford University Press, 1967).
2. Frank Kermode, *Romantic Image* (London: Routledge & Kegan Paul, 1957).
3. 'A Reply to Joseph Frank', *Critical Inquiry* 4 (Spring 1978) p. 584.
4. Thus, in *The Genesis for Secrecy* (Cambridge: Harvard University Press, 1979), he takes issue with deconstruction and maintains continuity with *The Sense of an Ending* when he argues that our search for order, for consonance, is an inevitable part of reading and living: 'We are all fulfillment men, *pleromatists*; we all seek the centre that will allow the senses to rest, at any rate for one moment' (pp. 72–3). And he concludes *The Genesis of Secrecy* by eloquently emphasizing how reading is a version of the interpretive activity that is central to living:

   > We do, living as reading, like to think of [the world] as a place where we can travel back and forth at will, divining congruences, conjunctions, opposites; extracting secrets from its secrecy, making understood relations, an appropriate algebra. This is the way we satisfy ourselves with explanations of the unfollowable world – as if it were a structured narrative, of which more might always be said by trained readers of it, by insiders. World and book, it may be, are hopelessly plural, endlessly disappointing; we stand alone before them, aware of their arbitrariness and impenetrability, knowing that they may be narratives only because of our impudent intervention, and susceptible of interpretation only by our hermetic tricks. Hot for secrets, our only conversation may be with guardians who know less and see less than we can; and our sole hope and pleasure is in the perception of a momentary radiance, before the door of disappointment is finally shut on us. (p. 145)

5. Joseph Frank, 'Spatial Form in Modern Literature', originally appeared in *The Sewanee Review*, 53 (1945) pp. 221–40, 435–56, 643–53. I am quoting from the revised and condensed version which appeared in *Criticism: The Foundation of Modern Literary Judgment*, ed. Mark Schorer *et al.* (New York: Harcourt Brace, rev. edn 1958) p. 392. A later revision of Frank's essay appeared in his *The Widening Gyre: Crisis and Mastery in Modern Literature* (New Brunswick, New Jersey: Rutgers University Press, 1963).
6. Joseph Frank, 'Spatial Form: An Answer to Critics', *Critical Inquiry*, 4 (Winter 1977) p. 246.
7. Quoted in William K. Wimsatt, Jr and Cleanth Brooks, *Literary Criticism* (New York: Vintage, 1967) 1st edn 1957, p. 29.
8. Erich Auerbach, *Mimesis*, trans. by Willard Trask (Garden City, New York: Doubleday, 1957) original edn 1953, p. 64.
9. Frank Lentricchia, *After the New Criticism* (University of Chicago Press, 1980) p. 33.
10. Lentricchia, pp. 33–4.
11. Lentricchia, p. 36.
12. Gerald Graff, *Literature Against Itself* (University of Chicago Press, 1979) p. 169.
13. Graff, p. 169.

9 Marxist Criticism of the English Novel: Arnold Kettle's *An Introduction to the English Novel* and Raymond Williams's *The English Novel from Dickens to Lawrence*

Although not only Edmund Wilson and *The Partisan Review* but even such formalists as Kenneth Burke and Dorothy Van Ghent approached the novel with a leftist political bias and included an ideological component in their critical perspective, Marxist criticism has not had a profound effect on traditional novel criticism in England and America. In this chapter I shall discuss two quite different figures: Arnold Kettle and Raymond Williams. For both, literature is related to the society that produced it. The two most significant Marxist critics of the English novel, they show both the expected focus on evaluating the degree to which a work mirrors a particular concept of reality. But they are also interested in the infinite variety and creativity of the artist. While the main focus of Marxist criticism is on art as representation of the socio-economic forces and the effects of those forces on human life, that is by no means the exclusive concern of Kettle or even Williams. Kettle's non-theoretical and less ideological Marxism is roughly similar to that of Wilson and *The Partisan Review* circle, whereas Williams represents a more ideological and theoretical strain Marxism that owes much to European Marxists such as Adorno, Althusser, Goldmann, and Gramsci.

Kettle's influential, vaguely Marxist two volume study entitled *An Introduction to the English Novel* (1951) lacks what we now think of as a theoretical argument. Reading Kettle, we feel the influence of Leavis's critical nominalism, as well as a quite contrary generalizing impulse which seeks to formulate broad ideas about literature as a *product* of society and about the behaviour of characters within novels as *products* of historical forces. Leavis deliberately eschewed abstractions and focused on the specific passage as a realistic depiction of a scene in the fabric of life, and Kettle is intellectually comfortable with that kind of nominalism. But, unlike Leavis, he also gropes for a system or theory to account for the socio-economic factors that shape not only the author, but the behaviour and destiny of the characters.

While the current generation of Marxists actually ignores Kettle, his work had significance for a generation of graduate students and teachers. During my education in the late 1950s and early 1960s in England and America, Kettle was held up as the example of Marxist novel criticism of the English novel. While I now realize it is his very lack of ideological purity that appealed to students of the novel, particularly in the Cold War era of my studies, Kettle has an important place in a book concerned with how the English novel has come to be read and taught. Kettle seems to have been purged from the consciousness of some recent Marxist criticism as if his lack of orthodoxy and his failure to articulate a theory had damned him to the twenty-sixth circle of the Marxist inferno. Although he is the one obvious precursor, he is not even mentioned in either Williams' *The English Novel* or *Marxism and Literature*. To be fair, Eagleton lists Kettle in his bibliography in *Criticism and Ideology*, but writes that Williams' strength is that he bypasses the 'vulgar Marxism' of his predecessors. While Williams does not acknowledge Kettle's influence, we shall discover striking similarities in their approach and concerns and see that both of them bear a strong Leavis influence. To be sure, compared to a Goldmann, a Lukacs, or even a Williams, Kettle seems a philosophic primitive, a kind of Grandma Moses of Marxism.

The rigour and scope of Williams' *The English Novel From Dickens to Lawrence* (1970), does not compare with that of his major works such as *Culture and Society* (1958), *The Country and the City* (1973), and *Keywords* (1976), or of his work on Marxist theory in the aforementioned *Marxism and Literature* (1977) and *Politics and Letters* (1979). Although read and discussed this book did not have the impact on the novel field that, given Williams's stature, one might have expected. For one thing, rather than probe new ground his readings modify and correct other readings, including those of Kettle and Leavis. His book – whatever his retrospective attempt in *Politics and Letters* to give it theoretical trappings – is a collection of lectures held together as much by a common personality as by a common theme; it is not, as he himself acknowledges, in *Politics and Letters*, 'a planned work'.[1] Perhaps because the lectures were originally written for the classroom, they lack the polemical edge which distinguishes Williams' best work. Moreover, interest on the frontier of novel criticism began to shift in 1970 from the kind of content problems that are Williams' main concern in *The English Novel* to more theoretical issues; thus, in the 1970s, this book seemed somewhat anachronistic even while his other works seemed to bring news from the intellectual front. Even to Williams' natural allies, including those touched by Marxist-oriented European criticism, Williams' book seemed rather naive. Thus, lacking the subject matter which would be of strong interest to proponents of similar positions, or the polemical edge necessary to engage potential opponents, *The English Novel From Dickens to Lawrence* never quite found an engaged audience.

II

While it is not our purpose to examine Marxist theory in detail, it is important to understand a few basic tenets. Marxists believe that material history – the history of labour and industry – is crucial. The oft-quoted Engels' 21 September 1890 letter to Joseph Bloch articulates crucial concepts in Marxist literary theory:

> According to the materialistic view of history, production and reproduction are *ultimately* the determining element in history in real life. . . . But now if someone twists that around to mean that the economic element is the *only* determining one, then he transforms that proposition into a meaningless, abstract, absurd phrase. The economic situation is the basis, but the various elements of the superstructure – political forms of the class struggle and its results, constitutions established by the victorious class after the battle has been won, and so on – legal forms – and even the reflexes of all these real struggles in the minds of those taking part in them, political, legal, and philosophical theories, religious ideas and their further development into systems of dogma – also have their effect upon the

course of the historical struggles and in many cases predominately determine their *form*.[2]

Lucien Goldmann has defined a crucial concept of Marxist epistemology: 'The knowledge of empirical facts remains abstract and superficial so long as it is not made concrete by its integration into a whole; only this act of integration can enable us to go beyond the incomplete and abstract phenomenon in order to arrive at its concrete essence.'[3] This flies in the face of the preoccupation with details in the work of Leavis and the New Critics. Marxist criticism believes that as Marx and Engels wrote in *The German Ideology*, 'Life is not determined by consciousness but consciousness by life'[4]; or as Marx puts it in *A Contribution to the Critique of Political Economy*: 'The mode of production of material life conditions the general process of social, political and intellectual life. It is not the consciousness of men that determines their existence, but their social existence that determines their consciousness.'[5] Thus the life we live from day to day is shaped by the material facts of our existence. Since art is deterministically affected by conditions in which the artist lives, the critic needs to understand these conditions. Milner nicely differentiates between determinism and mechanical causation: 'But if it is important to remember that the economic base does not mechanically "cause" the appropriate ideological forms, it is equally important to remember that it does, nonetheless, set certain very definite objective limits on the possibilities for their development.'[6]

Since Williams to date has been the most influential English Marxist literary theorist and since his theory provides an important context for his prior study of the English novel, I shall use his theoretical book *Marxism and Literature* as a major source of my brief introduction to Marxist literary theory. Marxism is based on two propositions which Williams defines in *Marxism and Literature*, the proposition that an economic base determines a social superstructure and the proposition that 'social being determines consciousness'.[7] He attributes the source for the first proposition to Marx's 1859 preface to *A Contribution to the Critique of Political Economy* which he quotes:

In the social production of their life, men enter into definite relations that are indispensable and independent of their will, relations of production which correspond to a definite stage of development of their material productive forces. The sum total of these relations of production constitutes the economic structure of society, the real foundation, on which rises a legal and political superstructure and to which corresponds definite forms of social consciousness. With the change of the economic foundation the entire immense superstructure is more or less rapidly transformed. In considering such transformations a distinction should always be made between the material transformation of the economic conditions of production, which can be determined with the precision of natural science, and the legal, political, religious, aesthetic or philosophic – in short, ideological – forms in which men become conscious of this conflict and fight it out.[8]

Williams isolates three areas of the superstructure: 'institutions', 'forms of consciousness', and 'political and cultural practices'.[9] For Williams the base is not static; he prefers to think of 'productive *activities*' as 'a dynamic and internally contradictory process – the specific activities and modes of activity, over a range from association to antagonism, of real men and classes of men. . . . The physical fixity of the terms [base and superstructure] exerts a constant pressure against just this realization'.[10] When Marxism takes account of the *dynamic* quality of the base, it is much more likely to avoid oversimplification, rigidity, and dogmatism in its analysis.

Marxist criticism proposes a scientific study of the relationship between society and literature. In art, representation or mimesis is conceived both as an ideological process and a goal. Modern Marxist aesthetic theory depends upon several concepts of representation. Let us begin with 'reflection', the most basic one, what Kettle calls 'life' – and move towards more complex concepts of mimesis:

What is already *and otherwise* known as the basic reality of the material social process is reflected, of course in its own ways, by art. If it is not (and the test is available, by comparison of this given knowledge of reality with any actual art produced), then it is a case of distortion, falsification, or superficiality: not art but ideology.[11]

Reflection, then, claims to be objective, but how do we determine what is 'already and otherwise known?' Isn't reflection a subjective standard posing as an objective one?

The next and somewhat more complex, concept of mimesis is 'mediation' by which art transforms and distorts the reality it expresses: 'All active relations between different kinds of being and consciousness are inevitably mediated, and this process is not a separable agency – a "medium" – but intrinsic to the properties of the related kinds.'[12] Mediation provides what Kettle would call pattern. Another important version of mimesis, one that seems to integrate reflection and mediation, is that of 'homology' – a term borrowed from the life sciences where it signifies 'correspondence in origin and development' in contrast to 'analogy' which signifies correspondence in 'appearance and function'.[13] Homology can be seen as 'Crystallizations, in superficially unrelated fields, of a social process which is nowhere fully represented but which is specifically present, in determinate forms, in a range of different works and activities.'[14] Because it relates ideology and cultural objects, homology becomes a structuralist concept. Thus the Marxist structuralist Lucien Goldmann, according to Milner, regards 'literature not as a reflection of reality, but rather as a distinct mode of practice, which stands in a relationship of *structural homology* to the various other modes of human practice'.[15]

But because homology is more a structure than a process, and because its analysis depends on something known prior to the homological relationship – depends, that is, on a kind of crystallized history, Williams prefers the concept of hegemony which he believes speaks to actual practice.

[Hegemony] sees the relations of domination and subordination, in their forms as practical consciousness, as in effect a saturation of the whole process of living – not only of political and economic activity, nor only of manifest social activity, but of the whole substance of lived identities and relationships, to such a depth that the pressures and limits of what can ultimately be seen as a specific economical, political, and cultural system seem to most of us the pressures and limits of simple experience and common sense. . . . It is a whole body of practices and expectations, over the whole of living: our senses and assignments of energy, our shaping perceptions of ourselves and our world. It is a lived system of meanings and values – constitutive and constituting – which as they are experienced as practices appear as reciprocally confirming. It thus constitutes a sense of reality for most people in the society, a sense of absolute because experienced reality beyond which it is very difficult for most members of the society to move, in most areas of their lives. It is, to say, in the strongest sense a 'culture' which has also to be seen as the lived dominance and subordination of particular classes.[16]

Thus, he perceives hegemony not as a crystallized structure but as a process: 'A lived hegemony is always a process. It is not, except analytically, a system or structure. It is a realized complex of experiences, relationships, and activities, with specific and changing pressures and limits.'[17] By thinking of hegemony as a process, we can account for 'the efforts and contributions of those who are in one way or another outside or at the edge of the terms of the specific hegemony'.[18] The danger, as Williams warns, is when the hegemonical explanation becomes reduced to 'a totalizing abstraction'.[19]

Beginning with Engels, Marxists preferred realistic literature, particularly the nineteenth-century novel, because that genre took as its goal – its aesthetic and moral and historical ideal – the most complete account of social reality. What gives this fiction its totality (a word Williams likes) is its ability to depict types. The concept of the 'typical' is central to Williams' concept of how imagined worlds imitate real ones – how art can reflect social reality – because a specific character or image can typify reality: 'The "typical" is the fully "characteristic" or fully "representative" character or situation: the specific figure from which we can reasonably extrapolate; or, to put it the other way round, the specific figure which concentrates and intensifies a much more general reality.'[20] Lukàcs takes this a step further when he argues in his later works that this totality must be in the service of 'a profound and serious, if not conscious, association with a progressive current in the evolution of mankind'.[21] From this and like kinds of legislative statement derives Soviet social realism which rejects 'modernism' as decadent. In social realism the typical becomes the ideal future man[22] or, to use Hillis Miller's terms, social realism becomes another version of Neo-Platonism, in the sense of iterating a specific paradigm, and a particularly rigid one at that.[23]

The novel, because it allows the critic to select arbitrarily paradigmatic passages, may be more amenable than lyric poetry to the kind of polemical criticism which uses evidence to support a particular political position. Marxists perceived that the novel could be an instrument for raising political consciousness. When Kettle wrote of effects, he was not thinking merely of the novel's formal rhetoric: 'Every novel we read must, to some extent (be it ever so little or ever so temporarily) change us. According to the degree of effect which it achieves it will (nearly always without our realizing it) influence our actions' (II. p. 39).[24] On one hand, the subject matter of novels – bourgeois life in an industrial, capitalist society – appealed to a wide audience. On the other, its characteristic critical dissection of society showed the audience the necessity of change. In theory, Marxist criticism gives priority to the controlling perspective rather than the experience of reading closely, but in practice the rigid paradigm breaks down. Once one experiences the texts of novels, one inevitably begins to see their infinite variety and their resilience to patterns and formulae. (One of post-structuralism's more valuable contributions has been to make us aware of those gaps and fissures which challenge unity and clarity.)

What Culler says of narratology is true of Marxist criticism *because* Marxist criticism – much more than other criticism – is a form of narratology: 'Positing the priority of events to the discourse which reports or presents them, narratology establishes a hierarchy which the functioning of narratives often subverts by presenting events not as givens but as the products of discursive forces or requirements.'[25] Of course this is true of all critical narratives, too, and particularly those of ideological criticism. If New Criticism emphasizes the priority of details or events (or story) at the expense of the narrativity or discourse, Marxist criticism reverses the hierarchy and stresses discourse at the expense of empirical data within a novel. In English Marxist criticism, the 'discursive forces' (and 'emergent' tradition) are the demands of Marxist dialectical explanations, while the priority of events (the dominant tradition) insists on discussing the novel in terms of characters' manners and motives, narrative voice, and organic form.

III

Kettle's Marxism is really a version of English positivism blended with English pastoralism, and his criticism lacks the strong theoretical grounding of European Marxist criticism. Because he is neither rigorous nor rigid, because his readings are only different in kind not degree from Leavis and his followers, he fits comfortably within the tradition of manners and morals. He is not content to take the ideological temperature of texts and to judge texts by what they reveal about Marx's dialectical materialism. Kettle's perspicacity and intelligence continually break out of a rigorous Marxist mould unlike,

say, Ralph Fox in *The Novel and the People* (1937) or the less rigorous
Christopher Caudwell, the best known of the 1930s British Marxist
critics. For Kettle has been influenced by Richards and Empson,
whose positivism and nominalism represent an English strain of New
Criticism. Thus he writes, '[T]he basis for all literary judgments must
be the actual words an author writes; and it is in the weight and choice
and arrangement of those words, carrying as they do the weight and
illumination of his view of life, that the qualities of a novelist are
revealed' (I. p. 107). As we shall see Kettle the Marxist competes with
both Kettle the humanist and Kettle the formalist.

Kettle continued Leavis's emphasis upon the importance of subject
matter in terms of its social and moral implications. Kettle follows
Leavis in his nostalgia for an organic rural community. He acknowledges his debt to Leavis in the Preface to his two volume *An
Introduction to the English Novel* (1951), and quotes Leavis with
approval a number of times. Kettle's version of Marxism tries, at
times, to cast off not only materialism but objectivity and to embrace
Leavis's (by way of Lawrence's) concept of 'life'. Like Leavis (and
Trilling), he believes that the novel is a central cultural statement of
our time. Thus he can write at the end of Volume II: 'The future of the
English novel . . . is a problem bound up inextricably with the whole
future, social and cultural, of the British people. The test of the future
novelist, like that of his predecessors, will lie in the depth and sincerity
of his response to the profoundest and most perilous issues of the time'
(II. p. 197). Kettle agrees with Leavis about the centrality of
Lawrence, whose life and work represent a protest against both
materialism and utilitarianism: 'The theme of *The Rainbow* is what
bourgeois society does to personal relationships. The pledge of *The
Rainbow* is that a new society will come about in which men and
women will be able to live whole and achieve vital, creative
relationships. But the relation of the theme to the pledge, of the earth
to the rainbow, is shrouded in wordiness and mysticism' (II. p. 129).

Kettle's distinction between life – the raw material perceived or
imagined by the writer – and pattern is his central aesthetic principle:

Pattern is not something narrowly 'aesthetic,' something which
critics like Clive Bell used to talk about as 'form' (as opposed to life
and content). Pattern is the quality in a book which gives it
wholeness and meaning, makes the reading of it a complete and
satisfying experience. . . . 'Form' is important only in so far as it
enhances significance; and it will enhance significance just in so far

as it bears a real relation to, that is to say symbolizes or clarifies, the aspect of life that is being conveyed. But form is not *in itself* significant; the central core of any novel is what it has to say about life . . . [T]he pattern which the writer imposes is the very essence of his vision of whatever in life he is dealing with. (I. p. 15–16)

While all novels consist of a relationship between life and pattern, most novels either emphasize one or the other. When the novelist begins with 'his pattern, his moral vision', Kettle calls the novel, borrowing one of Leavis's terms, 'a moral fable' (p. 17). By contrast, an alternative tradition, stressing 'life' and including Nashe, Defoe and Smollett, is 'less consciously concerned with the moral significance of life than with its surface texture. Their talent is devoted first and foremost to getting life on to the page, to conveying across to their readers the sense of what life as their characters live it really feels like' (I. p. 21).

Kettle contends that successful novels impose pattern onto life: 'Just as the moral fable fails unless the writer imbues his original moral concept with the stuff of life, so will the non-allegorical novel, which begins with the writer's undefined "sense of life", fail unless he gives his "slice of life" a moral significance, a satisfying pattern' (I. p. 25). Kettle, in 1951, sounds a theme similar to that of his American contemporaries Schorer and Van Ghent: 'The very act of artistic creation, that moulding into significant form of some thing or part of life, is in itself a discovery about the nature of life and ultimately its value will lie in the value of that discovery' (II. p. 68). Indeed, Kettle's pattern resembles Schorer's technique and Van Ghent's 'idea embodied in the cosmology'. Thus, he does not fault *Nostromo* for lacking a 'conscious, intellectualized solution', for 'the experience of the work of art is in itself a kind of solution, a synthesis, a discovery of the nature of the problem' (II. pp. 80–1).

Kettle's aesthetic values are often those of Anglo-American formalism. Van Ghent and Schorer would agree that terms like 'character' and 'atmosphere' or 'plot' 'can only be discussed in relation to the central core and purpose of each particular book' (I. p. 51). Following Leavis and James, Kettle prefers showing to telling: 'The statement of opinion replaces the revelation of actual human and social tensions in *Tono-Bungay* because Wells runs away from these actual tensions and takes refuge in his *ideas* about them' (II. p. 95). Kettle often sees the author as a presence in the text. On the whole Kettle is more attentive to the novel's rhetoric than Leavis; at times he is innovative about the relationships among author, text, and reader: 'Every novelist stands between the scene of his novel and the reader, controlling and directing our attention' (I. p. 157). He demonstrates that asking the right questions about genre helps us understand novels. Seeing *Jonathan Wild* as a moral fable makes it more comprehensible. Thus Defoe must be understood in terms of the picaresque tradition. And he reminds us that *Ulysses* is in the mock epic tradition of *Don Quixote* and the comic epic tradition of Fielding's *Joseph Andrews*.

Indeed Kettle's own immersion in the English novel tradition frequently overwhelms his dogma, as when he writes of realism in *Emma* in terms which appreciate it as a novel of manners: 'Our faculties are aroused, we are called upon to participate in life with an awareness, a fineness of feeling and a moral concern more intense than most of us normally bring to our everyday experiences' (I. p. 92). Finally, for Kettle, realism and depth of feeling are the standards by which Austen excels. But he insists on her limitations as a 'conventional member of her class', because she failed to recognize that the Hartfield world minority lives at the expense of the majority (I. p. 101). But for him the quality of the content – its inclusiveness and perspicacity – takes the form of attention to class division and class struggle. The discussion of *Emma* here and by Booth in *The Rhetoric of Fiction* did much to establish the orthodoxy of that novel in the Post-War period. For *Pride and Prejudice*, with its concern for money and property, had become the centrepiece of the Austen canon in the 1930s.

Let us examine Kettle's concept of realism. Within *The English Novel*, realism has three central meanings (a) truth to human nature; (b) understanding of class struggle at a specific time; (c) understanding of the evolutionary pattern of history. For Kettle, realism is not only a narrative mode, but an essential standard by which we judge texts; it means both verisimilitude in character analysis and a complex view of historical movements. Realism sometimes is a subjective criterion, as when he says of Angel's response to Tess's confession that it is 'unconvincingly realized' (II. p. 61). Here it reduces itself to the legislative or stipulative barometer of how a scene or character or plot conforms to Kettle's perception of human nature. Finally realism for Kettle, as for Leavis, also comes to be equated with 'mature' and serious even if verisimilitude is lacking. *Gulliver's Travels*, for Kettle, is 'realistic because it has to do with the actual problems and values of life', while 'romance was the non-realistic, aristocratic literature of feudalism' (I. pp. 28, 31). What distinguishes Kettle from traditional formalism and makes him a Marxist critic is his insistence that novels have ideological concerns, a sense of historical process, and characters who typify class problems in a socio-economic context.

Kettle gives high marks to those works which have identifiable ideological concerns. By ideological, he does not mean merely political, but a work that takes a position espousing a change in values. Kettle includes *The Way of All Flesh* because it is 'a propagandist novel', a 'novel with purpose'; 'the author is quite consciously concerned not merely to interpret facts but to change them' (II. pp. 38–9). Although Butler does not present 'a sense of the vitality of life itself', 'his bold and righteous indignation against the cant of conventional bourgeois life . . . gives the novel its unique and exhilarating flavour' (II. pp. 39–40). Yet Kettle acknowledges that we have the sense of Butler's opinions imposed on life and that those opinions limit 'the complexities and richness of life' (II. p. 47).

Kettle believes that history must be perceived as an organic process and that a novel must respond to the complexities of society as a dynamic force rather than as a static structure. Kettle measures a writer by asking whether the author understands the forces which create a dynamic social situation that shapes individuals. (As Christopher Hill's praise of Kettle's *Clarissa* discussion suggests, he is at his best when arguing that eighteenth-century novels such as *Clarissa* need to be understood in their social and economic context.)[26] He writes of Scott, whom he also praises for understanding the Industrial Revolution: 'What gives *The Heart of the Midlothian* its "body", its solid sense of real life and real issues, is Scott's ability to see his subject from the point of view of the peasantry, a point of view with its own limitations but one that is nevertheless neither idealistic nor dishonest' (I. p. 112).

Kettle does *not* always separate aesthetic judgments from political ones. He is at his most polemical discussing the imperialist novels of the early modern period. Kettle praises Conrad for achieving in *Nostromo* 'the presentation . . . of society in motion, history in the making' (II. p. 75). (Yet he does criticize Conrad's failure to define 'in its full theoretical and moral significance the process of imperialism' [II. p. 78].) Kettle shrewdly remarks of E. M. Forster: 'Such words as liberal, individualist, agnostic . . . refer more usefully to his *attitudes* than to a more specific, coherent philosophy' (II. p. 153). Aziz and Fielding are subjected to 'the strain of imperialism which, as in *Nostromo*, corrupts all it touches' (II. p. 154). (Kettle likes to link 'imperialism' and 'corrupts'.) He insists that one cannot 'divorce the values of art from those of life and consequently morality' (I. p. 99). For Kettle, *The Old Wives' Tale* is weak because Bennett lacks a sense of historical process. Thus he does not propose a more inclusive alternative than those of his characters and reduces life to Sophia's and Constance's views of life: 'What I am suggesting is that a novelist must have a really rich imaginative understanding of anything that he writes about and that if his subject involves, as Arnold Bennett's did, a sense of broad social change and development, the novelist's own understanding of these issues is most relevant' (II. p. 89).

Kettle believes in the importance of the type as 'the embodiment of certain forces which come together in a particular social situation to create a peculiar kind of vital energy' (I. p. 168). Invoking Lukàcs, he distinguishes between 'naturalism which concentrates on the typical in the sense of the average, the ordinary, the essentially casual, and that deeper realism which gets hold of the extreme possibilities inherent in a situation and gains a more profound typicality through a concentration on the truly significant tensions within that particular chunk of "life" ' (II. p. 108). Thus, Becky is an individual, but 'she is every woman of spirit rebelling against the humiliations forced on her by certain social assumptions' (I. p. 168). Note that 'type' does not indicate so much a representative moral figure as one who reflects a significant objective fact (or class) in social and historical reality. He rejects the view that *Emma* is a comedy of manners, as if that would consign it to the category of literary archaeology, and he stresses how Austen's 'realistic, unromantic and indeed, by orthodox standards, subversive concern with the position of women' informs Jane Fairfax's marriage (I. p. 97). For Kettle, '*Wuthering Heights* then is an expression in the imaginative terms of art of the stresses and tensions and conflicts, personal and spiritual, of nineteenth-century capitalist society' (I. p. 155).

Let us turn to Kettle's view of *Ulysses*. Insofar *Ulysses* is realistic, it succeeds. He praises 'Joyce's remarkable ability to bring a scene to life. *Ulysses*, despite some exasperating qualities and passages, tingles with life, with the physical feel of existence and with a sense of the vibrating reality of human relationships' (II. p. 143). *Ulysses's* greatness depends upon the intensity and range of its mimesis: 'The main purpose of the "Wandering Rocks" chapter is certainly the achievement on the surface level of a sense of the teeming life of Dublin and of a reality deeper than and independent of the individual consciousness' (II. p. 146). But *Ulysses* presents 'a society in hopeless disintegration extended between two masters – Catholic Church and British Empire –

which exploit and ruin it. . . . Not one character performs a single action that is not fundamentally sterile' (p. 148). Realism ought to be accompanied, apparently, by a melioristic vision that *Ulysses* lacks. But isn't Kettle condemning Joyce for not sharing Kettle's social vision, for not writing the novel he would write? Thus, according to Kettle, the tragedy of *Ulysses* is that 'Joyce's extraordinary powers, his prodigious sense of the possibilities of language, should be so deeply vitiated by the sterility of his vision of life. . . . The case against the use of the association method run mad is not simply that it is arbitrary and confusing and indeed often leads to unintelligibility, but that it actually builds up a false web of associations, a pattern which, like so many of the patterns of modern psychology, has not the kind of basis in reality which it is held up to have' (II. p. 149–50). Fundamentally, Joyce gives precedent to pattern and form, and ignores the complex social analyses which will point the way to a reordering of values. Kettle resents the lack of plot and does not admire what he feels is arbitrary association of language. Kettle feels that *Ulysses* lacks the 'feeling of the relationship of man to man and man to society in a great urban centre' (II. p. 149). But, in fact, *Ulysses* ends with hints that the relationship between Molly and Bloom will be re-established and that Stephen – fertilized by Bloom's humanistic values – will write the very book that Ireland requires. Kettle gives little *evidence* for his view that *Ulysses* does not end positively.

Marxist critics such as Lukàcs are hostile to the *alienation* they associate with modernism. As Milner notes, 'The whole of Lukàcs later writings are built about one all-embracing Manichean dualism, that is, the central opposition between *realism* and *modernism*.'[27] In the guise of criticizing arbitrary form, Kettle is really responding to what he perceives as a failure of Joyce's to achieve the evolutionary dialectic that Kettle prefers – a dialectic that sees the world evolving upward to a more efficient and humane economic organization. The view that realism should contain an image of ideal or future man to which history is progressing is derived from social realism, which was a dominant Soviet doctrine in 1951. This can lead to requirements for a propaganda component in art. Like social realism, Kettle is legislating what a novel should contain, but within a much more humanistic tradition derived from Leavis. That 'life' is a starting point puts a particularly benign implication to his stipulations.

Kettle believes that *Middlemarch* succeeds in its parts but not in its whole and that it is not a 'deeply moving book' because it lacks 'that final vibrant intensity of the living organism' and its 'various stories

. . . have no organic unity' (I. pp. 183–4). Eliot, he asserts, does not catch the subtle movement of society, 'that sense of the contradictions within every action and situation. . . . George Eliot's view of society is in the last analysis a mechanistic and determinist one. She has an absorbing sense of the power of society but very little sense of the way it changes' (I. pp. 183, 185). And Kettle in his study is trying to discover those changes for us. Marxists critics tend to 'use' criticism to discover not only the historical perspective that novels reveal but the historical conditions which produced them. Kettle does not accept the belief, which he attributes to George Eliot, that 'the individual is essentially passive, a recipient of impressions, changed by the outside world but scarcely able to change it' (I. p. 185). We note that Kettle admires characters who, by force of will, overcome materialism and implicitly reject the inevitability of dialectical materialism. But this of course is not quite the same as historical determinism. Kettle rejects the view, which he attributes to *Middlemarch*, that 'society [is] a static, invincible force outside the characters themselves' (I. p. 188). He admires Dorothea for encompassing 'that element in human experience for which in the determinist universe of mechanistic materialism there is no place – the need of man to change the world that he inherits' (I. p. 189).

Although Kettle does not give Hardy full points, he does implicitly speak to Leavis's dismissal of Hardy. One might have thought that the specificity of agrarian life and the dramatization of its conflict with external forces would win Kettle's admiration, but his attention is apparently deflected and disturbed by Hardy's propensity for vague philosophical meditation. '*Tess* . . . is a moral fable, [and therefore] the expression of a generalized human situation in history and neither . . . a purely personal tragedy nor . . . a philosophic comment on Life in general and the fate of Woman in particular' (II. p. 53). Kettle stresses the social and historical aspect of Tess's situation: '[Tess] survives because [Hardy's] imaginative understanding of the disintegration of the peasantry is more powerful than the limiting tendencies of his conscious outlook' (II. pp. 57–8). Perhaps influenced by Leavis, he faults Hardy for, like Butler, imposing a pattern that reduces life. Hardy is 'constantly weakening his apprehension of [the inner movement of life] by inadequate attitudes and judgments' (II. p. 62).

Objecting that James beats a retreat from social and historical reality and is inattentive to social and economic reality, Kettle notes that James's characters do not work: 'What the bourgeois world did for

James was to turn him into a moral idealist chasing a chimera of ideal conduct divorced from social reality. . . . [His characters'] sensibility becomes an end in itself, not a response to the actual issues of life. The freedom they seek turns out to be an idealized freedom; its ends, therefore, can only end in a desire not merely to be free *in* this world but to be free *of* this world (II. pp. 33–4). Woolf, too, ignores social and historical reality. After noting that *To the Lighthouse* 'convey[s] with extraordinary precision a certain intimate quality of felt life, . . . the impression of the momentary texture of experience', Kettle cannot resist asking 'So what? . . . Upon what vision of the world, what scale of human values, is it based?' (II. pp. 103–5).

Like his mentor Leavis, Kettle does not want to define theory and method, but prefers to write about individual works. At his best he begins with a response to a novel and asks why the book has come to be written as it has. On such occasions his focus on social issues enables him to catch a dimension of the novel's moral energy. Thus *Oliver Twist* involves us 'because every starved orphan in the world, and indeed, everyone who is poor and oppressed and hungry is involved, and the master of the workhouse (his name has not been revealed) is not anyone in particular but every agent of an oppressive system everywhere' (I. p. 125). He understands how Becky functions as a morally purposeful character: 'We know [Becky's] relationship, financial and social . . . with every other character in the book and we know the guiding principle of her conduct, that she wants to be mistress of her own life' (I. p. 167). Like Leavis, Kettle does not get bogged down in formal aesthetics or worry about separating author and narrator. Thus, in his discussion of Forster the expressive element in his criticism sometimes modifies the formal element: 'When E. M. Forster writes about India we are all the time aware of an outside observer battling with problems which he may not – he is quite aware – fully understand' (II. pp. 178–9). When Kettle praises Forster as 'a writer of scrupulous intelligence, of tough and abiding insights, who has never been afraid of the big issues or the difficult ones and has scorned to hide his doubts and weaknesses behind a façade of wordiness and self-protective conformity', we realize that Kettle is describing an ideal to which he aspires (II. p. 163).

But the real question of Kettle's criticism is whether one can have Marxism without the metaphysics of dialectical materialism. For Kettle's Marxism is, when compared to that of European critics such as Lukàcs and Lucien Goldmann, very much a garden variety – notwithstanding occasion rigorous moments, as when he applies the aforementioned Engels' 21 September 1890 letter to *Nostromo* – and avoids the rigidity of much continental post-war Marxism. His readings excel in their particular insights (their superstructure), but lack a theoretical grounding (a base). While Kettle is something of a Marxist critic, he frequently gives precedence to artistic values over political ones: 'Though we must see each novel as part of history and its value as the quality of its contribution to the achievement of man's freedom, yet it is important to remember that it is the book *itself* we are judging, not its intention, nor the amount of "social significance" to be got out of it, nor even its importance as a measurable historical influence' (I. pp. 12–13). Even if Kettle is reluctant to stress form, a man who quotes Henry James and T. E. Hulme to establish his position and who acknowledges that the source of his crucial distinction between life and pattern is E. M. Forster, has not completely allowed politics to subsume literary values.

Finally, Kettle's principal standard – the standard he most consistently applies – is not historical inclusiveness, which tends to stress class divisions and class struggle, but truth to his perception of human nature. Often Kettle's Marxism is really sentimental humanism in disguise, and his values are bourgeois and aesthetic. Marxism without metaphysics becomes a vague social attitude based on liberal and often sentimental principles of equity, and it is this Marxism that informs his history of the novel. But while he is not rigorous and scientific, his generalizations are often compelling. He argues that the ruling class culture relies on romance because it sustains its values even as it 'delights and entertains the rulers without bringing them face to face with realities they would sooner put behind them' (I. p. 33). The novel developed in the eighteenth century because 'bourgeois writers' wanted 'a medium which could express a realistic and objective curiosity about man and his world' (I. p. 37).

Yet his temperament and sensibility seem to resist such sweeping, provocative, vaguely Marxist generalizations which are neither examined nor discussed. 'The industrial bourgeoisie as a class . . . hated and feared the implications of any artistic effort of realism and integrity' (I. p. 88). But what is interesting, I think, is how such artists as Dickens, Hardy, and Joyce hated and feared the boundless confidence and practicality of the bourgeois, often while enjoying the comforts of that class. And Kettle seems aware of the iconoclastic stance of the artist and the effect of that stance on the creative imagination: 'The great novelists were rebels, and the measure of their greatness is found in the last analysis to correspond with the degree and consistency of their rebellion' (I. pp. 88–9). For Kettle, too, the artist is a dour fellow whose task is to reach or bear witness, not to delight: 'The task of the novelists was the same as it had always been – to achieve realism, to express (with whatever innovations of form and structure they needs must discover) the truth about life as it faced them. But to do this, to cut through the whole complex structure of inhumanity and false feeling that ate into the consciousness of the capitalist world, it was necessary to become a rebel' (I. p. 88).

Yet Kettle's contribution is important because he widened the discourse about novels. He takes much further Leavis's interests in the factors that create a novel. While Leavis addressed the moral seriousness of fiction, Kettle shows that books not only reflect and embody the society in which they were written but reveal and explore it. Building on the work of Leavis, he opened up the discussion of the novel form to include the external world. By eschewing an exclusive great tradition, he gives shape to the *realistic* tradition of the English novel. Like Auerbach he admires the dramatization of 'the complex relationship between personal and impersonal forces in a man's life' (I. p. 115). Like Auerbach he praises events which have a historical context; thus in *The Heart of the Midlothian* the trial of Effie is a 'significant event involving clashes of opposing cultures and differing values . . .' (I. pp. 112–13). Like Auerbach, Kettle likes to use a distinct passage to launch his discussion, although he is far less interested in style and more in content than Auerbach and is unable to show how style can crystallize a *Zeitgeist*. To be sure, measured against what Auerbach did for the European tradition, his accomplishments may seem limited and less brilliant. Unlike Auerbach, he cannot always make a sustained historical argument and often must settle for an historical *aperçu*.

Before turning to Williams, we should mention a few of Kettle's limitations.

(1) He makes an interesting admission that his characteristic method of quoting crystallizing passages is not responsive to a novel's movement. 'One tends to quote passages which show Conrad's consciously formulated understanding of the social situation he is recording; but the real test of a novel lies of course in its ability to convey artistically that understanding and for such a test the abstracted quotation is inadequate' (II. p. 74).

(2) Notwithstanding perceptive comment on Lockwood and Nelly

Dean in *Wuthering Heights*, Kettle does not do much with narrators.

(3) At times Kettle writes in the passive voice but neglects to identify the agent. Thus when he writes, 'Inferior art was elevated; great work treated in a way that shrouded its greatness', we need to know 'by whom'. Except for his vague allusion to 'those in authority', we do not know who is responsible for this outrage (I. p. 88).

(4) As his response to *Ulysses* indicates, Kettle does not like novels which fail to imply the possibility of progress towards a better day; Forster, too, is criticized for this failure. In Forster Kettle feels 'a limitation in the assessment of the capacity of human beings to change radically their consciousness. And this limitation reduces the book somehow, and all Forster's books. . . . The weakness of all Forster's novels lies in a failure to dramatize quite convincingly the positive values which he has to set against the destroyers of the morality of the heart' (II. pp. 160, 163). Thus in Part II of Volume II he feels that the most prominent writers – Huxley, Henry Green, Graham Greene, Cary, Compton-Burnett – working in 1951 (the year of Kettle's publication) are caught in the throes of 'pessimism and decadence' which are 'life-denying and in consequence art-denying' attitudes (II. p. 166).

IV

For Williams novels are economically determined cultural and historical phenomena that record, and even, at their most significant, anticipate historical processes. Williams understands the novel not merely as social criticism, but as part of the process of shaping and changing historical consciousness, by which he means 'a vision of the nature of man and the means of his liberation in a close and particular place and time . . . [A]t its most important [literature's] process is different and yet still inescapably social: a whole way of seeing that is communicable to others, and a dramatization of values that becomes an action' (pp. 58–9).[28] And this is the goal of the critic. Williams believes that the history of the novel makes the history of ideas look different: 'That sense of the problematic, in community and identity, in knowable relationships, is more deeply there and is earlier there than anywhere else in our recorded experience' (p. 191). Novels are for him what oral traditions are to students of primitive cultures. Art originates from '*social* experience . . . that's neglected, ignored, certainly at times repressed; that even when it's taken up, to be processed or to function as an official consciousness, is resistant, lively, still goes its own way, and eventually steps on its shadow . . .' (p. 192).

Understanding Williams' place in English literary history means seeing his place in an historical sequence that begins with Leavis, moves to Kettle, and then to Williams and, more recently, to Terry Eagleton. What is valuable in Williams' work is the attention to society as, in his words, 'not only the bearer but the active creator, the active destroyer, of the values of persons and relationships' (p. 26). As we move from Leavis to Kettle to Williams, we feel a growth in historical consciousness. Williams sees society in terms of a broader demographic perspective than Kettle, to say nothing of Leavis. His standard of 'totality' addresses not only the inclusiveness and quality of the mimetic process, but its intensity and unity. For Williams, quality and inclusiveness are objective standards that measure how a novel adheres to 'the nature of man and the means of his liberation in a close and particular place and time' (p. 58). But we realize that these are subjective standards disguised as objective ones and reductive ones at that. Williams's argument that a novelist's method is shaped by his experience seems to preserve continuity with James's concentration on technique as a means of expressing the author's life experience. His statement that 'Dickens's morality, his social criticism, is in the form of the novels' is not so different from Leavis or such American formalists as Booth, Van Ghent, or Mark Schorer (p. 48).

For our purposes, it is unfortunate that *The English Novel from Dickens to Lawrence* (1970) does not have the stature of his major work, such as *Culture and Society* or *The Country and the City*. Our approach will be to isolate the central threads of *The English Novel*'s argument and relate it to his critical values as revealed throughout his works. He relates the Victorian novel to historical and cultural developments in England which by the end of the 1840s was the world's first urban society. The writers discovered the meaning of that crisis, 'often quite personally felt and endured', in their novels (p. 11). The crucial achievement of the 1847–8 period, when a new generation of novelists emerged, was 'the exploration of community: the substance and meaning of community' (p. 11). In this period, society was no longer a framework or a standard, but 'a process that entered lives, to shape or to deform' (p. 13). Williams begins *his tradition* with Dickens whom he praises for the 'creation of consciousness – of recognitions and relationships' and for his ability 'to dramatize those social institutions and consequences which are not accessible to ordinary physical observation' (pp. 33–4). Rereading, we understand that Williams's own critical method is to *create consciousness* of new relations and to dramatize social relations in the face of industrialism and the social process it creates.

While Williams has been turned into a kind of cult figure by the British academic left, particularly Terry Eagleton, he, like Kettle, has affinities with the humanistic mould of Leavis and his followers. Certainly Leavis, Trilling, and probably such New Critical figures as Van Ghent and Guerard would have subscribed to the following comment by Eagleton: 'The novel, for Williams, is one medium among many in which men seek to master and absorb new experience by discovering new forms and rhythms, grasping and reconstructing the stuff of social change in the living substance of perceptions and relationships.'[29] It is strange that Williams does not mention Kettle in *The English Novel* for Kettle has, in many ways, anticipated Williams' approach. Nor does he mention Ian Watt who has created the kind of dialogue between individual and society, public and private, social and literary studies that Williams seeks. And both Watt and Kettle share with Williams the intellectual patrimony of Leavis.

In turning away from aesthetic criteria to issues of content, Williams is deeply indebted to Leavis. In *Politics and Letters*, he acknowledges the deliberate nature of the response to *The Great Tradition* which he 'knew . . . by heart'.[30] Like Kettle, Williams is influenced by Leavis's concept of 'life' as vitalistic, instinctive, and resistant to industrialism, rationalism, and materialism. Conscious of his working class origins, Williams felt himself an outsider to the academic establishment. Indeed he might have been drawn to Leavis, who was not merely a secret sharer of his social position, but someone who represented to him real social intelligence. Williams, too, saw himself as a cultural critic rather than as a specialist scholar or a member of an academic elite – an elite, in his mind, often drawn from the aristocracy – which imposes anachronistic and irrelevant social values, or rather, customs and amenities disguised as values.

His early perspective has been deeply influenced by Leavis's humanism in that he stressed the individual as the focus of interest. Indeed, Williams wrote in *Reading and Criticism* (1950) that literature, is 'valuable primarily as a record of detailed individual experience which has been coherently stated and valued'.[31] Leavis provided a model for dealing with the dialogue between self and society, although he emphasized the potential independence of the non-conformist conscience. Eagleton correctly notes that Williams's version of the English tradition, with little reference to the European novel, is marked by a provincialism that recalls that of Leavis; he also notes that, like Leavis and Lukàcs, Williams sees nineteenth-century realism as a paradigm of fiction.[32] When Williams writes of fiction that depends on 'adolescent nostalgia' as opposed to 'adult memories', (p. 129) of 'seriousness' and 'seriously' (for example: 'examine . . . with a seriousness' [p. 131], or 'very serious human actions are at the center of all [James's] best work' [p. 133]), we hear the influence of Leavis's voice. *The English Novel* must be understood in terms of his intellectual oedipal relationship with Leavis.

Because it is the Leavis tradition in which he has been educated, he must first and foremost come to terms with that tradition. Not only does Williams begin with Dickens, whom Leavis dismisses in *The Great Tradition*, but he rescues Hardy from Leavis's condescension. In the section on Hardy he deliberately classifies Hardy with the major figures in his great tradition and he objects to Hardy, Eliot, and Lawrence being patronized as autodidactic: 'They belong to a cultural tradition much older and more central in this country than the comparatively modern and deliberately exclusive circuit of what are called public schools' (p. 96). He objects to those 'influential critical accounts [that] have tries to push [Hardy] aside', referring undoubtedly to Leavis (p. 97). And in *Politics and Letters*, he deliberately appropriates Leavis's concept of the concrete in order to praise Hardy: '[Hardy] could reach a very wide range of social experience through a series of relations which were wholly knowable in manifest ways, and which he could render concrete in his fiction. That was not possible, for example, for Dickens, who had to devise different fictional strategies for a much more complex urban world, increasingly dominated by processes that could only be grasped statistically or analytically – a community unknowable in terms of manifest experience'.[33]

For Williams, as for Leavis and Kettle, Lawrence is a very strong figure. Thus he writes in *The English Novel*: 'What is new [in Lawrence], really new, is that the language of the writer is at one with the language of his characters, in a way that hadn't happened, though George Eliot and Hardy had tried, since the earlier smaller community of the novel had been extended and changed' (p. 173). Like Kettle and Leavis, he sees the major writers expressing his values and, like them, he sees Lawrence's rebellion against materialism and rationalism as central. Lawrence '[altered] the novelist's language of description and analysis to the colloquial and informal from the abstract and polite –

many writers have followed him; we have even got used to it' (p. 173).

Like Leavis, Williams is also indebted to the high seriousness of Arnold who felt that literature should be a criticism of life. Like Leavis, Williams rejected the Wildean tradition that art was play and had nothing to do with life. Like Leavis, Williams took issue with the Bloomsbury tradition that artists and others in the intellectual elite could cultivate their own sensibilities and fulfil their own needs in personal relations without worrying about the general population, the community, politics, history, or social and economic forces. But Williams goes much further than Leavis. For Williams, 'social criticism when it is most successful is always and inescapably a criticism of life' (p. 51). In *Marxism and Literature*, Williams specifically attacks Leavis's values. He notes that: 'What had been claimed for "art" and the "creative imagination" in the central Romantic arguments was now claimed for "criticism", as the central "humane" activity and discipline".'[34] Tradition became 'a selection which culminated in, and in a circular way defined, the "literary values" which "criticism" was asserting.'[35] Marxism, Williams contends, has tried to 'relate "literature" to the social and economic history within which "it" had been produced' and to include popular literature.[36] Thus Williams prides himself on seeing writers such as Dickens, Hardy, and even Joyce in the context of popular life.

It would be a mistake to consider the lectures published in 1970 as an illustration of the theoretical argument in *Marxism and Literature* (1977). Nevertheless, it is well to be attentive to the later volume because many of its major arguments are implicit assumptions in the earlier work. While the concepts on *Marxism and Literature* (1977) do not systematically inform the earlier book on the novel, Williams in *The English Novel* sees literary works in terms of 'recognition of a constitutive and constituting process of social and historical reality'.[37] Let us examine the basic tenets of Williams' Marxism, remembering that they only loosely inform the argument of *The English Novel*. According to Williams, 'The more significant Marxist position is a recognition of the radical and inevitable connection between a writer's real social relations (considered not only "individually" but in terms of the general social relations of "writing" in a specific society and period, and within these the social relations embodied in particular kinds of writing) and the "style" or "forms" or "content" of his work, not considered abstractly but as expressions of these relations'.[38]

Williams sees the development of an author 'as a complex of active relations, within which the emergence of an individual project, and the real history of other contemporary projects and of the developing forms and structures, are continuously and substantially interactive'.[39] The concept of alignment pre-empts the argument that writers express their subjectivity: 'Writing, like other practices, is in an important sense always aligned: that is to say, that it variously expresses, explicitly or implicitly, specifically selected experience from a specific point of view'.[40] This concept is crucial to refuting claims of 'objectivity' and 'neutrality' and 'fidelity to truth' 'which we must recognize as the ratifying formulas of those who offer their own senses and procedures as universal'.[41] He values 'commitment to social reality'; 'commitment, strictly, is conscious alignment, or conscious change of alignment'; but how can one measure commitment or what he calls 'profound understanding of the social and historical crisis'?[42] Following Lukàcs' distinction between 'actual' and 'possible' consciousness, Williams believes that great writers 'integrate a vision at the level of the possible ("complete") consciousness of a social formation, while most writers reproduce the contents of ("incomplete") actual consciousness'.[43]

Marxism believes that 'not only the forms but the contents of consciousness are socially produced'.[44] 'Specific authorship' must be seen 'in its true range: from the genuinely reproductive (in which the formation *is* the author), through the wholly or partly articulative (in which the authors are the formation), to the no less important cases of the relatively distanced articulation or innovation (often related to residual or emergent or pre-emergent formations) in which creativity may be relatively separated, or indeed may occur at the farthest end of that living continuum between the fully formed class or group and the active individual project'.[45] For Marxists, according to Williams, "Society" is . . . never only the "dead husk" which limits social and individual fulfillment. It is always also a constitutive process with very powerful pressures which are both expressed in political, economic, and cultural formations and, to take the full weight of "constitutive," are internalized and become "individual wills".'[46] Moreover, changes in form or medium (the artistic means of transforming the real world into art) develop from a changing relationship between the artist and society.

Williams is most innovative as a theorist when he speaks of language. For him, language is 'constitutive' and 'historically and socially *constituting*. What we can then define is a dialectical process: the *changing practical consciousness of human beings*, in which both the evolutionary and the historical processes can be given full weight, but also within which they can be distinguished, in the complex variations of actual language use'.[47] According to Williams, language 'is a socially shared and reciprocal activity, already embedded in active relationships, within which every move is an activation of what is already shared and reciprocal or may become so'.[48] He wants to insist that the 'sign' within language is not arbitrary but conventional and that the conventional is the result of a social process. He insists that man creates language systematically in his social relationships, and is not simply created by language. In other words, men, not language, speak, and this position makes him something more of a humanist than is realized. He acknowledges that, under certain conditions, the 'aesthetic function' of language becomes dominant, and the aesthetic intention and response displace the precise historical situation. But he objects to thinking of art as different in kind from 'mechanical' work.[49] This distinction occurred, he believes, from the time capitalism began to consider work as a commodity rather than as an expression of an organic relationship between self and the not-I world. Williams insists on the materiality of art: 'Literary production, then, is "creative", not in the ideological sense of "new vision", which takes a small part for the whole, but in the material social sense of a specific practice of self-making, which is in this sense socially neutral: *self-composition*'.[50] It may range 'from reproduction and illustration through embodiment and performance to new articulation and formation. . . . Writing is always in some sense self-composition and social composition . . . [T]he active struggle for new consciousness through new relationships [is] the ineradicable emphasis of the Marxist sense of self-creation'.[51]

We need to define two of Williams' key concepts: 'knowable community' and 'structure of feeling'. Williams claims that he bases his work 'on the indissoluble unity of individual and social experience'.[52] Rather than speak, as Hillis Miller does in *The Form of Victorian Fiction* (1968), of the narrator's knowledge of the imagined world, Williams speaks of novels as 'knowable communities': 'The knowable and therefore known relationships compose and are part of a wholly known social structure and . . . in and through the relationships the persons themselves can be wholly known. . . . Both society and persons are knowable' (pp. 14–15). We no longer believe, he argues, that persons are completely knowable. Nor do we believe that relationships are part of society; we now see that 'knowable relationships, so far from composing a community or a society, are the positive experience that has to be *contrasted* with the ordinarily negative experience of the society as a whole (or of the society as opposed to the local and immediate community') (p. 15). A knowable community depends on a perspicacious observer and coherent social data. 'What is knowable is not only a function of objects – of what is there to be known. It is also a function of subjects, of observers – of what is desired and what needs to be known' (p. 17). Society becomes not merely a background against which the drama of personal virtues and vices is enacted, but the creator of virtues and vices. What were once faults of the individual's soul becomes faults of society. In the recent *New Left Review* interviews published as *Politics and Letters*, he defines 'knowable community': 'Those novels which can attain an effective range of social experience by sufficiently manifest immediate relations possess a knowable community.'[53]

Perhaps the following statements in *Marxism and Literature* help clarify the concept of the 'knowable community': 'There is a persistent presupposition of a knowable (often wholly knowable) reality in terms of which the typification will be recognized and indeed (in a normal process in 'Marxist criticism') verified';[54] or, 'A cultural phenomenon acquires its full significance only when it is seen as a form of (known or knowable) general social process or structure.'[55] What is not clear is whether knowable community is a quality that belongs to the novel as perceived by the reader or to the world as perceived by the author. If the former, the 'unknowable' community would vary depending on the reader's experience. If the latter – in the sense of 'able to be known' and 'not able to be known' – isn't the reader's test of knowability dependent on a comparison of the text with a concept of the world that exists prior to the text? Aren't 'affective range' and 'manifest immediate relations' subjective terms? Are they different from quality and inconclusiveness? At times Williams seems to imply that we go to the imagined worlds of novels – to fictions – for the coherence that we lack now that knowable communities are not attainable; that, as we have seen, is the major point of Kermode's *The Sense of an Ending*.

Williams' concept 'structure of feeling' is not an entirely successful effort to fuse humanism and Marxism. Rather than define 'structure of feeling', Williams finds it easier to say what the concept includes: 'characteristic elements of impulse, restraint, and tone; specifically affective elements of consciousness and relationships: not feeling against thought, but thought as felt and feeling as thought: practical consciousness of a present kind, in a living and interrelating continuity . . .' (p. 132).[56] In the concept of felt thought we see the T. S. Eliot influence – which again gives away Williams' traditional training.

Knowable community can be defined in terms of 'structure of feeling that is lived and experienced but not yet quite arranged as institutions and ideas' (p. 192). Eagleton defines structure of feeling as 'that firm but intangible organization of values and perceptions which acts as a mediating category between the psychological 'set' of a social formation and the conventions embodied in its artifacts . . . [T]he novel, for Williams, is one medium among many in which men seek to master and absorb new experience by discovering new forms and rhythms, grasping and reconstructing the stuff of social change in the living substance of perceptions and relationships'.[57] We might ask whether we really see such an abstract, objective model in novels and, if we do, how can we isolate the data to prove it? And we should note that Eagleton's second sentence could easily describe Leavis's and Trilling's less rigid and ideological conceptions of fiction, and that Williams' concepts in *The English Novel* are often different from them in degree, not kind. Williams emphasizes that structure of feeling is a dynamic process. '[It] is a cultural hypothesis, actually derived from attempts to understand such elements and their connections in a generation or period, and needing always to be returned, interactively, to such evidence. . . . The idea of a structure of feeling can be specifically related to the evidence of forms and conventions – semantic figures – which, in art and literature, are often among the very first indications that such a new structure is forming.'[58]

Structures of feeling are 'social experiences *in solution*'.[59] Although Williams distinguishes 'structure of feeling' from 'world view' and 'ideology', he uses the term in a way that approximates Zeitgeist, as when he says: 'In England between 1660 and 1690, for example, two structures of feeling (among the defeated Puritans and in the restored Court) can be readily distinguished, though neither, in its literature and elsewhere, is reducible to the ideologies of these groups or to their formal (in fact complex) class relations.'[60] The efficacy of realism depends upon capturing the fabric of the structure of feeling. Thus while discussing Hardy's *The Return of the Native*, Williams remarks: 'As in all major realist fiction the quality and destiny of persons and the quality and destiny of a whole way of life are seen in the same dimension and not as separable issues' (p. 103). More than the other major Victorians, Hardy '[centred] his major novels in the ordinary process of life and work' (p. 116); thus, in Hardy's 'structure of feeling,' 'work and desire are very deeply connected' (p. 117). He praises Dickens for 'a structure of feeling, in its strengths and weaknesses, which he shares with the popular culture of his time'

(p. 55), and for capturing the actual crisis of values in the period in which he wrote.

Just like Kettle and Leavis, Williams sees George Eliot as a pivotal figure who shares many of his values. When Williams asserts that Eliot invented 'the analytic consciousness, that ordinary product of individual and social development, which comes in to enlighten and to qualify but above all to mediate the isolated desire and the general observation', he is making her his precursor as novelist and critic (p. 78). He sees in her work, for the first time, a schism between 'the narrative idiom of the novelist and the recorded language of her characters; between the analytic idiom and the overwhelming emphasis of emotion' – a schism which is central to his perception of a modern, industrial society and which he is trying to bridge (pp. 79–80). (It is curious how so many of our critics see Eliot as a precursor of, if not a mirror of, their own critical method.) Williams praises George Eliot for recording 'real history: indeed one of the clearest examples of literature enacting a history which is not otherwise, in any important way, articulated or recorded' (p. 78). By real history, he means the relationship of a typifying individual, who represents a social class, with other typifying individuals and the community. Williams attributes to Eliot the kind of vision on which he prides himself as critic: 'George Eliot became so conscious of history as a social and as a moral process that the problem of most of her work after *Mill on the Floss* is the discovery of an action which is capable of expressing it in its real connections' (p. 87). For Williams sees himself not as a literary critic but as a social historian in a tradition defined by Arnold and George Eliot, whose curiosity about, and conscious examination of, the structure of society are that of a critic: '[I]t is a social mode in which the observer, the signifier, is not himself at stake but is refined into a fictional process, indeed into a fiction . . . [It is] a mode in which we are all signifiers, all critics and judges, and can somehow afford to be because life – given life, creating life – goes on where it is supposed to, elsewhere' (p. 91). This seems to me a valuable insight, one which not only establishes an important parallel between the detached narrator as reader of society and the anxious self-doubting modern man as 'reader' of experience, but understands that the 'critic' partakes of both aspects. Thus, 'the knower has become a separated process in himself: a profoundly serious but also profoundly accepted alienation' (p. 92). Williams argues that while the perception of a network of relations by Dickens reconciles 'common humanity', Eliot's web or tangle sees 'human relationships as not only involving but comprising, limiting, mutually frustrating. And this is of course a radically different consciousness; what is still called a modern consciousness' (p. 88). Williams praises Eliot's later work – *Daniel Deronda*, *Middlemarch*, and *Felix Holt* – for its 'emphatic consciousness of historical *process*' as opposed to mere 'historical *change*' (p. 88).

Williams is not only interested in his authors as products of their culture but also as explorers of the frontiers of social awareness. Thus, he claims, Hardy needs to be seen 'in his real identity: both the educated observer and the passionate participant, in a period of general and radical change' (p. 106). Yet Williams understands that there is an important distinction between the biographical author and the formal presence. Williams uses biographical evidence to show that Hardy was not a peasant and that, as he puts it, 'Within [Hardy's writing], he is neither owner nor tenant, dealer nor labourer, but an observer and chronicler, often again with uncertainty about his actual relation' (p. 101). Or he remarks how the distance between Lawrence and his characters breaks down: 'What is new here, really new, is that the language of the writer is at one with the language of his characters, in a way that hadn't happened, though George Eliot and Hardy had tried, since the earlier smaller community of the novel had been extended and changed' (p. 173). And this last passage describes the relationship Williams seeks between himself and the authors he discusses, and explains why he speaks so frequently in the first person as he tries to come to grips with the novels he discusses. Williams insists throughout his discussion of Eliot and Hardy that 'Their novels are the records of struggle and difficulty, as was the life they wrote about', and that their novels may be the better for their lack of 'thematic unity' and 'unity of tone' (p. 85). The emphasis on quest is important to understanding not only his conception of the novelist, but his criticism in this study, as in all of his works. For Williams' subject is the subject he ascribes to the novelists he discusses: 'the exploration of community: the substance and meaning of community' (p. 11). That Williams defines himself in terms of those who came to the university from outside the public schools is a rhetorically effective prelude to tracing in Hardy the passage back and forth between the familiar and eduated worlds: '[T]he real Hardy country . . . is that border country so many of us have been living in between custom and education, between work and ideas, between love of place and an experience of change' (p. 98). What Eagleton writes of Williams's relationship to *Culture and Society* is also true of *The English Novel*: '[T]he key to that work is that Williams offers himself, not consciously or intrusively but implicitly and with every title to do so, as the latest figure in the lineage he traces, a character within his own drama'.[61] That Williams himself has written a number of novels may make him feel that he has a place in this lineage.

Williams is interested less in the way books present and reflect society than in the way books present the culture in which they are written and in the way they express and define that society. This interest takes him beyond the narrow formalism that sometimes restricts the focus of literary critics to a search for patterns of language or narrative modes. Part of Williams's originality stems from his seeing novels as explorations of social movement: '[The] new novelists of a rapidly changing England had to create, from their own resources, forms adequate to the experience at the new and critical stage it had reached' (p. 12). According to Williams, society's role changed: 'Society, now, was not just a code to measure, an institution to control, a standard to define or to change. It was a process that entered lives, to shape or to deform; a process personally known but then again suddenly distant, complex, incomprehensible, overwhelming' (p. 13).

The Brontës, he argues, were the first to be committed to 'passion'. Williams understands 'that the Brontë sisters knew directly a whole structure of repression in their time; knew it and in their own ways broke it with a strength and a courage that puts us all in their debt' (p. 63). Although he understands the role of form in containing 'passion', his interest in narration is related to the novel as social experience; for example, the first person narrator of *Jane Eyre* establishes an intimate relationship with the reader: 'What matters throughout is this private confidence, this mode of confession: the account given as if in a private letter, in private talk; the account given to a journal, a private journal, and then the act of writing includes – as it were involuntarily, yet it is very deliberate and conscious art – the awareness of the friend, the close one, the unknown but in this way intimate reader: the reader *as* the writer, while the urgent voice lasts' (p. 70). Williams's interest here is in the fundamental personal relationship, not in the ideological component.

It must be said that the Brontë discussion is typical of his tendency to construct an abstract polemical argument without too much attention to analysis of passages, albeit he quotes, following Leavis, long passages. What Williams tries to do is to create in his own criticism a concise 'structure of feeling' about a 'knowable community' created by the author. After all, if the novel is a structure of feeling so, at best, is the critical book. While his chapters explore the work's significance, they do not recreate a sense of the process of reading (or rereading) a novel. This is partly because his own method of pointing to quotations as representative passages of a larger pattern has limitations. (He has himself expressed doubt about this method.)

What Williams lacks is a middle level of discourse to connect his specific analyses with his abstractions. Quoting in place of an argument can actually distance the reader from the immediacy of the critical structure of feeling that must serve as the bond between critic and reader. Critical discourse requires argument, not simple recitation unaccompanied by analysis. Even if in the context of their sources, the long passages he cites dramatize 'a very complex structure of feeling' (p. 37) and dramatize a 'moral world in physical terms' (p. 40), it does not follow that they perform the same function when transplanted to the different environment of his critical discussion. Quotes from other writers do not necessarily have the same typifying value in an abstract argument as the passage had within the imagined world of the novel.

As *The English Novel* progresses, from Dickens, to the Brontës and Eliot and then to the late nineteenth and twentieth century, the sociological, if not the Marxist, perspective becomes more prominent. The Hardy chapter is a turning point. Williams's close analysis of a passage at Dairyman Crick's, describing the spring setting as Tess and Angel gradually get to know one another, is an example of his use of close analyses to show that at best Hardy fuses the educated and country culture: 'The mature style itself is unambiguously an educated style, in which the extension of vocabulary and the complication of construction are necessary to the intensity and precision of the observation which is Hardy's essential position and attribute' (p. 109). He contends – as Lawrence himself had – that Hardy saw before Lawrence 'the human nullity of that apparently articulate world' (p. 110). Hardy is 'caught by his personal history in the general structure and crisis of the relations between education and class, relations which in practice are between intelligence and fellow-feeling' (p. 111). Hardy's characters are affected by 'economic processes' interacting with 'the natural processes': 'The social process created in this interaction is one of class and separation, as well as of chronic insecurity' (p. 115). Hardy's fatalism derives from 'the decadent thought of his time' (p. 116).

That two of the last four chapters following the Hardy chapter are entitled 'A Parting of the Ways' and 'Alone in the City' rather than, as in prior chapters the names of authors, underlines his change in emphasis. (The other two of the last four are titled 'Joseph Conrad' and 'D. H. Lawrence'). In 'A Parting of the Ways' he speaks of the schism between the social and the personal between 1890 and the First World War. In this period, there was a tension between 'art as a vehicle', the position of Wells, and 'art as autonomous in its own clear circle', the position of James (p. 138). And, as I have been arguing, this has been an issue in the novel criticism since that period. Williams, like Leavis, feels that James sacrifices on the altar a full understanding of life. James has included in his novels 'very serious human actions', but he has excluded 'history' (p. 133). For James, 'The act of seeing, the act of making, the act of rendering and presenting is life itself of an intense kind. . . . What really matters in James is that act of signifying in which the novel itself becomes its own subject. . . . Consciousness in James, to put it another way, is the almost exclusive object and subject of consciousness' (p. 135).

Let us conclude with a summary of what a Marxist approach contributed to the aesthetic of fictions that we bring to the English novel.

(1) The concept of history as a dynamic and evolving process emphasizes that the reading and movement of a novel are not static but dynamic and constantly changing in shape and meaning.
(2) The Marxist critics have provided the English novel – in its practice and its criticism – with a larger perspective than its customary stress on manners and motive evokes.
(3) By focusing on art as content, Marxist criticism sees the continuities between the creation and consumption of art and other experiences.
(4) It resists the tendency to remove art from the context of other human activities and to see art as a special activity with its own rules produced by the elite for the cognoscenti. (Perhaps this view is best epitomized by Yeats's esoteric desire to be a golden bird removed from the conditions of morality, who would 'set upon a golden bough to sing / To Lords and ladies of Byzantium / of what is past, or passing, or to come'.) De-mystifying art was, and is, an important contribution of Marxist criticism.
(5) By urging criticism to think about economic and social – and by extension – intellectual backgrounds, it has been and is a factor in keeping literary studies from becoming narrow and provincial.

But we must also acknowledge the failures of Marxist criticism:

(a) All ideological criticism tends to be in what Hillis Miller calls the

'Platonic' tradition and to insist on resemblance to a paradigm.[62] It usually does not appreciate playfulness, creativity, and uniqueness for its own sake. Nor does it attend to the artistic and formal values of novels, except when they can be described in terms of the dominant historical and social patterns required by ideology, and Marxist criticism is no exception.

(b) Marxist criticism is often inattentive to the subtleties of the text and insists on broad generalization at the expense of close reading.

(c) It underestimates the irrational, emotional, magical, and epiphanical moments within a text.

(d) It tends to define historical contexts in exclusively or primarily economic terms.

(e) It often underplays the creative process of an artistic figure whose imagination is, no matter what other factors contribute to the artistic work, unique, idiosyncratic, and, in the best case, brilliant.

(f) Its theoretical apparatus (as outlined in a book such as *Marxism and Literature*) seems to be inappropriate and at times inapplicable to the reading of complex texts.

(g) It is guilty of a general neglect of poetry which is less responsive to the categorizing and abstracting sensibility.

(h) For fiction, it takes nineteenth-century realism as a paradigm, and ignores other kinds of fiction.

In its quest for ideology, Marxist criticism neglects what Lionel Trilling has called culture's 'hum and buzz of implication. I mean the whole evanescent context in which its explicit statements are made'.[63] Trilling notes 'that in proportion as we have committed ourselves to our particular idea of reality we have lost our interest in manners'.[64] Eloquently affirming the humanistic testament of fiction's social purpose, Trilling writes of the novel: 'Its greatness and its practical usefulness lay in its unremitting work of involving the reader himself in the moral life, inviting him to put his own motives under examination, suggesting that the reality is not as his conventional education has led him to see it. It taught us, as no other genre ever did, the extent of human variety and the value of this variety. It was the literary form to which the emotions of understanding and forgiveness were indigenous, as if by the definition of the form itself.'[65]

NOTES

1. *Politics and Letters* (London: New Left Books, 1979) p. 244.
2. Peter Demetz, *Marx, Engels, and The Poets* (University of Chicago Press, 1967), trans. Jeffrey L. Sammons, rev. edn pp. 142–3.
3. Lucien Goldmann, *The Hidden God*; quoted in Andrew Milner, *John Milton and the English Revolution* (New York: Barnes & Noble, 1981) p. 3.
4. Karl Marx and Frederick Engels, *The German Ideology*, Part I; quoted in Milner, p. 4.
5. Marx, *A Contribution to the Critique of Political Economy*; quoted in Milner, p. 4.
6. Milner, p. 6.
7. Raymond Williams, *Marxism and Literature* (Oxford University Press, 1977), p. 75.
8. Quoted in Williams, ibid., pp. 75–6.
9. Ibid., p. 77.
10. Ibid., pp. 81–2.
11. Ibid., p. 97.
12. Ibid., p. 98.
13. Ibid., p. 105.
14. Ibid., p. 106.
15. Milner, p. 9.
16. Williams, p. 110.
17. Ibid., p. 112.
18. Ibid., p. 113.
19. Ibid., p. 112.
20. Ibid., p. 101.
21. Georg Lukàcs, *The Meaning of Contemporary Realism*, quoted in Milner, p. 29.
22. See Williams, p. 102.
23. J. Hillis Miller, *Fiction and Repetition* (Harvard University Press; Cambridge University Press, 1982); see Chapter One.
24. Through section III, page numbers in parentheses refer to Arnold Kettle, *An Introduction to the English Novel*, 2 vols (New York: Harper, 1960) orig. edn 1951.
25. Jonathan Culler, *The Pursuit of Signs: Semiotics, Literature, Deconstruction* (Ithaca, New York: Cornell University Press, 1981) p. 172.
26. Christopher Hill, *Puritanism and Revolution* (New York: Schocken Books, 1964) first edn 1958, pp. 367–94.
27. Milner, p. 29.
28. In section IV, page numbers in parentheses refer to Raymond Williams, *The English Novel From Dickens to Lawrence* (New York: Oxford University Press, 1970).
29. Terry Eagleton, *Criticism and Ideology* (London: New Left Books, 1976) p. 34.
30. *Politics and Letters* (London: New Left Books, 1979) p. 245.
31. *Reading and Criticism*, p. 107; quoted in *Politics and Letters*, p. 238.
32. See Terry Eagleton, pp. 36–7.

33. *Politics and Letters*, p. 247.
34. Williams, *Marxism and Literature*, p. 51.
35. Ibid., p. 52.
36. Ibid., p. 52.
37. Ibid., p. 102.
38. Ibid., p. 203–4.
39. Ibid., p. 196.
40. Ibid., p. 199.
41. Ibid., p. 199.
42. Ibid., pp. 201, 204.
43. Ibid., p. 197.
44. Ibid., p. 193.
45. Ibid., p. 198.
46. Ibid., p. 87.
47. Ibid., p. 44.
48. Ibid., p. 166.
49. Ibid., p. 160.
50. Ibid., p. 210.
51. Ibid., pp. 210–12.
52. Williams, *Politics and Letters*, p. 252.
53. Ibid., p. 247.
54. Williams, *Marxism and Literature*, pp. 102–3.
55. Ibid., p. 105.
56. Ibid., p. 132.
57. Eagleton, *Criticism and Ideology*, pp. 33–4.
58. Williams, *Marxism and Literature*, pp. 132–3.
59. Ibid., p. 133.
60. Ibid., p. 134.
61. Eagleton, p. 73.
62. J. Hillis Miller, *Fiction and Repetition*, p. 6.
63. Lionel Trilling, 'Manners, Morals and the Novel', *The Liberal Imagination* (Viking: New York, 1951) p. 206.
64. Ibid., p. 216.
65. Ibid., p. 222.

10   The Fictional Theories of J. Hillis Miller: Humanism, Phenomenology, and Deconstruction in *The Form of Victorian Fiction* and *Fiction and Repetition*

I

With the publication of *Fiction and Repetition*, J. Hillis Miller has confirmed his place in the first ranks of American critics. His importance is not merely that he proposed the most important sustained argument for a way of reading fiction by one of the American post-structuralists, but that he entered into a serious dialogue with past criticism of fiction. Cumulatively, J. Hillis Miller's six critical books – *Charles Dickens: The World of His Novels* (1958), *The Disappearance of God* (1963), *Poets of Reality* (1965), *The Form of Victorian Fiction* (1968), *Thomas Hardy: Distance and Desire* (1970), and *Fiction and Repetition* (1982) – constitute one of the major critical achievements of the last two decades. These are primarily works of literary criticism, but they are also substantial methodological and theoretical statements. In my final chapter, I have chosen to focus on two of Hillis Miller's books, *The Form of Victorian Fiction* and *Fiction and Repetition*, because they are less concerned with specific authors and texts and more with theoretical and methodological questions about fiction. Despite Miller's denial that the latter book proposes a theory,

222

Fiction and Repetition is Miller's version of both Van Ghent's *The English Novel: Form and Function* and Brook's and Warren's *Understanding Fiction*. It contains the major premises of post-structuralist thinking about fiction and it places that thinking in the context of, and tries to integrate it with, prior criticism.

While Miller's subsequent intellectual journey took him to structuralism and post-structuralism, *The Form of Victorian Fiction* needs to be understood in the context in which it was written. The phenomenology of Georges Poulet dominated the thought of Hillis Miller from the late 1950s; and that influence, along with the influence of the more traditional formal criticism derived from the James tradition and New Criticism, informs his work on the novel, although by the late 1960s he was already being influenced by structural linguistics. Like Frye and Kermode, Miller desires to go beyond the positivism of the New Criticism and Neo-Aristotelianism; Poulet, with whom he taught at Johns Hopkins, provided an example of how this could be done.

In Poulet and Miller, the critic surrenders his ego in order to enter into the consciousness of the author and to relive his world and thoughts. As Frank Lentricchia notes, Poulet is committed 'to the *cogito*, or subject which possesses itself directly, without gap, lag or mediation, in a "moment" before or above time'.[1] For Poulet, the cogito is 'a moment in "solitary mental life", anterior to discourse and time, in which discourse becomes irrelevant; a moment in which, presumably, there is no need for discourse because the speaking subject is immediately present to itself without gap in the transcendence of the present'.[2] The reader opens himself to the cogito of the author in order to retrieve the subject.

In an important testament of how this works, Poulet describes a visit to Venice when he saw a room full of Tintorettos; he speaks of discovering the 'common essence present in all the works of a great master, an essence which I was not able to perceive, except when emptying my mind of all the particular images created by the artist. I became aware of a subjective power at work in all these pictures, and yet never so clearly understood by my mind as when I had forgotten all their particular figurations'.[3] Finally Poulet's work has a strong romantic component. Cogito is a version of the romantic imagination which half perceives and half creates and which by its energy transforms experience. Before we can perceive art intensely, we must empty our minds of all but the artist's work. If Poulet's idea that the reader empties himself can be thought of as having a kinship with Keats's negative capability, his anti-historicism resembles that of Frye.

The ontology of the work of art is no longer that of a well-wrought urn
which the critic sees as an object; almost like a person involved in a
spiritual quest, the reader enters into the ontology that exists apart
from the real world. Literature, as Poulet puts it, 'exists in itself
withdrawn from any power which might determine it from the
outside'.[4] The cogito is an ineffable presence approached by the
self-effacing reader. Familiarity with the author's other works helps us
to approach that presence, although experiencing the cogito is not
dependent upon knowing historical or biographical information, or
the author's canon, or even on the language he uses.

Already emerging in the Dickens book, phenomenology is the
dominant critical approach in *The Disappearance of God* and *Poets of
Reality*. In a pattern that we have seen before in this study, Miller turns
the authors he discusses into paradigms of his critical ideal. Thus in
Poets of Reality the author, as he approaches his subject, effaces his
ego just as the ideal reader and critic are supposed to do when they
approach a text. And he does the same thing in *Fiction and Repetition*
where the ideal reader, like the ideal author, discovers heterogeneity
in texts and avoids the logical and consistent position dependent on
historical or biographical explanations. Miller equates the author's
effacement of the ego with abandoning the will to power and
ultimately with spiritual grace: 'The effacement of the ego before
reality means abandoning the will to power over things. This is the
most difficult of acts for a modern man to perform. It goes counter to
all the penchants of our culture. To abandon its project of dominion
the will must will not to will. Only through an abnegation of the will can
objects begin to manifest themselves as they are, in the integrity of
their presence. When man is willing to let things be then they appear in
a space which is no longer that of an objective world opposed to the
mind. In this space the mind is dispersed everywhere in things and
forms one with them' (*PR*, p. 8).[5] And this, we realize, describes the
appropriate stance of the reader before the work of literature. For,
according to phenomenological criticism, the reader must abandon
'his will to power over things' to achieve the grace that is necessary to
enter into the privileged world of the author's consciousness or cogito
and thus to read with understanding and sensitivity. This consciousness or cogito is the revealed presence beyond the apparently real
presence. It is accessible to the privileged readers who can, because
they dispossess themselves of their ego, enter into the world of the
author as revealed in and through the text. In the reader's search for
the real, true author beyond the appearance in the text, we see an

unintentional parody of the Christian's search for the true spirit. The text is the mediating agency between reader and author just as the Catholic Church mediates between the Soul and God. Put another way: the reader is a kind of acolyte to the author.

In *Fiction and Repetition*, Miller has a different historical perspective from his other books. While *Poets of Reality* and *The Disappearance of God* propose panoramic historical arguments on which the reading of literary works depends, *Fiction and Repetition* disdains historical argument based on empirical evidence. Miller's denial of historical development strikingly cointrasts with his thesis in *The Disappearance of God* and *Poets of Reality*. In those works he sees a natural progression of increasing subjectivity from Romanticism to Victorianism to modernism. In *The Disappearance of God* he argued that 'Writers of the middle nineteenth century . . . tend to accept the romantic dichotomy of subject and object, but are no longer able to experience God as both immanent and transcendent' (*PR*, p. 2). In the sequel, *Poets of Reality*, he extends his historical perspective to the twentieth century: 'If the disappearance of God is presupposed by much Victorian poetry, the death of God is the starting point for many twentieth-century writers' (*PR*, p. 2). In *Poets of Reality* Miller assumes a gloomy, vatic tone to judge modern writers:

Romantic literature and modern technology are aspects of a world-embracing evolution of culture. As this development proceeds, man comes even to forget that he has been the murderer of God. . . . The triumph of technology is the forgetting of the death of God. (*PR*, pp. 4–5)

Poets of Reality uses Conrad to define the conditions of twentieth-century life and then turns to Yeats, Eliot, Thomas, Stevens and Williams: 'Each begins with an experience of nihilism or its concomitants, and each in his own way enters the new reality. . . . In their work reality comes to be present to the senses, present to the mind which possesses it through the senses, and present in the words of the poems which ratify this possession.' (*PR*, p. 11). In much criticism of consciousness, including Poulet and his Geneva school followers, brilliance and impressionism go hand in hand. Part of its original appeal was that it moved beyond the New Criticism's stress on close analysis of linguistic detail, which the advocates of phenomenology, among others, felt had degenerated into a search for obscure details for their own sake. Yet despite Miller's use of quotation, the essay on

Conrad in *Poets of Reality* seems to take us a step away from the text.

At times, rather than commenting on the specific thrust of a passage in the evolving context of a literary work, Miller allows the text to evoke ruminations on theoretical, historical, and philosophical problems. After explicating the image of the kernel and the haze in *Heart of Darkness*, he steps back and writes:

> But this is not really so. Writing can only oscillate perpetually between truth and falsehood, and endure endlessly its failure to bring what is real, the darkness, permanently into what is human, the light. Every story is necessarily a failure. In the moment that the darkness is caressed into appearing by the words of the story, it disappears. Though writing is the only action which escapes the imposture of the merely human, at the same time all literature is necessarily sham. It captures in its subtle pages not the reality of darkness but its verbal image. (*PR*, p. 38)

Well, yes, and Conrad probably knows this, but does this really have to do with Conrad's work? Miller is trying to recreate for his reader his responses to the text. But he homogenizes the diverse reading experiences of an author: 'Conrad's novels all say the same thing, and yet are all different, as all clouds differ and yet are all children of the same sky' (*PR*, p. 67).

While brilliant on intellectual patterns and the broad *Zeitgeist*, Miller does not have a feel for lived history – the way that language and thoughts become translated into actions that provide the energy for political and social movements. And this limitation carries over through *The Form of Victorian Fiction* and *Fiction and Repetition*. I am distinguishing between history as lived human events and speculative intellectual history, including Miller's generalizations about the disappearance of God or modern nihilism. Indeed, the failure on the part of the deconstructionists and phenomenologists to understand the fabric of social institutions, customs, and conventions that constitute the context of English and American literature at times gives their work a claustrophobic quality.

II

The argument in *The Form of Victorian Fiction* depends in part on the validity of the argument in *The Disappearance of God* that the nineteenth century saw a change from a god-centred universe to a universe in which man is the centre. In the nineteenth century God disappears, although he is still the creator; by contrast in *Poets of Reality*, he is no longer the creator. Picking up a strand of *The Disappearance of God*, Miller writes: 'Victorian fiction may be said to have as its fundamental theme an exploration of the various ways in which a man may seek to make a god of another person in a world without God, or at any rate in a world where the traditional ways in which the self may be related to God no longer seem open' (*FVF*, p. 96). Paradoxically, Miller notes that 'In the Victorian novel . . . each person comes into existence as a self only through his relations to others' (*FVF*, p. 45). According to Miller all fiction has a single pervasive theme: interpersonal relations. When God vanishes man, according to Miller, turns to personal relationships and each man creates his own putative order. Dorothea's marriage to Casaubon 'leads to her discovery that no man can be a god for another in a world without God. . . . Each man casts outward on the world patterns of value which have no existence except in his own mind' (*FVF*, pp. 115–16). Or, as Conrad would put it, 'Another man's truth is only a dismal lie to me.[6]'

Miller's argument depends on the interaction among what he isolates as the three principal components of Victorian fiction: the time structure, the interplay of the imaginary and real, and the patterns of interacting minds. In *The Form of Victorian Fiction*, Miller is as much a formalist as a phenomenologist and accepts some basic tenets of Anglo-American formalism. When we look at Miller's work, we are paradoxically struck both by his continuities with traditional criticism and his innovation and freshness. We can see how *The Form of Victorian Fiction* is midway between phenomenology and deconstruction, even while it bears the stamp of New Criticism. He knows that technique is discovery: 'Thackeray sees that a narrative style creates the reality it describes' (*FVF*, p. 71). Miller not only sees that the narrator is an important formal part of the novel but that he also assumes a living presence and becomes a character whose mind we know: 'The narrator is a personality created by the tempo, diction, and tone of the words. . . . He has ubiquity in time and space and knows everything there is to know within that all-embracing span' (*FVF*, p. 10). For the narrator the events are not imaginary but real: 'he has a superhuman power of memory and clairvoyance' (*FVF*, p. 11). Miller does not ignore the relation between art and the external world, as when he speaks of writers who overcome exclusion by playing the role of the narrator: 'When Marian Evans became George Eliot she did so by assuming the personality of a Feuerbachian general consciousness, the mind not of a specific society but of all humanity' (*FVF*, p. 113).

In *The Form of Victorian Fiction* Miller has not yet abandoned the author as a presence behind and within the text. He even speaks for the expressionistic function of art: 'In six of the most important Victorian novelists [George Eliot, Trollope, Dickens, Thackeray, Meredith and Hardy], some experience of detachment from the community, whether chosen or imposed, constitutes an originating moment which determines the writer's sense of himself and his stance in relation to the world' (*FVF*, p. 62). These writers used conventions 'to solve problems of their own. The writing of fiction was an indirect way for them to reenter the social world from which they had been excluded or which they were afraid to enter directly' (*FVF*, p. 63). The convention they use to enter is the omniscient narrator. This convention is 'the determining principle' of the form of Victorian fiction (*FVF*, p. 63). When he speaks about authors in this way, he has in mind the *cogito* of the author that informs the work, but, nevertheless he is offering a challenge to prevailing New Critical orthodoxies that preached that the author must be removed from the text. Indeed Poulet's and Miller's criticism of consciousness depends finally upon speculations about the original author: 'The words of a novel objectify the mind of an author and make that mind available to others' (*FVF*, p. 1). Miller defines reading as 'consciousness of the consciousness of another. . . . A novel is a structure of interpenetrating minds, the mind of the narrator as he beholds or enters into the characters, the minds of the characters as they behold or know one another' (*FVF*, p. 2). The narrator is a collective mind, a community consciousness which 'relives from within the thoughts and feelings of a character and registers these in his own language, or in a mixture of the character's language and his own language' (*FVF*, p. 3). In most Victorian novels, Miller notes, 'there is relatively little detached self-consciousness; . . . the characters are aware of themselves in terms of their relations to other people' (*FVF*, pp. 4–5).

Along with Kermode, Miller did much to refocus fiction away from the spatial notions of Frank and the archetypes of Frye and towards a sense of the novel as an evolving and developing temporal event: 'Time is a more important dimension of fiction than space' (*FVF*, p. 6). But for Miller the movement is defined both in terms of the characters' change and the narrator's: 'The dramatic action of a novel is the temporal pattern made of the sequence of interactions between minds, each with its own temporal flow, as they move toward some equilibrium or dispersal of their relationships' (*FVF*, p. 7). Contrary to the idea of form as static he argues that the novel is also 'a structure which is incomplete. . . . [It] exists in movement and openness' (*FVF*, pp. 29–30). According to Miller, time is crucial for writing novels, reading novels, and for understanding how characters live in the imagined world of novels:

> [N]ovels excel in expressing the temporality of the present as a reaching toward a future which will contain a reassimilation of the past. . . . The narrator stands in that future which possesses in potentiality the completed past, but he moves back through that past trying to bring it up to the future as a present actualized in words. The novelist seeks to comprehend his own past existence by moving away from it into an imaginary future which his story continuously generates, in one version of the hermeneutical circle of interpretation. The reader in his attempt to understand the novel is caught in another form of the temporal circle of interpretation, reaching toward a perfected understanding of the whole which is never attained, but which is presupposed as already existing in any partial explication. (*FVF*, pp. 15–16).

Thus of *Oliver Twist* he writes, 'the temporal sequence of the novel is the gradual approach of the mind of the protagonist toward that of the narrator' (*FVF*, p. 77). His discussion of time stresses that because all the aspects of temporal form are not finished, no moment can be the 'centre'; even the ending is only privileged by place but 'not because the circle is now at last brought round and full' (*FVF*, p. 47).

Yet paradoxically the temporality of fiction compromises the possibility of fulfilment of the characters' aspirations, the possibility of a significant form for the narrator, and thus the possibility of the reader's full and total comprehension of a text: 'The temporal structure of a novel, whether it is looked at from the point of view of the reader seeking to achieve a total grasp of the novel, or from the point of view of the narrator telling his story, or from the point of view of the characters seeking to fill the hollow in their hearts and come to coincide fully with themselves, is also an expression of the way man is alienated from the ground of his being, that proximity of the distant which haunts him like a tune he cannot quite remember, or like something half-glimpsed out of the corner of his eye' (*FVF*, p. 46). In a passage such as this, we can see the tendency to deny presence, meaning, and significance. But, surely, our own process of reading confirms that meaning is always a shadow in fiction, as in life, for time is erasing even as it creates. Thus in *Lord Jim* the absolute judgment of the omniscient narrator is gradually challenged by Marlow's self-doubting, anxious perspective.

In *The Form of Victorian Fiction* for the first time Miller tries to import linguistic models, particularly of Saussure, and to see literary plots and literary studies in terms of self-regulating linguistic structures. The systems of linguistics provide models for the perceptions and classifications of narrative modes, since literature is a form of language – in current terms, the *parole* (speech acts) that derives from the *langue* (system of language). As Josué V. Harari put it, 'Structural analysis describes and explains a text as a system of narrative transformations. It presents a picture of all possible narrative discourses, such that all existing narratives appear as particular instances of a general – although variable – hypothetical model.'[7] Thus novels are regarded as prolonged sentences where the meaning is determined by relationship to its other words rather than by reference to a meaning prior to the sentences. In this view, a novel is not supported epistemologically by anything 'outside itself' (*FVF*, p. 34).

An important analogy is the one that equates the role of words in a sentence to the role of interpersonal relationships in a plot. Just as the meaning of the plot depends on interaction between persons, 'The source of meaning which makes language possible can be located in no single word, but only in the interaction of words in syntactical patterns' (*FVF*, p. 136). He implies that a happy ending may disguise rather than reveal the meaning of a book, just as the perfected sentence may disguise more than it reveals. He questions 'whether the perfected sentence brings into the open the latent principle of meaning which makes language possible, or whether it hides it. Perhaps the power behind language is only brought to the surface in the gaps between words, in the failures of language, not in its completed articulations' (*FVF*, p. 137). In other words the plot as a long sentence has a deep structure beneath its surface conclusion. Thus we might argue that in *Bleak House*, despite the apparent happy ending of the 'plot' as a 'perfected sentence', the 'latent principle of meaning' is the spreading spiritual drought of the community which is neither healed nor contained by Esther's marriage to Allen Woodcourt.

Retrospectively, we can see how *The Form of Victorian Fiction* was a necessary prelude to *Fiction and Repetition*. What is important in terms of Miller's intellectual progress is that for the first time in his work Miller denies a traditional separation between the signifier and the signified, and refuses to grant that the novelist's words create an imagined world that reveals or represents an a priori world. This makes possible the equation of imagination and reality: 'Words liberated from their usual function as the names of independently existing objects, persons, actions, or qualities, recover their primordial power to create a reality of their own' (*FVF*, p. 40). Because, he argues, language creates its own reality within a self-enclosed system, fiction cannot mirror reality: 'Far from affirming the independent existence of what he describes, Dickens' narrator betrays in a number of ways the fact that fictional characters and their world are made only of words' (*FVF*, p. 36). Finally novels are fictive: 'Any novel is to some degree an antinovel, not a direct picture of reality but a work of art which reaches toward reality by going away from it. A novel inevitably contains in its language some revelation that it is a fiction. As such it generates its own linguistic reality rather than bearing a one to one correspondence to some objective reality' (*FVF*, pp. 71–2). Since fiction, according to Miller, 'may be a way of bringing into the open the imaginary quality of reality,' imaginary and real are no longer polar opposites (*FVF*, p. 35). And this, he believes, is appropriate in a relativistic world where each man creates his own reality, and where, since hopes and plans and dreams are hardly less real than the factual world, one person's real world may seem quite imaginary to the perceptions of another. The New Critical idea of an hermetically enclosed ontology is echoed in the structuralist model, but the latter denies that the ontology expresses an anterior world; 'Every element draws its meaning from the others, so that the novel must be described as a self-generating and self-sustaining system, like the society it mirrors' (*FVF*, p. 30). But indeed we might ask, can we *intellectually* afford books to be about language? Doesn't the reality of *Our Mutual Friend* or *Bleak House* derive from Dickens' view of Victorian England? Can we put aside or condescend to the subject matter of Dickens or other nineteenth-century novelists as if we were viewing Mondrian or Malevich – particularly since we are now learning that the supposedly abstract formalism of these painters is iconographic of their spiritual concerns?

Miller sees the lack of definite meaning in texts as a parallel to the incoherence of the world that the novels would imitate: 'In Victorian fiction there is a parallel movement from a view of society as a system in which each element has a center and foundation outside itself to a view of it as a system which founds itself, as a sentence generates its own meaning' (*FVF*, p. 34). A major premise is that the Victorian novels lack a priori 'ground' and 'centre' and that their meaning is defined only in relation to their parts. Basically the text as mimesis deconstructs the text as words and vice versa. But in the following passage Miller does not have the same forceful grasp of his concepts that he will later have: 'The reader of a Victorian novel, like the author of it, must be on both sides of the mirror at once, seeing the fiction as a fiction, as a cunning model in words of the society it reflects, and enjoying at the same time a sovereign inwardness gained through perfect coincidence with the collective awareness of the community' (*FVF*, p. 68). Yet his own view of the Victorian novels has a centre, and it is the traditional centre of the narrator. If in *Middlemarch* Eliot's narrator represents 'the universal experience of mankind', does that not provide a centre? (*FVF*, p. 83). If we can ground Victorian fiction in concepts, does it not have an informing centre or centres? Indeed the thematic centre is the same as in *The Disappearance of God* and *Poets of Reality*: how man defines himself and his relationship to other people in a moral and spiritual vacuum created by the disappearance of God. In *Fiction and Repetition*, Miller will propose the concept of heterogeneity to resolve the paradox of how a novel can have and not have 'ground' at the same time.

Miller understands the role of the reader not in terms of responding to specific linguistic effects created by the author to shape the reader, but in terms which suggest the self-effacing reader approaching the mystery of the cogito. For example, he speaks of the narrator's use of 'we' in *Vanity Fair* as the 'rhetoric of assimilation': 'We are asked to identify ourselves with one another and with the narrator who speaks for us until by a kind of magical sympathy we lose our identities, are drawn into the group, and taken all together come to form a ubiquitous chorus of judgment, the whole middle and upper class Victorian community surrounding the stories of Becky and Amelia, and judging them collectively or allowing the narrator to judge them in our names' (*FVF*, p. 72).

The Form of Victorian Fiction anticipates *Fiction and Repetition* in a number of important ways. Its argument is preoccupied with doubling and repetition. A work of fiction repeats the real world and it repeats the author's life. The present tense telling repeats the past. In first person narration, older narrators repeat the events of their lives and 'repeat' them in the sense of reliving them. As readers we are conscious of prior episodes which resonate in present ones. The consciousnesses of characters iterate their past. Reading, we repeat the lives of characters who, in turn, are repeating their lives as characters because the narrative is a repetition of already lived lives; since sometimes the characters are repeating the lives of their creators, our process of learning about the characters may repeat the author's process of growth and evolution. In *The Form of Victorian Fiction* what he will later call 'repetition' usually takes the name of 'doubling,' and doubling is a crucial concept in his argument. Thus the author 'doubl[es] his past' to the extent that he writes an autobiographical novel (*FVF*, p. 10). Doubling is a basic structural principle in the novels; of *Our Mutual Friend*, he writes, 'the basic structural principle . . . is a doubling, like that of a play within a play, or of a picture within a picture, by which different levels of language or of narrative consciousness are placed one inside the other to generate an oscillation between imagination and reality' (*FVF*, p. 37). Writing of *Henry Esmond*, he speaks 'of the doubling of mind within mind characteristic of the autobiographical novel', until 'doubleness' becomes the 'fundamental structuring principle' of *Henry Esmond*; and he speaks of the author's 'double displacement' by which he becomes part of 'the mirroring general consciousness' and 'the minds of the protagonists' (*FVF*, pp. 104, 23, 139–40).

Before turning to *Fiction and Repetition*, let us consider some problems in *The Form of Victorian Fiction*. Sometimes Miller's generalizations do not hold. Thus he writes, '*Henry Esmond* is poised between Thackeray's nostalgia for a time when the self and the community had an extra-human foundation and his confrontation of a new situation in which people must generate their own identities over the void within them by way of the interplay between one person and another in society' (*FVF*, p. 104). But when in the novel since Fielding and Richardson did self and community really have an extra-human foundation? Surely not in *Emma* when the heroine is an example of 'myself creating what I saw'. The brevity of *The Form of Victorian Fiction*, which was based on a series of lectures given at Notre Dame, does not give Miller much space to develop readings and give a sense of a novel's evolving linear structure. (The latter continues to be a problem in *Fiction and Repetition* when he has more space.)

Another problem is that Miller's selection of novels seems arbitrary. For example, Hardy's *A Pair of Blue Eyes* is neither well known nor is it the best example of Hardy's method. Unlike the later *Fiction and Repetition*, Miller does not give himself room to develop his concepts in a carefully argued capacious chapter. We should note that his attraction to abstract language sometimes leads him to imprecision as when he writes: 'Hardy's characters, like those of other Victorian novelists, often have a perfect intuition of the other person's heart' (*FVF*, p. 13). This is usually not true of Victorian fiction (Do Ada and Richard, or even Esther and Jarndyce, really understand one another?). It is even less true in Hardy where pairs of characters – Jude and Sue, Tess and Angel – often assume that their partial understanding of one another is a true one. Finally, terms like 'patterns of intersubjectivity', 'hermeneutical circle of interpretation', and 'incarnate' diminish the clarity of Miller's argument.

III

Miller announces that *Fiction and Repetition* is a 'series of readings of important nineteenth- and twentieth-century English novels. The readings are more concerned with the relation of rhetorical form to meaning than with thematic paraphrase, though of course it is impossible in practice to separate these wholly. The focus . . . [is on] "how does meaning arise from the reader's encounter with just these words on the page?"' (*FR*, p. 3). In *Fiction and Repetition* the title subject of each chapter becomes an individual work, rather than an author, as in *The Disappearance of God*, *Poets of Reality*, and *Thomas Hardy: Distance and Desire*, books in which he was trying – following Poulet – to recreate the consciousness of the author that informs several works.

Miller proposes two kinds of repetition. One version is ' "Platonic" repetition [which] is grounded in a solid archetypal model which is untouched by the effects of repetition. . . . The validity of the mimetic copy is established by its truth of correspondence to what it copies' (*FR*, p. 6). This is the major concept underlying Western literature, including nineteenth and twentieth-century English realistic fiction and the aesthetic standard by which critics as diverse as Aristotle, Auerbach, and James measure works. The world to which the author refers may be more or less a facsimile based on the principle of recreating a perceived image of what an aspect of the external world is really like. But the world represented in the novel is always anterior to the author's imaginative vision.

By contrast, 'the other, Nietzschean mode of repetition posits a world based on difference'. It assumes that 'each thing . . . is unique, intrinsically different from every other thing . . . [Repetitions] are ungrounded doublings which arise from differential interrelations among elements which are all on the same plane' (*FR*, p. 6). Miller describes the artistic process of writing and the perceptual process of reading in terms of mental processes – voluntary and involuntary memory – common to all. The first kind of repetition recalls 'willed memory' which 'works logically, by way of similarities which are seen as identities, one thing repeating another and grounded in a concept on the basis of which their likeness may be understood' (*FR*, p. 8). The second recalls the 'involuntary form of memory' which replaces the world of life with that of fiction and imagination in the form of dream: 'one thing is experienced as repeating something which is quite different from it and which it strangely resembles' (*FR*, p. 8). In this kind of repetition, the emphasis is more on similarity within difference than upon total resemblance. Yet we should note that the involuntary form of memory comes also in the first form of repetition when the individual selects and arranges the material from the anterior world, for that selection and arrangement inevitably produce a transformed world. Isn't that what Schorer means by technique as discovery? And we should also note that in the second kind of repetition, one can only have repetition when one has – if only for a moment – the stability of ground. For without the ground of a prior thing or word or event, how can a second thing echo or repeat the first? Thus can one ever have pure 'differential interrelations?'

These kinds of repetitions suggest traditional distinctions between vertical God-centred conceptions of the world and horizontal linear man-centred concepts. They have a kinship with Kermode's *kairos* and *chronos*. On the whole, the first kind of repetition is that of humanism; the second is of deconstruction; thus it is appropriate that the first finds its model in Plato and the second in Nietzsche. These forms of repetition are themselves figures for the division in Miller's mind between humanism and deconstruction, between interest in the way man is presented in novels and 'their manifest strangeness as integuments of words' (*FR*, p. 18). But we realize that we cannot rely on such simple distinctions. For humanism often implies a relativistic universe without ground, and the deconstructive mode uses arguments from authority, while referring beyond the text to anterior conceptions about language and how texts behave. In contrast to the vertical perspective of most Neo-Platonism, including Christian concepts of God, humanism has itself proposed a world based on 'differential interrelations among elements . . . on the same plane'. Even while proposing tentative ways of seeing those interrelations in a unified vision, it understands their recalcitrance and disorder – unless they are controlled by a dominant idea exercising authority, as in *Paradise Lost* or *The Divine Comedy*.

The concept of foreshadowing, the idea of discrete parts acquiring meaning from their relations to one another, is based as much on the second form of repetition as the first. For the 'ground' of the first is provisional and is shaped and modified by the second. Indeed, does not making sense of *Ulysses* or *Tristram Shandy* depend on a dialogue between these kinds of repetition? Certainly reading Bloom as a version of *Ulysses* depends not so much on the archetypal model of the Greek hero – what Miller calls Platonic imitation or willed memory – but on the strange resemblance – 'the differential interrelations' – between Bloom and Odysseus, both of whom exist for Joyce simultaneously in the spatial and temporal dimension. Thus Miller's categories are terms for critical concepts and strategies already in use, although his terms do give us a somewhat different critical perspective.

One might ask why Miller uses the term Nietzschean rather than Aristotelian. But isn't this because Aristotelian criticism seeks to examine the temporal linear world to create inductively a priori categories? Isn't classification in the *Poetics* based on anterior conceptions of what plays should be like, conceptions derived, to be sure, from the extant Greek drama? Indeed, in this one sense, Aristotle is a Platonist. Also Nietzsche is a figure who represents imaginative energy, madness, and rebellion against logic; finally, since Aristotle has been appropriated by the Chicago critics, perhaps Miller wants to propose a new and striking opposition.

In a stunning poetic leap worthy of Nietzsche, Miller claims – but does not argue – that 'Each form of repetition calls up the other, by an inevitable compulsion. The second is not the negation or opposite of the first, but its "counterpart," in a strange relation whereby the second is the subversive ghost of the first, always already present within it as a possibility which hollows it out' (*FR*, p. 9). But isn't this true of any dualism posited in terms of horizontal and vertical concepts of the world and, maybe, of any dualism? Once one accepts a binary division, doesn't 'A' always invoke the memory or shadow or trace of 'not-A'? I suppose one can say that Miller's readings, divided against themselves as they are, as they try to reconcile humanism and deconstruction, illustrate this inevitable presence of conceptual counterparts. For the relation between humanism and deconstruction enacts the premise that in the second form of repetition the image that is generated by the difference between the two things is a third thing which is not present in the other two. Miller believes that in his seven novels, 'each form of repetition inevitably calls up the other as its shadow companion. . . . The repetitive series is presented as both grounded and ungrounded at once. . . . The heterogeneity of these texts lies in the fact that both forms of repetition are present, though the two forms can be shown to be incompatible. The hypothesis of such a heterogeneity in literary and philosophical texts is a working principle of that form of criticism called "deconstruction" ' (*FR*, pp. 16–17).

In his introduction to illustrate the way humanism and deconstruction interact, Miller uses three examples of repetition – from *Henry Esmond*, *The Well Beloved*, and Benjamin's discussion of Proust. Recalling Benjamin's use of parable and figurative criticism, these illustrations of repetition take the place of formal argument. Like the second form of repetition, the meaning of a parable is not in the parable or in the material world to which the parable refers, but in something in between the two. In the second form of repetition, we have 'opaque similarity' which needs to be defined by parables and emblems: 'If the similarity is not logical or wakeful, but opaque, dreamlike, it cannot be defined logically, but only exemplified. The example will then only present again the opacity' (*FR*, p. 9).

Very much a humanist in interest and approach, Miller consistently returns for his grounding to human experience. Thus he knows that novels repeat persons – discover something that imitates real life – in language, in the 'figures' of persons. We as readers, he knows, are interested in the way that man is presented in literature because we believe that people resemble one another. In a sense, because we believe that man repeats the behaviour of those who preceded him, we read to discover models whose behaviour we want to repeat or to avoid. Authors create characters who 'repeat' themselves, or at times, wilfully try to create characters who live different lives and have different personalities from themselves.

Finally we realize that another meaning of *Fiction and Repetition* is that Miller repeats himself and develops major themes of his prior work in the 1970s. He well knows the irony of his title, for he repeats the subject matter in the English canon of prior criticism by including among his novels such major works as *Lord Jim*, *Wuthering Heights*, *Tess of the d'Urbervilles*, and *Mrs. Dalloway* as well as, of course, less analysed ones such as *Henry Esmond*, *The Well-Beloved*, and *Between the Acts*. Indeed, *Henry Esmond* had been one of the books on which he focused in *The Form of Victorian Fiction*. Hardy has been the subject of a prior book (*Thomas Hardy: Distance and Desire*), and Conrad and Bronte were the subjects of chapters in *Poets of Reality* and *The Disappearance of God*. Moreover, since he published *The Form of Victorian Fiction* and the Hardy book, he had published essays or, in the case of *The Well-Beloved*, a preface, on all but two of his novels (*Henry Esmond* and *Between the Acts*); the prior material is the basis for most chapters in *Fiction and Repetition*. He is aware of the problems of discussing repetition as a subject: 'Repetition cannot be analyzed without using it, in forms of language which inevitably turn back on themselves and lose their lucid or logical transparency' (*FR*, p. 8). Or, to use a valuable distinction Miller makes, repetition depends upon the use of language as a performance – upon language that enacts, rather than represents, its meaning.

Before we can understand *Fiction and Repetition* we must briefly discuss a number of the central concepts of deconstruction. Barbara Johnson, whom Miller quotes, has defined a central premise of deconstruction: 'Instead of a simple "either/or" structure . . . deconstruction attempts to elaborate a discourse that says *neither* "either/or" *nor* "both/and" nor even "neither/nor"', while at the same time not totally abandoning these logics either. The very word "deconstruction" is meant to undermine the either/or logic of the opposition "construction/deconstruction" ' (*FR*, p. 17).[8] The first of these concepts is the metaphysics of presence. Miller's chapter on *Wuthering Heights*, subtitled 'Fiction and the Uncanny' is really an attack on the metaphysics of presence: '[*Wuthering Heights*] creates both the intuition of unitary origin and the clues, in the unresolvable heterogeneity of the narration, to the fact that the origin may be an effect of language, not some pre-existing state or some "place" in or out of the world. The illusion is created by figures of one sort or another – substitutions, equivalences, representative displacements, synecdoches, emblematic invitations to totalization' (*FR*, p. 68). Miller follows Derrida in arguing that traditional analyses result from our *desire* 'to establish the center beyond fictive status as objective reality, the ground of all grounds, the metaphysical truth in itself that masters all anxiety and grants final reassurance'.[9] Lentricchia aptly summarizes the idea of centre: 'a metaphysical presence which abides through various fictive appellations, from subject to substance to *eidos* to *arché* to *telos*, transcendentality, conscience, structure, man, or the ultimate fiction of God, the fiction of indifference itself, the fiction of "exemption" from supplement'.[10]

Crucial to Miller's work is the Derridean concept of *différance*. According to Derrida: 'On the one hand, it indicates difference as distinction, inequality, or discernability; on the other, it expresses the interposition of delay, the interval of a *spacing* and *temporaliz-ing* that puts off until "later" what is presently denied, the possible that is presently impossible.'[11] As Lentricchia puts it, 'this second significa-tion, deferral, as "the possible that is presently impossible", is itself caught up in a movement of differentiation, for what is deferred has never been possible as the ontological ground of the sign. . . . The sense we have of a presence now deferred and waiting to be reappropriated is but an illusion created by the very process of linguistic deferral, an illusion continuously undercut by the cunning movement of signification as the structure of *differance*'.[12]

Miller stresses that presence or origin is always deferred. The text continually arouses the possiblity of presence, the expectation of a dominant pattern of meaning, only to postpone it. Put another way, it arouses the possibility of the first kind of repetition, based on similarity, only to substitute the second kind based on difference. But this is not so different from the Chomsky idea of a deep structure, latent beneath the surface of the sentence, that represents the supposedly more real meaning.

'Textuality' is another crucial premise. Lentricchia writes '[Textuality is] a potentially infinite and indefinite, all-inclusive series of networks of interrelation whose connections and boundaries are not securable because they are ruled by never-ending movements of linguistic energy that recognize neither the rights of private ownership nor the authority of structuralism's centralized government of interpretive norms'.[13] But haven't we known that the network of syntax and diction in a literary work creates its own system separate and distinct from the real world and that within that system the relation between syntax and diction has its own energy and coherence?

'Intertextuality' refers to both the relationship among literary texts and the dialogue between them and other writing. Each text takes its meaning from other texts, not merely prior texts, but other concomit-ant texts and expressions of culture and language. The blank and marble pages, the squiggly lines, the scrambled chapters, the skipped pages of *Tristram Shandy* are intertextual events because they respond not only to extant literary texts, but to contemporary and medieval ideas of logic, order, and rationality, particularly Locke's conception of how the mind develops ideas as presented in his *Essay Concerning Human Understanding*. But the intertextual network of *Tristram*

Shandy includes the subsequent texts like *Ulysses* and Beckett's novels, as well as recent theories of narrativity which give the contemporary reader a different perspective from the eighteenth-century reader on Sterne's experiments with form. Miller responds to texts in terms of other texts, sometimes in ahistorical terms and sometimes in historical terms. Even if one uses the term 'intertextuality' to define discussion of author's lives and literary convention, is this different from a traditional approach that stresses contexts and origins?

The concept of intertextuality – with its stress on echo, nuance, and difference – enables Miller, when discussing literary influences and psychological explanations to be more speculative and to provide less supporting empirical argument than traditional criticism. Such is the case when he discusses intertextual relations in Woolf. Woolf, he believes, had to break with past novels: 'Her anxiety [of influence] is therefore a determination not to write like all those fathers – Shakespeare, Johnson, Carlyle, and the rest' (*FR*, p. 223). According to Miller, the male writers 'believe in some original column of meaning from which all meanings have descended. They refuse to accept the silence and emptiness which is there, the hollow vase' (*FR*, p. 224). On the other hand, 'the talent of women, as writers and simply as women, may be for creative veiling of the emptiness': '[Men] believe in the existence, somewhere, of an original or conclusive head meaning, or an ur-word or an end word. They are inveterately logocentric, "phallogocentric", in their thinking, though this belief is undermined by their fear that behind the last veil there may be nothing. Women know that death, emptiness, silence underlie every surface' (*FR*, pp. 227–8). Miller is of course responding to Harold Bloom's oedipal and paternal version of the anxiety of influence. Women writers, according to Miller's extrapolation of Woolf, 'destroy the old false male rhythm and replace it with an authentic female rhythm. This new rhythm would be capable of filling the spaces and going out into the unknown, making the unknown into the known. Such a writer would be that androgyne of whom Woolf dreamed, possessed of male power and female sensitivity' (*FR*, pp. 229–30). Apparently then, the Platonic form of repetition is masculine, and at least more likely to be masculine, and the Nietzschean, one is feminine. But Miller does not sustain this dualism since his male writers are no less likely to use both kinds of repetition than his female ones.

Fiction and Repetition shows how post-structuralism is not so very far from the New Criticism and how different theories propose similar readings; it also shows that Miller has never left his humanistic roots. Indeed, the New Critical and deconstructive modes coexist in his book as an example of heterogeneity. Finally Miller acknowledges his ties to the New Criticism in his desire 'to account for the totality of a given work' (*FR*, p. 17). Miller's use of close readings of details to illustrate theme and character derives from the example of the New Critics. Where he parts company with Anglo-American formalism is in its 'presupposition that every detail is going to count by working harmoniously to confirm the "organic unity" of the poem or the novel' (*FR*, p. 19).

Miller speaks of novels in ways to which Van Ghent and Schorer could subscribe:

> Any novel is a complex tissue of repetitions and of repetitions within repetitions, or of repetitions linked in chain fashion to other repetitions. In each case there are repetitions making up the structure of the work within itself, as well as repetitions determining its multiple relations to what is outside it: the author's mind or his life; other works by the same author; psychological, social, or historical reality; other works by other authors; motifs from the mythological or fabulous past; elements from the purported past of the characters or of their ancestors; events which have occurred before the book begins. In all these kinds of recurrence the questions are the following: What controls the meaning these repetitions create? What methodological presuppositions will allow the critic, in the case of a particular novel, to control them in his turn in a valid interpretation? (*RF*, pp. 2–3)

Very much in the nominalistic tradition of Anglo-American humanism, Miller eschews theory and seeks to interpret 'as best I can the texts of my seven novels' (*FR*, p. 21). He makes traditionally modest claims for the critic rather than, as some recent critics have done, perceiving himself as a prophet and self-dramatizing himself as a seer and philosopher: 'In recent controversies about criticism there has been, so it seems to me, too much attention paid to this theory or that, to its terminology, and to its presumed or "theoretical" consequences, and not enough to the readings made possible by the theories in question' (*FR*, p. 21).[14] He affirms his belief in close reading for 'the teaching of reading, and the attempt in written criticism to facilitate the act of reading' (*FR*, p. 21). He understands that literary criticism must be the prelude to the next reading.

After discussing the limitations of New Criticism, he turns to his own prior allegiance to phenomenology or criticism of consciousness: 'In the hands of a master critic like Georges Poulet, it can facilitate recognition of the diversity of an author's work by way of the presupposition that the 'consciousness' of an author moves dialectically through a series of adventures' (*FR*, p. 19). He now contends that a shortcoming of that method is that the 'intimate grain of an author's language tends to disappear. . . . Civilized dialogue or even controversy about the meanings of a literary work is most aided by sticking to the words as the things to be accounted for' (*FR*, pp. 19–20). Of course, Poulet's idea of the cogito as an origin provides the kind of presence Miller is now trying to deconstruct.

Miller's definition of a novel as a 'representation of human reality in words' is an effort to account for the representational and linguistic duality of the novel (*FR*, p. 20). As Miller notes, the stress on human reality may lead one to 'speak of the characters as if they were "real people", and work out the "meaning" of their story in terms of ethical values, judgments of good and bad, happy and unhappy, and so on' (*FR*, p. 20). This is the method of Auerbach, Leavis, and Trilling. The emphasis on representation leads to discussion of narrative technique, or, as he puts it, 'on the conventions of storytelling in a given case as vehicles of meaning. . . . This will concern itself with the assumptions the novelist makes about the kind of consciousness of himself and of others the narrator has or the characters have, or with the temporal structures of consciousness the novel expresses, or with the elaborated emotional responses the story as a sequence of represented events arouses in the reader' (*FR*, p. 20). This includes James, Lubbock, and Booth, but also Kermode and Frye. Finally 'in words' implies that the novel is a dramatic poem and is concerned with 'local features of style, the "rhetoric of fiction", taking "rhetoric" not as modes of persuasion but in its other meaning as the discipline of the workings of tropes in its most inclusive sense of that word: all the turnings of language away from straightforward referential meaning . . . [T]he fact that they are made of words, inhibits the coherent or non-contradictory working of the other two dimensions of fiction. The result of this is that the critic can validate neither a wholly consistent thematic paraphrase of a given novel nor a wholly univocal phenomenological description of it as a system of assumptions about consciousnesses in their interrelation' (*FR*, pp. 20–1). This concept of words derives more from Derrida and post-structuralists than from the New Critics.

For Miller heterogeneity means attempting a traditional and a deconstructive reading, or, put another way, a grounded and un-grounded one. This enables Miller to argue that, at the same time, fiction is and is not mimetic of an anterior world. But does his acceptance of the law of non-contradiction really put him at odds with the more subtle of the New Critics and their formalist kin such as Empson or Burke? And wouldn't Booth approve of Miller's use of James as an example of how Anglo-American formalism acknow-ledged the contradictory patterns of language and form, demonstrated how the endings undermine what precedes, and discussed how the author's struggle to write a text can create a latent auxiliary text which – in a process akin to *pentimento* in painting – is in a tension with the actual text? Kermode, we recall, also proposed the concept of heterogeneity, the idea that two things could happen or two conditions prevail at the same time.

Miller deliberately eschews the historical progression of most books on the novel, and begins with *Lord Jim* which 'falls roughly midway in the historical span from which my seven novels come' (*FR*, p. 22). For most of us, *Lord Jim* is a paradigm of multiple meanings, a characteristic text of modernism. But to refute the accepted historical shibboleths Miller then proceeds to look backward to the Victorian novel, to show that there, too, we find heterogeneity. In each of his seven novels he insists that several meanings can co-exist 'related to one another in a system of mutual implication and mutual contradic-tion' (*FR*, p. 40). He does not want to tie his seven readings together with a narrative of the novel's historical development or evolution: 'It may be that the activity of reading, if it is carried out with rigor, tends to inhibit or even make impossible that sort of story we tell ourselves which is given the name "literary history" ' (*FR*, p. 23). Surely Miller's point that close reading subverts generalizations about literary history and authors' themes and technique is a truth, but a partial one. For the best critics, as we have seen, can create a dialogue between the specific and the general. In evaluating Miller we must distinguish between the way he uses texts to present his theory and what he presents as new readings of the novels. For his chapter on *Lord Jim* is as much a methodological introduction as an essay on *Lord Jim*.

First and foremost, the *Lord Jim* chapter should be read as an occasion to present Miller's theory and, secondly, as a reading of Conrad's novel. The chapter is much more significant in its first function. Subtitled 'Repetition as Subversion of Organic Form', it enables Miller to take issue with those who have adopted the principles of Coleridge and Aristotle to novel criticism; he has in mind of course the New Criticism and Chicago criticism respectively. The chapter also makes the crucial point that iteration creates patterns of meaning that undermine Jamesian and Coleridgean concepts of organic unity.

He shows how Coleridge takes the image of organic unity from his conception of 'the wholeness of a universe which circles in time around the motionless center of a God to whose eternal insight all times are co-present. . . . The concept of the organic unity of the work of art . . . cannot be detached from its theological basis. Nor can it separate itself from mimetic theories of art. . . . The creation, the soul, the work of art – all three have the same shape, the same movement, and the same relation to a generative center' (*FR*, p. 24). He proposes an alternative to the Coleridgean spatial conception of organic unity that informs the New Criticism. Iteration depends on linearity, on a horizontal dimension. One of his principle targets is the Aristotelian idea of the formal plot that enacts major themes. For him, Aristotle represents the presence of some 'sort of metaphysical certainty, . . . the confidence that some *logos* or underlying cause and ground supports the events' (*FR*, p. 35). It is not only *Lord Jim* that lacks the straightforward historical movement suggested by Aristotle's comments on beginning, middle, and end in the *Poetics*, for he later writes in the *Tess* chapter:

> This chapter attempts to identify this alogic or this alternative logic of plot and to justify giving it the Hardyan name of repetition as *immanent* design. Such a plot will be without an end in the Aristotelian sense, and the elements in the 'middle' will not be organized according to determined casual sequence (*FR*, p. 121).

Building upon the image of Penelope's weaving by day and unweaving by night, which he used as a parable for Proust's writing, he implies that each reader weaves *his own pattern*, which is then undermined and unwoven by his awareness that any pattern is unsatisfactory as a total explanation. Miller insistently stresses the continuity between reading and writing. He insists that reading is active and dynamic, and that a novel is perceived more temporally than spatially. He emphasizes that a text does not have a 'manifest pattern, like the design of a rug, which the eye of the critic can survey from the outside and describe as a spatial form. . . . The critic must enter into the text, follow its threads as they weave in and out, appearing and disappearing, crisscrossing with other threads. In doing this he adds his own thread of interpretation to the fabric, or he cuts it in one way or another, so becoming part of its textures or changing it' (*FR*, p. 23). But he accepts the Aristotelian idea that meaning is 'controlled by the text' (*FR*, p. 40). The reader looks for a centre, but has no assurance that one can be found. *Lord Jim* enables Miller to introduce the motif of repetition in a novel where every reader would have felt doubling as a structural and thematic ingredient: 'In the sequence of discrete episodes which makes up the novel, no episode serves as the point of origin, the arch-example of the *mythos* of the novel, but each is, by reason of its analogy to other episodes, a repetition of them, each example being as enigmatic as all the others' (*FR*, pp. 33–4). And here most readers would agree: 'Each enactment of a given episode echoes backward and forward indefinitely, creating a pattern of eddying repetition' (*FR*, p. 34).

Now let us turn to Miller's reading of *Lord Jim*. Miller does not buy Conrad's own idea of his novel as a progressively intensifying *progression d'effet* – a building of effects towards a climax; rather he sees that repetition implies that Jim's behaviour cannot be explained. 'The indeterminacy lies in the multiplicity of possible incompatible explanations given by the novel and in the lack of evidence justifying a choice of one over the others' (*FR*, p. 40). Surely the novel proposes – and Conrad expects the reader to perceive – a hierarchy of explanations. But to see the hierarchy, one has to take account of the absolute judgment proposed by the omniscient narrator at the outset. Does Miller see the implications of his valid perception that the omniscient narrator has the formal function of calling attention to the fact that Marlow is a teller? The omniscient narrator proposes an absolute judgment just as surely as Marlow proposes a relative one based on his complex and often sympathetic understanding of Jim, and this is surely part of a heterogeneous reading. Miller contends that *Lord Jim* lacks the reliable narrator of Victorian fiction: 'The novel is a complex design of interrelated minds, no one of which can be taken as a secure point of reference from which the others may be judged' (*RF*, p. 31). He is, I think, not only misreading the first four chapters, but is he not also forgetting that, in *Fiction and Repetition*, the narrators of all four of the Victorian novels turn out not to be so reliable? He shows that *Lord Jim* 'reveals itself to be a work which raises questions rather than answering them' (*FR*, p. 39), before concluding by asking whether 'the ambiguity of *Lord Jim* [is] a historical pheno-menon, a feature of the time in which it was written, or of the historical and social conditions of its author, or is its presentation of specific incompatible possibilities of meaning among which it is impossible to choose characteristic in one way or another of works of literature of any period in Western culture?' (*FR*, p. 41).

Like the New Critics, Miller eschews intentions and historical sources, but unlike them he discounts the possibility of resolving the ambiguity by reference to episodic parallels and imagery. Conrad's omniscient narrator certainly proposes in the early chapters a resolution of the problem about whether Jim's behaviour is, as Jim claims, gratuitous – something that could happen to anyone in his situation, as if he were acted upon by circumstances and only partially responsible – or whether his jump from the *Patna* was characteristic of his behaviour. The omniscient narrator provides a crucial series of four passages as evidence of Jim's inherent moral inferiority. The first is when he fails to respond to an emergency on the training ship; the second is his paralyzing fear, his anomie, during a storm, while as a First Mate, he is lying injured; the third is when he throws in his lot with those who have a soft spot – those who want an easier life than that of the British merchant marine and who enjoy their 'superior' racial status as white men among natives. The last is the revelation that while on duty his mind is preoccupied not with his responsibilities but with fantasies of heroism, fantasies that have become his secret life. And this series provides a ground that accompanies us through the reading of the novel and reminds us that Marlow's human, empathetic response is the result of his moral and psychological needs, and that we should not confuse Marlow's response with Conrad's judgment. Indeed, this series suggests to us the necessity of judging Marlow's humane, empathetic response and for looking for reasons to explain it. What Miller does not do in this chapter is to recreate what it is like to live in the imagined world of the novel when we take up residence as readers. Partly because of the plethora of critical material in the last twenty years, Miller's readings are not, as Van Ghent's were when published, among the best available ones; his reading of *Lord Jim* certainly does not compare with that of Watt's in *Conrad in the Nineteenth Century*.

Miller's historicism has both a traditional and deconstructive aspect. In this book he dislikes explaining texts in terms of literary and intellectual generalizations, the very technique he used in *Poets of Reality* and *The Disappearance of God*: 'Each period is itself equivocal. Periods differ from one another because there are different forms of heterogeneity, not because each period held a single coherent "view of the world" '.[15] But he cannot avoid proposing his own versions of literary history. For even if heterogeneity becomes a substitute for an ordered historical view, aren't his generalizations a kind of historicism? Does he – could he? – exclude a search for centres? The chapter on *Between the Acts* takes on an historical perspective in spite of itself, because one cannot discuss intertextuality without discussing influence and conventions. He not only discusses *The Well-Beloved* and *Tess* in the context of Hardy's other work, but he also relates *The Well-Beloved* to the twentieth-century novelist's interest in the 'fictionality of fiction' – his awareness 'of the dependence of his work on all sorts of conventions', and of the artificiality of conventions (*FR*, p. 152): 'If the *Well-Beloved* anticipates Fowles or Borges, it also brings into the open those subversions of the idea of a single ending which were already latent in one way or another in Victorian fiction' (*FR*, p. 156). Does Miller not slip into the idiom that assumes the historicism of the evolution of the novel in spite of himself? 'Each technical device contributing to the celebrated complexity of narration in *Wuthering Heights* has its precedents in modern fictional practice from Cervantes down to novelists contemporary with Brontë' (*FR*, p. 46). Or: 'Beatrix and Becky are Thackeray's contributions to the long line of selfish and destructive women presented in English fiction' (*FR*, p. 113). And he sees Thackeray's prototypes in eighteenth-century figures such as Hogarth and Fielding.

The discussion of 'extrapolation' from sequence depends on establishing at least as a tentative formation the 'ground' of a series: 'What are the grounds for evaluating another element added to a series? How can one know the new element is a valid repetition of the old ones, extending and continuing them?' (*FR*, p. 203). Extrapolation of meaning into a new tentative pattern recalls what Foucault calls *discursive formations*. According to Lentricchia, 'the discursive formation partakes simultaneously of the synchronic and diachronic: it rules time, but only in time and *for* a time. It exists, therefore, as a heterogeneous or "problematic unity" which contains the elements of its own transformation and appropriation'.[16] By contrast, rules of discourse exclude what they cannot integrate. Miller's historical view seems to accept Foucault's emphasis on discontinuity; or, as Lentricchia puts it, 'What Foucault calls "effective history" wants to preserve discontinuity, eruption, the moment of emergence, and to seek the point of "the reversal of a relationship of forces, the usurpation of power, the appropriation of a vocabulary turned against those who had once used it . . ." '.[17] If Miller has a historicism, it is one that proposes tentative patterns which contain their own undoing. He stresses the impossibility of absolute patterns by showing that each historical pattern contains the ingredients that undermine it.

Thus Miller's heterogeneous approach extends to his historicity. The chapter on *Between the Acts* subtitled 'Repetition as Extrapolation' argues that Woolf's novel is a repetition of prior English fiction but the chapter is also a repetition of Miller's prior arguments about kinds of repetition. 'Most of the modes of repetition which function in English fiction are not only present in *Between the Acts* but made overtly matters of interrogation' (*FR*, p. 231). He does not ignore Woolf's inclusion of the 'particularity of mental life, . . . the particular-and past tense] is one of the aspects of the novel which Woolf carries on unchanged from her eighteenth- and nineteenth-century predecessors' (*FR*, p. 186). But he denies traditional theories about the historical evolution when he groups Woolf with Trollope, whose characters know the minds of others, in contrast to Austen and Sartre for whom 'minds are opaque to one another' (*FR*, p. 191). He takes issue with the historical argument that twentieth-century literature is more nihilistic – an argument made in *Poets of Reality* – and he argues that in Woolf's inclusion of the 'particularity of mental life . . . the particularity of social behavior and customs, and the particularity of events in nature[,] . . . Woolf's work may be seen as firmly committed to traditional principles of "realism" in the novel' (*FR*, p. 208). But isn't he usually using an historical argument, as when he demonstrates that, among the novels he selects, we see in the twentieth century ones features similar to the nineteenth-century ones?

Since Miller's last chapters are on Woolf's *Mrs. Dalloway* and *Between the Acts*, his book concludes with the books with which we would have expected him to conclude. For after the opening chapter on *Lord Jim*, *Fiction and Repetition* is a chronologically ordered study, and he has a surprisingly traditional chronological perspective. Echoing T. S. Eliot in 'Tradition and the Individual Talent,' Miller concludes that *Between the Acts* makes explicit the way 'each new work in one way or another is a repetition of the long row of previous ones': 'Objective realism, the imitation of "life"; subjective realism, the imitation of the mind – these two goals have been those of the English novel since Fielding and Sterne, and before' (*FR*, pp. 231, 209). Yet his own ambivalence to historical patterns sometimes deflects him from proposing useful historical hypotheses. Thus, surprisingly, he does not link the 'fluid' boundaries 'between past and present' which he discerns in Woolf, to Contrad's Marlow or to Joyce (*FR*, p. 184).

IV

What is remarkable is Miller's scope, range, precision and clarity –
especially if one considers the complexity of the arguments and
abstract theory which he is trying to illustrate. Miller's major argument
is that 'heterogeneity . . . [is] characteristic of literature' – indeed, a
subtitle of the entire book could be 'Heterogeneous Readings of
English Novels' (*FR*, p. 128). By heterogeneity, he means that texts
convey multiple and even contradictory meanings, and the reader
must resist an urge to unify them into one coherent view. Miller
believes that heterogeneity allows one to 'account for the totality of a
given work' (*FR*, p. 17). Thus he presses what he calls 'the hypothesis
of possible heterogeneity' in contrast to an assumption that 'a good
novel is necessarily going to be homogeneous or organic in form' (*FR*,
p. 5). In the *Wuthering Heights* chapter, subtitled 'Repetition and the
"Uncanny," ' Miller proposed that 'The best readings will be the ones
which best account for the heterogeneity of the text, its presentation of
a definite group of possible meanings which are systematically
interconnected, determined by the text, but logically incompatible'
(*FR*, p. 51). In part because the uncanny and unexpected elements
that resist our urge for unity are part of our reading experience, books
are 'open' to multiple explanations. Hence he argues that a
characteristic of Hardy's novels is that they contain 'irreconcilable
elements': 'Criticism of Hardy has often erred by seizing on one
element in a given novel as the single explanation of the meaning of
what happens, leaving aside other explanations for which just as much
textual evidence can be given' (*FR*, p. 128).

Because meanings are open and problematic, the reader must be
supple and responsive. Miller stresses in his concluding remarks how
'each of the novels . . . alternates in its own way among different
possibilities of meaning . . . The novel renders impossible of solution
the problem of the truth behind the words, the problem of "truth" as
such. The critic can only in one way or another restate the alternatives
without resolving them into unity, moving back and forth from one to
another as one passage or another in the text is stressed as evidence. . . . My fundamental premise in this book is that the specific
heterogeneity of a given text can be exactly defined, even though a
univocal meaning cannot be justified by the text' (*FR*, pp. 230–1). Of
course given the length and variety of most novels, we should not be
surprised that at times inconsistency and contradiction will strive

against pattern and coherence. Few readers would expect the kind of organic structured form that one might find in a lyric.

It follows that a reading should be heterogeneous rather than seek to resolve alternate possibilities. We need not, Miller demonstrates, choose an either/or reading since a text may be open, unresolved, and problematic. An urge for order may falsify a text. Take *Jude the Obscure*, a Hardy novel that Miller does not discuss in *Fiction and Repetition*; traditionalists might say that Sue's character and sexual behaviour can be explained as the result of a stereotyped role imposed on her *or* as a result of compulsions and fixations she barely understands, but Miller teaches us that we can have both explanations. (Hardy is much clearer about the first of these meanings, but does not fully understand the psychological causes of her behaviour or at least lacks a vocabulary to describe it.) Or Esther in *Bleak House* can be seen as an overly sentimental bland passive figure whose formal function overwhelms her interest as a character. But one can also see a more complex psychological portrait whose victimized childhood shapes her telling and explains why she seeks refuge in the identity of Dame Durden, the hard-working drudge who enables the rest of the Jarndyce entourage to enjoy themselves. Because she needs the surrogate family to provide the childhood she lacked, she lives vicariously through others. Thus she loves Richard through a surrogate, Ada. Just as she is beginning to make progress towards achieving a sense of self-worth, her illness and subsequent disfigurement contribute to her sense of unworthiness. Finally, she must acknowledge and then reject the claims of Jarndyce before she can make a full commitment to Allen Woodcourt.

Again, my point is that Miller teaches us that we need not resolve the contradictions. Miller is proposing 'the notion of multiple valid but incompatible interpretations', but he stresses – more than reader response criticism – 'the coercive power of the sequence itself to determine the interpretation' (*FR*, p. 144). He rejects the assumption that a subtle reading need be a reading that resolves ambiguity. The great value of Miller's work is to teach us that the centre may be elusive or inexplicable or both. 'What is lost in the case of *Wuthering Heights* is the "origin" which would explain everything' (*FR*, p. 61). Miller argues that a novel can contain 'an energy of discontinuity which undoes the novel's coherence,' and it is a misreading to impose systems of order arbitrarily (*FR*, p. 110).

Building upon *The Form of Victorian Fiction*, he defines the parameters of discussing what happens to the reader and how the author becomes a presence in the text. For Miller the reader is a crucial figure acted upon by the action of writing produced by the author as he presents an imagined world. 'The situation of the reader of *Wuthering Heights* is inscribed within the novel in the situations of all these characters who are readers, tellers of tales, most elaborately in Lockwood. The lesson for the reader is to make him aware that he has by reading the novel incurred a responsibility like that of the other spectator-interpreters' (*FR*, p. 70). Since reading is a kind of interpreting, every character becomes a reader in *Tess*: 'Attention is insistently called to the act of reading, in the broad sense of deciphering' (*FR*, p. 143). Although the connection between the art of reading and of perceiving is not new, Miller gives it a felicitous turn. He shows us how the reader is involved in the very epistemological quest that occupies the character: 'All interpretation is the imposition of a pattern by a certain way of making cross-connections between one sign and those which come before and after. Any interpretation is an artistic form given to the true sequence of things. Meaning in such a process emerges from a reciprocal act in which both the interpreter and what is interpreted contribute to the making or the finding of a pattern' (*FR*, p. 144). For as readers we make sense of other people's lives – including their sense-making.

Repetition is a crucial concept that takes many forms. All novels have, of course, the 'power of a work of art to repeat itself indefinitely' (*FR*, p. 145); and to 'lead its readers through some version of the sequences of emotion for which it provides the notation' (*FR*, p. 146). And Booth would have approved of Miller's stress on how books create readers through a structure of effects. As Miller repeatedly urges, reading indeed is the ultimate repetition: 'The reading of the first present-tense words of the novel performs a multiple act of resurrection, an opening of graves or a raising of ghosts. . . . The words themselves, there on the page, both presuppose the deaths of that long line of personages and at the same time keep them from dying wholly, as long as a single copy of *Wuthering Heights* survives to be reread' (*FR*, pp. 71–2). Of course this kind of survival is true of any novel that is still read, but he stresses that the tradition of reading enables us to relive the past experience of others: 'Any reader, or anyone who writes a critical essay on *The Well-Beloved*, is momentarily the last in this line. He is no more able than any of the other links in the chain to put an end to it. He cannot provide a definitive explanation of the novel which will stop the passing on of its compulsion to repeat itself. What the critic says also in its own way keeps the generative force alive. This might be called the aporia of interminability' (*FR*, p. 173). Indeed, Miller might have stressed how such a chain is a formal component of *Heart of Darkness* or *Lord Jim* where Conrad has Marlow call attention to the difficulty of communicating within his tale; in *Heart of Darkness* the repetition by one of Marlow's listeners, in the very brooding tone Marlow had used, shows the possibility of communication.

Paradoxically, *Fiction and Repetition* illustrates the homogeneity of Miller's approach. For example, by the end of the book, we realize that what had seemed unique to the novel under discussion is true not only of every work he discusses but, if one accepts his assumptions, virtually every work that he might discuss. Take some of the comments on *Wuthering Heights*: 'Why is it that, an interpretive origin, *logos* in the sense of ground, measure, chief word, or accounting reason, cannot be identified for *Wuthering Heights*?' (*FR*, p. 63). Or: 'This missing center is the head referent. . . . There is no way to see or name this head referent because it cannot exist as present event, as a past which was once present, or as a future which will be present. It is something which has always already occurred and been forgotten' (*FR*, p. 67). For Miller, the key to *Wuthering Heights* is that the mind cannot order all the details, but isn't this inability to control significant detail what Eliot meant by a lack of objective correlative? According to Miller, 'The best readings, it may be, are those, like Charlotte Brontë's, which repeat in their own alogic the text's failure to satisfy the mind's desire for logical order with a demonstrable base' (*FR*, pp. 52–3). But isn't this claim true of the best readings of all novels? And we begin to realize that the distinctions between the kinds of repetition indicated in the subtitles are, if not distinctions without a difference, less important than their illustrations of the paradigmatic method that Miller is proposing. While he would probably contend that each of the seven paradigms of repetition defines one range of possibilities for a heterogeneous reading of other novels, does he really present those possibilities as distinct, separate models? I think not, in part because if he did, the models would become centres or origins.

Let us examine how the chapter on *Tess* becomes an occasion for Miller to speculate on how to read – which is the main theme of his book: 'The reader must execute a lateral dance of interpretation to explicate any given passage without ever reaching, in this sideways movement, a passage which is chief, original, or originating, a sovereign principle of explanation' (*FR*, p. 127). Miller's heterogeneous reading of *Tess* argues that 'A large group of incompatible causes or explanations are present'; the generation of meaning must come from repetitive sequences, because there is not a first cause or source (*FR*, pp. 140–1). But, as Aristotle understood, a repetitive sequence inevitably refers to an anterior cause, even if that cause may be contradicted by other anterior causes. The causes may be multiple and even contradictory – and prior readers have noticed the uneasy balance in Hardy between social, personal, and cosmic causes. Whether he prefers the term heterogeneous or pluralistic, Miller is very much in the tradition of calling for a subtle reading that refuses to accept one cause. But it does not follow that the search for explanations need necessarily be reductive or need describe 'the text as a process of totalization from the point of departure of some central principle that makes things happen as they happen' (*FR*, p. 140). Nor does it follow that the 'repetitions [in *Tess*] produce similarity out of difference and are controlled by no center, origin, or end outside the chain of recurrent elements' (*FR*, p. 142). Readers of *Tess* feel in fact the opposite pressure, the pressure of a centre of meaning in the form of an indifferent cosmos thwarting human expectations and producing its own plot. Isn't Miller's conception of Hardy's senseless or indeterminate universe itself an origin, an anterior explanation? 'The specifically theological or metaphysical aspect of Hardy's thought is his full understanding that only such a transcendent mind would guarantee the possibility of the rational order of beginning, middle, end, and determinate meaning either for human lives or for works of literature' (*FR*, p. 175). It is a combination of fate, of social laws shaped by misguided authority, and of individuals' own compulsions and anxieties that expresses Hardy's anterior reality. Yet Miller himself is interested in traditional, psychological and social explanations for behaviour. Ultimately, he seems to understand that one can talk about novels as if they had ground or essence, even while he recognized that in another sense novels do not have either.

Miller's heterogeneity also extends to the way that he approaches the author in the text. He approves of Walter Benjamin's contention that 'The self of the author is not the explanatory origin of the work. . . . This self is made by the work. The self exists only in the work and in the work's detachment from the "real life" of the author' (*FR*, pp. 11–12). (That, of course, the self behind the text has no real validity is also the view of the New Criticism.) Yet Miller also has a rather traditional interest in the way an author is embodied in the text. He understands that the artist deliberately makes artistic choices which will 'give him authoritative indirect command over his own life'

(*FR*, p. 76). He makes the argument most thoroughly in the *Henry Esmond* chapter subtitled 'Repetition and Irony': 'These repetitions reveal the presence of Thackeray himself, the artificer who has made it all. "Thackeray himself" in fact, insofar as the reader can know him in his writing, is this need to be himself by writing himself as someone else' (*FR*, p. 74). Irony is itself a means by which the author discovers his true self: 'Thackeray wanted to understand and control his life by taking ironic authority over that assumed role and by showing the imagined person to have made a false interpretation of himself. Thackeray will present by irony the true interpretation and so indirectly a true interpretation of himself. He will come by way of the detour back to himself and so join himself to himself, taking possession of himself in a sovereign exercise of power' (*FR*, p. 106). In arguing that Thackeray uses irony to establish himself, Miller is quite traditional; if irony is the moment when an author speaks in his own person and suspends 'the line of the action', this would establish a ground for irony, but then Miller slips out of the voice of authority that he has assumed: 'Irony is the mode of language which cannot be mastered. It cannot be used as an instrument of mastery. It always masters the one who tries to master it or to take power with it' (*FR*, pp. 105–6).

Miller rightly observes that the problem in Thackeray's novels is getting a handle on its irony, that is, knowing whether and when he is cynical and when he is idealistically applying moral standards. According to Miller, 'where there is irony, there is no authority, not even the authority to know for sure that there is no authority. . . . The meaning vibrates among various possible configurations, since there is no solid base on which to construct a definitive interpretation' (*FR*, pp. 108–9). Do these vibrations of meaning and lack of authority have to do with the length of a novel, the impossibility of keeping its totality in mind? Perhaps what he says of irony is true of any heterogeneous reading. Indeed, doesn't Miller's book have a structure not unlike the one he attributes to *Henry Esmond*? '*Henry Esmond* contains within itself, distributed here and there in the text, various emblems for this lack of ground and for the consequent fragmenting of any coherent line, even the line which puts into question the line' (*FR*, p. 109).

It may even be that the subject of the English novel domesticates or naturalizes Miller to speak more of manners and motives and community life than he would have done otherwise. Irony itself is inherent in the novel; major subjects in the criticism of the English novel are the incongruity between the teller and his tale and the ironic relationship between an omniscient narrator and the major characters.

In the first case, the tale recalls the imperceptiveness of the teller; in the second an omniscient narrator establishes the moral and spiritual limitations of a character who often must mature in the course of the novel to the position held by the narrator. To a reader steeped in the English novel tradition and its criticism, what seems a deconstructive reading is really not very different from what traditional criticism calls paradoxical and ironic readings. An example of the similarity would be the following comment of Miller's on a passage from *The Well-Beloved*: 'The reader can see both the affirmation of the human habit of seeing likes in unlikes and the demystification of this habit' (*FR*, p. 14).

Can we say that in *Fiction and Repetition* Miller is divided against himself and illustrates the *aporia* of undecidability? He very effectively uses the strategies of humanism to call into question their basic assumptions. For example, 'The Oedipus story is the archetype of the discovery that there is no archetype' (*FR*, p. 109). But are not archetypes a kind of neo-Platonic or vertical interpretation which depends on a 'ground' anterior to the text? His use of the Oedipus story may finally establish its function as an archetype, in other words, does precisely what he sets out not to do: 'Henry is indeed an Oedipus, but an Oedipus manqué whose eyes remain blinded. He is an Oedipus who never reads the oracles right in their application to himself' (*FR*, p. 102). Miller cannot avoid centres and origins whether it be Schlegel's and Kierkegaard's theories of irony or his own concept of literary history based on his impressive empirical knowledge. Speaking authoritatively, he chooses *Henry Esmond* because it 'is one of the best texts in English fiction by means of which to explore the working of irony in narrative' (*FR*, p. 106).

Miller himself depends on origin or ground in the various other ways he approaches the author. This can range from the traditional romantic idea that the author defines himself in the creative act to speculations about the author's relations to his characters. An example of the first is when he argues that: 'The "real" author, Thomas Hardy, attempts to give himself substance in his work. He does this by projecting himself into a fictive narrator who tells a fictive story which is a displacement of Hardy's own story. Instead of providing him with substance, the narrator, by doubling and depersonifying Thomas Hardy and by telling a story about the impossibility of novel or autonomous action, deprives him of originality. . . . The narrator and the story the narrator tells suggest that Hardy is created by the story he has his alter ego tell' (*FR*, pp. 171–2). Miller even suggests that the artistic Hardy borrows from the real one and thus deprives him of substance.

Speaking of Emily Brontë's pseudonymous author of *Wuthering Heights*, Ellis Bell, he writes: 'Ellis Bell is another representative of the reader, overhearing, overseeing, overthinking, and overfeeling what Lockwood says, sees, thinks, feels, and writing it down so we can in our turns evoke Lockwood again and raise also that thin and almost invisible ghost, effaced presupposition of the words of the novel, Ellis Bell himself. Behind Ellis Bell, finally is Brontë . . .' (*FR*, pp. 71–2). To be sure, in discussing the author's relationship to his work Miller uses current terms like 'recuperate his selfhood' to describe how an author uses his creative activity to discover and define himself. But is he not more in the tradition of Stevens – a tradition in which man's imagination enables him to escape himself by creating a supreme fiction – than that of Saussure and Derrida. For Miller seems to be arguing that in taking a vacation from the real self in imaginative literature, the author discovers a self in his work that may be *more* real and coherent. Certainly, such biographical explanations depend upon the belief that *a priori* facts or causes are part of the centre or origin. Miller accepts Woolf's suicide and depression as a centre when he quotes her anguished statement 'Nothing matters' as an acceptance of death in preference to life (*FR*, p. 197). He quotes from *A Writer's Diary* where she described *Mrs. Dalloway* as 'a study of insanity and suicide; the world seen by the sane and insane side by side' (*FR*, p. 198). In a quite traditional reading that relates the work to the psychology of the author, Miller argues that 'Septimus Smith's suicide anticipates Virginia Woolf's own death. Both deaths are a defiance, an attempt to communicate, a recognition that self-annihilation is the only possible way to embrace that center which evades one as long as one is alive. . . . Clarissa and Septimus seek the same thing: communication, wholeness, the oneness of reality, but only Septimus takes the sure way to reach it' (*FR*, pp. 197–8).

Miller's own style enacts his heterogeneous values – or, perhaps his divided self. One of Miller's rhetorical strategies is to ask a series of questions: 'Which character may be legitimately described as genuine gold, true sun? Who is possessor of intrinsic worth allowing him or her to rule as sovereign over the others? Who is qualified by divine right to serve as a model for others, as the source of their reflected light or transfused value?' (*FR*, p. 77). Such a series of questions is his strategy for showing the range and the complexity of the problems he is addressing. More importantly, Miller's technique engages the reader in the search for meaning in Miller's own text. But he does not provide answers because for him there are none. The interrogatives are a purchase on undecidability. These questions are not merely rhetorical, but part of his deliberate effort to open the text, to show how critical questions about even frequently discussed issues are not necessarily solved and, more importantly, to show what the questions should be. Indeed, isn't such a series of questions an *instance* of the second type of repetition, 'a world based on difference' (*FR*, p. 6)? While each question seems to repeat the prior one, each is really a substantive variation – 'unique, intrinsically different from every other thing': 'These are ungrounded doublings which arise from differential interrelations among elements which are all on the same plane' (*FR*, p. 6). The interrogatives urge that readers question 'authoritative' readings and invite them to find in literary works open and heterogeneous readings. In a sense, his questions illustrate a method of reading and teaching whatever subsequent novels we shall encounter. The method substitutes the interrogative for the traditional declarative, and questions the possibility and desirability of the order and control that traditionally resolve ambiguity and difficulty – although, as we have seen, Miller does not always practice what he teaches.

By contrast, the use of *definitions* is the use of a rhetorical style that is a version of his first kind of repetition, one that is based on origin or ground; indeed it is his attempt to create authoritative ground within his own argument and to establish continuity with traditional kinds of argument. Sometimes Miller's own certainty and his own rhetorical style – his poise, polish, and control – contradict his argument for heterogeneity: 'Parody is a form of homage. It is also a form of literary criticism' (*FR*, p. 80). He speaks *ex cathedra* as if future readers must accept his definitions. For example does he establish by argument the justification for adopting Kierkegaard's problematic definition of irony as 'infinite absolute negativity' (*FR*, p. 105)? And this is typical of a tendency of Miller throughout his work to rely on authority to establish argument and thus to establish a centre or origin. The argument from authority is of course an example of the first type of repetition. The argument from authority is also inherently both repetitive and tautological.

Let us examine some of the problems and shortcomings of Miller's approach.

(1) Many of his statements are generalizations appropriate for all texts even when they appear in the guise of observations about individual novels. Basically Miller uses texts to prove an *a priori*

theory about writing. Much of what he says is applicable to every novel and does not derive from the text under discussion. For Miller each of the novels he discusses '[is a version] of the invitation, generated by the words of the novel, to believe that there is some single explanatory principle or cause, outside the sequence of repetitive elements in the text, accompanied in one way or another by a frustration of the search that belief motivates' (*FR*, p. 142).

(2) He oscillates between theory and method, sometimes lurching from one to another. Thus in the chapter on *Mrs. Dalloway*, subtitled 'Repetition as the Raising of the Dead'; he writes of Woolf's use of the past tense: 'Everything that the characters do or think is placed firmly in an indefinite past as something which has always already happened when the reader encounters it. These events are resurrected from the past by the language of the narration and placed before the present moment of the reader's experience as something bearing the ineradicable mark of their pastness. . . . The revivification of the past performed by the characters becomes in its turn another past revivified, brought back from the dead, by the narrator' (*FR*, pp. 186–8).

(3) Indeed, even though this would be an anathema to deconstructionist principles, on some occasions the concept of heterogeneity might better be defined in terms of a hierarchy in which one reading is acknowledged as the dominant, another as secondary, and still a third as even more subordinate. Let us see how this might modify Miller's approach to *Mrs. Dalloway*. For example, in *Mrs. Dalloway* he proposes the 'theme of constructive action', and argues that Clarissa's parties are 'her offering to life' (*FR*, p. 193). He makes a compelling case for Woolf as an affirmative writer: 'For her there is a creative power in the mind which thrusts itself forward, in spite of obstacles and hesitations' (*FR*, p. 213). He writes without irony of the ending of *Mrs. Dalloway* as an affirmation: 'Clarissa's party transforms each guest from his usual self into a new social self, a self outside the self of participation in the general presence of others', and he uses diary evidence to support convincingly this view (*FR*, p. 193). His argument for heterogeneity, the need to balance the possibility of affirmation with its antithesis, helps him to acknowledge Clarissa's final failure: 'Clarissa has been attempting the impossible, to bring the values of death into the daylight world of life' (*FR*, p. 196).

Yet his concept of heterogeneity carries the illusion that the various readings can coexist as equally plausible explanations without a hierarchy. But do not the various possible readings that occur to a reader often establish a hierarchy, a hierarchy depending mostly on the text, but also upon our prior reading experience and the place and time in which us readers live? Each plausible reading is not equally central to a mature understanding of a work. Thus in Miller's reading of *Mrs. Dalloway*, the affirmative interpretation is more dominant than the negative one that depends on the view that Mrs. Dalloway can accomplish nothing since death is the place of true communion. But, for me, the reading that stresses the efficacy of Clarissa's social activity is subordinate to one that stresses the ineffectuality of her attempt to create unity in her life or that of others.

(4) Miller is often guilty of misleading summaries of prior critical positions. For example, Miller attributes to the traditional position an insistence on a monolithic reading: 'All literary criticism tends to be the presentation of what claims to be the definitive rational explanation of the text in question' (*FR*, p. 50). This distorts the traditional position; in fact I think, most critics know that any interpretation is bracketed by 'this is true, isn't it?' He claims that prior criticism has depended on the notion that a single truth can be unearthed. But few experienced critics labour under such a delusion. Thus his view that 'The secret truth about *Wuthering Heights*, rather, is that there is no secret truth which criticism might formulate in this way' is an instance of good-natured oversimplification (*FR*, p. 51). To take another example, do prior Hardy critics really believe that they can find a single 'original and originating' explanatory cause for Tess's sufferings? I think not. Indeed it has been the strength of Hardy criticism – including that of Ian Gregor, Michael Millgate, and Irving Howe – to understand that even if the remorseless process, the malevolent universe, may be such a cause, this does not exclude precise empirical explanations based on both the social codes that are indifferent to human aspirations and the psychological complexity of characters. While Miller might be able to point here or there to simplistic thematic analysis which stresses one theme at the expense of others, most critics reject such reductive or 'totalistic' explanations.

(5) Miller might have further explored the psychological phenomena that depend upon kinds of repetition – compulsions, anxieties,

transference – and related them to writing and reading. We recall that Freud believed that it 'is an urge inherent in organic life to restore an earlier state of things'.[18] Isn't that nostalgic search for ground part of the compulsion to repeat that is one cause of repetition in art? Repetition always has a grounded and un-grounded basis; the grounded aspect derives from the mind's focus upon something that exists prior to its activity – anterior to the mind's present moment. As Neil Hertz writes, 'repetition becomes "visible" when it is colored or tinged by something being repeated, which itself functions like vivid or heightened language, lending a kind of rhetorical consistency to what is otherwise quite literally unspeakable'.[19] Isn't the ungrounded aspect the fact that the mind's quest for the grounded is always unfulfilled because the mind seeks an idealized, fantasized version of the grounded repetition? Thus Hertz can write: '[I]n trying to come to terms with the repetition-compulsion one discovers that the irreducible figurativeness of one's language is indistinguishable from the ungrounded and apparently inexplic-able notion of the compulsion itself'.[20]

(6) Miller is divided about the need to understand the world anterior to the text. He sometimes neglects how the text is historically constituted by conditions that existed in the author's life and in the period when he wrote. But he does not develop the arguments to recreate or – in current terms – 'recuperate' these conditions; nor does he accept Derrida's premise that literary texts are self-reflective and refer to nothing beyond them-selves.

(7) Occasionally, the stress on patterns and alogic causes him to abandon common sense and propose hyperbolic critical conceits. Does it really make sense to argue of a character – in this case, Jocelyn in *The Well-Beloved* – that 'it may be impossible to die' (*FR*, p. 169)? And he repeats the current critical conceit which proposes that the text and reader always iterate the life of the character: '[Jocelyn's] avoidance of marriage does not, however, free him from the perpetuation of the pattern of his life. It is repeated in the imagination of the narrator and in the record of that imagination in the text of the novel' (*FR*, p. 171). But, if one wanted to be facetious, one might remark that this is another way of saying that the author imagines and creates and the reader reads.

(8) Despite his desire to introduce alogical explanations, Miller is, of

course, trapped in the linearity of syntax and must progress logically.

(9) Miller does not systematically apply the theory proposed in Chapter One to the novels that follow or show where the two kinds of repetitions occur separately and where they interact.

(10) His heterogeneity is itself a centre or a critical origin and his procedure and point of view become a 'totalization'. That finally every text becomes interchangeable as his method works its magic upon the novels he discusses emphasizes this point. If all these novels explore the absence of ground, does not absence of ground as a critical concept itself become an origin?

V

Miller has significant continuities with the traditional humanistic criticism that we have been examining. Even as he probes the possibilities of deconstruction, he shows his humanistic inclinations. While discussing *Between the Acts* and establishing continuity between Woolf and her predecessors, he is grounding his work within the tradition of *his* predecessors: 'Interpersonal relations as a theme, the use of an omniscient narrator who is a collective mind rising from the copresence of many individual minds, indirect discourse as the means by which that narrator dwells within the minds of individual characters and registers what goes on there, temporality as a determining principle of theme and technique – these are, I have argued elsewhere, among the most impotant elements of form in Victorian fiction' (*FR*, p. 177). While he is noticing that Woolf is very much in the tradition of the English novel in trying to resolve form and content, we realize that Miller is in the tradition of criticism of the English novel when he perceives this tension.

Miller subscribes to Schorer's doctrine of 'technique as discovery': 'The most important themes of a given novel are likely to lie not in anything which is explicitly affirmed, but in significances generated by the way in which the story is told' (*FR*, p. 176). Nor is he indifferent to the function of narrative voice. Woolf's 'ubiquitous all-knowing mind' speaks retrospectively and moves freely from one mind to another (*FR*, p. 179): 'The narrator tells the story in a present which moves forward toward the future by way of a recapitulation or repetition of the past. This retelling brings the past up to the present as a completed whole, or it moves toward such completion' (*FR*, p. 177). The analysis of the verbal texture is in the mode of the New Criticism which considers a work of fiction as a dramatic poem. For the essay on *Mrs. Dalloway* is really a fine essay on how indirect discourse works and how the relationship between the tenses work.

That Miller regards the narrator as a character is in the tradition of Anglo-American criticism. Moreover, he seeks to explain how and why people behave – including the narrator – in terms of psychological motives and moral preferences, and does not regard them simply as linguistic signs. He argues that *Between the Acts*, in the tradition of the English novel, 'is a straightforwardly mimetic story about a group of people in an English country house' and uses the 'basic technical resource of the English novel through more than three centuries, the omniscient narrator' – notwithstanding that 'both in her practice and in her theoretical statements Woolf recognizes a contrary intention, the attempt to create an intrinsic, musical, architectural form' (*FR*, pp. 208, 209).

In giving flesh to theory and method by means of nominalistic readings, Miller is in the tradition of Anglo-American humanistic criticism which eschews theory for close reading and particular demonstrations, and whose interest is in what and how books mean. Reflecting his training, Miller frequently uses the traditional strategies of Anglo-American novel criticism: the empirical approach, the atention to details, and the confident sense that there is an interpretive explanation to be discovered. No sooner does he take a deconstructionist tack than he shifts to a humanistic one. While the latter comes from his sense that a novel deals with relationships among people, the former comes from his perception that novels are made of words: 'The competent reader of a novel moves easily back and forth between attention to the complexities of a verbal texture and thinking of the characters as if they were real people among whom there are relations of one sort or another' (*FR*, p. 206). Nor is his concept of the form of *Tess* so different from traditional notions of organic form: 'In *Tess of the d'Urbervilles* each passage is a node, a point of intersection or focus, on which converge lines leading from many other passages in the novel and ultimately including them all . . . [T]he chains of connection or of repetition which converge on a given passage are numerous and complex. . . . Taken together, the elements form a system of mutually defining motifs, each of which exists as its relation to the others' (*FR*, pp. 126–7). Doesn't, finally, Miller's own technique depend on the same assumption of total recall of details that he ascribes to the New Criticism (*FR*, p. 114)? 'Only an interpretation which accounts for each item and puts it in relation to the whole will be at once specific enough and total enough' (*FR*, p. 53).

He tries to resolve a traditional reading and a deconstructive reading. He believes that the reader has a double response – both in terms of the novel's representative qualities, its correspondence to life, and also in terms of its 'intrinsic shape . . . its self-contained harmonies and recurrences' (*FR*, p. 209). Yet his stress on the tension between thematic and formal readings is hardly new. He takes issue with critics who believe that literary form is undermined or overdetermined; he knows that words and passages are rarely finite, but rather have nuances of meaning, ambiguity, resonance from prior words and passages, and separate meanings for different readers: 'Nor is a work of literature like a set of motionless points between which one could draw lines to make a duck or a rabbit, as one connects the numbered dots in a child's game' (*FR*, p. 215). (But, one might ask, who would disagree with this?)

Miller speaks often about the way texts imitate other texts; that kind of repetition surely depends on ground. His use of sources and contexts is another traditional way that Miller seeks ground or centre. Miller's discussion of a Strauss song as a Woolf source is an ingenious but traditional influence and context argument, although recent criticism would use the term 'intertextuality' to describe it: 'Like Strauss's song, *Mrs. Dalloway* has the form of an All Souls' Day in which Peter Walsh, Sally Seton, and the rest rise from the dead to come to Clarissa's party' (*FR*, p. 190). Of course the past does actually return to the present in the form of Peter's and Sally's reappearance. In the *Tess* chapter his use of the poem, 'Tess's Lament', is a traditional contextual argument and an effort to establish a ground or centre beyond the text, for anything beyond the text temporarily becomes an origin from the moment it is evoked.

Miller's handling of the Oedipus myth in *Henry Esmond* recalls Frye's archetypal theories; Miller shows how novels repeat earlier fictional, historical and mythological prototypes, often to test, modify, and even discard them. Thus the narrative design of *The Well-Beloved* includes the relation to Hardy's other works and 'the novel's relation to works by other writers before and after, both those by authors whose works Hardy knew or who knew his work and those by authors to whom the relation was indirect' (*FR*, p. 158). For Miller, what is most striking in *The Well-Beloved* are its two endings which undermine the traditional form of a neat ending: 'The double ending in The New Wessex Edition keeps the chain visibly open. It thereby corresponds to the meaning of the novel, which is its lack of definitive meaning' (*FR*, p. 174). But Miller realizes that any multiplotted novel proposes 'more or less openly, alternative workings out of the same narrative materials' (*FR*, p. 155). To be sure, the endings of many traditional Victorian novels are not the *telos* of the whole – the goal towards which the life of the protagonist has been tending – that they are supposed to be. Surely much traditional criticism has made that point about the plots and endings of Victorian novels. In another link to the Anglo-American tradition Miller sees analogies – repetitions – between the fictional process and life, and is, like Kermode, interested in the way we use fictions in our own lives: 'We have in real life the kind of relation to our past selves, it may be, that a novelist writing as a third-person omniscient narrator has to his protagonist' (*FR*, p. 88).

With its emphasis on literature as self-sufficient and not necessarily referential, literary criticism has caught up with cubism and Post-impressionism. For deconstruction is emphasizing the ontological reality of the text – the sentences and words themselves as objects, units of energy, textures, sounds, visual surfaces, spaces, and even distinct letters – as well as the perceiver's role in making sense of that reality. As turn-of-the-century European painting saw colour as decorative and shapes as forms, independent of referential meaning, so current criticism sees literary texts, like musical compositions, as having an identity separate from what they represent, and studies its self-enclosed formal relationships – to use Miller's words for Woolf – its 'intrinsic, musical, architectural form' (*FR*, p. 209). In his decon-structive voice, Miller is part of this movement to rescue the text from exclusive reliance upon a representational aesthetic.

While Kermode warns us in *A Sense of an Ending* that we always beieve that we live in a special era of crisis and change, such a belief seems particularly crucial to the contemporary critical environment. This feeling, central for decades to modern painting and literature, was not dominant in literary criticism until recently. Even as they interpreted the complexities of modern literature, Leavis, Trilling and the New Critics, with their conservative, nostalgic set of values and authoritative confident tone, provided a counterbalance to the uncertainty of modern literature. For we can now see that these critics looked for values in literature which would sustain what they regarded as essential humanistic traditions, traditions which were in danger of going astray in the modern world. They felt, as Arnold put it in 'Stanzas from the Grande Chartreuse', between one world 'dead' and 'the other powerless to be born', and yet, like Arnold, they found solace in the values that repeated themselves from the past through the present. At times Derrida and his followers, including Miller, speak as if they have passed beyond the bankruptcy of metaphysics to a new era when literary texts mean in quite different ways. Even if we resist their privileging the critic's mind over the author's, we should recognize that they have added important concepts to literary criticism and have been an important catalyst for helping traditional criticism to define its own theory and method.

NOTES

1. Frank Lentricchia, *After the New Criticism* (The University of Chicago Press, 1980) p. 66.
2. Lentricchia, p. 73.
3. Georges Poulet, 'Criticism and the Experience of Interiority', in *The Structuralist Controversy: the Languages of Criticism and the Sciences of Man*, eds Richard Macksey and Eugene Donato (Baltimore: Johns Hopkins University Press, 1970) p. 72. Lentricchia also cites this key passage, p. 75. See also Georges Poulet, 'Phenomenology of Reading', *New Literary History*, 1:1 (Oct. 1969) pp. 53–68.

    In rejecting the positivistic world of science, ignoring the external world, and privileging the imagination and sensibility of the perceiver, Poulet is in the tradition that seeks an artistic alternative to real life. That tradition includes French Symbolism, English aestheticism influenced by Pater's *The Renaissance*, and Romantic formalism, as practiced by Frye and Stevens.
4. Quoted in J. Hillis Miller, 'The Geneva School', in *Modern French Criticism: from Proust and Valéry to Structuralism*, ed. John F. Simon (University of Chicago Press, 1972) p. 292.
5. I have used *PR* to designate *Poets of Reality* (Cambridge, Mass.: Harvard University Press, 1965); *FVF* to designate *The Form of Victorian Fiction* (Notre Dame, Indiana: University of Notre Dame Press, 1968); and *FR* to designate *Fiction and Repetition* (Cambridge, Mass.: Harvard University Press, 1982). Page numbers in parentheses refer to those texts.
6. See Conrad's 2 Nov. 1895 letter to Edward Noble in Georges Jean Aubry, *Joseph Conrad: Life and Letters*, 2 vols (Garden City, New York: Doubleday, Page and Company, 1927) LL. I. 184.
7. *Textual Strategies: Perspectives in Post-Structuralism*, ed. and with an introduction by Josué V. Harari (Ithaca, New York: Cornell University, 1979) p. 26.
8. Barbara Johnson, 'Nothing Fails like Success', *Deconstructive Criticism: Directions: SCE Reports*, 8 (Fall 1980) pp. 9–10.

    Jonathan Culler, *On Deconstruction: Theory and Criticism after Structuralism* (Ithaca, New York: Cornell University Press, 1982), writes:

    Since deconstruction treats any position, theme, origin, or end as a construction and analyzes the discursive forces that produce it, deconstructive writings will try to put in question anything that might seem a positive conclusion and will try to make their own stopping points distinctively divided, paradoxical, arbitrary, or indeterminate. This is to say that these stopping points are not the payoff, though they may be emphasized by a summary exposition, whose logic leads one to reconstruct a reading *in view of* its end. (pp. 259–260)

9. Lentricchia, p. 165.
10. Lentricchia, p. 164.

In *On Deconstruction* Culler writes:

The authority of presence, its power of valorization, structures all our thinking . . . [T]he metaphysics of presence is pervasive, familiar, and powerful. There is, however, a problem that it characteristically encounters: when arguments cite particular instances of presence as grounds for further development, these instances invariably prove to be already complex constructions. What is proposed as a given, an elementary constituent, proves to be a product, dependent or derived in ways that deprive it of the authority of simple or pure presence . . .

A deconstruction would involve the demonstration that for presence to function as it said to, it must have the qualities that supposedly belong to its opposite, absence. Thus, instead of defining absence in terms of presence, as *its* negation, we can treat 'presence' as the effect of a generalized absence (pp. 94–5).

11. Lentricchia, p. 170; quoted from *Speech and Phenomena and Other Essays on Husserl's Theory of Signs*, trans. David B. Allison (Evanston, Ill.: Northwestern University Press, 1973) p. 129.

According to Culler, 'The term *différence* . . . alludes to this undecidable, nonsynthetic alternation between the perspectives of structure and event. The verb *différer* means to differ and to defer. *Différance* sounds exactly the same as *différence*, but the ending *ance*, which is used to produce verbal nouns, makes it a new form meaning 'difference–differing–deferring'. *Différance* thus designates both a 'passive' difference already in place as the condition of signification and an act of differing which produces differences' (*On Deconstruction*, p. 97).

12. Lentricchia, pp. 170–1.
13. Lentricchia, p. 189.
14. Thus I cannot accept Vincent B. Leitch's contention that 'in effect, [Miller] assumes the role of unrelenting destroyer – or nihilistic magician – who dances demonically upon the broken and scattered fragments of the Western tradition' ('The Lateral Dance: the Deconstructive Criticism of J. Hillis Miller', *Critical Inquiry* 6:4 [Summer, 1980], p. 603).
15. Miller, 'Deconstructing the Deconstructors', *Diacritics* 5 (Summer 1975) p. 31.
16. Lentricchia, p. 195.
17. Lentricchia, p. 204; he quotes from Michel Foucault, 'Nietzsche, Genealogy, History' in *Language, Counter-Memory, Practice: Selected Essays and Interviews*, trans. Donald F. Bouchard and Sherry Simon (Ithaca, New York: Cornell University Press, 1977) p. 154.
18. Quoted from Freud's *Beyond the Pleasure Principle* by Neil Hertz, 'Freud and the Sandman', in Harari, *Textual Strategies*, p. 318.
19. Hertz, p. 301.
20. Hertz, p. 321.

Selected Bibliography

The following list includes all critical and scholarly studies cited in the notes plus a number of seminal works for the study of the theory of the novel.

Abrams, M. H., *The Mirror and the Lamp: Romantic Theory and the Critical Tradition* (New York: Oxford University Press, 1953).
——, 'The Deconstructive Angel', *Critical Inquiry*, 4 (1977) 425–38.
——, 'How to Do Things with Texts', *Partisan Review*, 46 (1979) 366–88.
Aldridge, John W. ed., *Critiques and Essays on Modern Fiction 1920–51* (New York: Ronald Press, 1953).
Auerbach, Eric, *Literary Language and Its Public in Late Latin Antiquity and in the Middle Ages* (Princeton University Press, 1965).
——, *Mimesis: the Representation of Reality in Western Literature*, trans. Willard Trask (Princeton University Press, 1953; orig. edn 1946).
Barthes, Roland, *The Pleasure of the Text* (New York: Hill & Wang, 1974).
——, *S/Z* (New York: Hill & Wang, 1974).
Beach, Joseph Warren, *The Twentieth Century Novel: Studies in Technique* (New York: Appleton-Century, 1932).
Benjamin, Walter, *Illuminations*, Trans. Harry Zohn. 1968 (Rpt. New York: Schocken, 1969).
Bentley, Eric, ed. *The Importance of Scrutiny* (New York University, 1964).
Bilan, R. P., *The Literary Criticism of F. R. Leavis* (Cambridge University Press, 1979).
Blackmur, R. P., ed., *The Art of the Novel: Critical Prefaces by Henry James* (New York: Scribner, 1934).
——, *Eleven Essays in the European Novel* (New York: Harbinger, 1954).
Bloom, Harold, *The Anxiety of Influence: a Theory of Poetry* (New York: Oxford University Press, 1973).
——, *A Map of Misreading* (New York: Oxford University Press, 1975).
——, ed., *Romanticism and Consciousness* (New York: Norton, 1970).
Booth, Wayne C., 'Between Two Generations: the Heritage of the Chicago School', *Profession 82*, 19–26.
——, *Critical Understanding: the Powers and Limits of Pluralism* (University of Chicago Press, 1979).
——, *Now Don't Try to Reason With Me: Essays and Ironies for a Credulous Age* (University of Chicago Press, 1970).
——, *The Rhetoric of Fiction* (University of Chicago Press, 1961).

——, '*The Rhetoric of Fiction* and The Poetics of Fiction', *Novel*, 1:2 (Winter, 1968) 105–13.

——, *The Rhetoric of Irony* (University of Chicago Press, 1974).

Brooks, Cleanth, *A Shaping Joy: Studies in the Writer's Craft* (London: Methuen, 1971).

——, *The Well Wrought Urn* (New York: Harcourt Brace, 1947).

Brooks, Peter, *Reading for the Plot* (New York: Knopf, 1984).

Burke, Kenneth, *The Philosophy of Literary Form*, rev. edn (New York: Vintage, 1957).

Cassirer, Ernst, *The Logic of the Humanities*, trans. Clarence Smith Howe (New Haven, Conn.: Yale University Press, 1961).

Crane, R. S., 'The Concept of Plot and the Plot of *Tom Jones*', *Critics and Criticism*, ed. R. S. Crane (University of Chicago Press, 1952).

Culler, Jonathan, *On Deconstruction: Theory and Criticism after Structuralism* (Ithaca, New York: Cornell University Press, 1982).

——, *The Pursuit of Signs: Semiotics, Literature, Deconstruction* (Ithaca, New York: Cornell University Press, 1981).

——, *Structuralist Poetics: Structuralism, Linguistics, and the Study of Literature* (Ithaca, New York: Cornell University Press, 1975).

Daugherty, Sarah B., *The Literary Criticism of Henry James* (Ohio University Press, 1981).

De Man, Paul, *Allegories of Reading: Figural Language in Rousseau, Nietzsche and Proust* (New Haven, Conn.: Oxford University Press, 1979).

——, *Blindness and Insight: Essays in the Rhetoric of Contemporary Criticism* (New York: Oxford University Press, 1971).

Demetz, Peter, *Marx, Engels, and the Poets* (University of Chicago Press, 1967), trans. Jeffrey L. Sammons, rev. edn.

DePietro, Thomas M., 'Literary Criticism as History: the Example of Auerbach's *Mimesis*', *CLIO*, 8:3 (1979) 377–87.

Derrida, Jacques, *Writing and Difference* (University of Chicago Press, 1978).

Donoghue, Denis, 'Deconstructing Deconstruction', *New York Review of Books*, 27:10 (12 June 1980) 37–41.

Eagleton, Terry, *Criticism and Ideology* (London: New Left Books, 1976).

——, *Marxism and Literary Criticism* (London: Metheuen, 1976).

Ellmann, Richard and Feidelson, Charles, Jr, eds, *The Modern Tradition* (New York: Oxford University Press, 1965).

Eliot, T. S., *Selected Essays*, new edn (New York: Harcourt, Brace & World, 1950).

Fish, Stanley, *Is There a Text in the Class?* (Cambridge, Mass.: Harvard University Press, 1980).

Forster, E. M., *Aspects of the Novel* (New York: Harcourt, Brace & World, 1954; orig. edn 1927).

——, *Aspects of the Novel*, ed. Oliver Stallybrass. (London: Edward Arnold, 1974; orig. edn 1927).

——, *Howard's End*, Abinger edn (London: Edward Arnold, 1972; orig. edn 1910).

——, *Two Cheers for Democracy*, Abinger edn (London: Edward Arnold, 1972; orig. edn 1951).

Foucault, Michel, *Language, Counter-Memory, Practice: Selected Essays and*

Interviews, trans. Donald F. Bouchard and Sherry Simon. (Ithaca, New York: Cornell University Press, 1977).

Frank, Joseph, 'Spatial Form: an Answer to Critics', *Critical Inquiry* 4 (Winter 1977) 231–52.

——, 'Spatial Form in Modern Literature', *The Sewanee Review*, 53 (1943) 221–40, 435–56, 643–53.

——, *The Widening Gyre: Crisis and Mastery in Modern Literature* (New Brunswick, N.J.: Rutgers University Press, 1963).

Frye, Northrop, *Anatomy of Criticism: Four Essays* (New York: Atheneum, 1967; orig. edn 1957).

——, *Fables of Identity: Studies In Poetic Mythology* (New York: Harcourt, Brace & World, 1963).

——, *Fearful Symmetry* (Princeton University Press, 1947).

Genette Gerard, *Narrative Discourse: An Essay in Method*, trans. Jane E. Lewin (Ithaca, N.Y.: Cornell University Press, 1980).

Gilbert, Sandra M. & Susan Gubar, *The Madwoman in the Attic: the Woman Writer and the Nineteenth-Century Imagination* (New Haven, Conn.: Yale University Press, 1979).

Graff, Gerald, *Literature Against Itself: Literary Ideas in Modern Society* (University of Chicago Press, 1979).

Hardy, Barbara, 'Toward a Poetics of Fiction: 3) An Approach through Narrative', *Novel*, 2:1 (Fall, 1968) 5–14.

Harari, Josué V., ed., *Textual Strategies: Perspectives in Post-Structuralist Criticism* (Ithaca, N.Y.: Cornell University Press, 1979).

Herz, Judith Scherer, and Martin, Robert K., eds, *E. M. Forster: Centenary Revaluations* (London: Macmillan, 1982).

Heyman, Ronald, *Leavis* (Totowa, N.J.: Rowman & Littlefield, 1976).

Hill, Christopher, *Puritanism and Revolution* (New York: Schocken Books, 1964), first edn 1958.

Hirsch, David H., 'The Reality of Ian Watt', *Critical Quarterly*, 2:2 (Summer 1969) 164–79.

Hirsch, E. D., *The Aims of Interpretation* (University of Chicago Press, 1976).

——, *Validity in Interpretation* (New Haven, Conn.: Yale University Press, 1967).

Holdheim, W. Wolfgang, 'Auerbach's *Mimesis*: Aesthetics as Historical Understanding', *CLIO*, 10:2 (1981) 143–54.

Hyman, Stanley Edgar, *The Armed Vision* (New York: Alfred A. Knopf, 1948).

Howe, Irving, *Politics and the Novel* (New York: Horizon Press and Meridian Books, 1957).

Iser, Wolfgang, *The Act of Reading: a Theory of Aesthetic Response* (Baltimore: Johns Hopkins University Press, 1978).

——, *The Implied Reader: Patterns of Communication in Prose Fiction from Bunyan to Beckett* (Baltimore: Johns Hopkins University Press, 1974).

James, Henry, *Notes on Novelists* (New York: Charles Scribner's Sons, 1914).

Jameson, Frederic, *Marxism and Form* (Princeton University Press, 1972).

——, *The Political Unconscious* (Ithaca N.Y. Cornell University Press, 1981).

Johnson, Barbara, 'Nothing Fails like Success', *Deconstructive Criticism: Directions: SCE Reports*, 8 (1980) 7–16.

Kermode, Frank, *The Genesis of Secrecy* (Cambridge, Mass.: Harvard University Press, 1979).

——, 'A Reply to Joseph Frank', *Critical Inquiry* 4 (Spring 1978) 579–88.

——, *Romantic Image* (London: Routledge & Kegan Paul, 1957).

——, *The Sense of An Ending: Studies in the Theory of Fiction* (New York: Oxford University Press, 1967).

Kettle, Arnold, *An Introduction to the English Novel*, 2 vols (New York: Harper, 1960; orig. edn 1951).

Krieger, Murray, ed., *Northrop Frye in Modern Criticism* (New York: Columbia University Press, 1966).

Langbaum, Robert, *The Poetry of Experience* (New York: Norton & Company, 1963; orig. edn 1957).

——, *The Modern Spirit: Essays on the Continuity of Nineteenth and Twentieth Century Literature* (New York: Oxford University Press, 1970).

Langer, Susanne K., *Feeling and Form* (New York: Scribner, 1953).

Leavis, F. R., *The Common Pursuit* (New York: Penguin, 1962; orig. edn 1952).

——, *Dickens the Novelist* (Harmondsworth: Penguin Books, 1970).

——, *Education and the University* (London: Chatto & Windus, 1943).

——, *The Great Tradition: George Eliot, Henry James, Joseph Conrad* (London: Chatto & Windus, 1948).

——, *Reevaluation* (London: Chatto & Windus, 1936).

Leitch, Vincent B., 'The Lateral Dance: the Deconstructive Criticism of J. Hillis Miller', *Critical Inquiry*, 6:4 (Summer, 1980) 593–607.

Lentricchia, Frank, *After the New Criticism* (University of Chicago Press, 1980).

Levine, George, *The Realistic Imagination: English Fiction from Frankenstein to Lady Chatterley* (University of Chicago Press, 1981).

Lodge, David, *Language of Fiction* (New York: Columbia University Press, 1966).

Lubbock, Percy, *The Craft of Fiction* (New York: Viking, 1957; orig. edn 1921).

Lukacs, Georg, *Studies in the European Novel* (New York: Grossett & Dunlap, 1964).

McKeon, Richard, *Thought, Action, and Passion* (University of Chicago Press, 1954).

Mack, Maynard and Gregor, Ian, eds, *Imagined Worlds: Essays in Honour of John Butt* (London: Methuen, 1968).

Miller, James E., ed., *Theory and Fiction: Henry James* (Lincoln: University of Nebraska Press, 1972).

Miller, J. Hillis, 'Ariachne's Broken Woof', *Georgia Review*, 31 (1977) 44–60.

——, 'Ariadne's Thread: Repetition and the Narrative Line', *Critical Inquiry*, 3 (1976) 57–78.

——, 'A "Buchstäbliches" Reading of *The Elective Affinities*', *Glyph*, 6 (1979) 1–23.

——, 'The Critic as Host', *Critical Inquiry*, 3 (1977) 439–47.

——, 'Deconstructing the Deconstructors', *Diacritics*, 5:2 (1975) 24–31.

——, *The Disappearance of God* (Cambridge: The Belknap Press of Harvard University Press, 1963).

——, *Fiction and Repetition: Seven English Novels* (Cambridge, Mass.: Harvard University Press, 1982).

——, *The Form of Victorian Fiction* (University of Notre Dame Press, 1968).

——, 'The Geneva School', in *Modern French Criticism: from Proust and Valéry to Structuralism*, ed. John F. Simon (University of Chicago Press, 1972).

——, 'Narrative and History', *ELH*, 41 (1974) 455–73.

——, *Poets of Reality: Six Twentieth Century Writers* (Cambridge: The Belknap Press of Harvard University Press, 1965).

——, 'Stevens' Rock and Criticism as Cure', *Georgia Review* 30 (1976) 5–33 (part I) and 330–48 (part II).

Miller, Nancy K., 'Emphasis Added: Plots and Plausibilities in Women's Fiction', *PMLA*, 96 (1981) 36–48.

Millet, Kate, *Sexual Politics* (New York: Doubleday, 1979).

Milner, Andrew, *John Milton and the English Revolution* (New York: Barnes & Noble, 1981).

Mitchell, W. J. T., ed., *On Narrative* (University of Chicago Press, 1981), reprint of articles from *Critical Inquiry* 7:1 (Autumn 1980) and 7:4 (Summer 1981).

Muir, Edwin, *The Structure of the Novel* (London: The Hogarth Press, 1954; orig. edn 1928).

Poulet, Georges, 'Criticism and the Experience of Interiority', *The Structuralist Controversy: the Languages of Criticism and the Sciences of Man*, eds Richard Macksey and Eugene Donato (Baltimore: Johns Hopkins University Press, 1970).

——, 'Phenomenology of Reading', *New Literary History*, 1:1 (Oct. 1969) 53–68.

Rathbun, Robert C. and Steinmann, Martin, Jr, eds, *From Jane Austen to Joseph Conrad: Essays Collected in Memory of James T. Hillhouse* (Minneapolis, Minn.: University of Minnesota Press, 1958).

Richards, I. A., *Principles of Literary Criticism* (New York: Harcourt, Brace & World, 1925).

Rosen, Charles, 'The Ruins of Walter Benjamin', *New York Review of Books* 24:17 (27 Oct. 1977) 31–40; 24:18 (10 Nov. 1977) 30–8.

Said, Edward, *Beginnings: Intention and Method* (New York: Basic Books, 1975).

Scholes, Robert & Kellogg, Robert, *The Nature of Narrative* (London: Oxford University Press, 1966).

Schorer, Mark *et al.*, eds, *Criticism: the Foundation of Modern Literary Judgment* (New York: Harcourt, Brace, rev edn 1958).

——, *The World We Imagine* (New York: Farrar, Straus, Giroux, 1968).

Schwarz, Daniel R., ' "I Was the World in Which I Walked"; The Transformation of the British Novel', *The University of Toronto Quarterly*, 51:3 (Spring 1982) 279–97.

——, *Joseph Conrad: 'Almayer's Folly' through 'Under Western Eyes'* (Ithaca, New York: Cornell University Press, 1980).

——, 'The Originality of E. M. Forster's Novels', *Modern Fiction Studies*, 29:4 (Winter 1983) 623–41.

——, 'The Importance of E. M. Forster's *Aspects of the Novel'*, *The South Atlantic Quarterly*, 82 (Spring 1983) 189–208.

——, ' "The Idea Embodied in the Cosmology': The Significance of Dorothy Van Ghent', *Diacritics*, 8 (Fall 1978) 72–83.

——, 'The Consolation of Form: the Theoretical and Historical Significance of Frank Kermode's *The Sense of an Ending'*, *Centennial Review*, 38:4, 39:1 (Autumn 1984–Winter 1985), 29–47.

Searle, John R., *Speech Acts: an Essay in the Philosophy of Language* (London: Cambridge University Press, 1969).

Showalter, Elaine, *A Literature of Their Own: British Women Novelists from Brontë to Lessing* (Princeton: Princeton University Press, 1977).

Smith, Barbara Herrnstein, 'Narrative Versions, Narrative Theories', in Mitchell, W. J. T., ed. *On Narrative* (University of Chicago Press, 1981).

Spilka, Mark, 'Ian Watt on Intrusive Authors: or the Future of an Illusion', *Hebrew University Studies in English*, 1:1 (Spring 1973) 1–24.

Stone, Wilfred, *The Cave and the Mountain: a Study of E. M. Forster* (Stanford, Cal.: Stanford Univesity Press, 1966).

Suleiman, Susan, and Crosman, Inge, eds, *The Reader in the Text: Essays on Audience and Interpretation* (Princeton University Press, 1980).

Thornton, Gene, 'P. H. Polk's Genius versus Modernism', *New York Times, Arts and Leisure* (12 Feb. 1982) 25–8.

Tompkins, Jane P., ed., *Reader Response Criticism* (Baltimore: Johns Hopkins University Press, 1980).

Trilling, Lionel, *E. M. Forster* (New York: New Directions, 1964; orig. edn 1943).

——, *The Liberal Imagination* (Viking: New York, 1951).

Van Ghent, Dorothy, *The English Novel: Form and Function* (New York: Harper, 1961; orig. edn 1953).

Watson, Gary, *The Leavises, The 'Social' and the Left* (Swansea: Brynmill, 1977).

Watt, Ian, *Conrad in the Nineteenth Century* (University of California Press, 1979).

——, *The Rise of the Novel* (University of California Press, 1957).

——, 'Serious Reflections on *The Rise of the Novel'*, 1:3 (Spring, 1968) 205–18.

Wellek, Rene, 'Henry James's Literary Theory and Criticism', *American Literature*, 30:3 (Nov. 1958) 293–321.

Williams, Raymond, *The English Novel From Dickens to Lawrence* (New York: Oxford University Press, 1970).

——, *Marxism and Literature* (Oxford University Press, 1977).

——, *Politics and Letters* (London: New Left Books, 1979).

Wilson, Edmund, *Axel's Castle: a Study in the Imaginative Literature of 1870–1930* (New York: Charles Scribner's Sons, 1959).

Wimsatt, William K., Jr and Brooks, Cleanth, *Literary Criticism: a Short History* (New York: Vintage, 1967; first edn 1957).

Woolf, Virginia, 'Mr. Bennett and Mrs. Brown', *The Captain's Death Bed and Other Essays* (New York: Harcourt, Brace Company, 1950).

Index

Abrams, M. H., 139, 149n
Abstract expressionism, 9, 145
Adorno, Theodor, 187
Althusser, Louis, 187
American Jewish novel, 9
'Angry Young Men', 9
Aporia, 11, 252, 255
Aristotle, 42, 51, 104, 112, 135, 155–7,
    168n, 180–1, 234, 236, 243–4, 253
  Poetics, 138, 144, 236, 244
  Neo-Aristotelians (Chicago critics), 3,
    5, 7–8, 12, 18, 72, 100–1, 104,
    110, 112, 136–7, 154–7, 165,
    168n, 177, 180–1, 223, 236, 244
Arnold, Matthew, 6, 17, 42, 60, 64, 77,
    86, 157, 162, 182, 185, 209, 214,
    264
  'Stanzas on the Grand Chartreuse',
    264
Ayer, A. J., 182
Auerbach, Erich, 1, 7, 89, 96, 118–36,
    143, 145–9n, 152, 181–2, 186n, 204,
    234, 242
  personal history, 133
  'Introduction: Purpose and Method'
    to *Literary Language and its
    Public in Latin Antiquity and the
    Middle Ages*, 119–21, 148n–49n
  Mimesis, 1, 7, 89, 118–35, 146, 181
    (Biblical narrative, 124–5;
    compared to Frye, 145–8; figural
    interpretation, 124–5; history:
    161; Homeric and biblical styles
    contrasted, 122–5, 134;
    humanism, 132–3; limitations,
    134–5; modern realism, 126;
    narrative voice, 130–1; on *The
    Song of Roland*, 128; on Woolf,
    130–2; on Petronius, 122–3;
    teleology, 129–33; Vico's
    influence, 119–20)
Austen, Jane, 65, 67–8, 74, 76, 85, 88,
    102–3, 106, 114, 126, 154, 159–61,
    197, 199, 248

Emma, 15, 68, 111, 126, 138, 154–6,
    159–61, 168n, 197, 199, 233
  (Emma, 126; Knightley, 126,
    154, 159–61)
Pride and Prejudice, 88, 197

Balzac, Honoré, 28, 35, 77, 111, 129,
    131
  Eugénie Grandet, 35
Barthes, Roland, 2, 9, 12, 107, 166–7,
    169n, 177
  Le Plaisir du Text, 167
  S/Z, 167, 169n
Baudelaire, Charles, 18
Beach, Joseph Warren, 28
  The Method of Henry James, 28
  *The Twentieth Century Novel: Studies
    in Technique*, 28
Beckett, Samuel, 165, 240
  Company, 165
Bell, Clive, 45–6, 195
Bellow, Saul, 9
Benjamin, Walter, 86n, 92, 97, 98n, 237,
    253
Bennett, Arnold, 199
  The Old Wives' Tale, 199
Bentley, Eric, 78n, 116n
Besant, Walter, 20
  'The Art of Fiction', 20
Bible, 28, 122–3, 133–4, 140–1
  see Auerbach, 122–5, 134
  see Frye, 140–1
  see Kermode, 172, 181
Bilan, R. P., 66, 70, 78n–79n
  The Literary Criticism of F. R. Leavis,
    66, 70, 78n–79n
Bishop Gregory, 128
Blackmur, P. P., 12, 23, 24, 40n, 85–6,
    96, 98n
  'A Feather-Bed for Critics', 85
  The Art of the Novel: Critical Prefaces
    (ed.), 16–29, 40n, 74
  Eleven Essays in the European Novel,
    85, 98n

273

Blackmur, P. P. – *continued*
  Language as Gesture, 85
Blake, William, 42, 47, 61, 139, 141
Bloch, Joseph, 189
Bloom, Harold, 66, 91, 118, 149, 182,
  240
Bloomsbury, 5, 42, 45–6, 62, 209
Boccaccio, 165
Booth, Wayne, 1, 6–7, 12, 25, 40n, 50,
  80–1, 94, 96–7, 101, 115, 151–69n,
  184, 206, 242–3, 251
  'Between Two Generations: the
    Heritage of the Chicago School',
    168n
  *Critical Understanding: the Powers
    and Limits of Pluralism*, 151
  *Modern Dogma and the Rhetoric of
    Assent*, 151
  The Rhetoric of Fiction, 1, 6, 7, 40n,
    80, 151–169n, 197 (aesthetic and
    moral values, 160–5; Afterword
    to Second Edition, 164–5;
    Aristotelian Heritage, 154;
    'Implied Author', 158–9, 161–2,
    165–6; on *Emma*, 155–6;
    reliable and unreliable narrators,
    159; response to James,
    153–4)
  A Rhetoric of Irony, 6, 151, 153, 155,
    167n
  Now Don't Try to Reason with Me,
    151, 156–7, 169n ('How Not to
    Use Aristotle: the Poetics', 168n;
    'How to Use Aristotle', 168n;
    The Rhetoric of Fiction and the
    Poetics of Fiction', 151–2;
    167n–68n)
Borges, Jorge Luis, 247
Bradley, A. C., 51
  Shakespearean Tragedy, 51
Bradley, F. H., 8
  Appearance and Reality, 8
Brecht, Bertolt, 140
Brontë, Charlotte, 77, 216–17, 252
  Jane Eyre, 216
Brontë, Emily, 15, 54, 77, 118, 138, 149,
  104–5, 216–17, 237–8, 247, 249–52,
  256, 259
  Wuthering Heights, 15, 77, 91, 138,
    199, 204–5, 237–8, 247, 249–52,
    256, 259 (Nelly and Lockwood,
    204–5, 251, 256)
Brooks, Cleanth, 17, 21, 27, 40n, 85,
  137, 143, 149n, 153

  Literary Criticism: a Short History
    (with William Wimsatt), 17, 21,
    27, 40n, 137, 143, 149n
  Understanding Fiction (with Robert
    Penn Warren), 85, 153, 227
Brown, E. K., 56
  Rhythm in the Novel, 56
Browning, Robert, 51
Bunyan, John, 109
  The Pilgrim's Progress, 109
Burke, Kenneth, 9, 12, 85–6, 97, 98n,
  136, 156–7, 168n, 187, 243
  The Philosophy of Literary Form,
    98n, 157, 168n
Burney, Francis, 76
Burton, Robert, 139
  Anatomy of Melancholy, 139
Butler, Samuel, 198, 201
  The Way of All Flesh, 198

Cargill, Oscar, 21–2, 40n
  The Novels of Henry James, 21–2, 40n
Carlyle, Thomas, 240
Cary, Joyce, 205
Caudwell, Christopher, 195
Cecil, Lord David, 66–7, 70
Cervantes, Miguel de, 247
  Don Quixote, 86, 197
Cezanne, Paul, 19, 102
Chase, Richard, 2, 27
  *The American Novel and Its
    Traditions*, 2, 27
Chicago Critics, *see* Neo-Aristotelians
Chomsky, Noam, 239
Coleridge, Samuel Taylor, 19, 52, 65,
  68, 89, 91, 243–4
  The Ancient Mariner, 45
Compton-Burnett, Ivy, 205
Conrad, Joseph, 3, 15, 43, 49–50, 63,
  67–9, 71–4, 76, 102, 117n, 132,
  141–2, 144–5, 161, 198, 204, 217,
  225–7, 237–8, 243–8 *passim*, 252,
  265n
  Heart of Darkness, 72–3, 141, 226,
    252 (Kurtz, 141)
  Lord Jim, 3, 15, 73, 76, 141–2, 144,
    230, 243–6, 248 (Marlow [also in
    Heart of Darkness], 230, 245,
    248)
  Marlow tales, 73, 76, 101, 252
  Nostromo, 63, 72–3, 196, 198, 203
  Typhoon, 73

Crane, R. S., 7, 52, 112, 155–7, 168n
'The Concept of Plot and the Plot of
Tom Jones', 52, 112, 156, 168n
(in *Critics and Criticism*, 168n)
Cubism, 8, 19, 264
Culler, Jonathan, 10–15n, 100–1, 107,
116n, 166, 168n–69n, 194, 220n
On Deconstruction, 13, 15n, 265n–66n
The Pursuit of Signs, 12, 15n, 110–11,
116n, 194, 220n
Structuralist Poetics, 10–11, 14, 15n,
100–1, 107, 116n, 166,
168n–69n, 265n–66n

Dante, 236
The Divine Comedy, 236
Daudet, Alphonse, 26
Daugherty, Sarah B., 17, 20–2, 27,
39–40n
The Criticism of Henry James, 17,
20–2, 27, 39–40n
Deconstruction, 1, 5, 10–13, 137, 186n,
226–7, 234–65n
in Miller's *Fiction and Repetition*,
234–65n
Defoe, Daniel, 3, 76, 80, 99–106, 109–14
passim, 196–7
Moll Flanders, 80, 99, 105, 110–12
Demetz, Peter, 220n
DePietro, Thomas, 148n
De Quincey, Thomas, 185
Derrida, Jacques, 2, 9, 11–12, 165–6
169, 177, 238–9, 242, 256, 260
Writing and Difference, 169, 260
Dickens, Charles, 7, 15, 38 62–3, 67,
69–70, 72, 77, 79n, 93, 96, 163,
188–9, 203, 206, 208–9, 214, 217,
220n, 222, 224, 228–34, 250
Bleak House, 15, 163, 230–1, 234, 250
(Esther Summerson, 93, 230,
234, 250)
Great Expectations, 93
Hard Times, 67, 72
Little Dorritt, 69
Oliver Twist, 202, 229
Our Mutual Friend, 231–3
Disraeli, Benjamin, 83
Sybil, 83
Doctorow, E. L., 9
Book of Daniel, 9
Ragtime, 9
Donne, John, 127
The Anniversaries, 127
Donoghue, Dennis, 5–6, 15n

Dostoevsky, Fyodor, 54, 83, 90
The Brothers Karamazov, 54
Notes from Underground, 83
Drew, Elizabeth, 96
*The Novel: a Modern Guide to Fifteen
English Masterpieces*, 96

Eagleton, Terry, 75, 79n, 188, 206–8,
213, 215–16, 220n–21n
Criticism and Ideology, 75, 79n, 188,
206–8, 213, 215–16, 220n–21n
Eco, Umberto, 9
The Name of the Rose, 9
Eliade, Mircea, 179
Eliot, George (Marian Evans), 54, 63,
65–74, 76, 91, 111, 201, 208,
214–15, 217, 227–8, 232
Adam Bede, 68, 91
Daniel Deronda, 215
Felix Holt, 71, 215 (Mrs. Transome,
71)
Middlemarch, 72, 111, 200–1, 215, 232
(Casaubon, 72, 227; Dorothea,
201, 227)
The Mill on the Floss, 69, 214 (Maggie
Tulliver, 69)
Silas Marner, 72
Eliot, T. S., 8, 65–6, 69, 71, 78n, 84–5,
98n, 137, 139, 149n, 153, 162, 184,
212, 217, 225, 248
'The Function of Criticism', 65
'Tradition and the Individual Talent',
66, 78n, 84, 248
review of *Ulysses* (in *The Dial*), 137,
149n
After Strange Gods, 66
Selected Essays, 98n
Empson, William, 182, 195, 243
Engels, Friederich, 7, 189–90, 193, 203,
220n
1890 Letter to Joseph Bloch, 189–90
The German Ideology (with Karl
Marx), 190, 220n

Fauvism, 8, 19
Fielding, Henry, 15, 49, 52, 63, 69–70,
89–90, 99–103, 104, 109–14, 126,
159–61, 168n, 197, 233, 247–8
Jonathan Wilde, 197
Joseph Andrews, 53, 197
Tom Jones, 15, 52, 111–13, 126,
159–61, 168n
Flaubert, Gustave, 17, 19, 32, 34, 37, 71,
73–4, 76–7, 106, 121, 128–9, 152, 154

Flaubert, Gustave – *continued*
  Madame Bovary, 32, 34, 74
Fletcher, Angus, 119, 139–40, 145,
  148n–50n
Forster, E. M., 1, 6, 8, 38–9, 41–59n,
  62, 198, 202–3, 205
  'Anonymity: an Enquiry', 45, 47
  'Art for Art's Sake', 46, 59n
  Aspects of the Novel, 1, 6, 38, 41–59n,
    62 (dialogue between life and
    art, 47–8; endings, 52–3;
    limitations, 57–8; pattern, 54–5;
    plot and story, 46, 51; prophecy,
    54; response to Woolf, 42–3;
    result more important than
    technique, 48–9; rhythm, 55–6;
    stress on character, 46–51: flat
    and round characters, 49; style
    enacts humanistic values, 44–5;
    time, 52)
  'The Challenge of our Time,' 43
  Howards End, 43–4, 59n
  The Longest Journey, 43–4
  Passage to India, 43–4, 57, 198, 202
    (Aziz and Fielding, 98)
  A Room With A View, 43–4
  'Two Cheers for Democracy', 43,
    45–6, 59n
  Where Angels Fear to Tread, 43–4,
    48
Foucault, Michel, 11, 15n, 165, 247,
  266n
  'What Is an Author?', 11, 15n, 165
  discursive formations, 247
Fowles, John, 247
Fox, Ralph, 195
  The Novel and the People, 195
Frank, Joseph, 52, 156, 168n, 178–9,
  186n, 228
  'Spatial Form in Modern Literature',
    156, 168n, 178, 186n, 228
  'Spatial Form: an Answer to Critics',
    179, 186n
  *The Widening Gyre: Crisis and
    Mastery in Modern Literature*,
    168, 186n
Frazer, Sir James, 57
  The Golden Bough, 57
Freud, Sigmund, 57, 103, 107, 140, 260,
  266
  Beyond the Pleasure Principle, 266
Friedman, Alan, 52
  The Turn of the Novel, 52
Fry, Roger, 45–6

Frye, Northrop, 1, 4, 7, 9, 12, 50, 89, 92,
  118, 135–50n, 179–83, 223, 228,
  242, 263, 265n
  Anatomy of Criticism, 1, 7, 92, 118,
    135, 150n, 179 ('Archetypal
    Criticism: Theory of Myth', 141;
    archetypes, 136–8, 142–4, 146;
    compared to Auerbach, 145–8;
    continuities with Chicago
    criticism, 135–6; 'Historical
    Criticism: Theory of Modes',
    141; ignores real world, 144–7;
    limitations, 143–4; Menippean
    satire, 138–9; on Burton's
    Anatomy of Melancholy, 139;
    on *Lord Jim*, 141–2, 144; part
    of modernist movement, 142;
    role of theory, 135; spatial
    versus temporal, 146; 'Specific
    Continuous Forms (Prose
    Fiction)', 138, 140; 'Specific
    Encyclopedic Forms', 140)
  Fables of Identity, 137, 149n
  Fearful Symmetry, 149n
  Northrop Frye in Modern Criticism,
    142

Gautier, Théophile, 18
Genette, Gerard, 56
  Narrative Discourse, 56
Geneva School, 225
Gestalt Psychology, 56, 81, 84, 96, 178
Goldmann, Lucien, 187–8, 190, 194
  202, 220n
  The Hidden God, 190, 220n
Gordon, Caroline and Tate, Allen, 85,
  151–3
  The House of Fiction, 85, 151–3
Graff, Gerald, 183–4, 186n
  Literature Against Itself, 183–4, 186n
Gramsci, Antonio, 187
Green, Henry, 205
Greene, Graham, 205, 265n
Gregor, Ian, 259
Guerard, Albert, 108, 178, 207

Harari, Josué V., 15n, 230, 265–66n
Hardy, Barbara, 150n
Hardy, Thomas, 15, 49, 51, 63, 77, 83,
  93–4, 96, 111, 126, 145, 147, 162,
  197, 201, 203, 208–9, 213–17, 222,
  228, 233–4, 237–8, 244, 247,
  249–51, 253, 255–6, 258–60, 262–3

Hardy, Thomas – *continued*
  Jude the Obscure, 15, 111, 126, 162,
    250 (Jude, 126, 234; Sue, 126,
    234, 250)
  A Pair of Blue Eyes, 233
  The Return of the Native, 213
  Tess of the D'Urbervilles, 83, 93, 147,
    197, 201, 213, 217, 234, 237, 244,
    247, 251–3, 259, 262–3 (Angel,
    197, 217, 234; Tess, 147, 197,
    201, 217, 234, 259)
  The Well-Beloved, 237–8, 247, 251,
    255, 260, 263
Hartman, Geoffrey H., 137, 142–3, 149n
Hawthorne, Nathaniel, 27, 77, 145
  The Scarlet Letter, 27
Hegel, G. W. F., 118
Hertz, Neil, 260, 266n
Heyman, Ronald, 61, 78n
Hill, Christopher, 198, 220n
  Puritanism and Revolution, 198, 220n
Hirsch, David, 116n
Hirsch, E. D., 158–9, 163, 165, 167–69n
  The Aims of Interpretation, 158, 163,
    165, 168n–69n
  Validity in Interpretation, 158–9, 168n
Hogarth, William, 247
Holdheim, Wolfgang, 119–21,
    148n–49n
Holocaust, 9, 89–90, 133, 136, 152, 172
  National Socialism, 131, 133
Homer, 122–6, 175
  The Odyssey, 175
Horace, 26, 42, 47, 86, 157
Howe, Irving, 259
Hulme, T. E., 85, 139, 203
Humanistic Formalism, 5
Huxley, Aldous, 205
Hyman, Stanley Edgar, 98n, 168n
  The Armed Vision, 98n, 168n

Impressionism, 19, 102

James, Henry, 1, 5, 6, 8, 16–40n, 41–2,
    48–9, 51–3, 55, 62–3, 65, 67–8, 86,
    102, 106, 152–4, 162, 196, 201–3,
    208, 218, 223, 234, 242–3
  'The Art of Fiction', 17, 18–22
    passim, 27, 40n
  Criticism and Critical Theory, (form,
    23–4; interest, 24–5; on Daudet,
    26; on G. Flaubert, 20; on
    Trollope, 22; on Turgenev, 20;
    point of view, 25; Prefaces to the

  New York Edition [*see also The
    Art of the Novel*, ed. Blackmur,
    R. P.] 16–29, 40n, 74; Preface
    to *The American*, 27; Preface to
    The Awkward Age, 20; Preface
    to *The Portrait of the Lady*, 20;
    Preface to *Princess Casamassina*,
    21; Preface to *The Spoils of
    Poynton*, 18; Preface to *The
    Tragic Muse*, 24; Preface to *What
    Maisie Knew*, 21; 'The Present
    Literary Situation in France', 28,
    40n; Romance, 27)
  Works, (*The Ambassadors*, 33, 36, 55,
    75: Strether, 36, 55; *The
    American*, 77; *The Awkward
    Age*, 29, 36–7: Nanda, 36; *Daisy
    Miller*, 77; *The Golden Bowl*, 75;
    Portrait of a Lady, 75; *Roderick
    Hudson*, 72, 74; *The Turn of the
    Screw*, 114; *Washington Square*,
    63; *Wings of the Dove*, 33, 36)
Johnson, Barbara, 238, 265n
Johnson, Samuel, 64, 77, 115, 240, 248
Joyce, James, 3, 8, 15, 38, 42–4, 50,
    53, 58, 66, 80, 90–1, 96, 102, 132,
    137–40, 161–4, 175, 184, 197,
    199–200, 203–5, 209, 236, 240, 248
  'Clay', 157
  *A Portrait of the Artist as a Young
    Man*, 80, 90, 163–4 (Steven
    Dedalus (also character in
    Ulysses), 44, 90, 175, 200)
  Ulysses, 3, 15, 44, 53, 58, 137–9,
    161–3, 175, 197, 199–200, 205,
    236, 240 (Bloom, 175, 200, 236;
    Molly, 200)
Jung, Carl, 57, 103, 137

Kafka, Franz, 140, 148
  'The Hunter Gracchus', 148
Keats, John, 126, 223
  'Ode on a Grecian Urn', 126
Kenyon Review, The, 86
Kermode, Frank, 1, 7, 9, 48, 52, 92, 101,
    141, 170–86n, 212, 223, 225, 235,
    242–3, 264
  debate with Frank about time and
    space, 178–9
  fiction and myth, 179–80, 184
    (function of fictions, 173)
  The Genesis of Secrecy, 48, 175, 186n
  'A Reply to Joseph Frank', 176, 179,
    186n

Kermode, Frank – *continued*
  Romantic Image, 173, 186n
  *The Sense of an Ending: Studies in the
    Theory of Fiction*, 1, 7, 52, 92,
    141, 170–86n, 212, 264 (*aevum*,
    176, 179; as Aristotelian, 180–1;
    emphasis on reader, 177;
    historical background and
    influence on graduate study,
    170–2, 177; limitations, 184–5;
    time, 170–86n: *Chronos* and
    Kairos, 176, 179–83, 235)
Kettle, Arnold, 1, 5, 7, 51, 59, 62, 96,
    102, 108, 112, 152, 168n, 187–9,
    191–208, 214, 218–20n
  aesthetic values, 196–7
  background, 198–9
  concept of realism, 197
  An Introduction to the English Novel,
    7, 51, 59n, 62, 96, 102, 188,
    194–208, 218–20n
  limitations, 204–5, 218–19
  Marxism, 191–205
  moral fable, 196
  on *Ulysses*, 198–9
Kierkegaard, Sören, 255, 257
Krieger, Murray, 139, 148n–49n
  Ed., *Northrop Frye in Modern
    Criticism*, 148n–50n

Lacan, Jacques, 107
Lawrence, D. H., 2, 3, 7, 15, 27, 42–3,
    47, 50, 54, 58, 62, 65–7, 76–7, 90–1,
    94, 96, 132, 139, 162, 177, 188–9,
    195, 206, 208, 217, 220n
  Lady Chatterley's Lover, 162
  The Rainbow, 15, 77, 91, 139, 161–2,
    177, 198 (Tom and Lydia, 177,
    195)
  Sons and Lovers, 162 (Paul Morel,
    162)
  Studies in Classic American Literature,
    2, 27
  Women in Love, 77
Leavis, F. R., 1, 5–7, 9, 12, 60–79n, 86,
    101–2, 104, 108, 113, 115, 117n,
    119, 152, 155, 162, 182, 185,
    188–90, 194–7, 200–2, 204, 206–9,
    213–14, 216, 218, 242, 264
  The Common Pursuit, 65, 78n
  contribution of Leavis, 60–2, 77–8
  *Culture and Environment: the
    Training of Critical Awareness*,
    (Ed. with Thompson, Denys), 61

  D. H. Lawrence: Novelist, 62
  Dickens The Novelist, 62, 69, 72, 79n
  Education and the University, 60,
    78n
  The Great Tradition, 1, 60, 62, 66,
    67–79n, 102 (concept of form,
    68–9, 74; contribution, 77;
    disinterestedness, 70; Form and
    Humanism, 74; impersonality,
    69–70; 'interest', 100; limitations,
    75; literature as extension of life,
    68; maturity, 70; on authors, 72;
    on Conrad, 72–3: on *Nostromo*,
    73; on James, 74–5; prefers
    concrete to abstract, 71; prefers
    nineteenth-century realism, 70;
    seriousness, 70; shortcomings,
    75–7)
  influenced by Johnson and Arnold,
    64–5
  influence on Kettle, 194–6
  influenced by Lawrence, T. S. Eliot,
    and Richards, 65–6
  influence on Williams, 207–9
  Nor Shall my Sword, 64
  'The Novel as Dramatic Poem', 63
  'Retrospect of a Decade', 60
  Revaluation, 61, 79n
  Scrutiny, 6, 9, 60–4, 67, 75, 78n, 99,
    108, 116n, 117n
Leavis, Q. D., 62, 67, 108, 116n
  'The Discipline of Letters: a
    Sociological Note', 116n
  Fiction and the Reading Public, 108
Lehman, Ben, 89
Leitch, Vincent D., 266n
Lentricchia, Frank, 137, 149n, 182–3,
    186n, 223, 238–9, 247, 265n–66n
  After The New Criticism, 137, 149n,
    182–3, 186n, 223, 238–9, 247,
    265n–66n
Levine, George, 134–5
  The Realistic Imagination, 134–5,
    149n
Lévi-Strauss, Claude, 10, 15n, 137
  Anthropologie Structurale, 15n
Locke, John, 116n, 239
  *Essay Concerning Human
    Understanding*, 239
Lodge, David, 88
  The Language of Fiction, 88
Lubbock, Percy, 1, 5, 6, 8, 17, 28–40n,
    41–2, 48–9, 51, 53, 55, 62, 74, 86,
    153, 242

Lubbock, Percy – *continued*
  The Craft of Fiction, 1, 6, 28–40n,
    41–2, 48–9, 75, 153 (Balzac's
    Eugénie Grandet, 35;
    contribution summarized, 39;
    Henry James, 28–40n; on *The
    Awkward Age*, 36; on *Clarissa*,
    34; on dramatized consciousness
    of narrator, 30–1; on Flaubert,
    37; on *Madame Bovary*, 32, 34;
    on Thackeray, 33–4; on
    Tolstoy, 21–2: *Anna Karenina*,
    35; *War and Peace*; on Turgenev,
    31; on *The Wings of the Dove*,
    36; picture versus drama, 34–6:
    prefers drama, 37; shortcomings,
    38–9)
Lukàcs, Georg, 86, 92, 98n, 108, 118,
    188, 193, 199–200, 202, 208, 210,
    220n
  *The Meaning of Contemporary
    Realism*, 220n
  Studies in European Realism, 92, 98n

Malevich, Kazimir, 231
Mallárme, Stepháne, 18
Marx, Karl, 7, 182, 190, 194 (*A
    Contribution to the Critique of
    Political Economy*, 190, 220n; *The
    Germany Ideology* (with Engels),
    190, 220n; *see* Marxism *and* Engels)
Marxism, 1, 5, 7–8, 62, 96, 112, 152,
    187–221n (Marxist criticism, 7–8,
    96, 112, 187–221n: contribution,
    218–19; problems, 219–20, theory
    189–94; *see also* Kettle, Arnold,
    see also Williams, Raymond
Matisse, Henri, 8, 19
Maugham, Somerset, 42
  Cakes and Ales, 42
Mauron, Charles, 50
McKeon, Richard, 7, 112, 117n, 155–6,
    168n
  Thought, Action, Passion, 117n, 155,
    168n ('Imitation and Poetry',
    117n, 155, 168n)
Melville, Herman, 56, 77
  Moby Dick, 54
Meredith, 38, 77, 87, 228
  The Egoist, 87
  Harry Richmond, 38
Mill, James, 67

Miller, James E., 18–20, 22–3, 26, 40n
  Ed. *Theory of Fiction: Henry James*,
    17–29
Miller, J. Hillis, 1, 8–9, 12–13, 16, 25,
    39n, 56, 193, 210–11, 218–19,
    220n–66n
  *Charles Dickens: the World of His
    Novels*, 222, 224
  'Deconstructing the Deconstructers',
    266n
  The Disappearance of God, 222,
    224–7, 232, 234, 238, 246
  Fiction and Repetition, 1, 8, 12, 13,
    16, 25, 39n, 56, 211, 221n, 226,
    232–66n (concepts of
    deconstruction, 233–67n;
    discussion of *Lord Jim*, 243–6,
    252; heterogeneity, 242–3,
    247–9, 257; humanism, 237,
    239–41, 261–4; influence of New
    Criticism, 240–1; kinds of
    repetition (Platonic vs.
    Nietzschean), 16, 234–6, 240; on
    time, 228–9; shortcomings, 257–8,
    261; style enacts values, 256;
    textuality and intertextuality, 12,
    129–40, 232–67n *passim*)
  The Form of Victorian Fiction, 1, 8,
    211, 222–3, 226–34, 250, 265n
    ('The Geneva School', 265n;
    linguistic modes, 230–2;
    phenomenology, 222–2, 242;
    time, 228–30)
  Poets of Reality, 223–5, 227, 232,
    234, 238, 246, 248, 265n
  Thomas Hardy: Distance and Desire,
    222, 234, 236
Millgate, Michael, 259
Milner, Andrew, 190, 192, 200, 220n
  *John Milton and the English
    Revolution*, 190, 200, 220n
Milton, John, 109, 236
  Paradise Lost, 109, 236
Minimalism, 9
Mondrian, Piet, 231
Moore, G. E., 45
Moore, George, 67
Muir, Edwin, 41, 50, 55, 59n
  The Structure of the Novel, 41, 50, 55,
    59n

Nashe, Thomas, 196

New Criticism, 3, 5–10, 13, 17–18, 23, 58, 63, 72, 81–2, 84–6, 90, 99–102, 136, 139, 145, 152–3, 158, 171, 177–8, 190, 194–5, 207, 223, 225, 227–8, 231, 240–4, 246, 253, 261–2, 264

New Novel (France), 9

Nietzsche, Friederich, 16, 182, 234–6, 240

Partisan Review, The, 3, 5, 63, 152, 187

Pater, Walter, 8, 18, 40n, 42, 53, 56, 265n

The Renaissance, 8, 265n

Phelan, James, 164

Phenomenology, 8, 223–34
in Miller's *The Form of Victorian Fiction*, 223–34

Picasso, Pablo, 8, 19, 184

Plato, 86, 181
Platonism and neo-Platonism, 16, 25, 32, 42, 62, 143, 146, 148, 193, 234–6, 240

Poe, Edgar Allan, 145

Pollock, Jackson, 140

Pope, Alexander, 157

Post-Impressionism, 8, 19, 49, 264
1910–12 London post-Impressionist Exhibits, 49

Post-Structuralism, 2, 8, 12, 147, 194, 222–66n

Poulet, Georges, 223–5, 228, 234, 242, 265n
see Phenomenology

Pound, Ezra, 8, 85

Priestley, J. B., 66

Proust, Manuel, 56, 131, 176, 237, 244
Remembrance of Things Past, 56, 176

Rabinowitz, Peter, 165

Racine, Jean, 147

Rahv, Phillip, 5
see The Partisan Review

Raphael, 102

Richards, I. A., 5, 65–6, 78n, 82, 98n, 156, 182, 195
Coleridge on Imagination, 66
Practical Criticism, 5, 66, 95
Principles of Literary Criticism, 5, 82, 98n

Richardson, Samuel, 34, 38, 53, 63, 76, 99–105, 108–11, 113, 126–7, 163, 176, 198, 233

Clarissa, 34, 108–9, 111, 126–7, 163, 198 (Clarissa and Lovelace, 127)
Pamela, 53

Robbe-Grillet, Alain, 185

Rosen, Charles, 98n

Rosenbaum, S. P., 58n–59n

Sacks, Sheldon, 50

Sartre, Jean-Paul, 248

Saussure, Ferdinand, 230, 256

Schlegel, Friederich, 255

Schorer, Mark, 1, 17, 28, 40n, 69, 85, 88, 96, 98n, 108, 178, 186, 196, 206, 235, 241, 261
'Fiction and the Analogical Matrix', 85, 88
'Foreword' to Percy Lubbock, *The Craft of Fiction*, 28, 40n
'Technique as Discovery', 85
The World We Imagine, 98n

Schwarz, Daniel R., 3, 59n, 117n, 149, 168
Conrad: 'Almayer's Folly' Through 'Under Western Eyes', 149

Scott, Walter, 28, 58, 66–7, 87, 198, 204
The Heart of the Midlothian, 87, 198, 204

Scrutiny, see F. R. Leavis

Sewanee Review, 86, 93, 168n

Shakespeare, William, 38, 51, 71, 102, 145, 147, 240
Measure for Measure, 71 (Claudio, 71)

Shelley, Percy Bysshe, 42, 157

Smollett, Tobias, 113, 196

Social realism, 193

The Song of Roland (Chanson de Roland), 128

Spenser, Edmund, 109
Faerie Queene, 109

Spilka, Mark, 116n

Stallybrass, Oliver, 41–2, 55, 58
'Introduction' to *Aspects of the Novel* (Abinger edn.) 41–2, 55, 58n

Stein, Gertrude, 44

Stendhal, 77, 126, 129, 131

Sterne, Lawrence, 15, 57, 69–70, 76, 101, 113–14, 127, 139, 155, 236, 239–40, 248
Tristram Shandy, 15, 57, 114, 127, 139, 155, 236, 239–40

Stevens, Wallace, 9, 19, 42, 57, 118, 148, 183, 185, 225, 256, 265n

Stevens, Wallace – *continued*
  'An Ordinary Evening in New
    Haven', 57
  'Tea at the Palaz of Hoon', 148
Stone, Wilfred, 43–5, 54, 59n
  *The Cave and the Mountain: a Study
    of E. M. Forster*, 43–5, 54, 59n
Structuralism, 1, 2, 5, 8–10, 137, 142,
  147, 192, 231, 239
Surrealism, 140
Swift, Jonathan, 197
  Gulliver's Travels, 197
Swinburne, Algernon Charles, 40n

Tacitus, 123
Thackeray, Henry, 33–5, 38, 49, 63,
  76–7, 94–5, 144, 227–8, 233, 237–9,
  247, 254–5
  Henry Esmond, 233, 237–9, 254–5
  Vanity Fair, 15, 94, 111, 144, 202,
    232, 247 (Amelia, 94–5, 232;
    Becky, 94–5, 144, 202, 232;
    Dobbin, 97)
Theatre of the Absurd, 9
Thomas, D. M., 9
  The White Hotel, 9
Thomas, Dylan, 225
Thompson, Denys, 61
  Co-editor (with Leavis), *Culture and
    the Environment: the Training of
    Critical Awareness*, 61
Thoreau, Henry David, 141
Thornton, Gene, 3, 15n
Tintoretto, 223
Titian, 19
Tolstoy, Leo, 31–2, 35, 48, 56, 83, 111
  Anna Karenina, 35
  War and Peace, 24, 31–2, 56, 83
Trilling, Lionel, 5–6, 9, 44, 59n, 62, 86,
  98n, 185, 195, 207, 213, 219, 221n,
  242, 264
  E. M. Forster, 44, 59n
  The Liberal Imagination, 98n, 221n
  'Manners, Morals, and the Novel', 86,
    219, 221n
Trollope, Anthony, 22, 63, 76–7, 228,
  248
Turgenev, Ivan, 19, 31

Utilitarianism, 42–3, 47, 66–7, 69, 182,
  195

Van Ghent, Dorothy, 1, 7, 9, 12, 69,
  80–98n, 101, 108, 136, 178, 187,
  196, 206–7, 223, 241, 246
  'The Dickens World: a View from
    Todgers', 93
  *The English Novel: Form and
    Function*, 1, 80, 136, 223
    (aesthetic influence, 82–3;
    chronological sense, 84; form,
    86–7; humanism, 87; importance
    of Gestalt psychology, 81, 84, 96,
    178; influenced by New Criticism
    and Burke, 85; influence upon
    successors, 95–6; language, 87–8;
    limitations, 92–4; on form, 86–9;
    the reader's role, 86)
Vico, Giambattista, 119–20, 140, 148n

Warren, Robert Penn, 21, 63, 85, 153,
  223
  Understanding Fiction (with Cleanth
    Brooks), 85, 163, 223
Watson, Gary, 78n
Watt, Ian, 1, 7, 9, 99–117n, 207, 246
  Conrad in the Nineteenth Century,
    114, 246
  The Rise of the Novel, 1, 7, 99–117n
    (contextualism, 112; formalism,
    102; historical method, 99–101,
    102, 109, 112; humanism, 146;
    importance, 101–3; on Defoe,
    99–106, 109–14 *passim*; on
    Fielding, 99–104, 109–14; on
    Richardson, 99–105, 108–11;
    problems and limitations, 105–7;
    Protestantism, 100, 103; realism
    of assessment versus realism of
    presentation, 114; response to
    Aristotelians, 112–13; role of
    characters, 112–13; 'Serious
    Reflections on *The Rise of the
    Novel*', 9, 114, 116n, 117n;
    teleology, 101–2; Watt's concept
    of realism, 100, 103–7)
Wellek, Rene, 24, 28, 39, 39n–40n, 61,
  66
Wells, H. C., 71, 96, 218
  Tono-Bungay, 196
Wilde, Oscar, 8, 18, 19, 38, 40n, 42, 53,
  56, 209
Williams, Raymond, 1, 5, 7, 96, 112,
  187–221n

Williams, Raymond – *continued*
  The Country and the City, 188, 206
  Culture and Society, 188, 206, 215
  *The English Novel From Dickens to
    Lawrence*, 7, 96, 188–221n
    (contribution of Marxist
    criticism, 218; 'knowable
    community', 212–13; limitations,
    218–19; Marxist theory, 189–94;
    'structures of feeling', 213–14)
  identifies with George Eliot, 218–19
  influenced by Leavis, 207–9
  Keywords, 188
  Marxism and Literature, 188, 190,
    209–12, 219, 220n
  Politics and Letters, 188–9, 207–8,
    212, 220n–21n
  Reading and Criticism, 207, 220n
Williams, William Carlos, 225
Wilson, Edmund, 2, 9, 187
Wimsatt, William, 17, 21, 27, 40n,
  136–7, 142–4, 148n–49n, 186n
  Literary Criticism: a Short History
    (with Cleanth Brooks), 17, 21,
    27, 40n, 137, 143, 148n, 186n

Woolf, Virginia, 3, 38, 41–3, 45–6, 50,
  56, 58n–59n, 62, 77, 130–2, 145,
  202, 237, 240, 247–8, 256, 258–9,
  261–4
  A Writer's Diary, 256
  'Mr. Bennett and Mrs. Brown', 42–3,
    46, 58n, 59n (Georgian and
    Edwardian writers, 42–3)
  Between the Acts, 237–8, 247–8, 261–2
  The Common Reader, 41, 62
  Mrs. Dalloway, 237, 248, 256, 258–9,
    261, 263 (Clarissa, 256, 258–9,
    263; Septimus, 256)
  To The Lighthouse, 130–1, 202 (Mrs.
    Ramsay, 130–1)
World War II, 9

Yeats, W. B., 18, 38, 42, 57, 139, 184,
  218, 225
  'Sailing to Byzantium', 57, 218
  A Vision, 139

Zola, Emile, 28